Media in the Swirl

Media in the Swirl

Ravi K Dhar
Pooja Rana
Editors

PENTAGON PRESS

First Published in 2012

Published by

PENTAGON PRESS
206, Peacock Lane, Shahpur Jat,
New Delhi-110049
Phones: 011-64706243, 26491568
Telefax: 011-26490600
email: rajan@pentagonpress.in
website: www.pentagonpress.in

Cataloging in Publication Data—DK
Courtesy: D.K. Agencies (P) Ltd. <docinfo@dkagencies.com>

Media in the swirl / Ravi K. Dhar, Pooja Rana, editors.
p. cm.
Contributed articles.

ISBN 9788182746534

1. Mass media. 2. Mass media—Technological innovations. 3. Mass media and minorities. 4. Transnationalism. 5. Ethnicity. I. Dhar, Ravi K. II. Rana, Pooja.

DDC 302.23 23

Printed at Aegean Offset Printer Greater Noida (U.P)

To
THE MOTHER

Contents

	Foreword	*xi*
	Acknowledgements	*xiii*
	Contributors	*xv*
1.	Introduction	1

SECTION A
MEDIA IN TRANSITION

2.	Broadcast Culture Meets Role-Playing Culture Consequences for Audience Participation in a Cross-media Production *Marie Denward*	17
3.	Reject Now, Accept in the Future? A study of innovation resistance to websites and blogs *Yah-Huei Hong*	34
4.	Financialization of US Media System: Links and Dependencies *Nuria Almiron*	46
5.	Global Warming on Second Life: The Public Sphere and Free Discussion in Collaborative Virtual Environments *Yuval Karniel, Amit Lavie Dinur, and Doron Friedman*	65
6.	Emergence of Supplement Journalism in India: A Critique *Pooja Rana*	78

SECTION B
MEDIA AND THE KNOWLEDGE SOCIETY

7.	WIPO Development Agenda Forum and its Prospects *Sara Bannerman*	95

8. Knowledge Society as Pathway to Sustainable Development in the Arab World: An Islamic Cultural Perspective 102
Muhammad Ayish

9. Emerging Patterns in the Era of E-governance: A Study of Users of 'Swedish Public Employment Service' on Internet 114
Ernesto Abalo, Martin Danielsson, Håkan Johansson, and Tobias Olsson

10. Digital Divide in Contemporary Brazilian Society 126
Denize Correa Araujo

11. WSIS, Turkey and Information Society 135
Babacan Taşdemir and Funda Başaran Özdemir

SECTION C
MEDIA AND DEVELOPMENT

12. Opening up the Black Box of Participation: A Reception Study of Mediated Participatory Practices 155
Nico Carpentier

13. Encapsulating a Freirean Logic of Empowerment Examining the Sonagachi Project, a community-oriented peer outreach initiative among sex workers in Calcutta, India 174
Satarupa Dasgupta

14. Internet and Political Communication Dynamics in India 186
Navneet Anand

15. Women Empowerment and Poverty Reduction in Bangladesh A Study of the Village Pay Phone Program 199
Linda Hultberg

16. Possibility of Applying Universal Service Policy Principle on Mobile Phone Service in the case of South Korea 212
Hyunwoo Lee

SECTION D
MEDIA & THE NEGOTIATION OF IDENTITY

17. Being Cultural Citizen: Role of Media 227
Shan-Shan Li

18. Virtual Diasporas
Notion of 'Home' and Identity Formation in Cyberspace 238
Elitsa Ivanova

19. Identities and Media of Brazilian Diaspora 251
Fernando Kuhn

20. New Media and Oromo Diaspora
Quest for Democracy and Self-determination 261
Habtamu Dugo

21. New Media and the Redemption of the Other 278
Ravi K Dhar

SECTION E
MEDIA AND THE QUEST FOR TRUTH

22. Labourers of the Real "Authenticity Work" in Reality Television 295
Minna Aslama and Mervi Pantti

23. Super Girl and the Expediency of Hybridity 309
Robert Moses Peaslee, Shu-Ling Chen Berggreen and Sunyoung Kwak

24. Anime in Asia: Why not Japanese?
Rethinking the Local-Global Cultural Nexus 322
Umi Khattab and Gin Chee Tong

Index 333

Foreword

We had come to expect new media technologies to settle down in familiar ways after a period of excitement. That expectation was reasonable, as the pattern had predictably recurred since the beginning of industrial scale communication, which for long was mainly mass communication.For instance, when wireless telegraphy was tinkered into broadcasting by amateur radio enthusiasts, it perturbed the establishment. Corporations and government agencies saw value in wireless telegraph, as it extended the reach of the telegraph network to ships on high seas. For them, the tendency of the radio waves to spread in spite of efforts to generate straight-line transmissions was a nuisance. What was nuisance for the establishment, including Marconi himself, was a source of joy for amateurs, who started "broadcasting" music records, among other things, to amuse each other. This bottom-up exuberance was short-lived, as the establishment eventually rationalized broadcasting in accordance with the industrial logic. The powers that be thought of broadcasting as the "newspaper of the air" and it became just that. Later, when television service started, the framework developed for radio broadcasting was transferred to the new medium. In effect, from newspapers to broadcasting, the mass media were cast in the same mould.

There was logic to it, beyond the interests of the powers that be. Constraints of what was possible with the available technologies were very real. Just visualize the bulky television cameras of the post-Word War period. The costs and also the physical size and fragility of electronic components necessitated the concentration of all the intelligent functions—recording, editing, archiving, and others—in the center of the system (the studio) and the reduction of the TV set to a dumb terminal with limited capabilities such as channel selection and volume and contrast control. It is quite true that the level of centralization was a matter of deliberate choice. Instead of a national broadcasting system, which was the choice of elites in most countries, there could have been many more stations based on schools, colleges, religious centers, and other local institutions. But a smart TV set with recording, editing, archiving, and other such capabilities in the homes of all the viewers was not practical. Technological advancements have opened new possibilities. Whether or not these possibilities are exploited is a matter of choice, albeit not always individual choice. One only needs to think of North Korea to get the point. On the other hand, people have shown a marked proclivity to exploit these possibilities, even in North Korea, when they are afforded the slightest opportunity. These opportunities are growing, as the laptops, and even smart phones, are now mobile studios in hands of millions of people. It is this technological reality that is allowing for the emergence of novel sociological phenomena that are a defining feature of our times.

The old mould is now broken. And we know the broad contours of the emerging media environment. We know that technological advancements have made possible flatter media systems. In addition to the above-discussed smart end user devices, the rapidly declining computing costs have also made possible flatter system architectures. Contrast between the hierarchical structure of the conventional telephone network and the flatter structure of the Internet gets the point across. The hierarchy of the telephone network was borne out of constraint —limited processing power. The pre-defined routing paths of the hierarchical network minimized the need for processing. The Internet, on the other hand, deploys processing power with wanton abundance. But we do not care because now the processing costs are relatively low and the advantages of abundant processing power in a system are great—dynamic routing, lateral connectivity, and flexibility. The experience shows that given a choice, which technology now affords, people prefer the flexibility of the flatter systems, in spite of the accompanying complexity, to the rigidity of the hierarchy, even though it offers simplicity.

While we broadly understand the technological scaffolding of the emerging media environment and also the behavioral tendencies of people, which seem to be remarkably consistent across the globe, the particular manifestations of the new technological possibilities and the social practices that develop around them continue to surprise us. Twitter is a case in point. Who could have imagined that a quirky system that limits messages to 140 characters would become a global phenomenon? Twitter and other such technologies are material manifestations of a new order sprouting out of the cracks in the old mould. Even in the new era, we continue to have industrial scale communication such as customized but automated emails from various institutions. But it is non-institutional communications such as that on Twitter that are having a profound impact.

This book capturesthe exuberant activity or "media swirl" ushering in the new media environment through the widening cracks in the old mould. It covers a remarkable range of new media technologies and the social contexts of their use. They include use of alternate reality game for audience participation in cross-cultural production, global warming on Social Life, supplement journalism in India, financialization of media corporations, paradoxical nature of reality television which is both constructed and spontaneous, among others. Books on new media typically have a much narrower range because they are bound by a tight framework. This book, on the other hand, keeps the lens broad and thereby is able to capture a very wide range of new media innovations and practices around the world. The reader is likely to find something or other useful for his or her particular interest, often a surprising ingredient for a new line of thought.

HARMEET SAWHNEY

Editor-in-Chief, The Information Society

Acknowledgements

We wish to acknowledge the overwhelming response and cooperation we received to the proposal of this book from our worthy contributors. We are thankful to them for meeting the deadlines we had to impose on them. We would also like to acknowledge our gratitude to Prof Harmeet Sawhney, who was kind enough to squeeze out time for writing the foreword to this book. Our thanks are also due to Professors Jan Servaes, Shin Dong Kim and Arvind Singhal who were indulgent enough to appraise and appreciate the book. We would also like to put on record here our thanks to Mr. Rajan Arya, CEO, Pentagon Press, for reposing faith in us.

RAVI K DHAR
POOJA RANA
Editors

Contributors

Abalo, Ernesto is a PhD student in Media and Communications Studies at Örebro University, Sweden.

Almiron, Nuria is a lecturer and researcher in the Department of Communications at the Pompeu Fabra University (UPF), Barcelona, Spain. Almiron received a PhD in Journalism and Communications from the Autonomous University of Barcelona and also holds a degree in Communication Sciences and a degree in Political Sciences from the same university. Her research focuses on the political economy of media, stressing the role of corporate and market structures from a critical perspective. His last book is Journalism in Crisis. Corporate Media and financialization, Cresskill, NJ: Hampton Press (2010).

Anand, Navneet is a communication professional with 15 years spent in media, academics and corporate sector. Presently offering strategic communication advisory through his agency GreyMatters Communications, Anand's previous assignments include positions at Reliance Industries Limited, The Indian Express, The Times of India, The Pioneer and PC World. Anand blends vast professional experience with high-end academic training. A doctorate in Sociology from Jawaharlal Nehru University, Anand has authored two books including The Media Effect (2003) and frequently contributes academic papers. Anand teaches journalism, marketing & strategic communication, and public relations at many institutions including IIM Lucknow, IIMC, JNU. A keen blogger, he writes on development and communication.

Araujo, Denize Correa is a PhD in Comparative Literature, Cinema and Arts by the University of California, Riverside, USA, 1998. Master in Cinema and English by the Arizona State University, Tempe, USA, 1990. Coordinator of the Post-Graduate Studies in Cinema at the Universidade Tuiuti do Paraná, Brazil, since 1997. Coordinator of the Master and Doctorate in Communication and Languages at the Universidade Tuiuti do Paraná from 2004 to 2010. Member of the IAMCR SRC - Scholarly Review Committee. Author of the book "Revisited Images: essays about the Hipervention Aesthetics", Sulina Ed. 2007. Research themes: digital culture, cinema, hybrid images, intertextuality.

Aslama, Minna is Visiting Lecturer of Communication and Media Studies at Fordham University, New York, and Researcher at the University of Helsinki,

Department of Communication. Her interests include new conceptualizations of media audiences and the concept of 'participation' in the web 2.0 era, public service media and content diversity, and media policy flows in the globalizing media environment. In addition, she is interested in new forms of collaboration emerging in relation to the media justice and reform movements. Prior to and in between her academic career, she has worked at the Division of Advancement for Women of the UN Secretariat, the Finnish Broadcasting Company, and most recently, as the Program Officer for the Necessary Knowledge for a Democratic Public Sphere program at the Social Science Research Council. She divides her life between Brooklyn and the Bronx, Helsinki, and New Delhi.

Ayish, Muhammad is Media Advisor at the UAE National Media Council in Abu Dhabi. Until October 2010, he had worked both as Dean of the College of Communication and professor of communication at the University of Sharjah, United Arab Emirates. He holds a doctoral degree in international broadcasting and public diplomacy from the University of Minnesota-Twin Cities, USA (1986). He has over 50 articles and book chapters published in international journals and books. His most recent book is: *The New Arab Public Sphere* (2008) Berlin: Frank & Timme). He also writes in the daily The National newspaper published in Abu Dhabi, UAE.

Bannerman, Sara is a SSHRC postdoctoral fellow with the Centre for Governance of Knowledge and Development, a part of the Regulatory Institutions Network (RegNet) at the Australian National University in Canberra. From September 2009 to May 2010, she was a Fulbright postdoctoral researcher working as a Visiting Scholar at the Elliott School of International Affairs, George Washington University. She is currently working on a comparative history of international copyright. Her dissertation, a history of Canadian international copyright, is forthcoming with UBC Press.

Berggreen, **Shu-Ling Chen,** Ph.D. is an Associate Professor at the School of Journalism and Mass Communication at the University of Colorado, U.S.A. Her research areas include children and media, media and identity politics, and media, culture and globalization.

Carpentier, Nico is Senior Lecturer at the Social Sciences Department of the University of Loughborough and Associate Professor at the Communication Studies Department of the Vrije Universiteit Brussel (VUB - Free University of Brussels). He is also vice-president of the European Communication Research and Education Association (ECREA). His theoretical focus is on discourse theory, his research interests are situated in the relationship between media, journalism, politics and culture, especially towards social domains as war & conflict, ideology, participation and democracy. His latest book is entitled — Media and Participation: A Site of Ideological-Democratic Struggle (Intellect, 2011).

Danielsson, **Martin** is a Ph.D student in media and communication studies at

Halmstad University, Sweden. His research examines the significance of social class for how young Swedish men interpret and make use of digital media in everyday life.

Dasgupta, Satarupa is a doctoral candidate at the Mass Media and Communication department of Temple University, Philadelphia, USA. Her doctoral thesis is on participation oriented peer outreach based HIV/AIDS intervention research among sex workers in India. Her research interests include HIV/AIDS intervention communication, community health advocacy, gender studies, and popular culture. She has received the New York University Postdoctoral and Transition Program for Academic Diversity fellowship and will serve as an assistant professor and faculty fellow at the NYU College of Nursing starting in Fall 2011.

Denward, Marie is a media and games researcher at the Interactive Institute, Stockholm. She belongs to the Game Studio group where she researches pervasive games and other forms of participatory media. Her dissertation deals with the transmedia storytelling production Sanningen om Marika. With an ethnographic approach she studied convergence culture in the game, particularly focussing on the amalgamation of producer-consumer and on cultures of production; on how participation was designed and crafted and how this affected the outcome. 2011 she will complete her PhD in media studies at Malmö University, School of Arts and Communication.

Dugo, Habtamu holds MA in Journalism and Media Studies from Rhodes University in South Africa and is a Senior Fellow of Human Rights at the Independence Institute, Colorado, USA, where he concentrates on researching and reporting on human rights issues and trends in Africa. He is also the Executive Secretary of the Oromo Studies Association, a multi-disciplinary international scholarly organization registered in the United States. The Oromo Studies Association focuses on multi-disciplinary studies of the Oromo people of East Africa and other societies in Northeast African region. Habtamu Dugo is currently a graduate student and Research Assistant at Geroge Mason University, School for Conflict Analysis and Resolution.

Friedman, Doron is a Lecturer in the Sammy Ofer School of Communications, in the Interdisciplinary Center, Herzliya, Israel. He is the head of the Advanced Virtuality Lab (http://avl.idc.ac.il) – a interdisciplinary group of researchers including Postdoctoral fellows and students. Doron holds a PhD and MSc in Computer Science from Tel Aviv University, in the area of artificial intelligence and virtual environments. Doron has a few dozen publications in peer reviewed journals and conferences in the areas of human-computer interaction, virtual reality, and artificial intelligence. Doron is the co-author of several patent applications; he was the co-founder of two startup companies (in the areas of Internet and business intelligence) and is occasionally involved in "real-world" projects as a consultant.

Hong Yah-Huei, Alice is a faculty member in the Graduate Institute of Mass Communication of Fu Jen Catholic University (Taiwan). She got her Ph.D. degree in the University of Wisconsin-Madison, U.S. in 1996, and was a research fellow in the Asian Communication Research Centre (ACRC) in Nanyang Technological University (Singapore) in 2009. She has many years of practical experience in election campaigning and also is a reviewer of many renowned Journals in Taiwan and in the U.S. She has broad research interests and the areas of her specialization include Internet campaigning, political communication, advertising effects, and quantitative research methods.

Hultberg, Linda earned a MFS (Minor Field Study) scholarship by SIDA to perform a field study in Bangladesh in the year 2007. The study, Women Empowerment and Poverty Reduction in Bangladesh, sorts under political communication and evaluates women's experiences of empowerment as an outcome of the Village Pay Phone program under the Grameen Bank's micro credit program. The results were published in a Swedish scientific anthology distributed by Jönköping University. Currently Linda is working as a Communication Manager at the municipality of Sundbyberg, Sweden, enhancing citizen engagement and participation through the web.

Ivanova, Elitsa is a PhD candidate at the Department of Journalism, Media and Communication, Stockholm University. Her research interests include media and ethnicity, in particular journalism and ethnic minorities, and diaspora studies. She is also interested in discourse studies. Currently, she is working on her dissertation thesis which examines the discursive construction of ethnic minorities in Swedish and Bulgarian mainstream press, including the ways editorial conditions and journalistic practices influence the content.

Johansson, Håkan is an Associate Professor in social work, School of Social Work, Lund university, Sweden. His research interests are e-governance, participation and citizenship.

Karniel, Yuval is a senior lecturer at the Sammy Ofer School of Communications, IDC. He has extensive experience teaching law and communications courses. He co-directed the joint program in law and communications at the College of Management in Tel Aviv. Dr. Karniel is also on the Israel Broadcasting Authority's board and chair the ethics committee. He was the general counsel of Israel's commercial television and radio authority, and has served on many public committees. He earned a LL.M. in international law from the American University in Washington D.C. and a LL.D. from the Hebrew University of Jerusalem.

Khattab, Umi is currently senior lecturer in the School of Communication, University of Sunshine Coast, Australia. Prior to this, she taught and researched at the University of Melbourne, Australia, where she also coordinated the Honours and Postgraduate Diploma program in Media and Communications. Earlier, while at the National University of Malaysia, Khattab wrote as a columnist for *The New Straits Times* in Malaysia and continues to freelance. Some of her writings contributed to public debates and to a rethinking of social and educational policies in the country. In recognition of her work, Khattab was recently invited by the Malaysian Press Institute (MPI) as a panel judge for the 2010 National Journalism Award. Khattab's research largely focuses on Asian media and audience practices and public communication.

Kuhn, Fernando graduated in Journalism and worked as a reporter and editor for Brazilian newspapers and magazines. Master in Multimedia from the Brazilian Universidade Estadual de Campinas (Unicamp), and PhD in Social Communication from the Universidade Metodista de São Paulo (Umesp), also in Brazil (where he was twice awarded with a fellowship ofThe State of São Paulo Research Foundation – Fapesp). He was at the University of London's School of Oriental and African Studies (SOAS) in 2004 as visiting research student for his doctoral research "The Local and the Global Radio: Flow, Reverse Flow and Cultural Identity on the Internet". Professor Kuhn coordinated the implementation of the Digital Media course in the Faculdades Integradas Alcantara Machado (FIAM), in Sao Paulo, and took part in the Global Media research group, based in Umesp. He is currently a researcher in the Local and Community Communication research group at the same university. His other areas of interest are international communication, globalization, diasporas, community media, ethnic media, intercultural communication, media and sport, media and environment, popular culture and journalism.

Kwak, Sunyoung is a doctoral candidate at the School of Journalism and Mass Communication at the University of Colorado, U.S.A. Her research focuses on Asian media.

Lavie-Dinur, Amit is Vice-Dean and the director of the television studies program at the Sammy Ofer School of Communications. She has taught communications courses at leading Israeli universities and colleges, including Tel Aviv University, and served as the dean of student affairs at the Media School of the College of Management in Tel Aviv. Lavie-Dinur is serving as executive member of the Israel Film Council. She served as a selector for the New Israeli Foundation for Cinema and TV. Her research focuses on propaganda and persuasion in television and film, television genres, popular culture and cultural aspects of advertising.

Lee, Hyunwoo is a researcher of Institute for Communications Policy in Seoul National University. His main research interests are the major actors and their interaction patterns in media policy making process. He has published a dozen journal articles and two books. These publications reflect his research interests in media industry and regulation policy. Nowadays, he is delving into major media policy change cases in South Korea to investigate the characteristics and limitations of policy making process.

Li, Shan-Shan is associated with the Centre for Cultural Research at University of Western Sydney, Australia.

Olsson, Tobias is a Professor of Media and Communication Studies, Jönköping University, Sweden. Tobias Olsson has published a large number of journal articles and book chapters, most of them concerning issues of new media and citizenship.

Özdemir, Funda Basaran is an Associated Professor at the Faculty of Communications in Ankara University. Her research interests include telecommunications policy, innovation and technological changes, science and technology policy, political economy of information and communication technologies, ICT, internet diffusion and policy, information society policies and development economics and policy. She is the author of three books on the political economy of telecommunications and ICTs in Turkey and strategies of privatization in the telecommunication sector and the co-editor of one book on economy of communications networks. She also has published various articles on new information technologies, telecommunications and communication policies in EU and Turkey.

Pantti, Mervi is Associate Professor at the Department of Social Research/Media and Communication Studies, University of Helsinki, Finland. She is also director of the international Master's programme Media and Global Communication. Her research interests include mediated emotions, disaster reporting and participatory journalistic practices, amateur images in particular. Among her publications are Amateur Images and Global News (Intellect, 2011) and the forthcoming book Disasters and the Media (Peter Lang 2011), as well as articles in journals such as International Journal of Cultural Studies, Javnost/the Public, European Journal of Communication, and Media Culture & Society.

Peaslee, Robert Moses is an Assistant Professor of Electronic Media and Communication in the College of Mass Communication at Texas Tech University, U.S.A. He earned his doctorate in 2007 in the School of Journalism and Mass Communication at the University of Colorado, Boulder. His research focuses on discursive intersections of text, place and practice.

Tasdemir, Babacan graduated from Ankara University Communication Faculty in 2003 and completed Middle East Technical University (METU) Media and Cultural Studies Master's Program (MCS) in 2006 in Ankara, TURKEY. He is presently research assistant at MCS Program and PhD. candidate in Science and Technology Policy Studies Program at METU. His PhD. thesis is about Information Society and New Media Policies in the European Union. Information and communication technologies and policies, political economy of communication and documentary cinema are among his major academic interest fields.

Tong, Gin Chee is a PhD student in the Media and Communications program, University of Melbourne, Australia. Tong worked in the public relations industry in Malaysia prior to pursuing her studies in Australia. Tong's research focuses on media globalisation, identity and nation-building.

1

Introduction

The history of human civilization is the story of various turning points, most of them technology-based. As the technology has evolved, human society has climbed from one step of evolution to another. Every new paradigm of technological innovation has transformed the way human beings organize themselves for undertaking individual, social, economic and political activities. Of these technologies, the ones of immediate relevance for the emergence of the modern knowledge society are the *information* and *communication* technologies.

In the initial phase of their evolution, the two followed a disparate route. The information technology got a jump-start with the invention of the printing press. Enabling mass production of printed messages, it rid readers from the drudgery of hunting for manuscripts lying in monasteries and libraries. Communication technologies, on the other hand, were in the initial stages more in the nature of transportation technologies. With the passage of time, the focus of communication technologies shifted from physical entities to information. The communication of information received a shot in the arm with the invention of telegraph and telephone services. It facilitated the transportation of information across continents through deep sea cables and made possible the network of news agencies that we get to see to this day.

As time passed, each of these two technologies kept on undergoing major incremental changes. The printing press moved from the stage of lithography to that of the modern offset printing, revolutionizing the quality and the cost of printed texts. Newspapers, magazines, books and other forms of print media spawned as a result of these technological innovations. All strove to make information available to the common man as conveniently and cheaply as possible. The print media technology, however, remained only an information technology as its products had to be transported physically to the point of sale and consumption.

This media technology was followed by those of the radio, cinema and television. Of these three, while cinema was purely an information technology, the other two were communication technologies too. Cinema did away with a major disability of the print media. It sought to process information not in the form of orthographic symbols which called for literacy but in the form of iconic symbols like moving pictures of human beings and their environment. In this respect, it was a major technological innovation in information technology. Radio and the television too did away with the need for a literate user of information. But, they differed from the cinema as they ventured into the domain of communication technologies. They not only processed information in an audio visual form but also conveyed it to the location of the user. These two media technologies were the initial attempts at the marriage of information and communication technologies. In this sense, they were the first hybrid technologies.

Though radio and television were not merely information but also communication technologies, they didn't integrate all the forms of communication technology with information technology. Telecommunication remained for a long time outside the purview of this marriage. With the convergence of telecommunication, satellite communication and information technology in the form of the Internet and the World Wide Web, these disparate technologies were completely fused for the first time. This convergence led to the birth of the new information and communication technologies. These technologies have not only revolutionized the information and communication processes of the existing mass media technologies of print, radio, cinema and television but have also given birth to a new form of communication known variously as new media, web journalism, online communication, web media and cyber journalism.

The emergence of new information and communication technologies marks a signal turning point in the history of human communication. Hailed as a complete media, new media is completely different from the old mass media technologies. It enjoys not only all the advantages of the mass media such as mass reach and multiple replication of messages but also the privilege of being free from their disabilities such as the absence of interactivity and face to face communication. Besides, it has the potential of delivering all the mass media messages without being hamstrung with their limitations such as limited user participation and individual interaction. Apart from this, the new media enjoys the advantages of multimediality, asynchronicity and user independence. It gives a power to the user which no other mass media did till now. In fact, the user can access media content of his/her choice at any place and at any time, something that mass media couldn't. In fact, the shift from the old mass media technologies to the new media constitutes a paradigm shift in human communication.

To understand the implications of this paradigm shift for human society, we need to understand communication in its historical as well as its semantic contexts. Derived from the Latin verb, *communicare*, which means 'to impart a piece of information, an idea or a concept with a view to discovering/developing a commonality of thought and/or feeling' or 'to make something entirely common with another', communication may be defined as the process of interaction that helps in evolving a common ground of understanding between any two persons or entities. Interaction as defined by Oxford Advanced Learners' Dictionary means 'reciprocal action or influence'. It follows that the relationship between the two communicators is not fixed but dynamic. In other words, the roles of message production and agenda setting keep oscillating between the two communicators.

Viewed thus, communication becomes a process wherein there are no fixed producers or consumers of messages. The roles are dynamic and interchangeable. So, contrary to popular perception that communication implies speaking or writing or even showing signs to express oneself, communication involves listening as much as speaking, reading as much as writing and seeing as much as showing. It follows, therefore, that communication is dialogic. In other words, the communication message is not necessarily a pre-existing entity. It emerges from the dynamic exchange of verbal and non-verbal signals/symbols between the communicators.

And, what's more, the process of interaction could produce as many messages as are the number of communicators, depending on the idiosyncratic and cultural inputs each brings to bear on the process of interaction, leading to what has often been called the polysemy and polyphony of communication. However, as communication strives to create a common ground of understanding among the communicators, ideally it should produce one common message between the communicators. Furthermore, as communication involves the interaction of each communicator with the other, it is personalized and individualistic in nature. **Osgood and Schramm**, the Convergence model and in recent times, the Participatory School of Communication—all have attested to this interactive character of communication in their own ways.

But, this is not the way the Transmission School represents communication. Taking inspiration from the Aristotelian theory of rhetoric, it equates communication with the transmission of messages from a fixed speaker/sender to a fixed audience with a view to bringing about a behavioural change in the latter. Lasswell was the first to initiate this misrepresentation of communication. Being primarily concerned with propaganda, his model delineates the graph of communication as a linear route involving someone speaking in a certain channel to someone with a certain effect on the person(s) spoken to. As John Fiske observes, "This is a verbal version of Shannon and Weaver's original model. It is still linear: it sees communication as the transmission of messages: it raises the issue of 'effect' rather than meaning." Shannon and Weaver, two engineers concerned with the fidelity of the sound transmitted across telephone lines, gave a similar account of communication to explain the efficiency of the mechanical process that they had been working on. Their model consists of five elements: an information source, producing the message; a transmitter, encoding the message; a channel through which the encoded message is sent as signals; a receiver, decoding/reconstructing the message from the signals; and a destination/recipient receiving the message. All these elements are not unlike those spelt out by Lasswell. They, however, add a sixth element too in the form of the noise that subverts the message.

These two models also typically underlie many others in the American tradition of research, presenting Source-Message/Channel-Receiver as the basic process of communication. Gerbner's model of communication, a variation on Shannon and Weaver's model of communication, adds the perceptual dimension to the process of communication as envisioned by the Transmission School. In the words of John Fiske, 'it sees the communication process as consisting of two alternating dimensions—the perceptual or receptive, and the communicating or means and control dimension." This model is as linear as the other transmission school models are. Berlo, adds one more element to this model which makes it dyadic instead of being monadic. Berlo stresses the role of relationship between the source and the receiver as an important variable for ensuring the success of communication. Apart from this, he enumerates the factors to be taken into account at each 'end' of the communication for predicting the success of communication. These are the relative competence of the sender and the receiver in regard to communication skills, their relative levels of knowledge, the convergence/divergence of the social systems they belong to, their cultural affinities and their relative attitudes. Like others in the Transmission School, Halliday too subscribes to the linear model. However, his emphasis falls on the impact of the socio-cultural moorings of the communicators. According to him, no source communicates as a free agent without being influenced by his/her position in a socio-cultural system. Like the rest of the transmission models, Maletzke's model of mass media has linearity built into it. Maletzke's model comprises four major elements, whereas Lasswell's model, which underlies many communication models, comprises five. Maletzke argues that the 'with what effect?' component of Lasswell's model properly belongs to sociological and psychological study of the receiver and should therefore not be introduced as a fifth component. But, whatever be the variations worked out in each of these models, they ultimately endorse the basic model given by Shannon and Weaver and are hence unidirectional, linear and non-interactive.

In short, the transmission model distorts the very truth of communication. It distorts the conceptual basis of communication by killing the quintessential element of interactivity. As communication is interactive, it empowers both the participants in the process equally. None is privileged at the expense of the other. In other words, each citizen can put forward his/her views in the public sphere and influence the agenda of public discourse. This element of liberty, rather right to communicate, in the public sphere is taken away when the public sphere is captured by the mass media, making communication unidirectional and privileging the media owner as producer of mass media messages and passivizing the media user as a mere consumer. So, while communication creates communication equality between the citizens, mass communication creates communication inequality between media owners and media users.

So, when the Transmission School defines communication as a uni-directional process of sending messages from a producer to a consuming mass audience, it effects a basic distortion in the meaning of the term. What the Transmission

School speaks of is 'mass communication' and not 'communication'. This semantic shift has been basically facilitated by two important factors: the emergence of the mass media technologies like the printing press, the television, and the cinema and the expansion of the public sphere.

The birth of the mass media technologies helped not only in the mass replication of messages but also in the extension of the public sphere. While the mass production of messages brought down the unit cost of production, it also increased the efficient use of resources. In this respect, the mass media behaved like the other mass production technologies of the industrial age. With the increase in the output of communication products, it was possible to increase their circulation and/or subscription. In other words, enhanced production led to extended markets, which in turn extended the public sphere. The extended public sphere did not permit face to face communication, thereby killing interactivity. Besides, as the power of sending messages got fixed and localized with the media owners, communication became a one-way traffic of messages from powerful media owners to passive, faceless and heterogeneous mass of audiences. This gave birth to mass communication, a process at once opposed to that of communication.

The advent of mass media and its attendant phenomenon of mass communication turned communication upside down. It usurped the right of the citizen to communicate in the public domain and handed over the right, read power, to communicate to either the government or corporate houses that got to control the mass media. The communication equality that characterized interpersonal communication turned into a communication inequality in which the mass media owner monopolized the right to communicate as the 'sender' of mass media messages and the citizen was passivised as a mere recipient of those messages; the maximum extent to which (s)he could make his/her presence felt in the process of communication was to give a feedback. The content of public discourse got restricted to the agenda that the mass media organization decided, keeping in mind its editorial and business policy. It is this inequality that further led to power inequality between the privileged and the marginalized in human society, particularly in the developing world.

Besides, as the mass media messages had to reach out to a large audience, there could be no personalized communication. Mass audiences, which were heterogeneous and anonymous, called for mass messages that could appeal to the largest common denominator of such an audience. Obviously, like the factories which churned out 'standardised' products for mass consumption, the mass media came out with 'standardized' messages containing news pertaining to business ventures to begin with and political and social change in later times. Both reached out to heterogeneous mass of users submerging the small group proclivities and individual idiosyncrasies. Standardization was, therefore, a clever capitalistic euphemism for such a deterioration of quality.

The phenomena, which began with the print media, continued with the electronic media, especially television, with the exception of the radio. With a view to enhancing its TRPs, the TV channels sought to produce programmes that caught the attention of the greatest number of eyeballs. With the booming of business opportunities, and a fillip in advertising, the fight for viewers' attention became greater. In the attention economy of the twentieth century, television sold the attention of its audiences to the advertisers. Radio, though an exception to this trend, could do nothing to obviate it as it came under the guillotine of governments fearful of the power that it could give to the masses and corporate houses suspicious of its power to circumvent copyright provisions that ensure the trickling in of their revenues perennially.

Controlled by the governments, the radio too produced messages that empowered the government at the expense of the masses. In effect, mass media effectuated a breakdown in the continuity of the quintessential meaning of communication. It gave birth to models of communication that fixed the roles of the two communicators as sender and receiver and made the process largely unidirectional. The producer of mass messages was empowered at the expense of the consumer of those mass messages and the communication inequality was stabilized in the mass media for a long time to come.

The dominance of mass media technologies in the public sphere was facilitated by the structural changes in the latter. As long as (wo)men lived in small and geographically cohesive communities, it was possible for the members of the community to interact with each other face to face. But, as the community started disintegrating and giving way to the modern industrial societies, it was not possible to sustain interaction among its members to interact face to face. The void created by the disintegration of the community could set in centrifugal forces but for the role played by mass media to replace the geographical public sphere by the mediated one. Mass media supplanted the town hall/village green as the forum for public debate, discussion and information. Mass media sought to inform, educate and entertain its audiences. With its wide-sweeping reach, it could overcome the barriers of distance to connect the members of the community scattered over the length and breadth of a nation-state and create, thereby, the semblance of cultural cohesion. Along with the developed means of transportation, it became the instrument of building huge nation-states and of sustaining them administratively. Soon, communication that embraced interpersonal and group interaction got back-grounded from the public domain and the mass communication of messages by the mass media got foregrounded.

The Transmission School of Communication and the process of mass communication perpetuated a communication inequality wherein the sender of the messages got empowered at the expense of the recipient. The 'massification' of media messages was a pivotal element in the widespread prevalence of this model in theory and praxis. So, any attempt at restoring the balance in the communication inequality had to target this massification of messages. This got catalyzed through two important developments in mass media. One was the emergence of the new media consequent upon the advent of the new information and communication technologies and the other was the reinvention of the old media in response to the threat from the new media.

Emergence of New Media and the Resurrection of Communication

The New Media was at once a democratic media that pulled the rug from under the seat of power of the 'producer' of messages and rehabilitated the user as an equal participant in communication. Tim Berger Lee's Mosaic browser was designed to enable the Web surfers to communicate among themselves irrespective of who had hosted the site. For the first time, the difference between the producer and the consumer of messages had been made to evaporate and the quintessential spirit of communication as it obtained at the interpersonal and the small group level resurrected. Obviously, it resulted in the individuation/personalization of messages, which the old mass media could never achieve. For the first time, the lumpen mass of mass communication had acquired a face, a personal and individual character.

The old mass media reacted to this development through a number of measures. One was the co-opting of the new media and its incorporation within the matrix of the old media. Newspapers and TV channels increasingly resorted to the use of mobile messages for opinion polls and for narrowcasting. Some of them went online by hosting the print editions on the web as their news sites. But, though they went on the Web they little understood the character of the new media. As a result, they ended up hosting shovel ware on their sites. As understanding of the new media dawned, the interactive options available on the news sites increased, enabling the participation of the audience in the process of mass communication. The development of blogs was another step in the direction of the empowerment of the audience as an equal participant in the process of communication. Each of these developments had the fallout of greater acknowledgement of the personal/individual element in mass communication. As individual readers accessed the various interactive options available on the news sites or communicated their views through mobile phones to the media house, the personal element in communication got strengthened.

The reach of the new media has been further increased with the change in the platform of its usage. As long as desktop computers were the medium through which new media messages were processed and communicated, the reach of this medium was restricted to the academic elites. But with the ubiquitous cell phone taking over as the platform of new media, it has penetrated the common folk living at the base of the demographic pyramid. In other words, it has successfully extended the public sphere to include within its ambit people from socially and economically depressed backgrounds. This is an essential step in the direction of the democratization of communication in the national public sphere. Apart from the role, new media has started playing in the political process of nation-states, it has also impacted upon the ways in which people interact at the social, economic and cultural planes.

This book is an attempt to capture the path-breaking changes in the media landscape of the world, consequent upon the birth of the new media technologies and their impact upon the political and economic rubric of the various national societies. Reflecting this concern is the section-wise division of the book, with each section presenting the canvas of these changes and their impact through the prism of the respective national perspectives.

The first section **Media in Transition** represents five national perspectives. Marie Denward's 'Broadcast Culture Meets Role-Playing Culture: Consequences for Audience Participation in a Cross-Media Production' presents the Swedish perspective. In this chapter, Denward talks about how mass media is repositioning itself in the face of the challenge posed by the new media's total media experience. She exemplifies it through her study of an alternate reality game produced by the public broadcaster, Swedish Television, in collaboration with a small pervasive game company to provide online and live action role playing experiences in parallel with traditional TV drama, resulting in 'interaction for spectators.' Yah-Huei Hong in 'Reject Now, Accept in the Future?: A Study of Innovation Resistance to Candidate Web Sites and Blogs' explores the reasons underlying the rejection by voters in Taiwan of web sites and blogs hosted by candidates who participated in 2006 Taipei and Kaohsiung mayoral elections. The study is carried out with a view to understanding why users may reject a new technology and resist its adoption in certain unique situations. The author studies this unique problem within the twin frameworks of Technology Acceptance Model (TAM) and Innovation Resistance Theory. Nuria Almiron in 'The Financialization of the US Media System: Links and Dependencies (2007-08)' explores the recent phenomenon of financialization in the US media as contrasted with commoditization, with a view to uncovering the lexus between the financial markets and the media. She shows through her analysis of media ownership patterns, financial statements and top management control that media organizations in the US have become largely financial organizations with many of them having finance as their core business. The last chapter of Section A represents the Israeli perspective. Dr. Yuval Karmiel in 'Global Warming on Second Life: The Public Sphere and Free Discussion in Collaborative Virtual Environments' compares discussions among random participants in the real, physical world to those held with similar participants in the virtual environment of Second Life on global warming and finds the real world discussion to be far more serious and profound than that of the virtual world, though the latter was more liberal and participatory, indicating that virtual public space has not as yet matured to take the place of the existing public sphere, which is both geographical and mass-mediated. Dr. Pooja Rana in the 'Emergence of Supplement Journalism in India' presents a comparative analysis of the content of supplements brought out in two leading Indian dailies, one in English, The Times of India, and another in Hindi, Dainik Bhaskar. She shows how the emergence of supplement journalism in the post-liberalized phase of Indian economy has burst beyond the seams of political news pre-occupying Indian newspapers into the subjects of popular discourse due to the advertisers' desire to reach out to different segments of the market in the composite Indian reading public. She argues that this diversified engagement with the various aspects of social life, however, lacks depth of interrogation and involvement, as its sole purpose is to attract the attention of the various segments of the audience for the benefit of the marketers.

The second section **Media and the Knowledge Society** represents the Canadian, Islamic, Swedish, Brazilian and Turkish perspectives. In the chapter 'The WIPO-Development Agenda Forum and its Prospects for Taking into Account Different Levels of Development', Sara Bannerman discusses the merit of WIPO Development Agenda, as proposed in 2004, by a coalition of developing countries called the 'Friends of Development'. The chapter analyses how WIPO needs to be sensitive to the variety of levels of development of various countries while planning and implementing Intellectual Property Rights as the flow of information to developing counters is vital for their growth. She argues that the development agenda addresses a broad range of issues and proposes changes to WIPO's institutional procedures that could see the inclusion of a wider range of interests and perspectives in the organization's activities, with particular focus on transparency, participatory norm setting, member state consultation, and non-governmental organizations' participation. In the chapter 'Knowledge Society as a Pathway to Sustainable Development in the Arab World: An Islamic Cultural Perspective', Prof. Muhammad Ayish speaks of the imperatives of localizing particularity the notion of knowledge society to that of the Islamic cultural perspective underpinning life in the Arab world so that the Arab society can mark progress without disrupting continuity with its glorious past as expounded in The Holy Quran. He elaborates how knowledge acquisition and dissemination lies at the centre of Islamic thought and belief and goes on to present an Islamic Knowledge Model as an alternative to the Western knowledge Model. So even as he emphasizes the need for going beyond the traditional sources of knowledge, he emphasis the need for meeting the challenge to synthesize the cherished values of the Islamic culture with the innovations of thought emanating from the West. Ernesto Abalo and others in 'Emerging Patterns of Inclusion and Exclusion in the era of E-government' posits that patterns of inclusion and exclusion emerge as a government agency digitizes its information and services by making them increasingly Internet-based. Based on a survey of 762 unemployed citizens using the Swedish Public Employment Service, they conclude that these are no black-and-white compartmentalization between inclusion and exclusion, but degrees of them. The study shows that the degrees of exclusion are inversely related the level of education and directly related to age. So, unemployed people who are on the periphery of digital inclusion have less chances of availing of job opportunities online than those who are near the center of digital inclusion. Denize Correa Araujo in 'Digital Divide: Causes and effects in Contemporary Brazilian Society' analyzes the complexity of the digital divide and the social/ political/and economic divide. The author argues that it is easier to achieve digital inclusion than social, political and economic inclusion, with the help of his evaluative study of two projects, 'The lighthouses of knowledge' and 'The Streets of Citizenship', being run in Curitiba, Capital of Parana, a province of Brazil for offering the less privileged people opportunities to Communicate over the cyberspace. He, however, believes that access to online communication can play an instrumental role in removing social, economical and political inequalities and divides. In 'WSIS, Turkey and Information Society', Babacan Tasdemir and Funda Basaran Ozdemir discuss critical issues concerning both the conceptualization and the materialization of the Information Society discourse, within the framework of WSIS at the international level and TSIS at the national level, in the case of Turkey. The authors argue that both the documents strongly depend on the hegemonic discourses of global capitalism and that the euphoria created is a cover to hide the economic designs of global capitalism to take advantage of globally built information networks to make push for markets and profits.

The third section is on **Media and Development**. It presents four different national perspectives. Nico Carpentier in 'Opening Up the Black Box of Participation: A Reception Study into the Conditions of Possibility of Mediated Participatory Practices' strikes a cautionary note in reading too much into the participatory narrative of the new media. He opines that technology in itself cannot ensure participation; it is the people who ensure it. The chapter is based on a comparative case study of nine films posted on the online platform *16plus* and an access TV programme *Barometer* on the TV1 channel of the VRT in Belgium. He concludes that mediated participation is not enough for a programme to be positively valued. The case studies also show that respondents use social relevance as a key principle for evaluating media output. Satarupa Dasgupta in 'Encapsulating a Freirean Logic of Empowerment Examining the Sonagachi Project, a Community-oriented Peer Outreach Initiative among Sex Workers in Calcutta, India' undertakes evaluation of the Sonagachi Project, a peer outreach and participation-based programme, under the guidance of sex workers, from a Freirean perspective. The Sonagachi Project aimed at the uplift of the sex workers in Sonagachi through community, group and individual- based participatory communication strategies, wherein the sex workers themselves were equal participants as they acted as change agents. This could be possible only because mass media intervention was kept out of its preview. Embodying the Freirean postulates of dialogic action, the Sonagachi project shows how unmediated face-to-face communication can empower a marginalized community of people not only to rid themselves of social stigma but also to emancipate themselves economically and politically. Navneet Anand in his study on 'Internet and the Political Communication Dynamics in India' looks at the potential of new media to draw in both the political parties as well as the citizens into its networked public sphere, which unlike the mediated public sphere of the 20th century is non-hierarchical and open, though this promise is dependent on the resolution of the problem of citizens' access to the new media. Linda Hultberg in 'Women Empowerment and Poverty Reduction in Bangladesh: A Study of the Village Pay Phone System' examines the usage patterns and access of the mobile pay phones given to the women in rural Bangladesh and the consequent impact on men and women using and/or owning them. The study supports earlier finding on women's limited access to the mobile phones given to them through the agency of Grameen Bank. However, increased usage of the mobile pay phone, though in male custody, helped to shift these women from a purely private space into a public space as their houses became sites of social gatherings in which even strangers participated. Hyunwoo Lee in 'The Possibility of Applying Universal Service Policy Principle on Mobile Phone Service in South Korea' states that given the fact that 76.1 percent of Koreans use mobile phones as of 2004, it is rather worrisome that 72.4% of the underprivileged are unable to use them because of high costs of handsets and high call rates, resulting in the exclusion of a segment of the society from the communication sphere/space. To mitigate this social and political exclusion, USO was spoken of. However, economic efficiency based on market competitiveness and social equity do not always go hand in hand. In view of the efficacious role played by USO to mitigate this social and political exclusion, the author has explored how mobile phone communication has become a necessary route to social and political inclusion and how USO is compatible with economic efficiency particularly in the case of Korea where there is restricted competition leading to high profits and high call rates.

The fourth section **Media and the Negotiation of Identity** presents five different national perspectives. Shan-Shan Li in 'Being Cultural Citizen: the Role of Media' investigates the media experiences of Chinese students in Sydney, Australia with the purpose of understanding how they negotiate cultural differences between their native culture and the new culture and if at all, they develop a new hybrid cultural identity. It mainly focuses on their internet and television usage. Elitsa Ivanova explores the notion of 'home' away from 'home' in the chapter on Virtual Diasporas: The Notion of 'Home' and Identity Formation in Cyberspace. She argues that the notion of 'home' is still highly relevant in the formation of diasporic identity. More so in the modern informatized world where people can surpass geographical and political boundaries through the New Media. By enhancing the possibilities for simultaneity, it (New Media) improves their ability to stay connected with their erstwhile as well as host countries, and with each other. However, even if Internet opens up new opportunities of identity construction for the diasporic communities, it does not alter the social base of identity or the conventional constraints on social interaction discourse. Their offline activities and social behaviours both structure and reflect their on time community–building efforts. For most virtual diasporic communities, the notion of home has more of a symbolic value than any material one, as their social experience in the host country happens to structure the construction of their new hybrid identity in the host country. Thus, new media enables virtual diasporic communities to create a new form of imagined community that acts as a meeting point of dialogic encounter and 'home' as a place understood through memory, history and constructed cultural sites. Fernando Kuhn in 'Identities and Media of the Brazilian Diaspora' explores how a miniscule Brazilian immigrant population negotiates its identity in the various countries they have adopted, particularly in the USA with the help of the ethnic mass media and the new media. Kuhn identifies the difference new media has made to this process by constructing 'transnational and local diasporic spaces,' thereby making geographical and political redundant in Community-building. Habtamu Dugo in 'Oromo Diaspora: Quest for Freedom, Democracy and New Media' examines how the Oromo diasporic community makes use of the new media to keep in touch with each other for political activism leading to the national quest for freedom and self-determination. The paper discusses the role of new media as viable alternative in the face of state restrictions/ denials of press freedom and Oromo media ownership rights. Ravi K Dhar in 'New Media and the Redemption of the Other' traces the re-emergence of communication from out of the shadow of mass communication by virtue of the advent of the new information and communication technologies. He argues that, in sharp contrast with mass media, new media facilitates participation of all sections of the citizenry in the public sphere, thereby correcting the power inequality created by the mass media. He, however, cautions against the over-corporatization and excessive regulation of the cyber space apart from the spectre of the digital divide.

The fifth section **Media and the Quest for Truth** presents three national perspectives. In the chapter on 'Labourers of the Real: "Authenticity Work" in Reality Television'. Dr. Minna Aslama discusses an important trend in modern television broadcasting in the US concerning the documentation of the 'authentic' or the 'quest for reality' in Reality TV programming. She speaks of the complexity involved in analyzing this new trend due to its paradoxical nature of being both 'constructed' and 'spontaneous'. She explores the complexity still further by analyzing the 'discourses of authenticity' of the various stakeholders involved in Reality TV: the producers, the cast, the audiences, and the media. She delineates the nuances of each of these discourses to point towards the over-riding concern of Reality TV to engage in the age-old human quest of uncovering the truth of human existence. In the chapter on 'Super Girl and the Expediency of Hybridity', Robert Moses Peaslee and others examine the realty show, Super Girl, the Chinese variant of American Idol or Britain's Pop Idol, and observe that though modeled on them, this show represents the discourse of hybridity which negotiates the space between a creeping homogeneity and a struggling heterogeneity in the global sphere. In 'Anime in Asia: Why not Japanese?: Rethinking the Local-Global Cultural Nexus', Umi Khattab and Gin Chee Tong look at the reasons for the mass appeal of the anime to Asian viewers in the context of the contesting claims of the local-global 'scapes' and observe that anime does not propagate homogeneity, rather it depicts the hybrid, occi-oriental cultural icons, values and practices to better appeal to local, plural Asian audiences.

To conclude, new media has set off a chain of paradigmatic changes in not only the mediascape of nations across the globe but also the landscape of their social, political and economic spheres of activity. As the 21st century unfolds itself, the world we are accustomed to will change at so dramatic a pace that it will render all forms of human thought and behaviour redundant in a matter of months and the world unrecognizable in a matter of years. This rapid pace of technological change will privilege the young and tech-savvy generation at the expense of the middle-aged and the old unless they keep in step with the pace of these changes. Also, the world will become more technologically determined and people who suffer from technological disability will form the new 'outcastes'. But, going by the penetration rate of this technology and the desire of the marketer to make deep inroads into the mass at the bottom of the pyramid, the layer of such a class of 'outcastes' should be wafer-thin and at the extreme fringes of human society. All in all, the NICTs promise to make their world more democratic, more inclusive and more cohesive.

Section A

MEDIA IN TRANSITION

2

Broadcast Culture Meets Role-Playing Culture Consequences for Audience Participation in a Cross-media Production

Marie Denward

"*Role-playing nerds strike back*". This was the headline on 24th April 2008 in Svenska Dagbladet[1], one of the biggest Swedish daily newspapers, when reporting on a small anarchistic pervasive entertainment company, winning an iEmmy Award for Best Interactive Television Service 2008[2]. "*In the beginning we were all nerds and role-playing geeks*", says Christopher Sandberg, CEO at The company P. With roots in the subculture of Nordic live action role-playing[3], the company has been involved in a couple of experimental productions on a non-profit basis, now trying to earn a living on their hobby engagement. "*We ran around in the forests waiving rubber swords, and got teased by our older sisters. This movement has been underground for many years, and this prize is a kind of revenge*", he continues.

When public service broadcaster Swedish Television (SVT) wanted to create a drama beyond reality TV and docusoaps, the company P (P) played an important part. In close cooperation the two merged fiction and reality in a media production that would "*make the viewers get up from the TV sofas*". *Sanningen om Marika (SOM)*[4] was not only a television series, it was also a game that lasted a few months, played both on the net and in the real world. The drama and the game together with a series of debate programs were the main components of the production.

The *Sanningen om Marika* production had two teams, one working at the company P and the other at SVT. This article focuses the cooperating companies and their conflicting production cultures. The cultural differences could not have been larger – SVT being the oldest and most prestigious media company in Sweden with a reputation of objective reporting and civic education, and P being a very young, small, and quite anarchistic company relying partially on volunteers in their productions.

The production was one of the very few experiments to marry traditional broadcast culture with the 'participation culture'[5] fostered in the Nordic countries, primarily within the live action role-playing (LARP) subculture. But it was also an example of a public service broadcaster's attempt to keep pace with the fast changing media landscape, redefining their programme obligations, service commitments and changing audience expectations. One of the aims with *SOM* was to involve the audience in new ways using broadcasted television and radio, the Internet, mobile applications and a fictional universe that blurred the fictive and the real.

The *SOM* production can be seen in the light of the changing media landscape, changes that can be observed and experienced on all levels in society, in the way media companies operate and how users/consumers interact with and use media products and content (Jenkins & Deuze, 2008). What we can observe is an enormous expansion of new actors. Thus, the relationship between the media industry and its audience has changed, compared to a few decades back. Now, in the twenty first century media are converging to form a 'hybrid media ecology' (Benkler, 2006 in Jenkins, 2008), where almost any individual or group has the ability and the power to produce and distribute content. As a result of all of today's media technologies saturating our work and life environments "*no one is 'outside' anymore*", Deuze concludes (2007:38) arguing it is necessary to stop referring to our behaviour as consumption or production, instead acknowledging that we are "*working and living in the media*". This culturalisation of the new economy and everyday life aesthetisation produce consumers prepared and capable to modify, design and innovate products themselves to fit their needs. In turn, companies in several fields like media and cultural industries have begun to embed the productive activities of consumers in their business strategies.

This article focuses the meeting between two very different companies in the hybrid media ecology. It points at the clashing production cultures and processes, and the effects they had on their joint cross-medial production. Observations show that, due to their differing production cultures, the production teams carried underlying conflicting notions and opinions both of the audience and of the product to be designed and produced. This affected the game design and the output for the audience; the possibilities to interact and participate. The broadcaster used its traditional broadcast production processes and methods that resulted in 'interaction for spectators' while the pervasive games actor created more and different possibilities for the audience to participate.

The Production

Sanningen om Marika could be described as a cross-medial production – a production spanning several media types. The creators called it a "*participation drama*" (SVT, 2007a), indicating the intent to get the audience to actively participate in the storyline. Due to the size and structure of broadcast organisations the development of multi platform formats has been initiated and largely led by the broadcast industry (Ytreberg, 2007). It is easier for broadcasters to free and redirect resources towards digital media than the opposite; for digital media companies to start broadcasting. This was also the case with the *SOM* production; it was initiated by SVT. A freelancing SVT producer was employed with the mission to create a new type of drama production that would include new forms of audience participation; a novel format that would take off in a television drama that invited *"the audience* [...] *to step in to the fiction and take part in it in new ways"* (Lägersten, 2007) by exploiting the prospects of interweaving pervasive game components. A production that would target new audience groups in the problematic segment of youth and young adults that neither watched SVT's programmes nor watched television at all, but were more interested in digital games and other interactive media content and products.

The producer was inspired by the Canadian *ReGenesis*[7] production, where a television program was connected to a type of alternate reality game, ARG. According to Jane McGonigal, an ARG is

> "an interactive drama played out in online and real spaces, taking place over several weeks or months, in which dozens, hundreds or thousands of players come together online, form collaborative social networks, and work together to solve a mystery or problem [...] that would be absolutely impossible to solve alone." (McGonigal, 2004)

Highly skilled competence in game design and game production was needed and had to be found outside the SVT organisation. A workshop was held with participants from organisations with representatives from The company P and two IT research institutes[8] to develop early game concepts fall 2005. This resulted in a P representative getting a few months part time employment to write the first treatment of the entire *SOM* production, the television production and the game. Probably this is the first time in broadcast history where a television production and an ARG have been codesigned from day one.

During 2006 the television drama was recorded by SVT. Early 2007 The company P was brought in as a consultant to create and design the game that would offer the audience LARP experiences in parallel with traditional TV viewing. P had an outspoken goal to create a 'pervasive game' where the reality outside the game would blur and intervene with the game. P also had ideological and political goals; they intended the game to be a learning experience that would assist in the participants' personal development processes and encourage them to question values and behaviours that are considered 'normal' in today's society.

Pervasive games form a broad category of games that blur the boundaries of game and ordinary life; carried out in public spaces and urban environments (Montola & Stenros forthcoming). They involve outsiders and intertwine with participant's everyday living and ordinary routines, and as they are played in the physical surroundings of the participant they give extra flavour to a participant's ordinary life. Alternate reality games can be seen as one of many subgenres of pervasive games. Since pervasive games break up the boundary of gaming in terms of space, time and social relations, the actions in the game can be difficult to separate from nongame actions (Montola, 2005). This shapes ambiguous and unique 'brink' experiences (Poremba, 2007).

The production contained three main components. A televised drama series provided the hub for the storyline. It explained the background and developed the fictional world of the story. In parallel with this clearly fictional drama series, a second story was played out in the real world and on the Internet, where the participants were encouraged to *"pretend that it was real"* and to imagine and immerse into the fiction as if it was reality rather than just engagement in a game. The third core component of the production was a public debate program aired weekly directly after the drama series. This program, which was recorded a day before it was aired, served as a means to connect the fictional drama series (recorded a year in advance) to the ongoing game.

Due to the nature of the production with multiple modes of engagement, it is not possible to say precisely how many persons actually participated in the game. Our survey had 385 respondents, the central game site had 490 registered participants and the secret society[10] site, which was used to organise the most important real-world activities, had 751 registered participants. A rough estimate is that about 500 persons participated in the game to some extent. According to the web statistics the number of individuals participating in a lighter manner was much higher; browsing, reading and viewing material on conspirare.se, other production web pages, *YouTube* and *Flickr*.[11] The participant profiles ranged from television viewers to experienced role-players. The majority were between 17 to 40 years.

Modes of Participation

Sanningen om Marika offered multiple modes of participation. To make it possible to at the same time watch *SOM* as a TV viewer and participate in this intense role-playing experience, the game offered multiple layers of participation with gradually intensifying immersion and influence over the storyline.

Game activities in the real world were organised in different ways. *Conspirare* was used to invite to and organise larger events, visible for any visitor on the webpage. Other real world participation in the game was organised through a separate website for the fictional secret society. The participants were encouraged to enlist in the society, which would send them on different missions and tasks in the real world in order to rise in rank within the society. The secret society focused on self-organised play in smaller groups, "*cells*". This part was also technology-supported; the participants were encouraged to download a mobile phone application,

Figure 1. A matrix.

which enabled them to read two-dimensional bar codes, "*matrixes*" (see Figure 1), with their mobile phone camera. In return, the participants would get a mission to perform and document. Participants could also submit their documentation to SVT, which put some of it on their web site and selected some of it to show in the debate program. The plot and storylines were held open to a certain extent, so that participants could initiate and influence the story through online and live action role-playing.

A final component of the production consisted of a puzzle-solving quest. In the drama series, an SVT character had put in hidden "*subliminal messages*" that were not visible to the eye, and then SVT made a special tool available on the SVT website that allowed the participants to watch the entire TV series, step by step, and find these messages. These were puzzles that, when solved, gave a password for yet another site where a subplot could be explored. The purpose of this part of the production was to invite and offer television viewers a lighter form of participation through online puzzle-solving, in addition to the physical play offered by the secret society and the role-play offered at conspirare.se.

Production Cultures

There is no commonly accepted definition on the concept of media production culture as such. If connected to a particular organisation/corporate body then it can be considered part of that organisation's culture, and thus the production culture is developed and determined in this particular organisation. The problem still lingers if we try to sort out the definition of organisation culture. Küng-Shankleman (2000:6) states various definitions on culture in this context, such as the ability to decipher phenomena like myths, ceremonies and rituals, or that culture can define behaviour and resolve ambiguity or even legitimise organisational actions, ideas and demands as well as determine an organisation's ability to master environmental changes and even directly influence economic performance.

Here I define production culture as rooted in and part of an organisation's culture that determines how production will be carried out and is manifested. In this production process the shared ideas and notions about the products of the organisation and about the customers/audience shape what to produce and for whom.

Apart from the difference in production cultures formed by the particular organisations or corporations—SVT and P—there is another dimension of production culture determined by the specific medium; broadcast and role-playing.[13] This refers to the concept of 'media logic' defined by Altheide and Snow (1979 in McQuail 2005) and captures the systematic nature of pre-existing definitions of representative content. This in turn implies the existence of a 'media grammar', which governs how time should be used, how items of content should be sequenced and what devices of verbal and non-verbal content should be used (McQuail, 2005). Media logic has been especially useful for identifying the predilection of media producers for factors that they believe will increase audience attention and satisfaction. Taken up by and developed by Peter Dahlgren (1996) it refers to

> "... the particular institutionally structured features of a medium, the ensemble of technical and organizational attributes which impact on what gets represented in the medium and how it gets done. In other words, media logic points to specific forms and processes which organize the work done with in a particular medium. Yet, media logic also indicates the cultural competence and frames of perception of audiences/users, which in turn reinforces how production within the medium takes place." (1996:63)

Thus, to analyse the design and production of the audience participation in the *Sanningen om Marika* production, light has to be put on the different production processes and media logics, dependent on the corporations and the media used.

Organisations

SVT is the oldest Swedish television broadcaster with a history reaching back to the 1950's, when television was a novelty. During recent years, the organisation has undergone major changes, similar to other European broadcasters. The company's strategy to face economic challenges is to reduce costs by rationalizing of the organisation and its productions, SVT states in its policy documents (Enli, 2008). The complex and hierarchical structure of a television production process (Deuze, 2007) also shape SVT's productions, with changes towards project-based production processes and semi-employed staff mixed with consulting and freelancing specialists. Accordingly most of the *SOM* production team were professionals in their own specialised field in the broadcasting process. They worked as consultants or on contracts for a certain period of the production, such as the producer, web editor and the directors of the drama series and debates to mention a few. However, many of the technical and basic professionals were on the other hand SVT employees.

Today, part of SVT's public service remit is to guarantee a broad range of programs and services via television, Internet and other forms of publication (SVT, 2007b). Programs can be watched on the Internet, and the usage of new media (games, chats, program web sites) has increased. The *SOM* team was part of the Gothenburg division, one of the seven program production departments throughout Sweden that serve both the regional audience and the national scene. SVT recently moved into a large four-story glass covered building with top modern working areas, located in the old harbour of Gothenburg, on the west coast of Sweden.

By comparison, The company P is a small, newly founded pervasive games entertainer, staffed by individuals experienced in organising pervasive entertainment and other similar productions.[14] Most of these people belong to the Nordic role-playing culture community or had contacts through their personal networks. P is a small flexible organisation with less than twenty people project-employed in overlapping design and production teams. P's three-room office is situated in an old nineteen century building, in a central Stockholm back street, walls painted black, white chalked wooden flooring, white-painted curved door and deep window sills. A big brown leather suitcase catches your eye in the small entrance, filled with handwritten pieces of papers, small watercolour paintings, ripped out pages from old books and other interesting pieces of props like electric cords, dice, dolls, feathers, all used during the *Prosopopeia* LARPs.[15] The office furniture came from both IKEA—modern office chairs and tables—and a cheap purchase from the Royal Theatre's 'sell out' of not needed theatrical props—nineteen century wooden furniture with velvet and leather imitation cover, for 'round table' meetings and visitors as well as for the pleasure of the eye. The company tries to commercialise various kinds of experimental pervasive entertainment products and productions. This interest includes not only the commercialisation of the entertainment LARPs, it also held strong ideological political features, and P workers believed pervasive entertainment could be used as a personal transformative power for individuals and in society at large.

At P the features of non-profit production culture were strong. In this culture everybody is expected to be engaged and able to work constructively and creatively whenever needed. This clashed with the commercial production culture of SVT, with regulated working time. Non-profit production culture like this contains two driving forces for the producers: the belief in your own capacity to make a good result and the expectations that your own engagement and work will result in getting game experiences back from participants (IPERG, 2006). This was very obvious in how *SOM* was managed, i.e. 'game mastered'. The head game master carried out his game mastering to receive experiences and immersion from it, both for him and for the rest of the game mastering crew.

The two teams cooperated primarily through weekly phone meetings, and in online forum dialogues on the project's web portal. Due to the geographical distance between the teams (400 kms), only a few physical meetings were held, in Stockholm and Gothenburg. The original aim was to move to a joint office during the intense phase of the production (during airing of the TV series), but this could not be realised for economical reasons. The online web portal was used in the early phase of the production, but technical problems made it less useful in the end. As all team members could not participate in all meetings, information was sometimes lost or did not reach all people involved (Rados, 2007).

The teams thus differed not only in their physical environment and size, but also in their societal/institutional and organisational context and history. They also had quite different goals—profitable and non-profitable—for the production. The differences were acknowledged by both parties and created a strong motivation to understand each other's cultures and languages. They were the focus for many meetings, especially in the beginning of the design and production process.

Media Production

SVT had the producer's role but the two teams had agreed on how to divide the work, according to their specialities and responsibilities. SVT was responsible for the drama series, studio debates, trailers and other marketing activities. SVT produced a *SOM* program webpage and a web editorial staff worked with the interactive components. P, on the other hand, was subcontracted to design and produce the game parts. This included game mastering, managing of interactive actors and forum editorial staff, as well as producing the real life installations and online puzzles. P also produced props, sounds and choreography and subliminal images for key scenes of the drama series, and edited the script for both the series and debates. In a joint research venture with the Swedish Institute of Computer Science and The Interactive Institute, The company P developed the technology platform that enabled participation on all available media—web sites, forum, chat, mobile application, created the game parts—and the orchestration of the these activities. Two groups of participants also served as volunteer game masters, one in Stockholm and one in Gothenburg.

In many respects the production at SVT was uncontroversial and followed ordinary broadcast production processes. The production was divided in several parts and teams, depending on the type of content to be produced; drama series, fictional debates or promotional parts as trailer, marketing and web pages. However, in other respects it was very unusual and unique. Professionals from different departments worked tightly together, and high-level managers took part in the on-the-fly decisions usually carried out at lower levels (Engblom, 2007; Lägersten, 2007; Wikander, 2007). Compared with SVT the production process at P looked very different. The design process of the game was carried out by a software development method[16] promoting iterations throughout the life cycle of the production, which the team learned and that worked satisfactorily through out the design and production process. Every week the team had follow-up and planning meetings and during the intense runtime period from mid-October to end of November the meetings were daily. There was consensus of the design document as a dynamic piece and numerous iterations and game test were made along the design process.

The cultures of media workers have been frequently investigated (Mc Quail, 2005; Küng-Shankelman, 2000) since it is widely assumed that the social background and outlook of those responsible for media production will influence the content of their media products. The SVT key *SOM* crew was experienced broadcast professionals, but with little or no knowledge of role-playing games. For the P team the opposite ruled. It is also a familiar idea that amongst audiences the personality and values of the author will give the work its primary meaning, despite being processed in a media industry (McQuail, 2005). Deuze (2007) states that media logic can be medium-specific because it primarily relates to production patterns within a given technological and organizational context. He presupposes that the process of giving meaning to the actions and beliefs of media workers has consequences for how media are made. A P worker wrote the treatment, by purpose of course—the cooperation with P aimed at creating something SVT didn't have internal competence for, thus leaving strong traces of Nordic Larp design principles to create a role-playing experience for the participants/audience.

The processes of broadcast production and role-playing games are quite different both technically and practically. Figure 2 illustrates the differences in the main work processes. The broadcaster thinks in terms of transmission, creates a finished program and transmits it to an audience (Bardoel & Lowe, 2006), a one-way communicative activity. The audience is typically seen as passive spectators, a 'target', limited in influence and interaction with the storyline, and success is measured quantitatively in terms of viewer ratings. The program is seen as a performance, with a set narrative and plot. A director uses a written manuscript to direct and stage employed actors to implement the show. The performance is recorded and broadcasted to an audience. The result is a controlled, one-directional and easily broadcasted product.

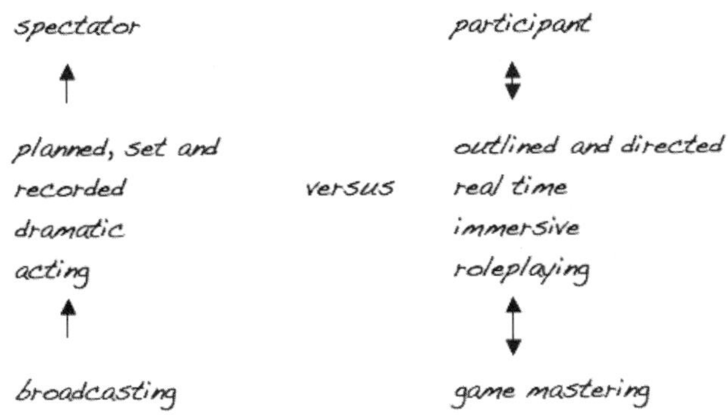

Figure 2: Broadcast and role-playing production.

On the other hand, in role-playing culture the individuals (both game masters and players) taking part are seen as participants and co-creators by the producers, and participants are expected to contribute to game masters' game experiences as well.

A flexible game design and open minded game masters are crucial to succeed with a role-playing game. The role-playing producer stages the scene, crafts the rules, and plans the core narratives, plots and characters (Montola & Stenros forthcoming). The producer is prepared for anything to happen in the game; participants often respond in surprising ways that can interfere with plans for later scenes, causing a demand for narratives, plots or characters to be changed, developed and carried out in unforeseen directions. This enables the creation of a planned but open-ended, interactive and multi-directional experience, played out online in chats, forums and in the physical world by LARPing in streets, parks, and nature.

SVT predicates to invite the audience to dialogue and participation on different levels in their activities (Enli, 2008) not only through the TV screen but by publishing its content on other platforms. This has also been pushed a lot internally (Rados, 2007; Lägersten, 2007). The audience participation offered to the *SOM* audience was intended to supply SVT with 'user generated content'.

By contrast, P aimed to foster participatory culture. Although the game part of *Sanningen om Marika* had a clear producer, the participants were expected to cocreate the game and storyline together with the game designers. The main mechanism worked to create a joint role-playing experience in which both the participants and organisers took part, and in which the roles by no means were fixed. As the participants got more involved in the game, they also gradually took on more and more of an organiser's role. The differences in attitudes between SVT and P were observed even in the details such as the wordings in blogs, the choice of pictures and photos and the selection of communication tools such as *Flickr*, *YouTube* and *GoogleMaps*.

These differences made cooperation complicated, as there was not a full agreement on what the production was—a recorded performance with Swedish Television's quality requirements and deeply conditioned understandings of broadcast practitioners of what to produce and for whom, or an open role-playing game, in which immersion in the game and a good player experience for both participant players and game masters were the most important things.

Observations

The observed consequences of the differences in production cultures and methods and thus views of the audience were vast and the list of examples lengthy. In spite of SVT coproducing with the subcontracted company one can very clearly observe the differences shining through in the produced material.

One of the most obvious examples is the televised debate, the fictionalised current affairs debate program, where the aim was to link the two very different components; the broadcasted drama and the participatory game activities online and in the real world. Early on, the companies had agreed on the goals of the current affairs debate program. The intent was to exhibit and contextualise the game for television viewers and to give the game participants a chance to appear nationwide on the television screen. However, when it was time to start producing the debate SVT recruited a director internally, who had other ideas for the program. The director would not bring in participants into the studio, and selected only a few video clips and photos from the contributed participant material. He had an explicit goal to produce "*good television*", which demanded a degree of quality he didn't feel the participant material had. Timing in broadcast production is difficult when different tasks are to be allocated and completed and in this case the director came in in the middle of the game design process. According to Tunstall (2001 in Deuze 2007) there is a tendency to think horizontally in terms of one's own speciality, not only difference in skills but also different sources of information, motivations and interests. To that can be added the at times different agendas, work practices and idea(l)s of freelance specialists and contracted or semi-permanent employers (Deuze, 2007). Still, the original idea of creating a live current affairs debate program was retained, and the director's re-planning of the debate made it a highly realistic side story to the television drama. He used his role-playing experiences and game mastered the actors separately, which strongly contributed to create a convincing fictionalised reality. This was a masterful move, and made the debate one of the most novel parts in the production, but it also lessened its relevance as a connection between the game and the TV show. From P's point of view though, this had a negative impact on the participatory elements of the game.

Common methods to 'pretend' audience participation and liveness in television were also used. This method of giving an appearance of liveness Bourdon calls 'continuity' to cover cases where television gives the appearance of liveness without being transmitted live in a strict meaning (2000 in Ytreberg, 2007). Studio-based shows like the public debate program are example of this. This common Swedish television genre—live current affairs debate programs (Örnebring, 2001)—entail possibilities for the audience to intervene and interact instantly, either by phoning, sending in questions via e-mail or SMS (Creber, 2000; Örnebring, 2001). But here the debate programs were part of the fiction and recorded one day in advance of the airing of the drama series. They were, promoted as 'live sent' by the program host in the trailers and only purposely indistinctly promoted as part of the *SOM* fiction in the program schedule. The survey answers and interviews show that many viewers/participants didn't perceive this and were unsure of if they were 'real' or not. The debate programs also contained prefabricated or previously sent in SMS appearing as SMS Ticker Tapes along the bottom of the screen, in this way giving an appearance of liveness and bypassing real time and authentic audience participation.

Similar observations were also made in the use of the Internet as one of the platforms in the production. The Internet is part of the digital development that has made interaction with the audience possible for broadcasters (Ytreberg, 2007). In spite of this digital medium's participatory potential and the fact that their close cooperator held knowledge and skills and used this potential, it was apparent that SVT continued its linear production methods. As mentioned earlier, a made up conflict between SVT and Adrijanna, staged on their two parallel homepages, was part of the narrative. On the SVT production homepage—SVT.se/marika —the web editor Eva Rados' blog was produced as small film snippets where Eva updated participants of how far SVT, with the help of the participants, had gone at the moment in the search for Maria. It served both as a way to update and to inform participants with small news items and documentary reports. These snippets were streamed through SVT Play application.[18] These instantly and quickly produced and 'broadcasted' video blogs served the means of keeping the liveness of the production.

The P crew on the other hand had totally different working and production methods. P worked very actively to include participants, following the designed ambitions of the game but also partly to cover up for the debate's low ambitions on audience participation. As LARP designers P had created several parallel sub stories to the main ones and open-ended plots; 'baits' that could be 'thrown out'. This was made to enhance and give room for participants' actions and ideas to codesign and create the development in the game—how, where and when they would like to take part and immerse into the game. As consequence the size of the sub story about the surveillance company[19] grew very big, with LARP activities around two of the participants. One participant attempted to infiltrate the surveillance company through contracting the company. The other participant tried to infiltrate the surveillance company through sending in her authentic CV thereby trying to become employed. This created huge interest and activities not only for these participants but also for the bigger group of participants that followed and took part in these sub stories in various ways. Participant material that the participants themselves had been urged to upload on *YouTube*, *Flickr* and other well known media applications were quickly published on *Conspirare*: video clips, pictures, photos and other material that could help in the search. This made participation accessible, relevant and game masters could thereby respond quickly. This meant a very varied quality but gave very high relevance for the game play—a conscious design principle of the game designers. This demanded game mastering seven days a week, almost 24 hours a day.

The two examples above are also good examples of the importance of making the game intervene into the participants own daily life's (Montola & Stenros forthcoming) Game masters personal communication with participants through chat messages, SMSes or phone calls made the experiences very strong and immersive and at the same time very participatory. To some extent SVT used the possibilities to interact personally with participants in game the same way. Eva Rados followed the *Conspirare* chat more or less every weekday and her participation was most appreciated by the active participants. Also the producer had e-mail contact with participants both in game and off game and took part a few times in the *Conspirare* chat and forum, using his nickname.

Figure 3: Encouragements at SVT.se (www.svt.se/marika)

Both companies used text and video blogs to encourage audience to interact. But a deeper examination shows large differences in how these blogs were used. At the SVT site, participants were asked to send in material: *"through sending material to the inbox" and "mailing to marika@svt.se"* (Figure 3). At

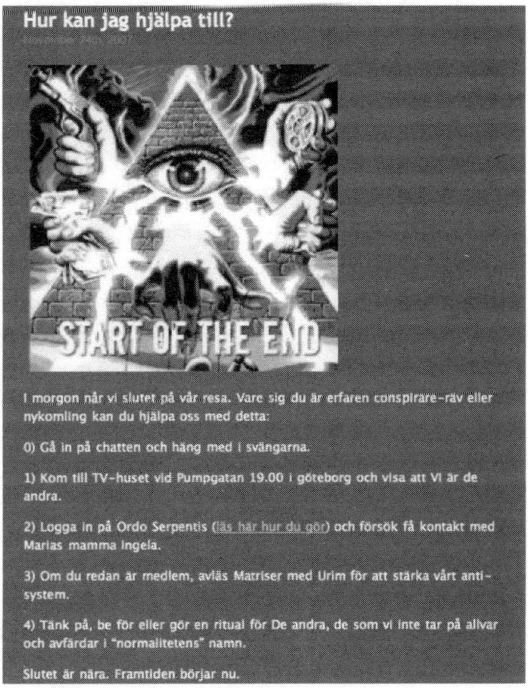

Figure 4: Encouragements at www.conspirare.se

Conspirare (Figure 4), participants could follow and take active part in online discussions, real time chatting and forum threads and together solve clues and mysteries as well as plan and prepare LARP events. Encouragements were pointed toward personal actions *"go to the chat and keep track of all the turns", "come to…the television building and show yourselves", "read matrixes using Urim*[20]*"* and *"think of, pray or make a ritual..".*

"EDITORIAL DIRECTOR RADOS I am the editorial director on this site and actively searching for the truth about what happened to Maria Klingbohm. The editing staff investigates in cooperation with conspirare.se. My blog will keep you updated. Through mailing to marika@svt.se or putting your own material in the inbox you will give us access of your traces and information that could help us in our search." (Translated by the author)

"How can I help? Tomorrow we are reaching the end of our journey. You can help us whether you are a Conspirite or a rookie:

1) Go to the chat and keep track of all the turns.
2) Come to the television building at 7 PM, Pump Street, Gothenburg and show everybody that WE are The Others.[21]
3) If already a member, read Matrixes using Urim to strengthen our anti system.
4) Think of, pray or make a ritual for the ones that we do not take seriously and dismiss in the name of "normality".
   The end is close. The future starts now."

(Translated by the author)

The chat applications exhibit a similar pattern. What SVT called a "*chat*" at the SVT site was, in fact, an FAQ.[22] No dates or times were shown and it was not possible to chat real time. Instead, you had to send in your question and it would (possibly) appear later together with an answer from the web editor. The SVT producer reflected on this during the production, but the application could not be changed at that stage. Examples from SVT chat:

"**Question**: You do not know if Ingela Klingbohm is alive or not?
Answer: As far as we know she has not existed."
And:
"**Question**: But then she is a character in your telly series? (I mean, it IS "based on a true story")][...]
Answer: The drama is not based on a true story. It is based on notes the authors found in town. If Adrijanna says it is the truth then that is up to her."

The chat application at conspirare.se was a freeware chat system[23] designed to displaying real time communication activities. Participants could choose to use their game characters like, "*mattlo*", "*Tomb*" or "*markzpot*", choose a different character for this purpose, or lurk (e.g. a person who only appear as "*lurker*"). The application showed the dates and times of contributions (e.g. messages, photos), allowed secret personal messages between participants while chatting, and so forth. It was an immediate and easy-to-use real-time chat. Participants could easily include URLs[24] and photos in their comments, which appeared in less than a second on the screen. This chat required instant moderation and hence P spent approximately 20 hours a day game mastering it.

These differences in approach towards the participants had a large impact. Interaction and contributions from participants were low on anything that looked as part of SVT and high at conspirare.se. SVT's expectations had been high, and there was considerable disappointment at the apparent lack of participant contributions—film snippets, photos, e-mails—as well as the low activity at the SVT chat and discussion forum.[25] *Conspirare* experienced the exact opposite—the forum grew quickly, constant discussions took place and participant material streamed in.

Still, not all of the activities coordinated by P were successful. The secret society did not gather as many participants as hoped, even though it was constructed to scale. The threshold for participating in the secret society was high. The story behind the game was complex, the participants were required to self-organise into groups, the missions were advanced, and on top of this, at least one participant in each group had to download and install the special mobile phone application that would only run on certain types of phones. In addition, the high level of interactive game mastering done at the real-time chat on conspirare.se required the game masters' undivided attention. As a result, the participants at the secret society got little reward for the completion of their missions. The effect was that the participants of the secret society were mostly the same as the crew that formed the core of *Conspirare* participants. The game failed to scale above the 100 to 300 active participants that could be effectively game mastered by more direct means.

Concluding Remarks

This article reports on observations of two media companies and how they coproduced a novel multi platform production. The *Sanningen om Marika* production is an example of how a Swedish public service broadcaster tries to address a changing media ecology, both in terms of the changing power relation to and enhanced interaction with its audience, and by means of cooperating with an expert in audience participation—a pervasive entertainment company. For public service broadcasters particularly, the new media ecology challenges the paternalistic heritage of public service and its tendency to stick to 'old' technology notwithstanding new and more efficient technology.

A closer look shows that the companies had different production cultures. Broadcast and pervasive games carry different views of what to produce and for whom as an effect of their differing organisation cultures and the differing media use. These differing cultures influenced the production both in how the audience participation was designed and in the outcome of the design—the possibilities to participate and the factual audience participation. The impact was seen both in the absence of participants in the televised debate programs and in the (absence in) user created material on SVT's platforms in the production. The culture clash between the teams was prevailing. However, the parties succeeded in their cooperation as a consequence of the two teams' strong personal engagement and driving force.

This was probably the first time the combination of an alternate reality game and a broadcast production was intentionally created, designed and produced from start to end and from idea to finished production. The fake current affairs debate programs included in the broadcast production also showed signs of novelty. The debate programs were directed, produced and marketed to deliberately blur the fictive and the real thereby dramatising a well-known television genre generally perceived to communicate serious and authentic issues of common interest to the public. In this way SVT, as a public service organisation, took a risk and challenged both itself and its audiences.

SOM also gave Swedish viewers/participants an opportunity to a totally new and never earlier experienced 'treat'; to take part in a Swedish countywide pervasive game at scale connected to a broadcast production. Possibilities to live action role-playing, both online and in the real world nationwide have not been given to an audience at large before.

In April 2008, the production received an international interactive Emmy Award, a well-deserved nomination. It was a truly innovative and original production, merging broadcast and pervasive gaming in a way that no previous production has done. It managed to create a win-win situation for the dedicated participants, for Swedish Television, and for The company P. All three had to extend and challenge their notions. P had to scale up their design, organisation, and work methods in order to create a large-scale production, and Swedish Television had to challenge its own production framework as well as the mainstream audience. Our early analysis of the participants' experience[26] speaks of a totally new and unexpected experience, irrespective of whether the participants were television viewers, experienced online role-players or live action role-players. Swedish Television expanded and challenged their traditional production methods, as well as experimented with traditional formats in new ways to create something novel. P managed to force their ideological and political demands to a great extent and to shake and challenge SVT's norms, rules and control, to design a game that enabled immersive participation. If a new media/television format or genre—participation drama—has been born is too early to say. But the fact is that this was a totally new experience for the SVT audience, which also adds to the difficulties for the audience to read, perceive and take part in this novel and unusual experience.

Other factors, which are not addressed here, but which probably also affected the interaction are the prototypical technology used, the width of the targeted audience(s) and the (poor) quality of the drama series. The very complex and not so easily graspable fictional universe (narrative) has to be added to this list. It intentionally blurred the real and the fictive including the mixing of well known/established television genres—which was time consuming and demanded efforts of the audience to be understood. The analysis of the production will continue concentrating on the participants' responses to the experience, which will shed more light on these factors.

Acknowledgements

This research was carried out within the Mobile Life Centre at Stockholm University[27] and also partly financed by IPerG[28]. I wish to thank the crews at SVT and P for their patience with me, and my constant questions. I am also indebted to all of the participants and others who took part in my interviews, wrote diaries, and answered the questionnaire.

NOTES

1. http://www.svd.se/kulturnoje/nyheter/artikel_1172943.svd (Accessed 15th May 2008)
2. Interactive Emmy Press Release: http://www.iemmys.tv/news_item.aspx?id=60 (Accessed 9th May 2008)
3. The Nordic role-playing community is experimental and usually advanced and has developed its own discourse about games and participatory culture. A further discussion will take us too far from this article topic, see Montola & Stenros (eds.) (2004).
4. Eng. "The Truth About Marika".
5. Here, this term is used with vaguely the same meaning as Interacting Arts does in Haggren, Kristoffer, Larsson, Elge & al (forthcoming) and less as defined by Jenkins (2006a & 2006b).
6. In media studies, audience participation as a concept has many meanings and connotations. For the purpose of the discussion here I stick to a definition of audience participation as new feedback possibilities provided by digital technology. These opportunities are incorporated in various combinations of traditional broadcasting and new media—multi-platform formats. It is a generic term, used in recent media studies, describing the convergence between mass media and personal media (Colombo 2004, Roscoe 2004).

7. Produced the first time 2004, see http://www.regenesistv.com/credits.html for further details on the televised production and the ARG.
8. Representatives from the two sister institutes—the Interactive Institute and the Swedish institute of Computer Science—were invited. See www.tii.se and www.sics.se .
9. A movie by David Fincher, produced by A&B Producoes Lda.
10. The secret society was called Ordo Serpentis. See www.ordoserpentis.org.
11. Further readings about the different layers of participation in ARGs can be found in Christy Dena (2008).
12. The S.O.M. Institute, a research and conference centre, studying society, opinion and media (S.O.M.) at Göteborg University carries out a nationwide survey every year, in which people are asked questions about politics, society, their use of media, public service, the environment, risks, new media technology and leisure-time activities. See www.som.gu.se.
13. Role-playing is not a medium, but pervasive larps such as *SOM*, use different kind of media like mobile phones, the Internet and other digital media. So to simplify, it is compared with broadcasting.
14. See www.thecompanyp.com.
15. *Prosopopeia Bardo I: Där vi föll* (Jonsson, Montola et al 2006, Montola and Jonsson 2006) and *Prosopopeia II: Momentum* (Jonsson, Montola et al 2007; Stenros, Montola et al 2007). P counts the *Sanningen om Marika* production as the third *Prosopopeia* production, with a storyline direct descendant to the two earlier ones. Resembling gaming structures and game mastering methods were also inherited from the earlier productions.
16. An agile software development method called SCRUM.
17. He had experiences of table top role-playing, but not larping or ARG experience (Jarnhed 2007).
18. SVT Play is an Internet application allowing viewers to watch sent programs on their computer screens through streaming media technology.
19. The surveillance company was called Kerberos. See http://www.sics.se/prosopopeia/kerberos.html
20. The mobile phone application was named Urim.
21. The Others is another name for the secret society, used in the game.
22. Frequently asked questions.
23. Lingr.com
24. A web page address (Uniform Resource Locator).
25. After airing of the first drama piece the discussion on the SVT *SOM* web was moved to SVT's ordinary web discussion forum, but a discussion never took off there though, to the disappointment of the producer.
26. To be published.
27. See www.mobile-life.org
28. Integrated Project on Pervasive Gaming. See www.pervasive-gaming.org

3

Reject Now, Accept in the Future?
A study of innovation resistance to websites and blogs

Yah-Huei Hong

The adaptation of candidate web sites and blogs has turned the Internet into one of the key battlegrounds in election campaigns. The new medium not only offers voters access to more campaign information in greater depth, but also gives candidates greater opportunities and space to communicate with the people. Moreover, it helps candidates to target their electors for direct interaction (Schweitzer, 2005). With low cost, big coverage, strong interactivity and high controllability as its main characteristics, the medium certainly exerts a strong pull on political candidates.

In his study on the 1998 US Senate and House elections, Dulio (1999) found that two-thirds of the candidates had their own web sites. For state-level races in the US in 2000, Kamarck (2003) found that over 90 per cent of the major parties' candidates owned personal web sites. In Finland, a nation that claims to have more Internet users per capita than any other country, in the European Parliament Election of 1996, 28 per cent of the candidates had personal web sites, and more than 100 candidate web sites were set up for the 1999 elections (Carlson and Djupsund, 2001). According to the newspaper association of Finland, in the 2004 EP election, 1/3 of the candidates believed that the web was a very important tool for propaganda running (Carlson and Strandberg, 2005).

The popularity of political blogs also is widely acknowledged. According to the survey published by the Pew Internet and American Life Project in 2004, the growth of blog readers was driven mainly by elections, on account of the large increase of readers of political blogs during the campaigns (Lee, 2005), turning the blog into the fastest growing phenomenon in Internet communication (Lee, 2006).

From the flourishing development of Internet campaigning in the West, it is clear how important the new medium of the Internet has become as a propaganda tool in political communication. In Taiwan, online campaigning has also gained in intensity in recent years. From the use of the bulletin board system in the 1994 Taipei mayoral election, to the "blog war" in the 2006 Taipei and Kaohsiung mayoral elections, political propaganda on the Internet has outgrown its early immaturity to become highly diversified. Researches show that the percentage of candidates owning web sites was 74.1 per cent in the 1998 Taipei and Kaohsiung mayoral elections, 31.3 per cent in the two cities' council elections, and 25.2 per cent in the legislative elections (Chung, 1999). The number of sites related to that year's "three-in-one" election was about 200, an almost threefold increase from the accumulated total of 75 from the previous elections (Peng, 2000). By the time of the 2006 Taipei mayoral elections, both the Hau Lung-pin and Hsieh Chang-ting camps made full use of blogs, with each of the two candidates owning more than one site (Hong, 2006).

Although the above demonstrates the fervor of online campaigning in Taiwan, it does not appear that the candidates' enthusiasm has successfully captivated Internet users. Zhang (2004) analyzed the various sources of campaign news relied on by audiences in the 2004 presidential elections, and found that for the 668 university students interviewed, television remained the chief source of information, followed by friends and relatives, newspapers, and lastly the Internet; their usage of candidate web sites was also relatively infrequent. Su (2007) posted a questionnaire on a candidate's blog to investigate the usage and satisfaction of Internet users with this type of blogs in 2006, but received fewer than 100 replies after three weeks.

In the past, the web sites of local election candidates may have been crudely set up, presenting only basic messages that simply repeated those on printed materials (Cheng and Chuang, 1996). However, in recent times, the content of candidate web sites and blogs nowadays is rich and highly varied. So, the continued indifference of the voters seems baffling. This research is motivated by the author's attempt to understand this phenomenon.

Roger's Diffusion of Innovation (DOI) theory (1983) is a popular model for explaining user adoption of new technologies (Carter and Belanger, 2005). The theory postulates that an idea or object that is perceived as new must be communicated through certain channels over time to be finally accepted by the adopters. Many studies confirmed the theory, presenting a large body of related evidence.

Most of the existing literature on new technology adoption focuses on how the audience diffuses innovation (e.g. Rogers, 1983; Mahajan and Eitan, 1979), or on how the diffusion of innovation can be measured correctly (e.g. Moore and Menbasat, 1991). Although many studies have paid attention to the process of new technology adoption, they fail to explain why an audience might reject new technology and resist its adoption. In fact, the "rejection of innovation" is as important as the "diffusion of innovation." In particular, while candidate web sites are widely used as a campaign channel, voters' acceptance of this kind of new web tool remains far below expectation. This study will try to unveil the possible reasons behind this interesting phenomenon.

To understand this phenomenon, Ram proposed the concept of innovation resistance (1987). Ram and Sheth (1989) further identified the major barriers that cause innovation resistance, which include "usage barrier," "value barrier," "risk barrier," and "image barrier." In another approach, Davis (1986) proposed the Technology Acceptance Model (TAM) to explain the process by which users accept a new technology. Davis, et al. (1989) believed that in that model user adoption is determined by the technology's "perceived usefulness" and "perceived ease of use." This study will adopt the viewpoints proposed by Ram and Sheth (1989) on innovation resistance and use a standard form of TAM to explore the reasons why Internet users resist adopting candidate web sites and blogs. In addition, this study will attempt to explore the factors that significantly predict users' intention to use the same technology in the future.

Cyber-campaigning in the West

The adoption of the Internet as a campaign weapon began with the 1992 US presidential election (Lusoli, 2005). However, it was not until the 1996 US presidential election that cyber-campaigning started in earnest (Gibon, 2004).

Dulio (1999) found that two-thirds of the candidates had their own web sites in the 1998 U.S. Senate and House elections. And Kamarck (2003) found that over 90 per cent of the major parties' candidates owned personal web sites in the 2000 local election. In the 2004 presidential election, blogging became another campaigning tool for the 2004 US presidential election, where every candidate relied on blogs to recruit volunteers, raise funds, and communicate with the voters. George W. Bush and John Kerry both used the web as an important campaigning tool (Williams, et al., 2005).

The trend of cyber-campaigning has also spread to Europe. In the 1998 German national election, political parties hopped onto the Internet bandwagon, aiming to increase voter turnout (Schweitzer, 2005). Nevertheless, in this election, the parties used web sites only as an electronic brochure (Kamarck, 1998) rather than a platform to interact with voters, as campaigners in the US did.

A revolution in cyber-campaigning took place in Germany for the 2005 election. Candidate web sites served the purpose of fund raising and allowed users to sign up for participation. The parties used their web sites as a rapid response tool, and also to criticize opponents. In the end, the Internet played an important role in that election (Guldenzopf and Voigt, 2006).

In the recent French presidential election, the two candidates Nicolas Sarkozy and Ségolène Royal both made good use of the Internet in their campaigns. Sarkozy shot almost one video a day, making up a total of about 200 videos on his web site, allowing voters to watch his campaign minute by minute and around the clock. Royal built a social-networking-like site for the purpose of "participatory democracy," inviting people to submit their opinion on what policies should be discussed in her forum, and to set up personal pro-Royal blogs to form a network of similar blogs. By the end of the six-month campaign, 1,500 pro-Royal blogs had been set up (Melillo, 2007). Although Sarkozy won the election, the participatory democracy Royal enacted on the Internet showed the importance and influence of the new media in France's political arena.

However, we can argue that while cyber-campaigning has become popular with political parties and candidates, it has not been as widely embraced by voters as expected. With respect to the 2000 US presidential election, Gibson (2004) found that only 30 per cent of Internet users had searched for election information on the web. In her study of the 2002 German national election, Schweitzer (2005) found that visitors to a particular party's web site tended to be supporters of the party. In addition, Carlson and Strandberg (2005) conducted a survey after the 2004 EP election in Finland, and found that few voters had visited campaigning web sites: 41 per cent of the respondents obtained information on election issues through television news and political programs, 36 per cent did so through newspapers, and only 10 per cent had experience accessing party and candidate web sites. Overall, compared to television and newspapers, the web remained an insignificant channel for gathering political information (Carlson and Strandberg, 2005).

Cyber-campaigning in Taiwan

The Internet has become a fancy wagon for campaigning not only in the West but also in Taiwan. In 1994, candidates in Taiwan's provincial governor and mayoral elections made vigorous use of cyber-campaigning through the bulletin board system (Chuang, 1999). In 1996, all candidates in Taiwan's first-ever direct presidential election had their own official web sites. In the 2000 presidential election, sophisticated and highly interactive candidate web sites were born, and every candidate had more than one web site to promote him or herself (Hong and Chang, 2002). By 2004, most of the candidate web sites included games as another way for users to interact with the web site (Hong, 2006).

For the 2005 local elections, blog campaigns became the latest fad in cyber-campaigning, and all the candidates made an effort in blog building. In the 2006 Taipei and Kaohsiung mayoral elections, the candidates each owned several blogs targeting different audiences (Hong, 2006).

In the past, candidate web sites could be resisted because of their unappealing content and lack of interactive design. However, sites today are full of diverse and rich multimedia contents, so why do voters still resist their adoption? This study is motivated by voters' neglect of the new cyber-campaigning tools, in an attempt to comprehend the behavior of resistance.

Innovation Resistance

Ram proposed the theory of innovation resistance (1987) as a response to the limitation of previous studies in focusing mainly on the successful adoption and diffusion of innovations and ignoring the behavior of resistance. However, as innovation brings about "change," resistance to change should be a common reaction. Moreover, the majority of individuals who stick to their old habits may be more typical and even more rational than those who seek change. Therefore, resistance to innovation forms a topic that is worthy of further research (Ram, 1987).

Why do people resist innovation? Sheth (1981) studied the psychological process of innovation resistance and named risk awareness and habit conflict as the reasons behind rejection of change.

According to Ram (1987), innovation resistance in consumers is dependent on three sets of factors: Perceived Innovation Characteristics, Consumer Characteristics, and Characteristics of Propagation Mechanisms. The first set of characteristics includes relative advantage, compatibility, complexity and perceived risk, the second set includes psychological variables (e.g. perception, motivation) and demographic variables, and the third set includes credibility and informativeness.

Based on the usage patterns, value, risk and image barriers noted by Ram and Sheth (1989), and the factor of perceived innovation characteristics proposed by Ram (1987), this study will attempt to explain the resistance of Internet users to candidate web sites and blogs.

Technology Acceptance Model (TAM)

Technology Acceptance Model (TAM) was designed to figure out the factors of user acceptance of a wide range of end-user computing technologies (Davis, 1986). The model posits that people's acceptance of information technology is determined by the two factors of perceived ease of use (PEOU) and perceived usefulness (PU) (Davis, et al., 1989).

Scholars have also integrated TAM and other communication models to explain the behavior of Internet adoption. For instance, in studying consumers' acceptance of virtual stores, Chen and Tan (2004) expanded TAM and IDT (Innovation Diffusion Theory) to propose a new theoretical model, which again found PEOU and PU to be the dominant determinants affecting consumer attitude and behavioral intention toward using virtual stores. In their study, PEOU is defined as the degree to which a consumer expects using the target virtual store to be free of effort, and PU refers to a consumer's subjective probability that using a specific virtual store will increase his or her performance in purchase or information searching. The results showed that both these factors significantly affected consumers' attitude toward using the virtual store, with PU a significant predictor of consumers' behavioral intention toward using the new technology.

The perceived ease of use (PEOU) in TAM is similar to the concept of complexity proposed by Ram (1987) in his model of innovation resistance. Consumers will adopt an innovation when they are aware that it is easy to handle (Taylor and Todd, 1995). The perceived usefulness (PU) in TAM is similar to the value barrier proposed by Ram and Sheth (1989). Since value barrier is concerned with relative advantage, when an innovation offers a stronger value compared to other substitutes, consumers will perceive the innovation to be useful and adopt it (Taylor and Todd, 1995).

Based on the assumptions in innovation resistance theory and technology acceptance model, the study will present several hypotheses as follows.

Hypotheses

H1: Higher levels of perceived complexity/perceived ease of use will be positively related to lower levels of intention to use candidate web sites and blogs in the future.

H2: Higher levels of perceived relative advantage/perceived usefulness will be positively related to higher levels of intention to use candidate web sites and blogs in the future.

H3: Higher levels of perceived incompatibility will be positively related to lower levels of intention to use candidate web sites and blogs in the future.

H4: Higher levels of perceived negative image will be positively related to lower levels of intention to use candidate web sites and blogs in the future.

H5: Lower levels of realization will be positively related to lower levels of intention to use candidate web sites and blogs in the future.

Controlled Variables

Davis, et al. (1989) proposed that perceived ease of use (PEOU) and perceived usefulness (PU) are mitigated by other external variables. In this study, the external variables, namely, Internet use, political interest and demographics, will be controlled, to allow us to identify the major factors that have significant impacts on people's intention to use candidate web sites and blogs.

In studying the impact of external variables on technology usage behavior, Hubona and Geitz (1997) found that prior experience has an impact on the frequency of usage. In a study of the diffusion of e-commerce, Eastin (2002) found that Internet use could predict the adoption of online service and online banking. Accordingly, Internet use may also have an impact on the adoption of candidate web sites and blogs, making Internet use the first external variable to be controlled in this study.

In addition, Hubona and Geitz (1997) discovered the existence of a negative correlation between age and PEOU, and the significant impact of education on using attitude and using frequency. In identifying the factors that may influence the adoption of interactive television in Hong Kong, Leung and Wei (1998) concluded that young and better-educated male respondents were more likely to be the early adopters. In light of the results shown above, this study will treat demographic variables, such as age, gender and education, as another set of external variables that will be controlled.

According to Kaye and Johnson (2002), when a user is more interested in politics, he or she tends to be more reliant on the Internet, as the Internet provides an opportunity for people to pass their points of view onto the politicians and communicate with other high political involvement users. Thus, political interest will also need to be controlled as the study examines the relationship between the independent variables and the dependent variables.

Research Method

Two research methods were adopted for this study: focus group discussion and e-mail survey. The focus group discussion was aimed at finding out the possible reasons behind people's resistance to using candidate web sites and blogs, through which some preliminary reasons behind voters' resistance to innovation were extracted. Next, a pre-test was conducted prior to the e-mail survey. Based on the results of focus group discussion and the suggestions of prior literatures, the questionnaire for the pre-test was constructed. The objective of the pre-test was to see whether the questionnaire is of proper length and whether the meaning of the questions is clear. The subjects of the focus group discussion and the pre-test not only included college students but also interviewees of other age groups.

We commissioned InsightXplorer Limited to conduct the formal survey. Electronic leaflets were sent to voters in Taipei City and Kaohsiung City one week after Election Day. The sample was drawn from InsightXplorer's Cyber Panel database; the biggest database in Taiwan that contains detailed data on more than 100,000 Internet users (Jiang, et al. 2004) covering the whole spectrum of professions and age groups. Respondents were randomly selected according to the age range specified by the author, and reviewed to ensure they had the right to vote in the coming mayoral elections. To take part in the survey, respondents only needed to click the 'Start' link in the e-leaflet to be directed to the web questionnaire interface. Respondents were prevented from filling out the questionnaire more than once by the login function.

The Survey

The survey lasted one week. On the first day, 2,786 e-leaflets were sent out to members in InsightXplorer's Cyber Panel database. In the first batch of questionnaires returned, 425 out of the 459 were valid, and 34 were invalid. Eventually, a total of 3,794 e-leaflets were sent out, returning 718 questionnaires, of which the valid sample was 608.

Descriptives

InsightXplorer Ltd. was asked to use the method of Stratified Proportional Random Sampling to collect a sample of 50 per cent male and 50 per cent female based on the distribution of age variation in its database. Out of the valid sample of 608, 414 of the respondents had never used candidate web sites or blogs. In terms of age distribution, 25 per cent of the sample was aged 20-24, 23.7 per cent was aged 25-29, 15.8 per cent was aged 30-34, 13.8 per cent was aged 35-39, 14 per cent was aged 40-49 and 7.7 per cent was aged 50 and up. Since the purpose of this study was to examine why Internet users resist using candidate web sites and blogs, these 414 respondents became the study's major sample.

Results and Discussion

In order to figure out why Internet users resist adopting candidate web sites and blogs, factor analysis was applied, using principle components with promax rotation to evaluate construct validity. Five factors were generated with Eigen values that are larger than one. The first factor was labeled Negative Image, the second Relative Advantage/Perceived Usefulness, the third Incompatibility, the fourth Realization, and the last Complexity/Perceived Ease of Use. 77.08 per cent of variability can be explained by the above five factors.

Table 1: Eigen Values, Explained Variability per cent and Cronbach's Alpha Value

	Eigen values	Explained variability	Cumulated variability	Cronbach's alpha
Factor 1 Negative Image	2.96	24.25%	24.25%	.82
Factor 2 Perceived Relative Advantage / Perceived Usefulness	2.01	16.47%	40.72%	.94
Factor 3 Incompatibility	1.75	14.33%	55.05%	.80
Factor 4 Realization	1.63	13.82%	68.87%	.70
Factor 5 Complexity/Perceived Ease of Use	1.01	8.21%	77.08%	.72

Hypothesis Testing

Hierarchical regression analysis was used for hypothesis testing. In the first stage of the analysis, the demographic covariate set was entered in order to hold the individual differences in age, education and sex. The results showed that demographics accounted for a non-significant .6 per cent of the variance in the dependent variable. In other words, demographic characteristics were not good predictors of respondents' intention to use candidate web sites and blogs in the future.

In the second stage, the political interest variable was entered, with the result that about an additional 11.1 per cent of the variance of the dependent variable was explained by this variable. Consequently, political interest was a significant predictor of the dependent variable (Beta =.335, p<.001), in other words, people with higher political interest were more likely to have higher intention to use related technology in the future.

In the third stage, the Internet use variable was entered. From Block 3, it is clear that only "discussed political issues with other people" had significant impact on the dependent variable (Beta=.123, p<.05): the more frequent the discussion was, the higher the intention to use candidate web sites and blogs in the future would be.

In order to find out whether resistance to candidate web sites and blogs had significant impact on respondents' intention to use the new technology in the future, all of the possible factors behind user resistance (negative image, incompatibility, perceived relative advantage, complexity and realization) were entered in the fourth stage of the hierarchical regression. As the five possible factors (independent variables) are significantly correlated (as shown in the correlation analysis), multicollinearity may be a problem, so the factors were all entered in Block 4 separately and run in different regression models.

Hypothesis 1

We can tell that after controlling for the demographics, political interest and Internet use variables, the result showed that complexity/perceived ease of use had significant impact on respondents' intention to use the new technology in the future. When people felt that it was not convenient or easy to use candidate web sites and blogs, the intention of innovation resistant in the future was high (Beta= -.094, p<.05). The Hypothesis 1 was supported.

Hypothesis 2

Again, after controlling for the external variables (demographics, political interest and Internet use variables), the result showed perceived relative advantage/ perceived usefulness to be a significant predictor of respondents' intention to use candidate web sites and blogs in the future. The higher people agreed with the statement that political information obtained from traditional media was enough, the higher the intention of innovation resistance in the future would be (Beta= -.102, p<.05). The Hypothesis 2 was also supported.

Hypothesis 3

The result also showed that incompatibility was a significant predictor of the dependent variable after controlling for the external variables. When respondents said they were not in the habit of using the Internet to obtain political information but were used to obtaining it from traditional media (e.g., television and newspapers), they would have low intention to use candidate web sites and blogs in the future (Beta= -.101, p<.05). The Hypothesis 3 was accepted by the above finding.

Hypothesis 4

Again, after the external variables were under control, the analysis result showed that negative image had significant impact on respondents' intention to use the new technology in the future. When people carried a negative image of candidate web sites and blogs, the intention of innovation resistance in the future was high (Beta= -.303, $p<.001$). The Hypothesis 4 was strongly supported.

Hypothesis 5

Finally, it is clear that realization was not a significant predictor of respondents' intention to use candidate web sites and blogs in the future (Beta= .062, $p>.05$). The Hypothesis 5 was rejected.

Discussion

The findings showed that incompatibility, perceived relative advantage/perceived usefulness, negative image, complexity/perceived ease of use and realization were the factors behind voters' resistance to using candidate web sites and blogs. In other words, when Internet users perceived that using candidate web sites and blogs was inconsistent with their existing habit, that the new media was no better than traditional media, had a negative impression of the new technology, perceived that it was not convenient to use the related products, or were uncertain about what kinds of information the candidates web sites and blogs would provide, they tended to not use the candidate web sites and blogs.

However, after controlling for the external variables, only the factors of incompatibility, perceived relative advantage/perceived usefulness, negative image, complexity/perceived ease of use were shown to have significant impacts on voters' intention to use candidate web sites and blogs in the future.

The more a voter was accustomed to obtaining political information from traditional media as opposed to from the Internet, the lower his or her intention to using candidate web sites and blogs in the future would be. This result clearly supported the conclusion of prior literatures that as consumers refuse to change the status quo or long established habits, the behavior of innovation resistance ensues (e.g. Sheth, 1981; Ram, 1989).

The results also pointed out that when voters judged that the information provided by web sites and blogs is not superior to that by traditional media, or when they believed that the information they obtain from traditional media is good and substantial enough, they would not have the intention to adopt the new technology This finding confirmed the thinking of Ram and Sheth (1989) and also proved Ram's hypothesis (1987) that the lower the perceived relative advantage is, the higher the innovation resistance will be.

In addition, when voters held a negative image of candidate web sites and blogs, such as when they perceived that the information provided by the sites is not credible or complete, the intention to use the new technology in the future would be low. This finding confirmed Ram's hypothesis (1987) that the higher the credibility (perceived expertise) of the propagation mechanism is, the lower the innovation resistance will be.

Further, the findings also showed that when the voters perceived that using candidate web sites and blogs was complicated and troublesome, their intention to use the technology would be low. This confirmed the findings of Schaupp and Carter (2005) that complexity is an important factor influencing voters' willingness to use e-voting service. In the same study, Schaupp and Carter suggested that government should emphasize the benefits of e-voting to new voters, so that by demonstrating the ease of use of the e-voting service, the young, politically apathetic group may be motivated. Accordingly, the author of this study also suggests that in building a web site, candidates should pay attention to its simplicity and user friendliness.

Among the factors behind voters' resistance to using candidate web sites and blog, only 'realization' did not have a significant influence on adoption in the future. The reason could be that the operationalization (e.g. I was not aware of the existence of candidate web sites and blogs) of 'realization' in this study belongs to a surface level of understanding, still far away from the 'real understanding' pointed out by Ram (1987). The above explanation needs further exploration in future studies to prove.

Besides, the results showed that people with higher political interest and those who discussed political issues more often with the other people on the Internet were more likely to have higher intention to use related technology in the future. This confirmed the conclusions of Bucy, et al. (1999) that political interest may have impact on media use. As people are more interested or involved in politics, they will try to get more related information from the media. As a prior research pointed out, most visitors agree that their motives to visit candidates' Web sites are to acquire candidate-related information and to better understand candidates' political opinions and policy standing (Hong and Chang, 2002). Since "big coverage" is one of the main characteristics of the candidate sites and blogs, in seeking more information, those political fans inevitably hop on the sites and blogs; hence use the new technology along the way.

Conclusion

To conclude, the author would like to propose some suggestions for related research in the future. According to Ram and Sheth (1989), innovation resistance has an impact on the timing of "adoption," by which adopters can be divided into five groups: innovators, early adopters, early majority, late majority and laggards. The timing of technology adoption is an important topic in innovation diffusion research (Pae and Lehmann, 2003), and as future research, the author may attempt to discern the timing of voters' initial use of candidate web sites and blogs, and compare the different characteristics of early and late adopters to provide more user information to web site owners.

In addition, in studying innovation resistance to the new campaigning tools, the author did not make a distinction between the web sites and the blogs. This is because the respondents were unable to differentiate between the two kinds of tools in the pre-test, which could be attributed to their lack of experiences with such products or the fact that they did not remember what they have used before.

Thus, in the beginning of the formal survey, the author used a question to filter the subjects, so that only if the respondent had not used both candidate web sites and blogs before, would he (or she) become one of the subjects. Since the text and technical features of the two Internet products are different (Trammell et al., 2006), in putting them into one category, the author may have created one of the limitations of this study. Future research is encouraged to differentiate the two kinds of campaign tools, especially when cyber-campaigning has become more mature and more popular among Internet users.

Furthermore, although the sample of this study is drawn from InsightXplorer's Cyber Panel database, the biggest database in Taiwan that covers the whole spectrum of professions and age groups, it is a non-probability sample and does not include all Internet users. This is a limitation not only in this study but also in all World Wide Web surveys (Schillewaert, et al., 1998), and requires further research to overcome.

4

Financialization of US Media System: Links and Dependencies

Nuria Almiron

This chapter analyses the role financialization has been playing in determining the fortunes of corporate US media, in the immediate context of the US financial crisis of 2007-08 and its fallout on the corporate US media system.

In the last three decades, the economies of the world have undergone huge transformations. Many economists have categorised these changes under neoliberalism, globalization and financialization—as is the case of the Political Economy Research Institute (PERI) at the University of Massachusetts (Epstein, 2005). While neoliberalism and globalization have been widely researched, financialization has received far less attention. In general terms, financialization means "the increasing role of financial motives, financial markets, financial actors and financial institutions in the operation of the domestic and international economies" (Epstein, 2005: 3). In other words, it refers to a "pattern of accumulation in which profit making occurs increasingly through financial channels rather than through trade and commodity production" (Krippner, 2005). And this growing dominance of shareholder values and capital market is taking place nowadays in every industry.

As early as 30 years ago, Cees Hamelink depicted the early financialization of modern late 20th century media corporations—although he did not use this term then. In his research, the Dutch professor found a highly oligopolistic scenario for the transnational information and banking industries till the mid-1980s. According to him, the increasing funding and information interests and needs of the information and banking sectors revealed both industries to be on the path to convergence in three respects: technological, operative and financial. The most important consequence of this being that the finance sector controls information resources through fund assignment (Hamelink, 1983).

Hamelink's contribution showed significant financial influence and dependence in the transnational information industry of late 1970s and early

1980s, an influence and dependence that was larger than that existing in other industrial activities. Nonetheless, the expansion of financial investment in this industry was not the focus of much attention from scholarly communication research until very recently (with some exceptions like Zallo's approach, 1992). In 2002, a group of French researchers from the Centre National de la Cinématographie in Paris took a huge leap into this field of research by studying the mutation of cultural industries and its financial consequences. In doing so, they started using the term 'financialization' for the new stage of the information and communication sector (Bouquillion, Miège and Pradié, 2003; Pradié, 2005).

In this chapter, we will present the results of research conducted on top US media conglomerates to assess the degree of their Financialization—that is, to which extent finance has assumed a dominant position in the corporate US media. The aim is to identify the main links between the media and the financial systems, far beyond the classical patterns of ownership-focused research. To do so, the chapter has been divided into a number of sections. Section 1 briefly introduces the tools used to measure financialization. Section 2 presents a comparative statement of the data on the six big conglomerates selected for the purpose and section 3 presents the results of research into the extent of Financialization in each conglomerate. The final section summarises and concludes the findings, with the ultimate aim of identifying factors that explain the impact of global financial turmoil starting in 2007on media economics.

Tools to Measure Financialization

Based on the case study of Almiron (2006; 2007), we identified the following variables for measuring and assessing the extent of Financialization in corporate US media: ownership/capital structure, stock prices, indebtedness, financial innovations, board of directors, and corporate goals.

That ownership matters in media groups is a widely researched issue (Hamelink, 1999; Doyle, 2002; Baker, 2007). We will add to this notion that the kind of corporate ownership (whether the company has stayed private or gone public) and the type of private or public shareholding are the clues to a company's primary connection with the financial system. It is not unusual for banking companies to hold stocks directly in publicly owned companies. For over one decade, many international financial players, mainly custodian banks,[1] have been investing in corporate media public stocks—among many other core assets. These last entities are committed to institutional investment portfolios and look for the maximum profitability in the shortest period of time. For that reason, the presence of one of these global financial investors in the capital structure of a publicly owned media company means expectations of high profit rates—usually as a result of stock market fluctuations. A useful scheme of ownership structure classification was provided by Kaserer and Moldenhauer (2005):

Table 1: Kaserer and Moldenhauer's Ownership Structure Classification Scheme

Category	Description
Managerial Ownership /Insider Ownership	
Management board member	Active member of the management board, including family members
Supervisory board member	Active member of the supervisory board, including family members
Former board member	Former member of the management and supervisory boards, including family members
Outsider Block Ownership	
Corporates	Non-financial company
Investment companies	Venture capital and buyout companies
Banks	Mortgage, credit or investment bank (for own account)
Institutionals	Institutional investors (asset management company, pension funds, banks (for third party account), etc.)
Insurance companies	Insurance companies
Government	Municipal, provincial, federal, sate government
Outside individuals	Individual persons which are not insiders
Treasury shares	Shares hold by the company itself
Employees	Employees of the company excluding members of the boards
Others	All shareholders which can not be assigned to another category
Outsider Dispersed Ownership	
Freefloat	Free float portion of the shares calculated as 100 per cent less sum of the shareholdings of all other categories

Source: Kaserer and Moldenhauer (2005).

As a result, the presence in the stock markets (growing increasingly in the media industry as depicted by Picard, 2002) is, obviously, the second most important sign of financialization. And this is what generates Crotty's neoliberal paradox (Crotty, 2005): intense product market competition makes it very difficult, if not impossible, for most media corporations to achieve high increases in earnings most of the time; but financial markets demand ever-increasing earnings all the time, or face falling stock prices and the threat of hostile takeover. Thus, financial goals become the primarily obsession of the top staff of a publicly held company. And, consequently, the whole corporate strategy is subordinated to short-term profitability targets. Additionally, the company is immersed in a scenario of major instability and of larger fragility (Chesnais, 2004) that, ultimately, we must not forget, increases financial competition (every player wants to win the funding race) and generates a wide gap between the virtual value in the stock markets (market capitalization) and the real accountable value (shown in the balance sheet) of a publicly held company.

Third, we must look at indebtedness. Throughout the last two decades, the financial indebtedness of corporate media increased (as compared to the commercial debt) to represent most of its global debt. Since the 1980s, the most common suppliers of credit are banks, raising capital in the stock market, and issuing debt (we look in depth in this in next paragraph). Given that current media groups have developed through a highly capital-intensive growth process, most of them accumulated an unprecedented financial debt, one of the largest in the whole international corporative arena.

This unparalleled corporate media indebtedness is directly related with the financial innovations that brought about the new finance regime that emerged in the late 20th century, summarized by Leonard Seabroke by the term *direct financing* (Seabroke, 2001). This concept aims to describe a process that is changing the structure of finance in the international political economy through what is also known as *financial disintermediation*, although it has not removed intermediaries but led intermediaries to expand the variety of financial services on offer to their clients, particularity for security trading. Thus, direct financing, which has been fiercely promoted by the US government, according to Seabroke, allows the financial sector to offer more credit to the public and receive more in trading revenues. For commercial banking that means a radical move: shifting away from bank held debt and direct bank loans toward security trading and securitization.[2] By this, banks act less as depositories of capital (their traditional role in the productive economy) and more as brokerage houses (as speculators in the finance markets). Companies that make widespread use of securitisation (in order to raise capital from their own illiquid assets through the emission of bonds or titles)[3] or that make intense use of other late 20th century financial innovations (such as stock options or offshore tax haven regimes) are deeply financialized.[4]

Another issue that accounts for the financialization of corporate media is, of course, the composition of the board of directors. Rather than all of its members being related to a direct ownership stock, corporate media can also involve banking or financial-related staff members that do not own any stock of shares being placed on their boards of directors. Reversely, we can find corporate media representatives that do not own any (or any relevant) stock of shares of a specific bank entity, but sit on the financial entity's board of directors. Interlocking directorates are a means by which corporations exercise political and economic influence. [5]

Actually, boards of directors, mainly through the study of interlocking directorates, have received enormous attention from economic scholars since Sweezy published "Interest groups in the American Economy"—what has been considered by most the first systematic study of interlocking directorates (Sweezy, 1939) and Selznick (1949) first described co-optation as the incorporation of representatives of external groups into the internal decision-making or advisory structure of an organization.

Finally, and sometimes primarily, we must also account for the ultimate corporation goals of media conglomerates, as many media giants have integrated play in the financial markets as a main, or at least relevant, regular activity. Thus, they have become financial actors that play with assets in the new international finance arena, rather than focusing on their communication and information aims, or they are mainly financial-driven conglomerates, with communication assets being only a segment of their diversified business.

Top Six US Media Conglomerates

Six huge corporations, made of successive mergers and acquisitions throughout history, dominate the current US media industry. They are General Electric, Time Warner, Walt Disney, News Corporation, CBS Corporation and Viacom.[6]

Table 2. The Top Six US Media Conglomerates by Revenues (2007)

Corporation		2007 Revenues ($ in millions)	Percentage of revenues coming from media industry activities (%)	Difference from 2006 revenues (%)
1.	General Electric Co.	172,738	9.21 (1)	5.71
2.	Time Warner Inc.	46,482	100.00	5.16
3.	The Walt Disney Co.	35,510	63.47 (2)	3.83
4.	News Corp.	28,655	100.00	13.26
5.	CBS Corp.	14,072	100.00	(1.59)
6.	Viacom Inc.	13,423	100.00	16.72

Source: SEC Annual Reports Filings. Negative values in brackets.
(1) NBC Universal operating segment. (2) Media Network and Studio Entertainment.

Almost all the six media US giants have holdings in all main communication sectors: television, radio, film, publishing and Internet (although, most of them focus their media empires in broadcasting). However the six conglomerates are quite different as corporate dimension is concerned.

Table 3. The Top Six US Media Conglomerates Data Comparison by Net Earnings (2007)

Corporation		Net earnings (Millions of $)	Number of employees	Average stock market price ($)
1.	General Electric Co.	22,208[(1)]	327,000	36.96
2.	The Walt Disney Co.	4,687[(2)]	137,000	33.95
3.	Time Warner Inc.	4,387	4,400	19.19
4.	News Corp.	3,426	53,000	21.64*
5.	Viacom Inc.	1,630	10,800	41.04*
6.	CBS Corp.	1,247	23,970	29.51*

(1) $3,107 millions (13.9%) belonging to the NBC Universal division. (2) $3,285 millions (70.9%) belonging to the Media Networks and Studio Entertainment divisions.
*: Free floating type of shares; NWS.A, VIA.B, CBS.B (without voting rights).
Source: SEC Annual Reports Filings and *Business Week* quotes service.

As Table 2 shows (footnote), media and communication divisions of General Electric and Walt Disney account for an important and large proportion, respectively, of their global net earnings and represent, if we were to consider only their media divisions, the fourth and third corporations by net earnings in the US media business.

Top Six US Media Conglomerates' Financialization

It is beyond the scope of this paper to offer a comprehensive analysis of this six conglomerates' financialisation degree, as every measuring tool we mentioned (ownership, quotation, indebtedness, financial innovations, board of directors, and corporate goals) could account for a whole research paper in itself. Nevertheless, we are able to provide some useful insight for each media group on the main issues.

Ownership

In early June of 2008, the six big media conglomerates' ownership distributed as follows:

Table 4. Top Six Media Conglomerates' Ownership 2008 (1)

Ownership's main traits (2)	GE	DIS	TWX	NWS	VIA	CBS
Free Floating (%)	99.17	92.43	99.68	72.47*	87.80*	86.15*
Institutional Class A ownership or only one class (%)	**60.73**	**64.00**	**81.97**	**85.80***	**13.04**	**15.28**
Top 10 institutions non-MF (%)	19.70	25.27	34.19	45.9*	11.70	14.20
Mutual Funds (%)	6.26	7.63	13.01	1.20*	3.95	1.28
Large class A holders (number)	**6,684**	**3,824**	**3,594**	**2,092***	**152**	**153**
Institutions	2,257	1,369	1,160	655*	90	82
Mutual Funds	4,400	2,434	2,406	1,421*	58	69
Others	27	21	28	16*	4	2
Institutional Class B ownership (%)	-	-	-	**22.88**	**80.68***	**81.62***
Top 10 institutions non-MF (%)	-	-	-	13.70	41.20*	39.40*
Mutual Funds (%)	-	-	-	0.87	1.26*	2.09*
Large class B holders (number)	-	-	-	**160**	**2,167***	**2,039**
Institutions	-	-	-	68	694*	688
Mutual Funds	-	-	-	79	1,458*	1,334
Others	-	-	-	13	15*	17
Board of Directors	0.22	7.57	0,32	40.00	82.00	80.00
Top Shareholder's stake	3.29	7.20	5.10	40.00	81.64	79.80

(1) Figures gathered the 10th June 2008. *: Stock without voting rights.
(2) GE: General Electric; DIS: Walt Disney; TWX: Time Warner; NWS: News Corp; VIA: Viacom; CBS: CBS
Source: AOL Finance, MSN Money, Business Week, Yahoo Finance and SEC.

As we can see in Table 4, all these conglomerates are listed companies — some of them in several stock exchange markets in the US, Europe and Asia, and the majority of them have almost all their shares listed (free float is between

70 per cent and 100 per cent), although three of them, News Corp, Viacom and CBS, have a dual stock system, as we will see.

The number of large holders, also called institutional ownership, shows firms' potential of growth, at least from the investors perception. The presence of strong institutional ownership usually is, as we said in section 1, a sign of a stock being considered a candidate for growth. And the reality is that most well known big firm's stocks are mostly hold by big institutions. Big institutions are pension funds, trust funds, mutual funds, hedge funds, private equity firms and large accounts in general, very often owned by, or related to, financial institutions. Mutual funds, although not holding the majority of outstanding shares are commonly the most numerous type of institutions. Mutual funds are investment companies classed as *open-end investment companies* by the Securities Exchange Commission (SEC). That means that they are professionally managed firms of collective investments that collects money from many investors to invest it in securities (stocks, bonds, short-term money market instruments and others). Mutual funds, as well as the majority of institutional holders, are mainly (though not only) interested in listed companies in order to get as much financial profit as possible in the shortest period of time.

General Electric (GE) is by far the largest conglomerate of our group of interest, with the biggest number of large institutions, which control more than the 60 per cent of GE ownership. At the time of our research, June 2008, amongst the top 20 GE institutional shareholders we could find divisions of at least six banking entities: Barclays (the first GE institutional shareholder, with the 3.94 per cent of shares) and State Street (the second GE institutional shareholder, with the 3.28 per cent of shares), but also Northern Trust, Fidelity, Mellon and Wells Fargo. With this high percentage of institutional ownership and such a representation of banking entities in the top positions, it is easy to conclude that financial-driven shareholders hold the main stock of GE ownership.

In the case of The Walt Disney Company (DIS), institutional investors control 64 per cent of the Company ownership. Amongst the top 20 June 2008 institutional shareholders, we could find divisions of at least seven banking entities: Fidelity (the first Disney institutional shareholder, with the 4.76 per cent of shares), Barclays (4.03 per cent of shares), and State Street (3.80) but also Northern, Black Rock, JP Morgan and Mellon. Thus, we must again conclude that financial-driven shareholders hold the main stock of Disney ownership. Only the presence of an outstanding non-financial individual shareholder (Steve Jobs, Apple's CEO, with more than 7 per cent of stock) restrains this trend.

Time Warner (TWX), in their turn, shows the largest figure in institutional ownership in a publicly held media company: 82 per cent of his stock is distributed into 3,594 institutional owners. Amongst the top 20 institutional shareholders we can find divisions of at least six banking entities: Barclays (4.62 per cent of shares), Fidelity (3.80 per cent) and State Street (3.40) but also Goldman Sachs, Northern and Black Rock. A mutual Fund company, Dodge & Cox (5.10 per cent of TW ownership), is the only investor with more than 5 per cent of shares and is the main TWX shareholder. With such a strong presence of institutional holders and financial entities, we must again conclude that financial-driven shareholders hold the main stock of TWX ownership.

In spite of being listed companies, the three remaining conglomerates are privately controlled groups with two different classes of stock: non-free floating shares with voting rights (class A for Viacom and CBS; class B for News Corp) and free floating shares without voting rights (class B for Viacom and CBS; class A for News Corp). Each one of this media conglomerates has a sole and main stockholder controlling the majority of voting shares; and, thus, controlling the board of directors regardless the trading movements in the free floating stock. Nevertheless, the publicly held stock packages without voting rights also represent a group of very important financial partners (as they are contributing to the company capitalization) for their respective controlling shareholders—and it is very common to find the latter holding also shares in the non-voting stock. It is needless to add that we can also find other interests—financial as well—amongst the voting shares that are not in the hands of the controlling shareholder.

Around 72 per cent of News Corp (NWS) shares are currently free floating shares without voting rights, while up to 86 per cent of them are on institutional hands. As far as the class B shares is concerned, the stock with voting rights, 23 per cent is held by institutions while 40 per cent belongs to an individual shareholder, Rupert Murdoch, through the Murdoch Family Trust. This percentage of control was achieved in February 2008, after the US Justice Department and FCC respective approvals of the stock buyback to Liberty Media (until then the second main stockholder with 16 per cent of voting shares). This swap between Liberty Media and News Corp meant the exchange of 16.3 per cent stake in NWS for shares of DirecTV, three regional sports networks and $550 million in cash.

Amongst the top 20 institutional shareholders of NWS, in both classes of stocks, we can find divisions of at least six banking entities: Fidelity, Mellon, Citigroup, J.P. Morgan and Barclays. While a mutual fund, Dodge & Cox, holds the 12 per cent of class A shares (non-voting). The remaining top institutional shareholders are private equity firms and large funds. Thus, we must conclude that financial-driven shareholders have also a vigorous presence in NWS ownership.

After the 2006 split of Viacom (VIA) and CBS, both companies are controlled by Sumner M. Redstone through National Amusements, Inc., the firm who controls NAIRI, Inc., the main Viacom and CBS stockholder. Through these companies, Redstone has around 80 per cent of the voting rights at each board of directors. Both firms include, nevertheless, large stockholders in their two types of shares, whom represent around the 80 per cent of Viacom and CBS ownership, in the non-voting shares stock, and between 13 per cent and 15 per cent in the voting stock.

Amongst the top 20 institutional shareholders of Viacom, in both classes of stocks, we can find divisions of at least three banking entities: UBS, Barclays and State Street. The remaining institutions are investment firms and large funds, while the second largest investor with voting stock in Viacom is Mario J. Gabelli, with the 8.5 per cent of class A shares. Gabelli is also the Chairman, Chief Executive Officer of GAMCO Investors, Inc., a New York Stock Exchange listed company that is a provider of investment advice to alternative investments, mutual funds, institutional and high net worth investors.

Finally, amongst the top 20 institutional shareholders of CBS, in both classes of stocks, we can find divisions of at least four banking entities: State Street, Goldman Sachs, Credit Suisse and UBS. The remaining institutions are investment firms and large funds, while the second largest investor with voting stock in CBS is again Mario J. Gabelli, with the 7.7 per cent of class A shares. According to CBS annual report, Gamco Investors, Gabelli's firm, received $274,120 in 2007 from CBS for investment management services.

From the above we can observe a very important presence of financial institutions of all kinds, with an outstanding position of banking entities, inside the institutional ownership of the big media conglomerates—an institutional ownership which, according to *Business Week* website analyses in June 2008, represent a greater percentage than is typically held for stocks in the media conglomerates industry. In fact, the vast majority of institutional entities, let aside banking related entities, are also financially driven: mutual or hedge funds, equity firms or investment firms aren't industrial partners but capitalist partners, and, thus, in their investments they do not seek to improve the invested firms' industrial know-how but to maximize their capital investments as fast as possible. This is true even in those cases with media moguls controlling the majority of stock.

Quotation

As we have seen in the previous section, financial entities have mainly penetrated into large media conglomerates' ownership through stock exchange markets, where the capitalization of every firm is synonym of strength, a measurement of corporate and economic power size (high market capitalizations allows for industrial expansion, competitors buyouts, hostile bids avoidance, etc.).

Table 5: Top Six Media Conglomerates by Market Capitalization, 2008

	Quote	Outstanding shares	Capitalization ($)
GE	29.78	9,967,400,000	296.83 B
DIS	33.61	1,905,182,000	64.03 B
TWX	15.07	3,578,336,000	53.93 B
VIA.A*	33.06	57,363,000	16.65 B
NWS.B*	17.87	798,521,000	14.27 B
CBS.B*	20.65	622,446,000	12.85 B

*: Free floating type of shares (without voting rights).

Source: New York stock exchange market, 12nd June 2008.

Table 5 shows a huge difference in market capitalization amongst the top 6 US media conglomerates. In June 2008, GE is the second largest US corporation by market capitalization, only after Exxon Mobile (464.65 B). But GE is not a full media conglomerate; media revenues representing only a portion of their global business, as we saw before. Nevertheless, although unlikely because its diversified business, GE has the financial power by market capitalization to take over any of its media competitors. This is probably why the three smallest actors—News Corp, CBS and Viacom—keep the free floating market out of the controlling ownership (the stock with the voting rights); while Walt Disney and Time Warner, with an akin market capitalization, are too similarly seized for each other and maybe too big for GE, for which the media business is only a small fraction of its global interests. This sort of equilibrium in the market capitalization arena could explain the relative stability of recent US media sector, with a number of big conglomerates that has stayed more or less the same since year 2000.

Corporate goals

In this section we will analyse to what extent the corporate goals of these big conglomerates have become financialised, that is, to what degree they have incorporated financial goals and/or have become financial actors, as well as media actors, in their corporate strategies.

Starting by the largest conglomerate, GE exhibits the most radical case. GE's operating business is divided into six segments: infrastructure, commercial finance, GE Money, Healthcare, NBC Universal and Industrial. According to the 2007 annual report, the commercial finance segment offers loans, leases and other financial services to customers for a variety of assets; while GE Money provides private-label credit cards, personal loans, bank cards, auto loans and leases, mortgages, corporate travel and purchasing cards, debt consolidation, home equity loans, deposits and other savings products, as well as credit insurance on a global basis. These two financial segments accounted for the 35.41 per cent of the total revenues in 2007 and for the 35.54 per cent of GE's net earnings in that year. That means that the financial business of GE even beat its aircraft business (Infrastructure segment in Table 4) in revenues and it provides almost the same profits as its flagship business.

Table 6: General Electric Operating Segments

	% On 2007 Revenues		% on 2007 Profit
Infrastructure	34.61	Infrastructure	37.23
Commercial Finance	20.49	Commercial Finance	20.80
GE Money	14.92	GE Money	14.74
Industrial	10.59	NBC Universal	10.70
Healthcare	10.16	Healthcare	10.53
NBC Universal	9.21	Industrial	6.00

Source: GE annual report.

Actually, the financial business of GE is so relevant for the company that the

GE Inc. consolidated group divides its corporative structure in two main affiliates: General Electric Inc. (GE) and General Electric Capital Services Inc. (GECS); where the later owns all the financial services while the former owns all the non-financial ones. GE recognizes the fundamental differences of both businesses in its annual reports, and this is the reason why it offers the review of certain information separately.

Disney's case is different. This company has a diversified business but keeps inside the worldwide entertainment field business. The company operates in four segments: Media Networks, Parks and Resorts, Studio Entertainment and Consumer Products. Media Networks is the segment operating television, radio and cable while Studio Entertainment holds the motion pictures interests. As Table 7 shows, Media segment is the main operating segment both in revenues and in profits.

Table 7: Walt Disney Operating Segments

	% on 2007 Revenues		% on 2007 Profit
Media Networks	42.37	Media Networks	54.75
Parks and Resorts	29.92	Parks and Resorts	21.85
Studio Entertainment	21.10	Studio Entertainment	15.34
Consumer Products	6.61	Consumer Products	8.06

Source: Walt Disney annual report.

In spite of this focus on the entertainment and media business, Disney Company declared in 2007 annual report $1,052 millions in gains on sales of equity investments and businesses (that accounted for the 3 per cent of revenues), and $995 millions in equity investments. Thus, as it has become a common situation amongst big corporations, Disney participates in the capital market or does financial investments as a regular business activity.

Time Warner is a fully devoted media and entertainment company divided into five business segment: AOL (interactive consumer and advertising services); Cable (cable systems that provide video, highs-peed data and voice services); Film entertainment (film, television, and home video production and distribution); Networks (cable television networks). The company doesn't provide information by segments but by type of revenues, where Subscriptions outstand as the main source of revenues to TW, while Content sales is the second source and in third place we find Advertising revenues.

Table 8: Time Warner Operating Segments

	% on 2007 Revenues (*)
Subscription	53.58
Content	25.19
Advertising	18.93
Other	2.30

Source: Time Warner annual report. (*) TWX does not provide net earnings or profit by segments.

However, as it was the case of The Walt Disney Corp, Time Warner shows a significant activity in financial investments, with $360 million in net gains in 2007, $1.045 billion in 2006 and $1.081 billion in 2005.

News Corp. defines itself as a diversified entertainment company with operations in eight industry segments, including: (i) Filmed Entertainment, (ii) Television, (iii) Cable Network Programming, (iv) Direct Broadcast Satellite Television, (v) Magazines and Inserts, (vi) Newspapers, (vii) Book Publishing and (viii) Other (NDS group). Almost half per cent of the revenues and net earnings come from Filmed entertainment and television segments.

Table 9: News Corp Operating Segments

% on 2007 Revenues			% on 2007 Profit
Filmed entertainment	23.50	Filmed entertainment	27.52
Television	19.90	Television	21.61
Newspapers	15.66	Newspapers	14.67
Cable Network Programming	13.62	Cable Network Programming	24.48
Direct Broadcast Sat. TV	10.73	Direct Broadcast Sat. TV	4.96
Book Publishing	4.70	Book Publishing	3.57
Magazines & Inserts	3.91	Magazines & Inserts	7.50
Others	7.98	Others	(4.33)

Source: News Corp. annual report. Negative figures between brackets.

Nevertheless, News Corp's equity investments are so relevant to its business that changes in the stock market prices can affect the company final results, regardless the media and entertainment segments outcome.

Viacom operates through two reporting segments: Media Networks, which includes MTV Networks and BET Networks, and Filmed Entertainment. Media Networks, although progressively decreasing, accounts for 60 per cent of the total revenues (Media Networks represented 64 per cent and 71 per cent of total revenues in 2006 and 2005, respectively). Viacom annual report does not provide profit information by segments.

Table 10: Viacom Operating Segments

	% on 2007 Revenues
Media Network	60.00
Filmed Entertainment	40.00

Source: Viacom annual report.

Again, we find relevant equity investments or capital gains. In their annual report, Viacom declares equity method investments totalling $265.7 millions in 2007, and recognizes a pre-tax gain on the sale of the non-controlling investment in MTV Russia of $151 million.

Finally, CBS Corporation operates in four business segments: Television, radio,

Outdoor (advertising), and publishing. The Television segment is clearly the main operative segment of CBS, accounting for 66 per cent of the revenues. CBS does not provide net earning information by segments.

Table 11: CBS Operating Segments

	% On 2007 Revenues
Television	66.00
Radio	12.00
Outdoor	16.00
Publishing	6.00

Source: CBS annual report.

According to CBS annual report, at December 31, 2007, the Company had $147.8 million of equity investments and recorded loses of $62.9 million after market declines of value of the Company's equity investments, principally Westwood One (a large radio network).

From these analyses we can observe that all the conglomerates have, to a greater or lesser extent, a not formally declared (with the exception of GE) segment of business which operates in a purely financial level and which revenues come mainly from buying and selling equity stocks. The financial sector is such an important source of revenues for GE that, adopting a much larger form of activity than merely equity investments, it even overcomes the rest of business segments in this company. Thus, we can conclude that GE business is the most financialized, while the rest of the studied conglomerates include the activity in the capital markets as a regular business alongside their core business.

Indebtedness and Financial Innovation

The growing debt of media conglomerates isn't something new at all. Nevertheless, throughout the last highly capital-intensive two decades, this debt has become unprecedented in scale at the financial level. At the same time, we observe a very intense use of financial tools for rising capital or for recapitalisation[7] that even outcome commercial loan—financial tools like public debt, notes and commercial paper.[8]

As GE case is quite different we will take a part its analysis from the rest of conglomerates. GE total borrowings of the consolidated group amounted to $525,878 millions at December 31, 2007, compared with $443,884 millions at the end of 2006. Most of its giant debt accounts for GECS division (General Electric Capital Services Inc) and its consolidated affiliates borrowings (97 per cent of total borrowings in 2007), which have been increasing in a regular and growing basis in the last years (a 58 per cent between 2003 and 2007).

Table 12: General Electric 2007 Financial Debt (millions of dollars)

	GE	GECS	Total
Short Term Borrowings	4,106	195,101	199,207
Long Term Borrowings	11,656	319,015	330,671
Total Borrowings	15,762	514,116	529,878

Source: GE annual report.

Due to the above, almost all GE debt is a financial debt, mainly senior debt (unsecured and asset-backed) and commercial papers (US and Non-US), while the borrowings payable to banks through loans represents 13.663 millions of dollars (2.58 per cent of total borrowings). The intensive use of financial instruments by GE has meant in recent years an increased cost, primarily because of the changes in general markets conditions (mainly increased interest rates attributable to rising credit). Proceeds of these borrowings were used in part to finance asset growth and acquisitions, according to GE annual report.

As far as the remaining conglomerates' indebtedness is concerned, their respective annual reports provide the following information:

Table 13. Financial Debt in 2007 (millions of dollars)

	TWX	DIS	NWS	VIA	CBS
Short Term Borrowings	126	3,280	355	667	124
Long Term Borrowings	37,300	11,892	12,147	7,943	7,006
Total Borrowings	**37,426**	**15,172**	**12,502**	**8,610**	**7,130**

Source: Time Warner, Walt Disney, News Corp., Viacom and CBS annual reports.

With regard to Time Warner (TW) indebtedness, total borrowings of the consolidated group amounted to $37,426 millions at December 31, 2007, compared with $35,300 millions at the end of 2006.

Disney total borrowings of the consolidated group amounted to $15,172 millions at September 30, 2007, compared with $13,525 millions at the end of 2006:

> According to Disney Annual Report, at 2007 the Company had $2.7 billion of commercial paper debt outstanding and bank facilities totalling $4.5 billion to support its commercial paper borrowings, with half of the facilities scheduled to expire in 2010 and the other half in 2011. From these fillings one can glimpse the intensive use of financial tools made by Disney, mainly through notes and commercial papers, while only a minor portion of debt is due to direct banking borrowings. In this respect, the main banking facilities are concerned to a syndicate banking credit signed in 1994 when a financial restructuring of the Company took place. Through this credit facility, Euro Disney borrowed funds that are collateralized primarily by the theme park, hotels, and land assets of Disneyland Resort Paris.

News Corp total borrowings of the consolidated group amounted to $12,502 millions at June 30, 2007, compared with $11,427 millions at the end of 2006 fiscal term.

Viacom total borrowings of the consolidated group amounted to $8,610 millions at end 2007, almost the same figure they amounted at end of 2006:

> According to NWS Annual Report, at 2007 the Company raised fixed rate debt of $744.6 million through the issuance of Senior Notes and Debentures (certificate of agreement of loans) and borrowed $750.0 million of bank debt under a revolving credit facility.[9] These proceeds were used to repay $1.04 billion of commercial paper. Interest expense on debt borrowings was $453.7 million and $425.4 million for the years ended December 31, 2007 and 2006, respectively.

CBS total borrowings of the consolidated group amounted to $7,130 millions at end 2007, compared with $7,125 millions at the end of 2006:

> According to CBS Annual Report, at 2007 the Company had a $3.0 billion revolving credit facility due December 2010 whose primary purpose is to support future commercial paper borrowings. In January and May 2007, the Company issued senior notes, $800 and $700 million. The CBS financial statements for 2007 also mention an amended and restated five-year Credit Agreement, dated as of December 8, 2005, with JPMorgan Chase Bank, as Administrative Agent; Citibank, as Syndication Agent; and Bank of America, UBS Securities and The Bank of Tokyo-Mitsubishi, New York Branch, as Co-Documentation Agents.

The above shows a generous use of modern financial tools for rising capital amongst media conglomerates and it is an incomplete glimpse, as it does not take into account the employ of offshore territories (tax havens) as a means of reducing tax paying, of avoiding legal requirements and of increasing opacity in some corporation activities. Many authors, as stated in section 1, consider tax havens' use as one of the main signs of contemporary financialization (for instance Seabroke, 2001 or Hdez. Vigueras, 2007).

Finally, if we compare the figures for global debt of these six conglomerates with the total debt accumulated by the US largest companies we can observe that media sector conglomerates are strongly indebted in comparison.

Table 14. Largest US Companies vs. Media Conglomerate by Financial Debt 2007 (billions of dollars)

	Revenues	Market Capitalisation	Total Debt
Bank of America	52.01	120.67	613.39
GE	172.74	296.83	529.87
JP Morgan Chase	59.01	129.73	491.56
AT&T	120.70	204.55	73.49
Wal Mart Stores	387.69	221.87	48.07
Time Warner	46.48	53.93	37.43

	Revenues	Market Capitalisation	Total Debt
Berkshire Hathaway	110.44	191.95	36.18
Procter & Gamble	81.51	192.83	36.96
IBM	101.26	168.58	35.19
Walt Disney	35.51	64.03	15.17
News Corp.	28.66	14.27	12.50
Johnson and Johnson	62.25	180.53	11.42
Exxon Mobile	389.30	448.64	10.01
Viacom	13.42	16.65	8.61
CBS	14.07	12.85	7.13
Chevron	222.33	199.85	6.79
Microsoft	57.95	262.91	0.00

Source: Yahoo finance and media conglomerates' annual reports.

Board of Directors

Finally, if we look at board of directors we can observe quite an amount of interlocks with other directorates. Due to the shortage of time and space, we considered only ties with financial entities of the three major media conglomerates.

Table 15. Main Financial Entities connected to Board of Directors o General Electric, Disney and Time Warner (2008)

GE	American Express, Arvest Bank, Banco Popular de Puerto Rico, Berckshire Hathaway, Bolsa Mexicana de Valores, Citigroup, Danske Bank, JP Morgan Chase, Lazard, Lehman Brothers, Merrill Lynch, Metropolitan Life, Morgan Stanley, New York Federal Reserve Bank, Rothschild, Scotiabank, SunTrust Banks, Goldman Sachs, The Reserve Bank of Australia, UBS.
DIS	American Express Company, Banco Santander, Berkshire Hathaway, Citigroup, Deloitte Touche Tohmatsu, Dow Jones, Ernst & Young, Federal Reserve Bank of Dallas, HomeStreet Bank, HSH Nordbank, J.P. Morgan Chase, KPMG, Merrill Lynch, Morgan Stanley, NIBC Bank, PricewaterhouseCoopers, Rabobank, Scotiabank, The Goldman Sachs Group, U.S. Bancorp, Visa, Wells Fargo.
TWX	American Express Compay, Banco Nacional de México, Bank of America Corporation, Bank of Israel, Carver Bancorp, China Development Bank, Citigroup, CitiStreet, Citizens Trust Bank, Deutsche Bank Group, Dow nes, Duff & Phelps, EuroHypo, European Central Bank, Federal Reserve Bank of New York, Goldman Sachs, J.P. morgan Chase, National Bank of Poland, Rabobank, Rockefeller Foundation, UMB Financial Corporation, World Bank.

Source: Annual Reports and corporate websites.

The results of this research show a minimum of 88 different financial entities connected to GE through board of directors interlocking in a direct or first stage.[10] Amongst them, we may point out the list provided in Table 15.

The 88 financial entities connected to the GE board of directors are mainly retail, commercial and investment banking firms, insurance companies (most of them owned by banking firms), asset managers, venture capital firms and financial authorities. Several of them were in the US Federal Reserve List of 2007 largest commercial banks in US, as is the case of JP Morgan Chase (first position in the Fed List), Citygroup (3rd position in the Fed List) and SunTrust Banks (8th position in the Fed List). And many others are amongst the top world financial institutions in their respective fields as Morgan Stanley securities, asset management and credit services firm; Lehman Brothers, Rothschild, Goldman Sachs, Lazard and Merrill Lynch investment banks; Zurich or Metropolitan Life insurances companies; or USB Swiss banking firm. The links with Federal Reserve boards (national Central Banks) are also tight, not being the least the case of GE Chairman, Jeffrey R. Immelt, who serves as director in the New York Federal Reserve Bank.

The former is what we can obtain from the analysis of the 2008 direct links of GE Board of Directors. Nevertheless, we could come across much more interlocks if we were to consider further relations (beyond the first level of linkage) and former directorships. In this last respect, we must not forget that old positions can also be worthwhile assets as is the case of GE director Douglas A. Warner. Warner, former chairman of J.P. Morgan Chase & Co, The Chase Manhattan Bank and Morgan Guaranty Trust Company between 1990 and 2001, serves as director in GE since 1992. Despite of its retirement in 2001 from his last banking position, he was still featured by it in 2008 in all the directorships positions he held. And this is the case as well for Roberto Hernández Ramiro, former Chairman of Banco Nacional de México and current director of Grupo Televisa. An analysis in depth including current and past positions is beyond the scope of this paper but it would provide an even clearer understanding of the extent of the interlocking directorates between the financial system and media conglomerates.

If we look at Disney board of directors we can also find an important amount of interlocks with financial directorates, as it was the case with GE, despite Disney much more media-focused business compared with GE. The research shows a minimum of 59 different financial entities connected to Disney through board of directors interlocking in a direct or first stage.

Regarding Time Warner board of directors, interlocking with financial directorates of the members of TW board is also outstanding. We found 86 financial entities connected to the Time Warner board of directors; again they are mainly retail, commercial and investment banking firms, insurance companies (most of them owned by banking firms), asset managers, venture capital firms and financial authorities. And again this is only a short list, as it does not include neither former positions nor further relations (beyond the firs level of linkage).

Conclusion

From this analysis of ownership, indebtedness, boards of directors, corporate goals and use of financial tools, a strongly financialized profile arises for the US media system. These conglomerates are characterized by financially-driven shareholders, an intense use of financial instruments (to the extent that finance has become a core business in some conglomerates), a large financial debt (sometimes huge, for example in the case of GE), and deeply interlocked directorships with financing firms. Thus, we may begin to consider that at the end of 20th Century we entered a new stage far beyond the commoditization of culture and communication, a stage in which corporate media is a financialized business in its structure, logic, and goals. It may not be a coincidence that the deregulation and privatization that built the current media conglomerates were largely policy-intensive processes conducted under the dictate of intense lobbying on the part of the elites of the financial leadership. And it may not be a coincidence, either, if the unprecedented financial fragility of the current economic regime—shown by its financial burst starting in 2007 and the resulting international crisis—is going to have a strong impact on global media structure and economics.

Notes

1. According to the US Federal Reserve, a custodian bank is a financial institution whose business, at its most basic level, "is defined as the providing safekeeping and settlement for client assets. Custodians are responsible for holding a broad range of financial assets, including equities and bonds on behalf of their clients, and for handling the back-office portion (settlement) of a securities trade which involves the exchange of a financial instrument for cash. Typical custody clients include pension and retirement funds, asset managers, insurance companies, and banks." (Fed, 2005).
2. Securitization can be defined as the packaging of pools of loans or receivables with an appropriate level of credit enhancement, and the subsequent redistribution of these packages to investors. Investors buy the repackaged assets in the form of securities (or secured loans). Securitization thereby converts illiquid assets (assets that cannot easily be sold) into liquid assets (Picard, 2002; Hernández Vigueras, 2007).
3. Robert Picard provides a very useful summary of the most common types of security available to media industry through the banking system (collateral, inventory loans and accounts receivable in the secured debt type; and commercial loans, commercial papers, lines of credit, revolving credits and trade credits in the unsecured debt type) (Picard, 2002:162-169).
4. The currently increasing financial debt of private corporations and public institutions is one of the main characteristics of the hegemony of the new finance regime, according to Seabroke (2001).
5. Interlocking directorates are defined as the linkages among corporations created by individuals who sit on two or more corporate boards (Domhoff, 2005)
6. As it is known, according to Ben H. Bagdikian, 50 corporations controlled the vast majority of all news media in the U.S. in 1983 (Bagdikian, 1983). In 1992 the number had squeezed to a couple of dozen (Bagdikian, 1992), while in 2000 they were already only six (Bagdikian, 2000); 5 in 2004 (Bagdikian, 2004). Nevertheless, the five conglomerates appointed by Bagdikian in 2004 didn't completely match the current scenario. Bagdikian left out General Electric (with NBC as a close sixth) and included Bertelsmann (due to its position as the largest printer of English books), while Viacom and CBS hadn't split yet.

7. By recapitalisation we mean the restructuring of a company's debt and equity mixture often with the aim of making a company's capital structure more stable.
8. While commercial loan is designed to providing working capital to purchase supplies or finance production or distribution of products, and it typically comes from a bank and its long-termed; commercial paper represent a means of raising short-term cash at a rate lower than bank interest rates. Commercial paper or notes are unsecured promises to pay a debt and interest made by corporations (Picard, 2002: 163-170). The financial nature of all these non commercial tools is clearly shown in the fact that all of them, whether they are notes, papers or warrants issued by a corporation, need the presence of a financial entity as a legal mediator.
9. A revolving credit is a type of credit between a bank and customer that operates much like a credit card, with the customer borrowing and repaying up to a limit established by the bank and according to agreed/upon terms for interest and payment dates (Picard, 2002).
10. That is, through boards of directors of others entities where GE directors serve and which belong either as to financial firms or to non financial firms where others directors related to financial firms serve.

5

Global Warming on Second Life: The Public Sphere and Free Discussion in Collaborative Virtual Environments

Yuval Karniel, Amit Lavie Dinur, and Doron Friedman

In recent years, Collaborative Virtual Environments (CVE) have become something much more than mere entertainment or a leisure time game for bored youngsters. These environments are the scene of encounters between people who develop conversations and discussions on a variety of topics. These discussions are grounded in norms and rules of conduct which, in part, are determined by the external service provider or the websites operators, and also by the participants. Meetings in virtual environments resemble real-life, physical ones but are not identical to them, and they pose us with interesting questions about this newly emerging culture, the nature and quality of the resulting discussions, the option to set up and manage a community and to formulate agreed norms of conduct among participants. In the physical world, discussion occurs through the encounter between people, which then enables conversation, discussion, an exchange of opinions and, eventually, the consolidation of agreements. Lacking the physical presence of its participants, the virtual environment constitutes a new and different world. We chose to look at the *Second Life* virtual environment, whose participants go by the name of *avatars*, and we conducted discussion groups on the subject of global warming. The discussion groups were held both in the real world and in the virtual environment. The latter type of discussion is essentially similar to the one that takes place in Habermas's (1989) "public sphere". Such a public sphere is not necessarily physical and in the case of the virtual environment, differences in power and status between the participants, are temporarily suspended. All participants have equal status and each is entitled to express her or his position regarding any issue of public interest (Werman, 1997: 35). Habermas's public sphere is considered a good, perhaps even utopian, basis for conducting a democratic discourse.

The Public Sphere

According to Habermas (1962/1989), the public sphere arose in the social and political context of 18th and 19th century Europe around the discourse that evolved in salons and cafes, as well as in newspapers and other printed forms. This sphere allowed for citizens' true democratic participation in political processes. It emerges in the encounter between private individuals, with social status, who have a certain, joint power to resist the establishment. Participants in the Habermasian public sphere conduct a rational, methodical discussion, entirely aimed at the general good and in the absence of any element of personal interest. This results in a critical consensus vis a vis the establishment. Successful discussion depends on autonomy from the authorities.

The public sphere offered a voice to members of the public who were not included in government and it constituted a new and evolving type of democracy. For Habermas, this ideal sphere was destroyed with the advance of capitalism and with growing state intervention. This robbed the bourgeoisie of its power in the public sphere (through the weakening of social movements and lobbies) as well as in the private one (by means of welfare policies which interfered with the family's autonomy). Habermas also argued that by maintaining its self-image in the media, the establishment undermines the rational basis of the discourse thus resulting in the subversion of public discussion. The public sphere, as a result, reverted to an earlier, pre-democratic mode of functioning, namely, as a staged presentation of public relations which aims to distract lay people from political action.

However, the public sphere that Habermas described was a "bourgeois" public space only. Offering a new space to a part of the population, it was a restricted space in terms of gender and class in which only bourgeois men could participate (Fraser 1992; Schneider 1997). The democratic nature of the public sphere is questionable since it excluded certain groups.

Habermas's original approach to the nature of the public discourse suits our research frame. He mentions three important elements that shape the public sphere: the first of these is that the public sphere was formed through discussion, often mediated. Second, it represented a new space of discussion for many who had previously been excluded. And third, ideas presented in the public sphere were considered on the basis of their merits, and not on the social standing of the speaker. (Kellner, 2000). Since Habermas's original work, there have been various reformulations of and additions to the idea of the public sphere (Calhoun, 1992), and in fact the literature on the public sphere has become quite large (as noted, e.g., by Dahlgren, 2001 and Sparks, 2001). One important addition to the public sphere theory is the notion of multiple publics, rather than of one overarching public sphere (Asen & Brouwer, 2001; Dahlgren, 2001; Fraser, 1992). To our research, this notion of plural spaces is relevant: Internet discussion groups and forums fit well with the notion of diverse public groups with different fields of interest.

The question that interests us is about the features that characterize an online public sphere, and to what extent such a space can be subsumed under critical theory.

The Public Sphere Online

Schneider's study (Schneider, 1997) has developed specific measures that can assess the degree to which the public sphere satisfies the conditions of democratic theory. Those measures can be applied in the context of an ongoing conversation that contributes to the informal zone of the public sphere. The four dimensions that comprise the idealized public sphere are equality, diversity, reciprocity and quality.

Equality—The equal distribution of voice among the speakers in the discussion.

Diversity—The presence of a range of conversational patterns by the participants.

Reciprocity—The possibility of reflecting upon and discussing messages in the discussion by others.

Quality—Quality in the public sphere requires that participants stay on the topic discussed.

According to Dahlberg (2001), if an online space is to be considered a public sphere, it must satisfy the following six criteria:

- Exchange and critique of reasoned moral-practical validity claims. Deliberation involves engaging in reciprocal critique of normative positions that are provided with reasons rather than simply asserted.
- Reflexivity. Participants must critically examine their cultural values, assumptions and interests, as well as the larger social context.
- Ideal role taking. Participants must attempt to understand the argument from the other's perspective.
- Sincerity. Each participant must make a sincere effort to provide all information relevant to the particular problem under consideration.
- Discursive inclusion and equality. Every participant affected by the validity claims under consideration is equally entitled to introduce and question any assertion whatsoever.
- Autonomy from state and economic power. Discourse must be driven by the concerns of publicly-oriented citizens rather than by money or administrative power. (ibid, p. 623).

Based on the research detailed above, Poor (2005) came to a useful definition of a public sphere that may be applied to the Internet, and that may allow us to identify a space for analysis. Drawing from Habermas's original conception (as noted above), he gave the four following criteria of public sphere on the Internet:

1. Public spheres are spaces of discourse, often mediated.
2. Public spheres often allow for new, previously excluded, discussants.

3. Issues discussed are often political in nature.
4. Ideas are judged by their merit, not by the standing of the speaker.

In spite of various cyber-liberal rhetorics, virtual space has never been free of external supervision. On different levels, the Internet has been developed, controlled and administered by governments. Nor do virtual interactions steer clear of corporate power (Papacharissi, 2004). The Internet, at this point in time, is mainly being developed and controlled by corporate interests, and it is dominated by online trade. Still, a huge amount of discussions are being conducted on the net—discussions which are relatively independent of state or economic influence (Al-Saggaf, 2006; Poor, 2005).

A large share of public interaction online involves participation in virtual communities. These are online groups in which people connect with others who share the same values, interests, or concerns, with the aim to exchange information, to make friends and provide emotional support (Wellman & Gulia, 1999). There are tens of thousands of virtual communities in virtual space—communities which flourish on list serves, electronic bulletin boards, online chat groups, and role playing sites (Madison, 2006; Papacharissi, 2002). Communities arise on the basis of diverse fields of interest, some of them extreme, like pornography sites that determine their own limits and modes of conduct (ethical, normative, etc.) (Karniel & Wismonsky, 2004). Many of these communities, again, are linked with mega-communities, which are sites that host thousands of online communities (Al-Saggaf, 2006; Beers, 2006).

Collaborative Virtual Environments and Second Life

Collaborative Virtual Environments have been in existence from the early 1990s (in fact, the first that could be properly so called started in 1987) (Johnston, 1987). Some of them began even before that in early basic versions which offered certain limited capacities (text-based Multi User Dungeons or MUDS, for example) (Joslin, 2004). Some of the recent research has focused on technological or architectural aspects of virtual worlds like presence, mode of development, the role of the user and other functions (Joslin, 2004; Quax, 2007). Others looked at behavioral, democratic and other aspects (Bailenson et al. 2004; Fabrie & Moore, 2005; Parsons et al 2004).

When considering them from the perspective of Computer Mediated Communications (CMC), virtual environments enable verbal as well as non-verbal communication in virtual space and in real time, between individuals who are geographically remote (Bailenson et al. 2004).

Among the most-used virtual environments *Second Life* (SL) is prominent. This Internet-based world, which has gained much media attention worldwide, started in 2006. SL allows its users (also known as "residents") to interact with one another and it serves in fact as an advanced social network by means of *avatars* who are capable to move and explore the cyber space of SL. The innovation that SL introduces is in terms of the diverse activities it offers: it combines community life with contents created by surfers, and to this is added a business component in the form of a local currency, which has actually created a virtual economy. The number of "registered residents" in SL is still on the increase (so far reaching about 20 million). Because of its financial basis participants can make money, and about 25 per cent of the companies appearing in *Fortune 100* (Sivan, 2008) are present on SL as well. Today, SL is a complete virtual world which in many senses resembles the physical world. It reflects the community, society and culture of the Internet, using media that include written and spoken communications and movement in a rich and varied virtual environment. It is SL, as said, which we have chosen as the virtual space for the discussions under study.

Democratic Public Discussion on CVE

Much has recently been said about the possibility of the Internet enhancing democracy (Dahlberg, 2001; Papacharissi, 2004; Zhang, 2004). Despite considerable speculation, many claims have been based upon actual online practices. Within these rhetorics and practices, three dominant 'camps' have emerged. First, a communitarian camp, which stresses the possibility of the Internet enhancing communal spirit and values. Second, a liberal individualist camp, which sees the Internet as assisting the expression of individual interests. Third, a deliberative camp, which promotes the Internet as the means for an expansion of the public sphere of rational-critical citizen discourse—discourse autonomous from state and corporate power through which public opinion may be formed and can hold official decision makers accountable. (Cammaerts & Van Audenhove, 2005).

The third camp is less prominent than the other two within Internet rhetoric and practice, yet the decentralized communications enabled through Web publishing, electronic bulletin boards, e-mail lists and chat rooms does seem to provide public spaces for rational-critical discourse. The deliberative position also offers a more powerful democratic model. Both liberal individualist and communitarian models posit a unitary subject, whether the isolated ego or the undifferentiated communal subject. In contrast, dialogue and difference are central to the deliberative model. The model assumes that difference always exists between subjects, difference which necessitates a process of rational-critical discourse in order for privately-oriented individuals to become publicly-oriented citizens and for public opinion to develop that can rationally guide democratic decision-making (Dahlberg 2001; Zhang 2004). This deliberative model informs our research, which comes to examine the question whether it is possible to conduct significant and qualitative discussion in CVE.

Research Hypothesis

A rational and critical discussion which allows public opinion to become mature and democratically operative and which yields publically oriented individuals needs to be conducted at a certain level of quality, seriousness, depth and relevance. This will enable the emergence of a diversity of high-quality arguments and the transmission of new information and data. Such a discussion must also be democratic and free, allowing all participants an equal voice, an equal opportunity to express their opinion, position and response, and it should offer regular feedback to participants and their different arguments—that is to say: an open and critical discussion which has the capacity to change views and bring about agreements.

We suppose that it is possible to conduct a democratic discussion in SL about controversial public issues, but only under certain conditions, as Schneider (1997) elaborated them (quality, diversity, equality, and reciprocity). We also assume that though discussion on a public issue is possible in virtual worlds, and specifically among a group of participants in *Second Life*, we believe—on the basis of the published research—that such discussion will typically be of reduced **quality**; they will be less **divested** in the used arguments compared to a real-life discussion—with arguments also being **qualitatively** inferior. The degree of **relevance** of the arguments, too, is bound to suffer. Yet at the same time we hypothesize that the discussion on SL will be more democratic, especially in terms of the share of participants and **equality** between them. We hypothesize that a virtual discussion will allow participants to have more equal slots of time and arguments (**reciprocity**) than in real-life discussions because certain aspects of face to face communication are absent, such as nonverbal features (body language, facial expression) as well as verbal ones (tone, intonation, etc.). There is more social pressure on the speaker, in face to face discussions, not to diverge, and usually one speaker takes the upper hand. Our assumption is that in SL, social pressure will be reduced, which implies that the level of relevance of the arguments and other things said will be lower, and that arguments and other expressions will be more equally distributed among the speakers.

Research Questions

1. Is there a difference between real life and virtual discussion in terms of quality and character of the discussion?
   - i Does the discussion in the real world have a deeper and more serious nature than that in the virtual environment?
   - ii Which discussions will have more sentences? Which will have more words?
2. Can a CVE such as SL be a public sphere for group discussions?
   - i Which discussion includes more sentences that are relevant to the issue?
   - ii Which discussion raises more arguments?
   - iii Which discussion raises more complicated arguments?
   - iv Which discussion shows more equal participation?
3. Which of the discussions has more impact on its participants?
   - i Following the discussions, which discussion will increase the participant's involvement and interest in the topic?

Research Design and Methods

We conducted four discussions in the framework of this study: two of these were online, on SL, and two were held face to face, in a conference room. Each discussion included between 8 to 12 participants, which resulted in a total of 36 participants who each only took part in one discussion only. Participants did not know each other by name. On SL, participants' identity was unknown because each participant adopted an avatar with neutral name and appearance from a group of avatars that were created earlier by us. The participants had 20 minutes right before the beginning of the experiment to wander about, change physical appearance etc, in order to get accustomed to the virtual environment. Interestingly, none of the participants chose to adopt an avatar of a different gender. The participants were checked to ascertain they had a similar level of knowledge about virtual worlds and that they are capable of conduction an on-line discussion. Each discussion took 50 minutes.

In order to be able to draw comparisons with previously published research and for data analysis participants were asked to use English in their discussions. Their English was examined and they were found to be on a similar level of familiarity with and competence in the language.

The topic of the discussions was *global warming*, a key public issue which has political, social, technological, cultural as well as economical implications and concerns all. Participants were presented with a specific, detailed question. As said, they had 50 minutes to discuss the issue.

All participants where recruited among the students of the *Interdisciplinary Center in Herzliya*. All participants were between the ages of 21 to 27, with similar demographic background.

All discussions were conducted in a conference room—physical of virtual—and they were videotaped and audio recorded. We aimed to maintain a level of similarity between the discussion groups in both methods in order to have optimal comparative results.

Questionnaire

Participants filled out a questionnaire both before and after the procedure. The questionnaire consisted of 7 questions tapping participants' opinions and concerns about global warming and awareness of the issue.

Findings

The first research question was whether there was a difference between the discussions, and we decided to use the basic qualitative measure of number of sentences per discussion. The basic statistical data of the findings, therefore, concern word and sentence counts for each discussion and speaker. Discussions SL3 and SL4 (face to face) rendered a total of 688 and 524 sentences respectively, while discussions SL1 and SL2 (online) produced a total of 855 and 537 sentences respectively.

We found a further indication concerning the quality of the discussions through word counts. When we divided word counts by number of sentences for each discussion we obtained average length of sentence for each speaker. In discussions SL1 and SL2 (online) the average sentence consisted of on average 5.0 words (both discussions showed an identical average), while in discussion SL3 (face-to-face) the average sentence consisted of on average 8.9 words, and this figure was 12.7 in discussion SL4 (face-to-face). The face to face discussions, as expected, included more words.

The second research question concerned the relevance of the spoken sentences. From a look at the number of relevant sentences and their percentage in the whole discussion, another difference emerged. Discussions SL3 and SL4 yielded 659 and 507 relevant sentences respectively; the percentages of relevant sentences were 95.8 per cent and 96.8 per cent respectively. Discussions SL1 and SL2 produced—respectively—a total of 297 and 221 relevant sentences, and this translated into the following percentages: 34.7 per cent and 41.2 per cent.

Research question 2 (4) asked about a dominant speaker and about equality between participating speakers. We analyzed both the number of sentences and the number of relevant sentences for each speaker. The outcome was as follows: discussion SL1 (online) featured one clearly dominant speaker who was responsible for 36.6 per cent of the sentences; of these only 25 per cent were relevant. This speaker has the lowest rate of relevant sentences in this discussion. We can therefore say that the dominant speaker here is the one who drew the discussion into irrelevant directions. Discussion SL2 (online) showed a more equal distribution of speakers, who used a relatively equal number of sentences.

In both face to face discussions, SL3 and SL4, we found dominant speakers (for SL3: 31 per cent and 17.3 per cent of the sentences; for SL4: 22.1 per cent and 21 per cent of the sentences), while the rest of the participants were responsible, in relatively equal proportions, for the rest of the sentences. SL3, however, included two participants who hardly spoke (each contributed 4 sentences only). This underperformance may have been the result of their weak command of English, though they had both claimed that they would be able to participate in a discussion in that language.

Content Analysis

We content-analyzed the four discussions in order to find out how many topics each of them had raised, and at what level of depth and quality the discussions had been conducted. For this purpose we constructed a list of topics relating to global warming that were mentioned during the discussions. We then rated the depth and comprehensiveness of discussion on each topic according to three categories: *topic was raised* (1); *topic was raised and comprehensively discussed* (2), *topic was not raised at all* (0). Then, we summed up the score that was given to each topic and came up with a final score for each discussion.

Discussion SL1 (online), especially, was superficial and full of fun; the opening questions were: Who really cares about this issue? Who among us actually knows something about it? Who is to be blamed? Does global warming really mean the end of humanity? The ensuing discussion was mainly about cars and about the concern that we might lose cars in our attempt to save the environment. Most of the discussion consisted of irrelevant topics such as: What's the real reason for us conducting this discussion on global warming on SL? What's better—talking on SL or face to face? One interesting, irrelevant comment was: "It's not fun, talking here." A total of 8 different arguments were recorded, and the discussion scored only 12 points on the above presented scale—which is quite a low score and the lowest we awarded in all the discussions.

SL2 (online) was a more profound discussion than SL1, yet superficial even so. The special question that was raised was whether global warming is a natural process taking place in nature. This came as an addition to other topics: The need to change opinions regarding global warming; cars; the Mafia's role in Israel's recycling business; legislation for fining people who don't recycle; the role of Yom Kippur in reducing pollution[1] ; Tel Aviv and Haifa as Israel top-polluted cities. Most of this discussion, nevertheless, consisted of irrelevant arguments, like: group members reported they were bored only 10 minutes into the discussion. They also argued that the discussion on SL was very frustrating and that they would much prefer to discuss the subject in real life. "Rather than sitting here and talking about it," they said, "let's just get up and do something about it in real life." And there were remarks like: "Who wants coffee?" (An intriguing question because it is unclear whether this referred to virtual coffee in the world of SL, or to real coffee in the computer lab in which participants were seated.)

A total of 13 different arguments were raised, and the discussion scored 17 points, which is rather low.

In addition to the content analysis, the physical situations of the avatars were also analyzed. Here we should mention discussion SL2 which ended with a swimming pool party, attended by some of the avatars who abandoned the conference room and went wandering. In face to face discussions, by contrast, all participants were active: talked simultaneously at times, and remained seated around the table throughout.

Discussion SL3 revolved entirely around global warming. Many interesting issues were raised, like for instance: sharing a car as a practical way of saving petrol and protecting the environment; to reduce the working week to four days so as to diminish pollution; medical and commercial experiments on animals; raising funds to put a halt to global warming; water shortage in Israel. The number of arguments raised was 13—out of the 20 included in the table. The discussion scored 24 points, which is significantly higher than the scores received by SL1 and SL2.

Discussion SL4 dealt emphatically with education and possible solutions: it had a decidedly practical focus. Specific issues that emerged were: the meat industry as a significant contributor to global warming; economic aspects of global warming. One suggested solution was the creation of alternative, cheaper and greener products to replace expensive and polluting ones; coping with global warming, initially, on the level of the super-powers (e.g., the USA and China). Of all four discussions, this one was the most organized. Sentences were longer and topics were the most relevant. Here the total of arguments raised were 13 out of 20; but the discussion scored a mark of 25, which is the highest of all marks awarded.

Examining Opinion Change

Participants filled out a questionnaire—before and after the discussions. The questionnaire included 7 questions about global warming that tapped their general knowledge, their opinions about global warming and how important they rate the issue. We constructed the questionnaire with the aim of measuring the influence of the discussions on these matters. We assumed that a serious, meaningful discussion which would also expose participants to new and reasoned facts and opinions would also entail a certain shift in their opinions.

The average scores for the 7 questions of all participants were combined to form a general response average for each participant. We then calculated the average for the each group discussion and gave each one of them a score representing the group's current position. SL1 participants gave an average score of 3.8 (on a scale between 1 and 7) before the discussion, while this score was 3.9 (on a scale between 1 and 7) after it. The change that was found as a result of the discussion's influence on the participants was 0.1.

SL2 participants gave an average score of 4.7 (on a scale between 1 and 7) prior to the discussion, and this score dropped to 4.7 after it. Basicly there was no change before and after the discussion. These two discussions, it would seem, did not leave much of an impression on their participants.

Participants in SL3, by contrast, initially rated the discussion at 4.7 (on a scale between 1 and 7) before, and 5.1 after, so that the change resulting from the discussion was 0.4. Similarly, participants in SL4 gave an initial rating of 4.8 (on a scale between 1 and 7) which changed into 5.3 after the discussion. This yields a change of 0.5 due to the discussion.

Paired sample T-test that was conducted to the 4 discussion groups indicated no significant difference at the general position of the groups. Yet, the two face to face discussions show a sharper rise in the group's average scores, from first administration of the questionnaire, to the second, while the discussions conducted on SL show smaller changes. These data indicate that participants were more affected by real-life, face to face discussion than by discussion on Second Life.

Discussion

The present findings confirm our hypothesis—which was based on the current literature—that there are considerable differences between a group discussion held in face to face format and a similar one conducted in the Collaborative Virtual

Environment of *Second Life*. We should first mention that we did succeed in running discussions on a key public issue—global warming—in the virtual environment of SL, in spite of participants' anonymity and their partial familiarity with the environmental issues. The discussion in real life was more profound and of higher quality, however, in all parameters checked. The difference did not necessarily inhere in the number of sentences spoken in the course of the discussion. In this respect we found a general resemblance between the discussions. Rather, it was related to the main parameter of the study, which was the number of sentences relevant to the discussion on the public issue selected. During the face to face meetings there was serious discussion which did not divert from or abandon the professional, topical focus. Obviously, participants were experienced in discussing a public issue when seated around a table in a conference room. Moreover, this situation was not anonymous, and lacked the serious obstacles experienced by participants who were being filmed and were directly exposed to someone who observed their behavior critically. Face to face participants showed no difficulty about spending nearly one hour discussing a current public interest issue which was not of their choice. They raised many and varied arguments and did so at length and in depth. Our hypothesis that a real-life discussion would be more serious and profound, would come up with more arguments and be more substantial on the whole as well as in terms of its specific arguments was confirmed.

Most notable was the finding that in the SL discussions only a small part of the spoken sentences was relevant and focused on the issue at hand. Anonymity and the alien visual virtual environment, enabled participants to stray from the topic at hand, and allowed them instead to engage in lighthearted chat.

The data we collected in this research did not allow us to gain a full understanding of the cause of the found differences, and we associate the findings with the specific set of conditions constituted by our experiment. Surely, the partial anonymity was an important factor in the freedoms participants allowed themselves in straying from the subject and the task. However, we also attach importance to the visual nature of the virtual environment, and to this being a relatively new type of environment for most participants. The visual stimulus constituted by the new virtual environment, and the use of avatars to replace the real physical body loosened up the participants and allowed them to conduct a spontaneous conversation. The topic of global warming, it transpired, was not of itself sufficiently attractive, and failed to arouse discussion. This also suggests that face to face participants stuck to the subject matter not because it was important and aroused much interest, but mainly as a result of the format of a conference room meeting. We do not ignore, either, that the face to face encounter was filmed in the unconcealed presence of a cameraman who was present during considerable part of the experiment. And though SL participants were also aware that their discussion was being recorded, the presence of the recording device in the virtual environment was less pronounced.

The other data, too, that were presented above confirm the conclusion that the face to face discussion was deeper and more varied than that in the virtual environment. Time apportioned to the topic as well as the relevant sentences produced allowed participants to come up with more, and more diverse, arguments and issues. The relatively greater freedom that marks the virtual world did not translate into unusual arguments and in a more free, critical, or diverse discussion. Rather, the opposite was the case: the discussion was insubstantial, superficial, touched on known issues and failed to meet the level of the face to face discussion.

We are of course aware that some of this difference should be related to the differences between face to face vs. written discussion, but this difference alone cannot explain the large gap between the two types of discussion. The findings clearly invite further research into differences between spoken vs. written discussion, and challenge us to isolate the component of physical reality vs. virtual environments—in the context of spoken discussion as well as in that of a written discussion.

Another hypothesis which the study confirmed, but only partly, concerns the equal distribution of expressions and speaking turns among the participants. The assumption is that virtual discussion offers a freer and more equal environment which allows every participant to join in, even those whose real, physical presence is minor and shy. Here, findings are not unambiguous. One of the virtual discussions involved a dominant speaker, but the other had a relatively equal distribution of speakers. This, too, requires further research, but our findings seem to suggest that virtual worlds offer more of a possibility to have open discussions with a wider participation in the public sphere. Both real-life discussions featured more prominent participants while the rest were less active. The more equal discussion occurred in the virtual mode. Moreover, our findings suggest that dominance in the real-life environment—which is determined, among other things, by physical presence, body language, quality of voice and self-confidence—differs from dominance in the virtual environment, where it is the result of familiarity with virtual worlds and writing skills. Interestingly, dominance in real life discussions was mainly in the form of dealing with and contributing to the issue at hand, while the dominant speaker in SL was the one who contributed less to the topic and pulled the discussion away to other areas.

The face-to-face discussions did not only deal more profoundly with the chosen topic—they also had more impact on participants. The questionnaires that came to examine the extent to which the discussion had affected participants' attitudes and in which way, revealed a significant difference between SL participants, who hardly changed their ideas and attitudes at all, and the face to face participants, who changed some of their responses to the questionnaires to some extent. This finding, too, fits in with the others which were indicating that the real life discussion was more serious and meaningful in terms of dealing with the issue of global warming. Here, too, however, we would like to add that our finding requires further study, especially to probe whether or not discussions in SL that do stick to the chosen topic and are more serious and profound, would still affect their participants less. Clearly, when the discussion is fairly poor and the experience mainly one of "yet another game in the virtual environment", one can hardly expect it to have an impact on participants' attitudes.

Conclusion

The public sphere is changing. The internet at large, and virtual environments with many participants more specifically, constitute a new platform for conducting and managing free public discussion on political and social issues. We may well, in the future, try to conduct a considerable part of discussions, conversations and decision making processes by means of new technologies and of computer-mediated communications, instead of face to face communication and direct, real life encounters. In the present study we compared discussions among random participants in the real, physical world to those held with similar participants in the virtual environment of *Second Life*. The topic of the discussions was global warming. The study's findings and outcomes are not surprising: The face to face discussion was more serious and profound and left more of an impression on participants. In the virtual SL environment, the discussion was more superficial, unfocused, lightweight, and it had very little impact on participants. Still, we found that even those who were inexperienced with the medium were able to take part in a public discussion on a current issue, even when it was by means of anonymous avatars in a virtual world, conducted in a conference room.

Our challenge is to find the ways, conditions and circumstances that will enable more substantial, in-depth and high-quality discussion, and to make decisions on public issues by means of virtual technology as well. The present study indicates the need for further work that examines how we can, also, conduct a free, equal, serious, profound and influential discussion in SL. Further research might, among other things, look into the effect of anonymity; the possibility of conducting spoken discussions in SL, as well as the significance and contribution of participants' previous experience with the virtual environment, as well as the impact of the discussion's rules and general framework. The present study indicates that SL has a real potential for offering an appropriate public space for the free discussion of public issues.

Note

1. Yom Kippur is the Jewish "day of atonement", when people fast and ask for atonement. In Israel, there is a reduced usage of electricity, and almost no use of cars of public transportation, and therefore less pollution.References

6

Emergence of Supplement Journalism in India: A Critique

Pooja Rana

This study attempts to interrogate the emergence of the phenomenon of newspaper supplement journalism in the wake of the liberalization of the Indian economy. In principle, the emergence of newspaper supplements in post liberalized India represents a move aimed at greater engagement with and more comprehensive coverage of information circulating in the public and personal spheres. This assumes significance in view of the fact that in the pre-liberalized phase of the Indian economy, newspapers were predominantly occupied with the coverage of politics alone. With the liberalization of the Indian economy, not only did the manufacturing and services sectors rediscover themselves but also the media and entertainment industry. While newspapers gave up their staid and formal look, newspaper supplements introduced Chaucerian plenty in terms of the coverage of all kinds of information right from spirituality to health, beauty and fashion. At the theoretical level, this shift and polyphonic diversity in newspaper content was a welcome development in the direction of removing anomalies in the communication equality between the media content producers and the media content users, thereby. This study interrogates the extent to which this theoretical premise has worked out in practice and to analyse the reasons for the gulf between theory and praxis, if any.

Though newspaper supplements have been there for the last over fifty years, there has scarcely been any serious attempt to analyze them. When we take a look back in time at the various instances when supplements have attracted notice, we find that most such efforts have either been in the form of newspaper reports/ reviews or articles. Here again, the focus of study for the most part has been commercial. Furthermore, even these analyses have been mostly carried out in the USA. Besides, some of these studies were based on magazines instead of newspaper supplements/pull outs. This section examines all these efforts to analyze newspaper supplements with a view to justify the raison d'être of carrying out this study.

A study on how people used and absorbed media in UK came up with interesting findings on the use of supplements vis-à-vis other media[1]. According to the study, weekend newspaper packages are regarded as a welcome alternative to the week's bite-sized news items—fleshing out and providing analysis of current affairs.

An Indian study, 'Fourth Dimension of the Fourth Estate'[2] argues that daily supplements like *Delhi Times. HT City*, *Express Newsline* and *Delhi Age* have changed reading habits and created a new young and vibrant readership which is career, health and leisure conscious. It has not only increased the readership with corresponding circulation but even the advertisement revenue generated from consumer durables.

According to another study[3] that was conducted to find attitudes towards advertising in various media, although many people have a negative attitude to advertising, the three forms of print media—magazines, newspapers and newspaper supplements—fared much better, with relatively low levels of negative comments. Seven per cent of the readers agreed that they were more likely to pay attention to an advertisement if it appeared in newspaper supplements.

A study[4] was conducted by the Media Research Users Council (MRUC) to provide an understanding of the nuances of readers' habits towards newspaper pullouts and sections. MRUC's Roda Mehta delivered a presentation saying that daily pullouts behaved differently from weekly pullouts. An interesting find was that for The Times of India, the average issue readership was 55 per cent of the claimed readership.

According to Karen Robock[5] during the late 1960s and early 1970s, the weekend supplements were instrumental in introducing the country to narrative journalism. The supplements were not of the most impressive quality, but for a time they contained journalism of the highest standard.

Deepti Mahajan[6] contends that supplements are products of the advertisers' need to reach out to the consumers. The print media are functioning in a 'dual-product market'. Journalists and editors produce "popular" newspaper content in order to attract readers, and access to readers is then priced and sold to advertisers.

According to another study,[7] newspaper supplements are one of the most effective ways of spreading planning and design ideas to large numbers of people and generating public debate. They are particularly useful for presenting proposals from action planning events, especially if combined with other coverage before and afterwards. Newspaper supplements are particularly relevant in cultures where newspapers are a popular media, adapted and accessible to all layers in the population and where freedom of expression is well respected.

None of these studies undertakes a comprehensive analysis of the content of newspaper supplements, based as these are on either opinion or the exploration of a point of view.

Research Design and Methods

By virtue of the nature of the objectives of this research study, quantitative research was found most suitable. The technique of content analysis was adopted to fulfill the research objectives.

Methods of Data Collection

In order that a content analysis of newspaper supplements could be undertaken, it was necessary to go in for multi-stage sampling. In the first instance, it was necessary to select the sample out of the plethora of newspapers published and registered with the Registrar of Newspapers in India (RNI). On the basis of the circulation figures released by the RNI, the researcher selected the English news daily with the maximum circulation.

On the basis of the parameter so fixed, *The Times of India* (TOI) was selected for the purposes of this study. *The Times of India* is an English daily that comes out of the stable of Bennett Coleman & Co Ltd., a media conglomerate with interests in print, electronic and online media. *The Times of India* has been a leading paper from its inception prior to the independence of the country. For purposes of convenience, that edition of *Times of India* as got circulated in Gurgaon, a part of Delhi National Capital Region, was selected for the purposes of this study.

Once the newspaper had been identified, the next stage was of sampling the number of issues released by the selected newspaper. As it was a study of newspaper supplements and not the main newspaper, the number of issues required for an authentic study was limited. Here, it is pertinent to note that while the news covered in the main newspaper changes on a daily basis, the subjects covered in a supplement have a greater permanence. In other words, mapping the content of a supplement is possible with a fewer number of issues. Besides, that also takes care of redundancy of data. Keeping in mind this reality, it was decided to take all the supplements issued in one month.

Identification of Variables for Data Collection

Both formal and semantic variables were identified for data collection.

Coding and Tabulation of Data

These were then coded and data collected from the sample was entered on the code sheet for tabulation. Small tables were then prepared from the master table.

Data Analysis

The data obtained was analysed for each of the supplements and then these were compared across the spectrum of all the supplements of TOI.

Results and Discussion

This section presents a discussion of the results obtained from the content analysis of the supplements of the paper under study.

General Information about TOI Supplements

Table 1 gives a synoptic view of the general characteristics of the various supplements of TOI.

Table 1: General Characteristics of TOI Supplements

Name of Supplement	Periodicity	Paper Quality	Paper Size
Delhi Times	Everyday	Newsprint	Broadsheet
Education Times	Weekly	Newsprint	Broadsheet
What's Hot	Weekly	Newsprint	Tabloid
Times Life	Weekly	Glossy	Broadsheet
Gurgaon Plus	Bi-weekly	Glossy/newsprint	Broadsheet
Times Ascent	Weekly	Newsprint	Broadsheet
Times Property	Weekly	Newsprint	Broadsheet

Of the seven supplements brought out by TOI, DT is the only supplement that comes out every day with the main paper. Five supplements come out on newsprint, one on glossy paper and one at times on newsprint and at times on glossy paper. While *Times Life (TL)* comes out on glossy paper, *Gurgaon Plus*, the local supplement of TOI, comes out sometimes on glossy paper and sometimes on newsprint. The variation in the quality of paper used is prompted by the marketing concerns of the newspaper. As TL focuses on lifestyle features and products, it has to attract attention to the products advertised therein. This is possible only with glossy paper. Though Times Ascent and Times Property are advertising supplements, they do not come out on glossy paper as the products and services advertised therein do not have to be marketed.

All the supplements of TOI but for one come out on broadsheet. The only exception is *What's Hot* which comes out as a tabloid. As broadsheet supplements, they integrate well with the main newspaper.

Ad-Edit Space Distribution

Table 2 presents the results of the advertisement-edit space ratio distribution in each of the newspaper supplements.

Table 2: Ad-Edit Space Distribution (in percentage terms)

Name of Supplement	Ad Space	Edit Space
Delhi Times	40.37	59.63
Education Times	62.67	37.33
What's Hot	33.98	66.02
Times Life	40.74	59.26
Gurgaon Plus	55.83	44.17
Times Ascent	97.8	2.2
Times Property	74.5	25.5

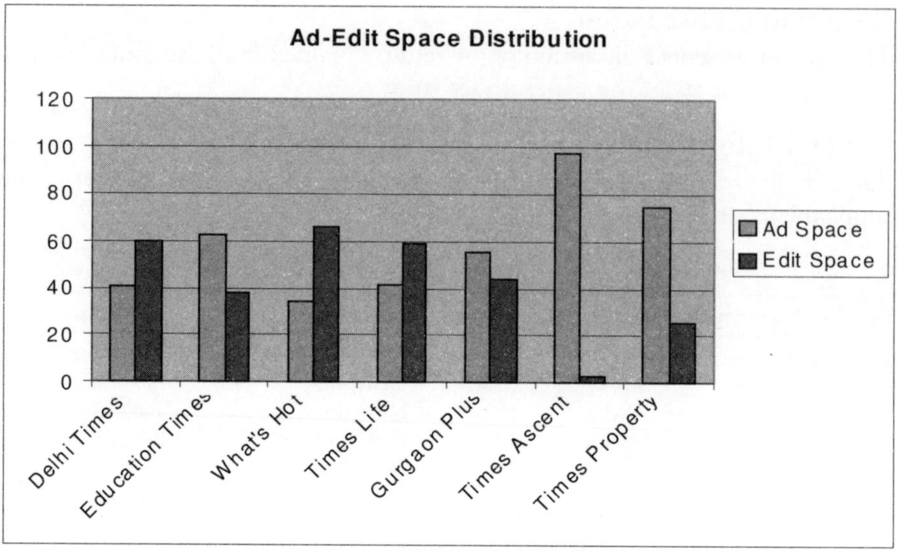

Figure 1: Ad-Edit Space Distribution

The ad-edit ratio is the highest in Times Ascent where advertisements take up 97.8 per cent of the supplement space, followed by Times Property (74.5 per cent ad space), Education Times (62.67 per cent ad space), Gurgaon Plus (55.83 per cent ad space), Times Life (40.74 per cent), Delhi Times (40.37 per cent) and finally What's Hot (33.98 per cent). The scaling down of the advertising space in each of these supplements is indicative of the overall purpose of publication of these supplements. As Times Ascent and Times Property are primarily advertising supplements, the high percentage of advertising space in each of them is understandable.

Distribution of Text-Visual Space

Table 3 presents the results of the text-visual space distribution in each of the various supplements of TOI.

Table 3: Text-Visual Space Distribution (in percentage terms)

Name of Supplement	Text Space	Visual Space
Delhi Times	73.84	26.16
Education Times	87.59	12.41
What's Hot	70.81	29.19
Times Life	71.99	28.01
Gurgaon Plus	56.49	43.51
Times Ascent	73.18	26.82
Times Property	82.25	17.75

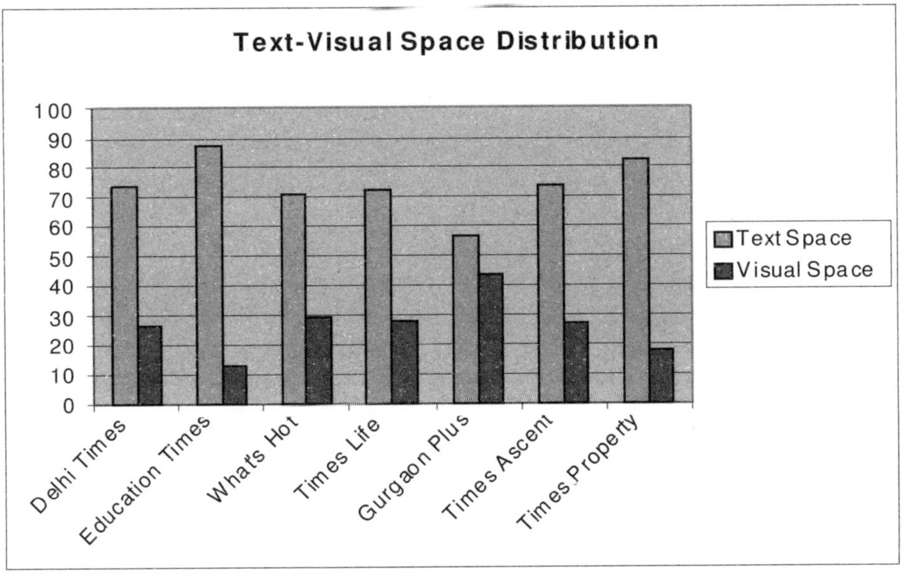

Figure 2: Text-Visual Space Distribution

Text-visual space distribution ratio among the various supplements of TOI is again non-uniform. While the text-visual ratio (T/V ratio) is the highest in Education Times (7.06:1), it is the lowest in Gurgaon Plus (1.3:1). Between these two extremities, the T/V ratio descends from Education Times to Times Property, then to Delhi Times, later to Times Ascent, still later to Times Life and penultimately What's Hot. The preponderance of visuals in Gurgaon Plus followed by What's Hot and Times Life owes to the rise of page-3 journalism which relies on people and lifestyle.

Distribution of Edit Space in TOI Supplements

Table 4 presents the results of edit space distribution across different textual forms in each of the supplements of TOI.

Table 4: Edit Space Distribution (in percentage terms)

Parameters	DT	ET	WH	TL	GP	TA	TP
Interviews	9.3	4.7	0	7.07	0	0	0
Soft Stories	27.25	0	0	0	0	0	0
Features	12.18	19.56	34.79	60.5	64.03	100	61.8
Memoirs	0.38	6.81	0.39	0	0	0	0
Review	0	1.32	13.35	0	0	0	0
Tech News	0	0	3.23	6.45	0	0	0
Print Promos	0	0	6.19	0	0	0	0
Hard News	0	22.78	0	0	2.36	0	21.1
Soft News	0	7.61	0	0	22.03	0	0
Miscellany	50.89	37.22	42.05	25.98	11.58	0	17.1

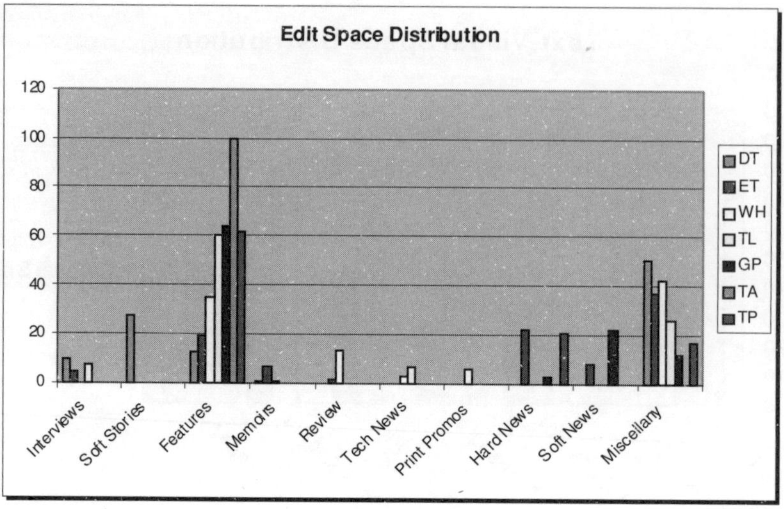

Figure 3

The edit space distribution in each of the supplements of TOI tends to be more or less skewed in favour of features, if one were to leave out the sundry items of jokes, cartoons, zodiac, handy tips, snippets etc from our comparison. While features occupied 34.79 per cent of the editorial space in What's Hot, they occupied 60.5 per cent of the space in Times Life, 64.03 per cent space in Gurgaon Plus, 19.56 per cent space in Education Times, 61.8 per cent space in Times Property and 100 per cent of the total edit space in Times Ascent. Only in DT and Education Times did features not take up maximum space. The high priority accorded to features in the editorial space of most of the supplements of TOI shows the need for leisure reading among the TOI supplement readers.

Feature Space Distribution in TOI Supplements

Table 5 presents the results of feature space distribution across various semantic categories in each of the supplements of TOI.

Table 5: Feature Space Distribution (in percentage terms)

Feature Type	DT	ET	WH	TL	GP	TA	TP
Wellbeing	3.19	0	10.11	9.29	13.38	0	0
Photo	7.96	0	0	0	3.65	0	0
Celebrity	17.96	12.9	7.66	15.27	0	0	0
Beauty	10.71	0	13.88	0	0	0	0
Culinary	9.33	0	21.94	0	11.99	0	0
Lifestyle	16.73	0	17.54	16.13	1.76	0	18.6
Crime	8.08	0	0	0	4.53	0	0
Politics	6.28	0	0	0	0	0	0
Relationships	7.71	0	12.06	28.42	0	0	0
Children	2.18	0	0	0	0	0	0
B'wood	9.87	0	0	0	0	0	0

Feature Type	DT	ET	WH	TL	GP	TA	TP
Travel	0	0	14.4	0	0	0	0
Art	0	0	2.41	0	0	0	0
Social Issues	0	0	0	22.94	0	0	0
Spirituality	0	0	0	7.95	0	0	0
Utility	0	19.79	0	0	0	0	0
Career	0	67.31	0	0	0	0	0
Development	0	0	0	0	33.86	0	37.5
Technology	0	0	0	0	9.28	0	0
Education	0	0	0	0	4.41	0	0
Grievances	0	0	0	0	11.68	0	0
HRD	0	0	0	0	0	100	0
Property	0	0	0	0	0	0	43.9

The feature space distribution in each of the supplements of TOI shows a variegated fare. While in DT, the top three slots are taken up by celebrity, lifestyle and beauty features in a descending order, in What's Hot culinary, lifestyle and travel features occupy the maximum feature space in the descending order. In Times Life, relationships, social issues and lifestyle occupy the maximum feature space, while in Education Times career, utility and celebrity features occupy most of the feature space in a descending order. In GP development, well being and culinary features occupy the maximum feature space while in Times Property, development and lifestyle features occupy the maximum feature space in a descending order. In Times Ascent, only HR development features figure, thereby taking up 100 per cent feature space. The wide distribution of the kind of subjects features focus on in each of the supplements of TOI shows a general preference

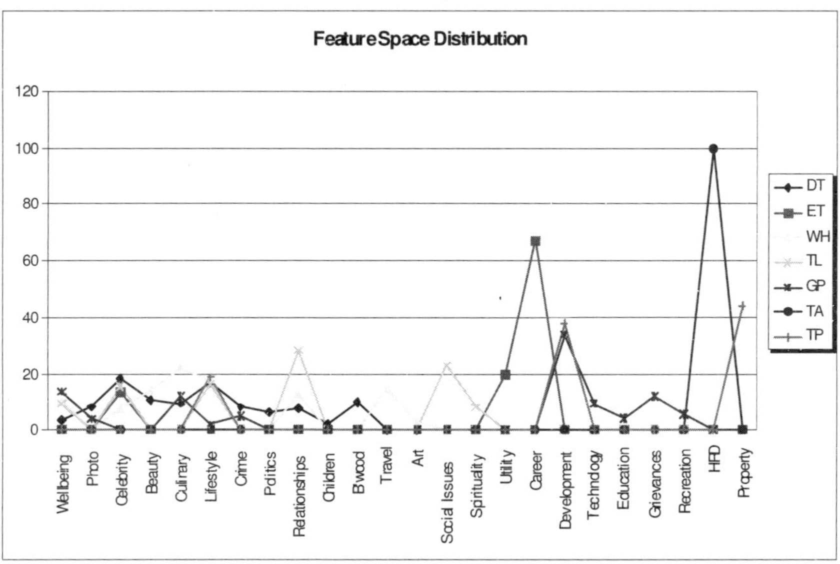

Figure 4

for lifestyle, relationship, culinary, celebrity, beauty and Bollywood features. The inference is obvious: the TOI supplements highlight the pleasing and beautiful aspect of life with a view to relieve the stress and the boredom of a harried metropolitan audience by focusing on such subjects as attract the readers' eyeballs, the paper is able to sell the attention of its wide readership to the marketers. The paper, therefore, fulfills both the entertainment and the commercial functions of mass media.

Feature Space Accorded to Relationship Features

Table 6 presents the distribution of relationship features across the different semantic categories in each of the various supplements of TOI.

Table 6: Relationship Feature Space Distribution (in percentage terms)

Name of Supplement	Formal	Informal	Intimate
Delhi Times	0	41.89	58.11
Education Times	0	0	0
What's Hot	0	0	100
Times Life	0	33	67
Gurgaon Plus	0	0	0
Times Ascent	0	0	0
Times Property	0	0	0

An analysis of relationship features highlighted in TOI supplements like DT, What's Hot and Times Life shows that the paper dares to bare the nature of

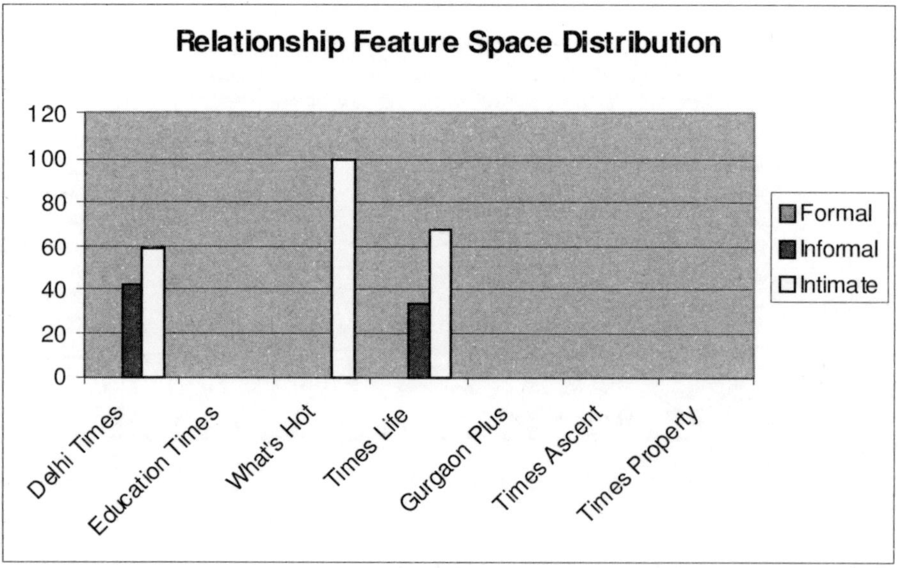

Figure 5

intimate relationships more than the informal and formal relationships obtaining in the society. While Times Life devotes 67 per cent of the relationship feature space to the discussion of intimate subjects, considered taboo in a traditional society, What's Hot apportions cent per cent of its relationship feature space to intimate subjects. Similarly, DT sets apart 58.11 per cent of the relationship feature space for the discussion of such issues. Interestingly, relationship features in none of the three supplements discussed formal relationships. Again, only DT and Times Life set apart space for informal features, but this space was far less than that given to intimate relationships. TOI, true to the popular perception, comes out as an avant-garde newspaper by stepping in to the territory of the profane and the prohibited.

Societal Role- Based Human Visual Categorisation

Table 7 presents the results of the kind of societal role models highlighted in the various TOI supplements.

Table 7: Human Visual Categorisation (in percentage terms)

Name of Supplement	Page-3	TV & Films	Political	Sports	Non-Celebrities
Delhi Times	24.83	55.37	1.68	3.02	15.1
Education Times	0	3.57	7.14	0	89.29
What's Hot	0	50	0	0	50
Times Life	4.4	16.98	0	0	78.62
Gurgaon Plus	12.5	0	0	6.25	81.25
Times Ascent	0	0	0	0	100
Times Property	0	0	0	0	0

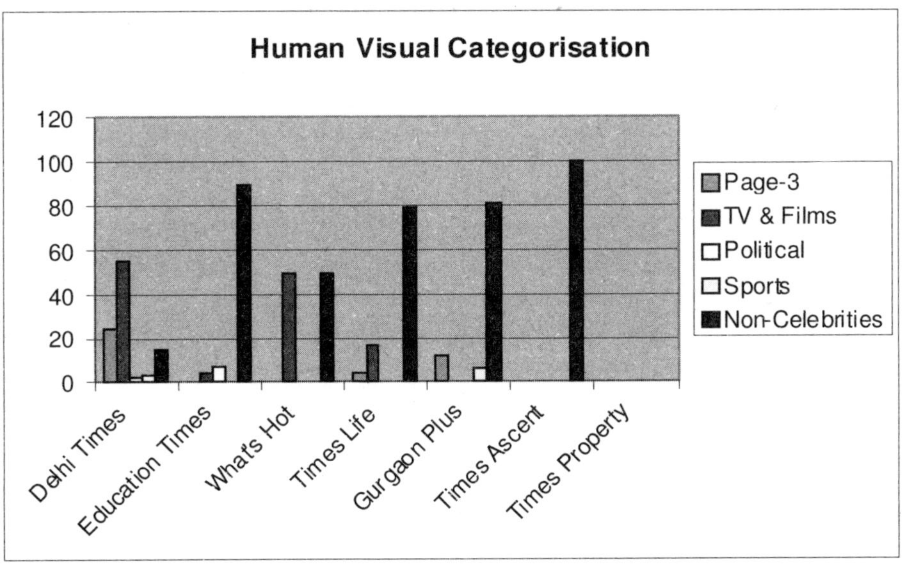

Figure 6

TOI gives a high priority to the visuals of TV and film personalities in its supplements, particularly DT (55.3 per cent) and What's Hot (50 per cent). Even in Times Life, if we were to set aside the non-descript visuals of sundry roles which account for 78.62 per cent, the visuals of TV and film personalities (16.98 per cent) are the highest among all the categories of roles.

Human Visual Categorisation on the Basis of Gender

Table 8 presents the results of the distribution of human visuals across the two genders in the various supplements.

Table 8: Gender-Based Visual Categorisation (in percentage terms)

Name of Supplement	Male	Female
Delhi Times	49.79	50.21
Education Times	52.63	47.37
What's Hot	42.5	57.5
Times Life	38.46	61.54
Gurgaon Plus	22.22	77.78
Times Ascent	55	45
Times Property	0	0

An analysis of the visuals in the supplements of TOI reveals that all the supplements of TOI but for two accord high priority to female visuals (all female/solo). The female visual percentage in various supplements ranges from 77.78 per cent to 45 per cent. Male-female visual ratio in Gurgaon Plus is as high as—2:7 followed by Times Life where the ratio is ~2:3. In What's Hot, 57.5 per cent of the human visuals are that of females followed by DT (50.21 per cent). Interestingly, DT has almost the same number of male and female visuals with

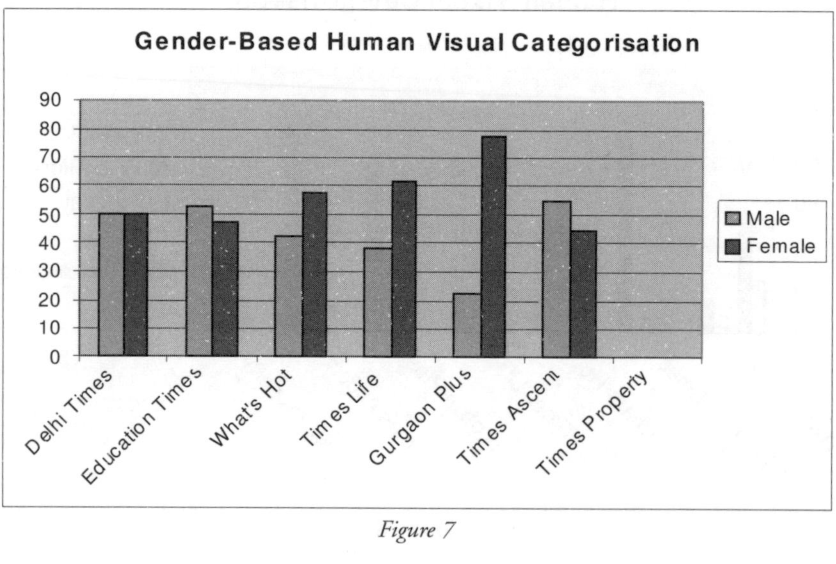

Figure 7

a very slight tilt towards female visuals. Education Times and Times Ascent —the only two supplements where the male visuals are more than the female visuals also do not depict wide variation. The message is loud and clear—TOI supplements use female visuals liberally to instantly grab the attention of readers.

Human Visual Presentation

Table 9 presents the results of distribution of men and women with different degrees of exposure in the various supplements of TOI.

Table 9: Manner of Human Visual Presentation (in percentage terms)

Name of Supplement	Minimally Exposed	Moderately Exposed	Maximally Exposed
Delhi Times	76.88	15.58	7.54
Education Times	100	0	0
What's Hot	68.06	25	6.94
Times Life	62.5	25	12.5
Gurgaon Plus	81.25	18.75	0
Times Ascent	100	0	0
Times Property	0	0	0

Interestingly, the TOI supplements may highlight female visuals and even may be bold enough to talk about taboo subjects, but the maximum number of human visuals in all the TOI supplements does not highlight the contours of human body. Unlike the prevalent public image of TOI splashing explicit female visuals unscrupulously, maximum number of human visuals in all the TOI supplements fall in the category of minimally exposed visuals. Only three TOI supplements out of seven, Times Life, Delhi Times and What's Hot, carry explicit human

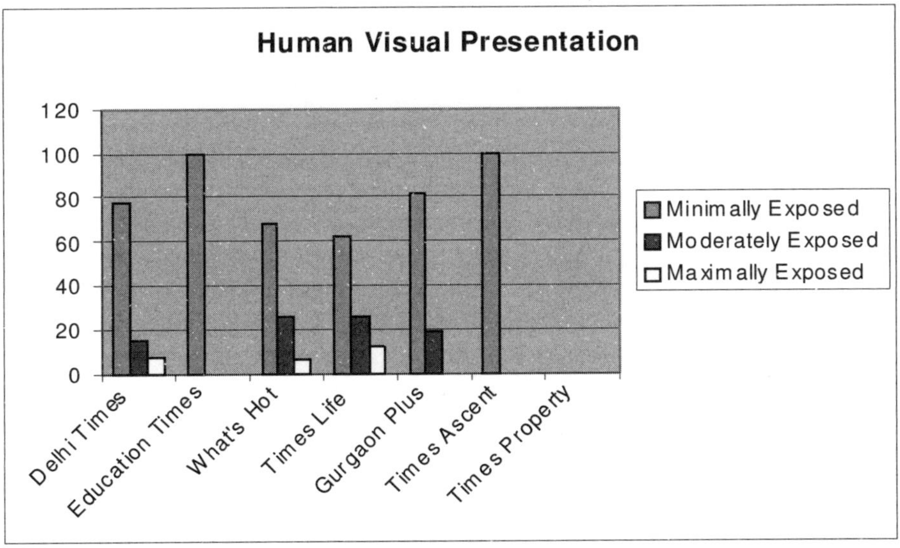

Figure 8

visuals. Here also, the percentage of maximally exposed human visuals ranges from 6.94 per cent to 12.5 per cent of the human visuals.

Layout of Visuals

Table 10 presents the results of the manner of visual presentation in the supplements of TOI.

Table 10

Name of Supplement	Bordered	Borderless
Delhi Times	83.39	16.61
Education Times	100	0
What's Hot	48.94	51.06
Times Life	22.22	77.78
Gurgaon Plus	38.71	61.29
Times Ascent	65	35
Times Property	100	0

The treatment accorded to visuals in various supplements of TOI doesn't depict any consistency. Three supplements of TOI—What's Hot, Times Life and Gurgaon Plus—are modern in terms of visual presentation. Here, the number of visuals merging with the text is more with TL taking the lead with 77.78 per cent of the total number of visuals integrating with text. On the other hand, we have Delhi Times, Education Times, Times Ascent and Times Property which are still conservative in their visual treatment.

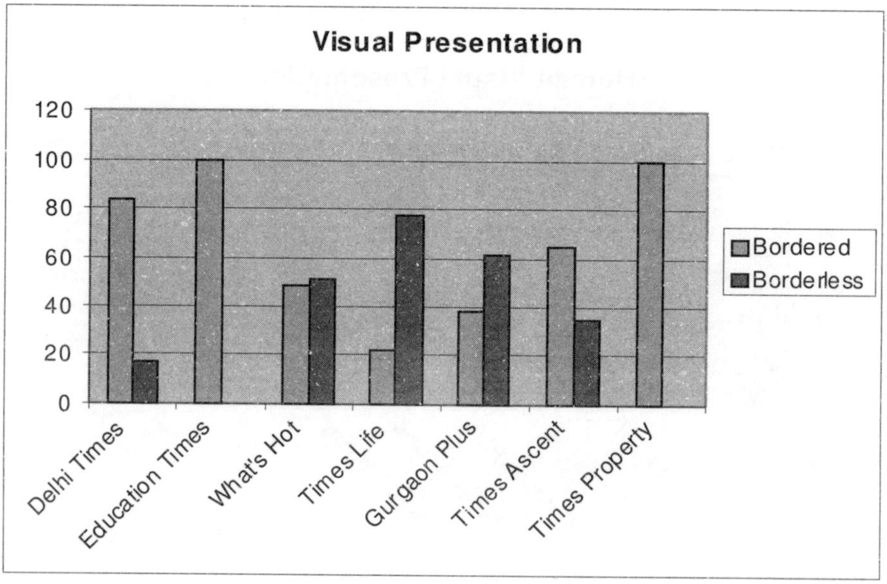

Figure 9

Conclusion

The study reveals that supplement journalism caters to three major players—the advertiser, the media house and the reader/consumer—through segmentation of information and a consequent fragmentation of mass audience/readers into identifiable homogeneous sub groups. By bringing out a variety of supplements on a variety of subjects ranging from fashion, beauty, lifestyle, and tourism on the one hand to careers, education and investments on the other hand, supplements reach out to different sub groups within the faceless heterogeneous mass audience. The media sells the attention of these sub groups to the advertiser at a price profitable to it. In view of the atomization of the society and high levels of stress in an industrialized/urbanized society, the readers' demand for amusement, information updating and lifestyle updating is met by the newspapers in their subject-specific, mixed and geographically-specific supplements. In terms of a serious engagement with the social, cultural and economic changes occurring in the society, the supplements have nothing to showcase.

In other words, the trend of supplement journalism unleashed in the post-liberalization phase of Indian economy has done nothing to make the public sphere interrogate questions of vital significance to the survival and welfare of the citizens. Rather, the trend targets the thin layer of the elite section of the society which is of significance to the marketers of lifestyle and FMCG products. The study, therefore, debunks the thesis that greater number of newspaper supplements leads to greater number of voices or greater level of engagement with citizens' concerns in the public sphere. It also posits that an increase in the index of economic growth makes the mass media more sensitive to the needs of the advertisers rather than the interests of the citizens. In such a scenario, alternative forms of media such as online communication become much more reliable facilitators of mainstreaming the masses in public debate and discussion and ensuring their right to communicate in the public sphere.

NOTES

1. Absorbing Media, http://www.magazinescanada.ca/files/Absorbing% 20Media %20Booklet.pdf
2. Om Gupta, (2002) Media Rewind: Fourth Dimension of the Fourth Estate, Vidura Volume 37, Issue 2
3. http://www.ppamarketing.net/cgi-bin/wms.pl/714
4. Indiantelevision.com's Breaking News, Posted on Dec 02, 2003 at 8.00 PM on http://us.indiantelevision.com/headlines/y2k3/dec/dec20.htm
5. *A look back at "a brief and shining moment that will never come again." How the freebie inserts changed Canadian journalism* http://www.rrj.ca/issue/2004/spring/423/
6. *Advertorials: blurring the dividing line,* Available at URL: http://209.85.175.104/search?q=cache:ONFOkOEo5YYJ:www.indiatogether.org/2004/aug/med-advert.htm+effect+of+advertising+on+newspaper+supple ments&hl=en&ct=clnk&cd=39&gl=in&client=firefox-a
7. Strategic Principles-Participation-Methods, Available at: http://www.ilo. org/ciaris/pages/english/tos/strprinc/particip/methodes/fiche_5.htm

Conclusion

Section B

MEDIA AND THE KNOWLEDGE SOCIETY

7

WIPO Development Agenda Forum and its Prospects

Sara Bannerman

The World Intellectual Property Organization (WIPO) Development Agenda was first proposed in 2004 by a coalition of developing countries called the "Friends of Development" as a set of reforms intended to make WIPO more responsive to the needs of developing countries. Over the next three years the proposal generated a rich and heated debate over the role of WIPO and intellectual property (IP) in development. By September 2007, when a set of forty-five proposals relating to a Development Agenda was agreed upon by member states, a place for wide-reaching discussion and critique on IP and development had been established within WIPO. This chapter argues that this forum is as important to WIPO and the Development Agenda as are the proposals themselves.

On the one hand, the Development Agenda can be seen in terms of its concrete and specific proposals for change. On the other hand, the Development Agenda can be viewed as an expansion of dialogue intended to better address the needs of developing countries within WIPO. Seen purely as a set of proposals for reform, the Development Agenda might be viewed as being fairly weak. In comparison with the World Trade Organization (WTO)'s Doha Ministerial Declaration on the Agreement on Trade-Related Aspects of Intellectual Property and public health, which was released as a result of the fourth session of the WTO Ministerial Conference in 2001, the Development Agenda proposes little in terms of substantial change (WTO, 2001). While the Development Agenda suggests that norm-setting activities at WIPO should, in one form or another, "take into account different levels of development," concrete measures for adjustments on par with those made under the Doha Ministerial Declaration have not been specified (WIPO, 2007b, Annex, No. 15).

If the Development Agenda is weak in terms of proposed changes to IP norms, it is strong in terms of the breadth of issues it has addressed and in the proposals it has introduced for including a broader range of interests in norm-setting processes and other WIPO activities (ibid., Nos. 5, 6, 15, 21, 42, and 44).

Whereas the Doha Ministerial Declaration led to fairly specific and narrow changes to IP norms for least-developed countries, the Development Agenda addresses a broad range of issues and proposes changes to WIPO's institutional procedures that could see the inclusion of a wider range of interests and perspectives in the organization's activities, with particular focus on transparency, participatory norm setting, member state consultation, and non-governmental organizations' participation (ibid., Nos. 5, 6, 15, 21, 42, and 44). These strengths are as important as any concrete measures proposed because, if taken seriously, they could help to ensure that the Development Agenda evolves as an ongoing project that will bring into WIPO the information and insights necessary to challenge and improve WIPO's practices and norms with regard to developing countries.

In this chapter I argue, first, that one of the most important battles of the Development Agenda at WIPO—the battle over the inclusion of development in WIPO's mandate—has already been won. Second, I show that there are opposing interpretations of the Development Agenda and how it should now be implemented. Although WIPO has agreed to take into account different levels of development in its norm-setting activities, some groups envision relatively minor changes, while others envision more radical change. Third, I argue that WIPO's mandate in promoting IP protection around the world originated as an idea from the eighteenth-century Enlightenment, which today stands open both to critique and reformulation. Finally, I conclude that, while great obstacles stand in the way of a true re-envisioning of WIPO's approach to IP, such a shift is possible and necessary.

The Battle Already Won

The Friends of Development have already won what is perhaps the biggest contest of principles to have faced WIPO in the past forty years—the question of whether WIPO's mandate includes development. During the three years of talks on a Development Agenda, it has been necessary to shift the thinking of some member states, and perhaps the secretariat itself, on this issue.

However, by July 2005, after protracted discussions on the issue of WIPO's mandate, a consensus had been achieved that there was room within WIPO's current mandate for development issues (WIPO, 2005c). The issue was not raised again substantively as a way of blocking further discussion of WIPO's role in development.

As Christopher May (2006, 4) notes, "this attempt to shift the WIPO's priorities [was] underpinned by the argument that as the WIPO is a specialized agency of the UN it should share the UN's focus on global developmental issues rather than a more technical focus on the governance and protection of IPRs [IP rights]." WIPO's formal commitment as a United Nations (UN) specialized agency to facilitate technology transfer "in order to accelerate economic, social and cultural development" was what allowed the Friends of Development to counter claims that development was not the domain of WIPO.[1] As such, WIPO's agreement with the UN has begun to be inscribed onto WIPO's practices and translated into a broader mandate for development within the organization.

The Development Agenda: Optimists and Pessimists

When it comes to the future of the Development Agenda, there are both optimists and pessimists. Pessimists (or realists) might generally predict that more powerful states will ultimately prevail over weaker ones, with the international IP regime maintaining its rights-centred focus. The Development Agenda forum is seen by pessimists as being an extension of, and infused with, international power relations—a struggle through which developing countries are unlikely to achieve substantial gains. The views of pessimists are substantiated by the fact that some of the most concrete proposals for change, such as those involving major institutional changes at WIPO (WIPO, 2007c, Nos. 42 and 60), those strongly encouraging the exploitation of public interest flexibilities in IP treaties (ibid., Annex A: No. 23; Annex B: Nos. 3 and 37), and those calling for a treaty on access to knowledge (ibid., Annex B: No. 35), were not included in the Development Agenda. The inclusion of proposals to encourage and assist developing countries with implementation and enforcement of current IP treaties further buttresses the concerns of pessimists (WIPO, 2007a).

Optimists, on the other hand, focus on the potential for international institutions to solve problems in international relations. They would argue that the active involvement of less powerful countries and interests in the discussions held as part of the Development Agenda has the effect, at least, of encouraging efforts to call to light and address the problems experienced by developing countries in the international IP system and, at most, to adjust the international IP system in a more concrete way.

The optimist/pessimist debate is already beginning to manifest itself as WIPO sets about the task of implementing the Development Agenda. One notable example concerns the agenda's Recommendation No. 15, which states:

Norm-setting activities shall:

- be inclusive and member driven;
- take into account different levels of development;
- take into consideration a balance between costs and benefits;
- be a participatory process, which takes into consideration the interests and priorities of all WIPO Member States and the viewpoints of other stakeholders, including accredited inter-governmental organizations and non-governmental organizations; and
- be in line with the principle of neutrality of the WIPO Secretariat. (WIPO, 2007b, Annex, No. 15)

The second element of Recommendation No. 15—that norm-setting activities should take into account different levels of development—is a central purpose of the Development Agenda. It focuses on WIPO's principle task of norm setting and inextricably links this task to considerations of the level of development of WIPO member states. While Recommendation No. 15 is an agreed principle, its translation into concrete measures will be hotly contested by those who wish to maintain the status quo at WIPO and those who call for more fundamental transformation.

The idea that norm-setting activities should take into account different levels of development is connected to the observation made by the Friends of Development in their 2004 proposal that "[IP] protection is a policy instrument the operation of which may, in actual practice, produce benefits as well as costs, *which may vary in accordance with a country's level of development*" (WIPO, 2004, Annex, No. 2; emphasis added). HaJoon Chang (2001, 303), who is a proponent of more radical change in IP regimes, similarly notes that

> [t]he domestic benefits of a stronger [IP rights] system—namely, increased knowledge generation by nationals—are likely to be very small for most developing countries, given that they do little [research and development] and a lot of the new knowledge that they generate is not patentable. The "international" benefits of such a regime—greater technology transfer, greater [foreign direct investment], greater efforts at innovation in the developed countries—are also close to zero, if any. On the other hand, the costs of such system are likely to be considerable—increased royalty payments, monopolistic abuses, the human (and financial) resource costs of administering an elaborate [IP rights] system, and so on.

The inclusion of special treatment or greater flexibilities in WIPO treaties would be a radical change that, in the past, has been difficult to achieve at WIPO. Although there are a few provisions available under the current WIPO agreements that are specifically for developing countries, these have been little used and have come to be viewed as largely ineffectual (Ricketson and Ginsberg, 2005, 956–60). WIPO treaties generally require signatory states, whether developed or developing, to meet similar standards and to operate under the same IP rights provisions.

Other relatively radical changes that could benefit developing countries (and perhaps developed ones too) have also been proposed that would alter or adjust international IP norms. A treaty on access to knowledge has been proposed that would have countries agree to adopt a minimum set of limitations and exceptions, invest in a knowledge commons, promote open standards, and allow copyright collecting societies in developing countries to direct a larger portion of their distributions to domestic rights-holders, among other things (WIPO, 2007c, No. 35). As well, the formulation of a minimum set of limitations and exceptions has been proposed as a way of ensuring a minimum level of access to works, "not only to guarantee the right of humankind to participate in cultural activity and scientific and economic progress, but also to facilitate and promote the creative activity of authors and cultural industries which require those exceptions to carry out a part of their activities" (WIPO, 2005a, Annex, page 2). Although neither of these proposals were included directly in the Development Agenda, further discussion on access to knowledge was agreed upon under the Development Agenda. Discussions regarding a minimum set of limitations and exceptions continues at WIPO (New, 2008).

What is clear is that there are differing views on the meaning of accounting for differing levels of development in the WIPO context. One view involves a substantial change to existing international treaties or new treaties, while the other involves concessions that are as minor as accepting paper instead of digital documents in patent filing processes. Under one interpretation, the fundamental norms of international IP would be either significantly adjusted or reformulated. Under another interpretation, the current system would remain the same, and different levels of development would continue to be taken into account in WIPO processes such as its technical assistance programs, which can often serve to extend and reinforce the current system.

Enlightenment and Critique

IP and its role in development must be viewed in the context of a long history of intellectual and political change. IP emerged in connection with the Enlightenment in eighteenth-century Western Europe (Wood-mansee, 1984, 425–48; Hesse, 1990, 109–37), and international institutions such as WIPO and its predecessors followed. That is, intellectual property and the idea that an author owned his or her own work emerged along with the commercial book trade and valorization of the individual intellectual work (Woodmansee, 1984, 425–48; Hesse, 1990, 110). International institutions in general have been seen as a product of the Enlightenment's optimism about the possibility of creating a rational and harmonious international system (Howard, 2001, 113).

Concerns about international development were integrated into the mandates of international institutions after the Second World War as industrialized countries began to formulate policies toward their former colonies, which had emerged as newly independent countries. WIPO was also faced with this new reality beginning in the 1960s when developing countries' issues began to be addressed in the organization and in modifications of the Berne Convention for the Protection of Literary and Artistic Works (Berne Convention) itself (Ricketson and Ginsberg, 2005, 887–963).

As with the Enlightenment and its various projects, the intellectual rationale with respect to international development and international institutions has been criticized for its potential to sanction and extend forms of hidden domination and dependency (Horkheimer and Adorno, 2002, 282). Such domination could occur by imposing the political ideals and institutions of the powerful on less powerful countries or by making use of a system of thought and discourse that tends to recreate and extend dependency and domination (Stiglitz, 2002, 282; Escobar, 1995, 290).

Some thinkers are nevertheless optimistic about the ongoing potential to reformulate structures of power through dialogue (Habermas, 1983). Some view the conceptual foundations of the Enlightenment, and of IP, as being fundamentally unstable and therefore open to renegotiation and rebalancing (Hesse, 1990, 130). It is for this reason that the acceptance of the development dimension in WIPO's mandate is seen as an achievement by those who believe that it is a necessary tool for reform at WIPO. The Development Agenda, while rightly viewed with skepticism by pessimists, is also rightly seen by optimists as a vehicle for re-examining WIPO's view of the policy goals of IP in general and for evaluating and critiquing the current contribution of WIPO in developing countries in particular. The Development Agenda, as a forum in which challenges, evidence, and new insight can be brought to light, is extremely important to this process.

There is reason for a certain degree of optimism, based on historical experience. WIPO's historical antecedent originated, in the case of copyright, in the nineteenth century as a project initiated by a highly particular set of interests: authors and publishers. What began as a pact between a few countries acting mainly in the interests of their authors and publishers slowly expanded into the broad international system that we know today (Ricketson and Ginsberg, 2005, ch. 2). Various interests, originally on the periphery of the international IP system, engaged in national and international forums and have since been accommodated in very concrete ways. Gramophone companies, photographers, broadcasters, performers, and producers of phonograms each had special interests that had to be accommodated by fairly major changes to the international IP system (ibid., chs. 3 and 4). The special interests of early twentieth-century Canada, a country that was in the unique situation of being the neighbour to the United States when it stood outside the Berne Convention, were accommodated in 1914 via a special protocol to the Berne Convention that took this situation into account (ibid., 102–3). Newly independent countries entering in the 1960s were also met with (limited) accommodations (ibid., 887–963). In each of these cases, it was necessary for new knowledge about the conditions experienced by various interest groups under the international IP system to be internalized through information and challenges brought forward by various fora.

At the same time, it could be said that some of these interests have adapted more to WIPO than WIPO has adapted to them. As Christopher May (2006, 65) notes, the education of diplomats and elites within WIPO—a process that can take place in many formats, including development agenda discussions—along with its technical assistance and education programs, serves to extend and strengthen the dominant WIPO views among less powerful countries and their interests. In order for the real challenges facing the international IP system in developing countries to be met, WIPO must ensure that the dialogue taking place in the forums and projects of the Development Agenda is really a two-way dialogue—one that is open to hearing about, and addressing, problems, challenges, and opportunities for change.

Conclusion

Optimists see an opportunity in the Development Agenda to initiate real transformation at WIPO, to re-evaluate and reformulate long-held ideas, to change minds, reformulate interests, and eventually to adjust the international IP system in ways that will serve the interests of both developed and developing countries. Such a transformation is seen to have already begun through the more widespread recognition of development as an important aspect of WIPO's mandate, which is a direct result of the Development Agenda's discussions.

Others are pessimistic about the potential for the Development Agenda to lead to concrete change. The most potent proposals that emerged as part of the discussions between 2004 and 2007 did not survive to become part of the Development Agenda, and powerful interests objected strongly to fundamental changes to the international IP system. Indeed, there is room for concern that a forum such as the one created for the Development Agenda discussions could serve as a tool for advancing and extending already-dominant views, with little room left for views that raise challenges and critique. WIPO, its member states, and observers must guard against this type of stagnation as the Development Agenda moves forward. Great obstacles stand in the way of significantly adjusting WIPO's approach to IP. However, the international IP system has undergone continuous adjustment since its establishment in the nineteenth century, and these changes have come about as a result of dialogues such as the one fostered through the Development Agenda forum.

Note

1. Agreement between the United Nations and the World Intellectual Property Organization, 27 September 1974, in *Treaties and International Agreements Registered or Filed or Reported with the Secretariat of the United Nations,* 956, no. 729.

8

Knowledge Society as Pathway to Sustainable Development in the Arab World: An Islamic Cultural Perspective

Muhammad Ayish

According to UNESCO, knowledge societies describe capabilities to identify, produce, process, transform, disseminate, and use information to build and apply knowledge for human development (UNESCO, 2005). In their basic configuration, knowledge societies draw on an empowering social vision that encompasses diversity, inclusion, solidarity and participation. In the past two decades, the phrase has gained skyrocketing popularity around the world in light of democratic and communications transformations in the post-Cold War era. Traditionally, knowledge has been equated with power and a nation's knowledge has been instrumental in defining its stature at national and global fronts (Carnoy & Castelles, 2001). Although the phrase "knowledge society" was initially coined in the late 1960s to describe the role of education in promoting community development around the world, its basic foundations have come to be grounded in the information and communication revolution as well as in democratic orientations taking shape since the late 1980s (Mansell & Wehn, 1998). The knowledge society has gradually come to replace the widely-reputed 'information society,' conceived as the successor to agricultural and industrial societies (Bell, 1976). Knowledge societies are believed to be distinctive for embracing significant social and human components that view individuals and groups as far more than 'wired' communities.

Like information societies, knowledge societies owe their defining power for early 21st Century development to a wide range of variables, the most outstanding of which are cultural. In knowledge societies, the value of information derives primarily from how it is brought to bear on social and economic community needs in the context of sustainable development. Yet, to fully comprehend the dynamics of knowledge creation, acquisition, and diffusions, we need also to consider the cultural foundations that give rise to knowledge societies as such.

Among other things, this argument suggests that while societies around the world share significant common features of knowledge-based endeavors and strategies, they are also bound to exhibit different conceptions of knowledge.

This paper addresses knowledge societies in the contemporary Arab World with an emphasis on the cultural foundations that define the region's attitudes towards knowledge creation, diffusion and application in its living experiences. It argues that it is culture rather than technology that shapes the elaboration of an Arab-Islamic knowledge society model that both reflects normative social and religious traditions and empowers communities in the 21st Century. As noted by numerous national and international reports, the Western-style knowledge paradigm in the Arab World is faltering because it has failed to account for the region's cultural values as well as its rich historical experiences in science innovations in different fields. The Glorious Qur'an and the Honorable traditions of Prophet Muhammad (PBUH) furnish us with a rich normative heritage for promoting knowledge as an act of worship a Muslim does to fulfill his/her religious duties. Arab-Islamic history is also rife with wide ranging experiences in scientific innovation in the fields of medicine, astronomy, physics, chemistry, biology and other fields. The defining feature of this heritage is the synthesis of science and morality in knowledge acquisition and diffusion. This chapter harnesses this moral-scientific synthesis to evolve an Islamic knowledge model in the Arab World, a model that both resonates with the region's cultural identity and addresses its emerging sustainable development needs.

Knowledge Society: The Dominant Paradigm

The phrase 'knowledge society' was first coined in 1966 by Robert Lane who saw it as a society having its roots in the epistemology and the logic of inquiry. Such a society, according to Lane, needs to be open enough to allow discussion on every topic, stable enough to maintain the order necessary for inquiry, rich enough to educate its population and dissatisfied or curious enough to want to know more (1966). Lane (1966:653) also claims that 'the knowledgeable society is characterized by a relative emphasis upon certain ways of thinking, a certain epistemology, or certain knowledge about knowledge'. In 1962, Fritz Machlup addressed the impact of knowledge and the emerging 'knowledge industry' on changes in occupational structures. Peter Drucker (1969), in association with educational and social studies, carried out by researchers such as Robin Mansell and Nico Stehr. Drucker noted that that 'knowledge has become the central factor of production in an advanced, developed society' (1969: 248). He observed that 'the key to producing more work was to work smarter (instead of harder); the key to productivity was knowledge (instead of sweat) (1969:255).

In recent years, the use of the concept of the knowledge society has turned more political and normative, as something that needs to be aspired for, often portrayed as the way forward for developed as well as developing nations and regions (Beerkins, 2006). Several analyses of the concept by Stehr (1994) and Böhme & Stehr (1986) indicate that the term 'knowledge society' owes its denotation to the constitutive mechanism or the identity of modern society as increasingly driven by knowledge.

The notion of 'knowledge society' is sometimes used interchangeably with the phrase 'information society'. Daniel Bell (1974) conceived of information society as a 'post-industrial society' in which the creation, distribution, diffusion, use, integration and manipulation of information is a significant economic, political, and cultural activity. He notes that 'the concept of the post-industrial society deals primarily with changes in the social structure, the way in which the economy is being transformed and the occupational system reworked, and with the new relations between theory and empiricism, particularly science and technology' (Bell, 1974:13).

UNESCO has been at the forefront of a global drive to promote the concept of knowledge societies as an empowering social umbrella for sustainable development in the 21st Century by integrating the term 'knowledge society', or its variant, 'knowledge societies', within its institutional policies. Ever since, there has been a great deal of debate on the issue, which strives to incorporate a more integral conception that is not only related to the economic dimension, but to the social and cultural as well.

One leading UNESCO report on knowledge societies has been initiated with the central question: Does the aim of building knowledge societies make any sense when history and anthropology teach us that since ancient times, all societies have probably been, each in its own way, knowledge societies? (UNSECO, 2005). To answer this question, the report notes that the control of knowledge can go hand in hand with serious inequality, exclusion, and social conflict. In ancient civilizations, knowledge was long the exclusive domain of tight circles of wise men and the initiated few. In the 18th and 19th centuries, however, the drive for democracy, political and social liberalism and the gradual emergence of a public sphere for knowledge fostered the spread of the ideas of universality, liberty and equality. The diffusion of knowledge through telegraphy, books, and the printing press, as well as the extension of an education for all through schools and universities, accompanied this historical development. The importance of education and critical thinking underscores that in building real knowledge societies, the new prospects held out by the internet and multimedia tools must not cause us to lose interest in traditional knowledge sources such as the press, radio, television and, above all, the school (UNESCO, 2005).

Cultural diversity or the visibility of cultural distinctions within communities in the context of freedom and participatory democracy is an outstanding feature of UNESCO-envisioned knowledge societies. Fostering diversity also means nurturing the creativity of emerging knowledge societies to fulfill not only an abstract ethical imperative, but rather to raise in each society an awareness of the wealth of the forms of knowledge and capacities it possesses, in order to increase their value and take advantage of what they have to offer. In this sense, a knowledge society should be able to integrate all its members and to promote new forms of cohesion involving both present and future generations. Since knowledge society is an inclusive concept, nobody should be excluded from knowledge societies, where knowledge is a public domain, available to each and every individual. Young people are bound to play a major role because they are often among the first to use new technologies and to help establish them as familiar features of everyday life. But older people also have an important part to play. They possess the experience required to offset the relative superficiality of "real-time" communication and remind us that knowledge is but a road to wisdom.

From an economic point of view, the emergence of knowledge societies is bringing about fundamental restructurings in the the economy and state in a way that knowledge has always been a factor of production, and a driver of economic and social development. Earlier economies depended, for example, on knowledge about how to farm, how to build, and how to manufacture. However, as the experience of the past decade has shown, the capacity to manipulate, store, and transmit large quantities of information cheaply has increased at a staggering rate over recent years (Neef, Siesfeld & Cefola, 1998). The digitization of information and the associated pervasiveness of the Internet are facilitating a new intensity in the application of knowledge to economic activity, to the extent that it has become the predominant factor in the creation of wealth. As much as 70 to 80 percent of economic growth is now said to be due to more advanced knowledge. In an increasingly global economy, where knowledge about how to excel competitively and information about who excels are both more readily available, the effective creation, use and dissemination of knowledge is increasingly the key to success, and thus to sustainable economic and social development that benefits us all. Innovation, which fuels new job creation and economic growth, is quickly becoming the key factor in global competitiveness.

Knowledge Realities in the Arab World: A Bleak Landscape

In 2002, the United Nations Development Program published its first Arab Human Development Report entitled *Creating Opportunities for Future Generations* (UNDP, 2002) in which it called for the consolidation of knowledge acquisition and its effective utilization. As a key driver of progress, knowledge must be brought to bear efficiently and productively in all aspects of society, with the goal of enhancing human well being across the region. In 2003, the UN Development Program published its *Arab Human Development Report* on building knowledge societies in the Arab World that evolves an "Arab knowledge model" based on the understanding of knowledge as a commodity, thus disregarding the diversity of knowledge found in the Arab region (UNDP, 2003). An investigation of the proposed role of information and communication technologies (ICT) in the Report indicates that, because ICT is biased towards the transfer of commodified knowledge and not the cultivation of the diversity of indigenous cultures and traditions, it may intensify this neglect to the point of epistemic violence. The suppression of cognitive justice may eventually lead to the failure in building just and prosperous Arab societies. The authors of the *Report* argued that the development challenges of the Arab region are the result of deficits in the area of knowledge, women's empowerment, and freedom. The dire realities of knowledge in the Arab world were also addressed in the 2009 Arab Cultural Development Report issued by the Beirut-based Arab Thought Foundation. The Report lamented the dominance of outdated educational norms and practices as well as an inhibitive Arab World environment not conducive to innovation in the various field of knowledge (Fikr, 2009).

In early 2008, the World Bank (2008: 2) issued its report '*The Road Not Traveled; Education Reform in the Middle East and Africa*' in which it noted that the MENA region has made significant strides in the education sector, having started in the 1960s and 1970s from very low levels of human capital accumulation. However, it has not capitalized fully on past investments in education, let alone developed education systems capable of meeting new challenges. According to the Report, the education systems did not produce what the markets needed, and the markets were not sufficiently developed to absorb the educated labor force into the most efficient uses.

The 2009 report on knowledge societies in the Arab world produced by the New York-based Brookings Institute noted Access to education has expanded markedly over the past five years. Jordan exceeded the international average on eighth grade science scores for the first time ever. It concluded that Arab countries, as a group, have made significant progress in most of these areas, especially compared with their own history. Yet, other regions have advanced even faster and tremendous challenges—such as creating 100 million new jobs for the region's mushrooming youth population—loom ahead. The Arab world must reinvigorate its efforts or be left behind. Many new initiatives are underway, but it is too soon to assess their impact. Success, ultimately, will be judged by what is achieved, not by what is invested. Arab societies have achieved success in some areas. Access to education improved markedly in the past several years. An Arab country surpassed the global average in 8th grade science scores for the first time; others show new commitment to assessment and change. New universities with global standards are enrolling students. Governments are investing more in research and development. Economic growth is robust across much of the region and high technology exports are rising. More oil wealth now stays in the region, invested in education, research, innovation, and productive industry. New philanthropy supports these ends.

An important facet of knowledge conditions in the Arab world is that they owe much of their inception and development to Western-informed philosophical visions of science and technology as functional tools of economic prosperity. In fact most of the leading knowledge society initiatives undertaken by Arab countries like the Mohammed bin Rashid Foundation, the Arab Science and Technology Foundation, the Arab Thought Forum, Qatar Foundation as well as leading science and technology universities are driven by beliefs in the power of knowledge to bring about sustainable transformations in the region's communities.

Normative Islamic Knowledge Values and Historical Experiences

While the dominant paradigm defining knowledge creation, acquisition, and diffusion in the Arab world is shaped by Western-style functional notions of knowledge as an economic asset and a commercial commodity, the Islamic conception of knowledge views it as an integral part of worship *Ibadah* or religious duties that are mandatory on all Muslims to do. Islam unquestionably urges people to seek knowledge and to establish knowledge societies. The centrality of *Ilm* or knowledge in Islam derives from teachings embedded in the Glorious Qur'an and the Honorable traditions of Prophet Muhammad (PBUH) as well as form historical evidence showing rich Arab-Muslims' contributions to the advancement of science and technology.

(a) Normative Islamic Conceptions of Knowledge

Knowledge in Islam, referred to as *Ilm*, is a central component of Islamic culture. Islamic heritage abounds with rich normative and experiential evidence supporting the promotion of knowledge. The text of the Glorious Quran is replete with verses inviting Man to use his intellect, to ponder, to think and to know, for the goal of human life is to discover the truth which is none other than worshipping Allah in His Oneness. Islam is the religion of knowledge. The first verse of the Qur'an enjoined reading as the key to knowledge. Allah says: *Read! In the Name of your Lord Who has created (all that exists). He has created man from a clot (a piece of thick coagulated blood). Read! And your Lord is the Most Generous. Who has taught (the writing) by the pen. He has taught man that which he knew not)* [al-'Alaq 96:1-5]. Allah created man and provided him with the tools for acquiring knowledge, namely hearing, sight and wisdom. Allah says: *And Allâh has brought you out from the wombs of your mothers while you know nothing. And He gave you hearing, sight, and hearts that you might give thanks (to Allâh)* [al-Nahl 16:78]. Because of the importance of knowledge, Allah commanded His Messenger to seek more of it. Allah says: *"My Lord! Increase me in knowledge"* [Ta-Ha 20:114]. The best of all branches of knowledge are the sciences of sharee'ah through which man comes to know his Lord, and his Prophet and religion. This is the knowledge with which Allah honored His Messenger; He taught it to him so that he might teach it to mankind: *Indeed, Allâh conferred a great favor on the believers when He sent among them a Messenger (Muhammad) from among themselves, reciting unto them His Verses (the Qur'ân), and purifying them (from sins by their following him), and instructing them (in) the Book (the Qur'an) and Al-Hikmah [the wisdom and the Sunnah of the Prophet (i.e. his legal ways, statements and acts of worship)], while before that they had been in manifest error"* [Aal 'Imraan 3:164]There is no goodness in knowledge which is not confirmed by action, or words which are not confirmed by deeds: *"O you who believe! Why do you say that which you do not do? Most hateful it is with Allâh that you say that which you do not do"* [al-Saff :2-3]. Knowledge brings a great reward. The one who points the way to something good is like the one who does it. When the knowledgeable person dies, his reward with Allah does not cease when he dies, rather it continues to increase so long as people benefit from his knowledge.

Beside various Qur'anic emphases on the importance of knowledge, there are hundreds of Prophetic traditions that encourage Muslims to acquire all types of knowledge from any corner of the world. The *Hadith* (Prophet's traditions) is also full of references to the importance of knowledge. Such sayings of the Prophet as '*Seek knowledge even in China*', '*Seek knowledge from the cradle to the grave*', *"Verily the men of knowledge are the inheritors of the prophets"*, and 'When a man dies, all his deeds come to an end except for three – an ongoing charity, beneficial knowledge or a righteous son who will pray for him' (Narrated by Muslim, 1631). The Prophet (PBUH) made seeking knowledge an obligation upon every Muslim, and he explained that the superiority of the one who has knowledge over the one who merely worships is like the superiority of the moon over every other heavenly body. He said that the scholars are the heirs of the Prophets and that the Prophets did not leave behind dinars and dirhams (i.e., money), rather their inheritance was knowledge, so whoever acquires it has gained a great share. The Prophe (PBUH) said that seeking knowledge is a way to Paradise. He (PBUH) said: 'whoever follows a path in the pursuit of knowledge, Allah (SWT) will make a path to Paradise easy for him.' (Narrated by al-Bukhaari, Kitaab al-'Ilm, 10)

(b) Historical Evidence

During most of its history, the Arab-Islamic civilization has generated outstanding types of knowledge in the different fields of life. Every traditional Islamic city possessed public and private libraries and some cities like Cordoba and Baghdad boasted of libraries with over 400,000 books. Such cities also had bookstores, some of which sold a large number of titles. That is also why the scholar has always been held in the highest esteem in Islamic society. While the domain of knowledge in the pre-Islamic period was confined mainly to literary and folkloric modes of expression, the advent of Islam heralded remarkable developments not only in the scope of knowledge, but in its epistemology. The Qur'an represents a linguistic achievement so high that Arabs were unable to match despite their record of distinguished literary craftsmanship. Baffled by the linguistic miracle of the Holy Book, Arabs were steered by Islam to explore areas of knowledge other than poetry and prose. Arab Muslims were also enjoined to draw on a multiplicity of knowledge acquisition methods other than imagination and oral transmission. An all encompassing scientific and information revolution was unleashed with far-reaching repercussions not only for Arabs, but for other peoples as well.

The concept of *ilm* implied different, but important sources of knowledge acquisition. The primary source is revelation as in the case of the Qur'an. Muslims are enjoined to submit to revealed knowledge by heart-based belief. In the meantime, Islam emphasizes the role of the intellect or reason *Aql* in leading man to the Divine. Mahmoud (1977: 89-90) notes that a good deal of rationality had marked Arab culture as evident in Arabs' approaches to language codification, Islamic jurisprudence Fiqh, and receptivity to Greek writings, mathematics and philosophy. Islamic jurisprudence-based works were centered on four schools of interpretation of the Qur'an and the Sunna: Shafieyya, (after Muhammad ibn Idris al-Shafi'i, d. 820); Hanbalyya, (after Ahmad ibn Hanbal, d. 855); Malikyaa (after Malik ibn Anas, d. 795); and Hanafiyya (after Abu Hanifa, d. 767). The philosophical stream of thought was concerned with establishing harmony between reason and revelation. Affected by translated Greek works of Plato and Aristotle, Muslim-Arab thinkers such as al-Farabi, Ibn Sina, Ibn Hazm, Ibn Tufayl, and Ibn Rushd laid down foundations for a new philosophical orientation in which intellect and reason were elevated to a higher status. In his utopia, The Perfect State, al-Farabi (d. 950) was greatly influenced by Plato's writings as he elaborated a theory of civil administration based on the concept of emanation of power from an absolute center, namely Allah. In Hay bin Yaqthan (The Alive Son of the Awake), Ibn Tufayl (d. 1185) narrated a story about a baby who was left alone on a desert land. From contemplation and observation, he got to know some natural phenomena, and in the end he discovered the existence of Allah together with a large body of ethical values. In other words, he independently reached the main principles of Islam which suggests human mind and divine revelation converged on a single point.

The Muslim mind has always been attracted to the mathematical sciences in accordance with the "abstract" character of the doctrine of Oneness which lies at the heart of Islam. The mathematical sciences have traditionally included astronomy, mathematics itself and much of what is called physics today. In astronomy the Muslims integrated the astronomical traditions of the Indians, Persians, the ancient Near East and especially the Greeks into a synthesis which began to chart a new chapter in the history of astronomy from the 8th century onward. The vast expanse of the Islamic world enabled the Muslims to develop natural history based not only on the Mediterranean world, as was the case of the Greek natural historians, but also on most of the Eurasian and even African land masses.

Muslims also inherited a wide range of technological knowledge, from the building of water wheels by the Romans to the underground water system by the Persians, became part and parcel of the technology of the newly founded order. Muslims also imported items from China before transmitting them later to the West. They also developed many forms of technology on the basis of earlier existing knowledge related to the metallurgical art of making the famous Damascene swords, an art which goes back to the making of steel several thousand years before on the Iranian Plateau. One of the major achievements of Islamic civilization was architecture which combines technology and art. The great masterpieces of Islamic architecture from the Cordoba Mosque and the Dome of the Rock in Jerusalem to the Taj Mahal in India display this perfect wedding between the artistic principles of Islam and remarkable technological know-how. Much of the outstanding medieval architecture of the West is in fact indebted to the techniques of Islamic architecture. When one views the Notre Dame in Paris or some other Gothic cathedral, one is reminded of the building techniques which traveled from Muslim Cordoba northward. Gothic arches as well as interior courtyards' of so many medieval and Renaissance European structures remind the viewer of the Islamic architectural examples from which they originally drew.

Suggested Knowledge Model

It is clear that knowledge is a deeply-rooted concept in Islamic beliefs and historical traditions. But unlike the Western conception which views knowledge as economic asset, the Islamic view of knowledge is embedded in religious duties, always taken as an integral part of worship in its broadest sense. According to this view, the power of knowledge is already recognized; yet, the forces that drive its creation, diffusion and application are intrinsically spiritual despite the significance of their physical manifestations. This religious ingredient in *Ilm* is bound to have important implications for how the issue of knowledge society has to be addressed. If you create knowledge and harness to promote values of good and inhibit values of evil, then you are fulfilling an important religious duty. This means of course that knowledge should not be subject to monopoly or commercialization, but should be accessible to the public to explore and generate innovative ideas and projects. Islam recognizes intellectual property rights as fundamental ingredients of individual and corporate creativity; yet, the monopoly of knowledge resources to inflict damage on community interests is forbidden. It is like holding merchandise to raise prices and make the highest of profits at a time when the community is unable to afford buying them. If the innovation has a promising potential for the institution of good values and practices in the community, then its owner would see it within Islamic faith as an opportunity to win Allah's rewards. This applies to all types of knowledge like media content, computer software, and publishing outputs. The synthesis of science and morality is very central in the Islamic theory of knowledge. Science should be steered towards community service and promoting the highest of moral values.

When juxtaposed against the functional Western model of knowledge society, the Islamic model looks as follows:

Western Knowledge Model	Islamic Knowledge Model
Knowledge processes are functional	Knowledge processes are religious rituals
Drive for knowledge is material/social	Drive for knowledge is moral
Knowledge is existential	Knowledge is transcendental
Knowledge promote individualism	Knowledge promotes community
Knowledge is empirical	Knowledge is revealed

Following is an elaboration of each set of dualities:

- **Functional-Ritual Knowledge Processes:** In Western-inspired models, knowledge has some functions to fulfill in economic, social and political life. From their inception, ideas are tailored o served specific functionalities that seek to promote economic production, political management, and social welfare. This suggests that the creation and diffusion of knowledge is very much tied to a concrete and sensible purpose which defines the value of knowledge processes. In Islam, however, knowledge is vital for the advancement of society in social, economic and political fields; yet, the value of the knowledge process is not derived solely from its functions and how it bears on our concrete living experiences, but also from the spiritual dynamics of its conceptions and applications. Muslims engage in knowledge processes because they are enjoined to do so as part of their religious duties. The value of knowledge-based innovations derives from being a fulfillment of religious duties as much as from their contributions to improving the quality of our life.
- **Material/Social-Moral Knowledge Drive:** In Western models, knowledge is conceived as an asset or an economic commodity whose value is subject to market forces and dynamics. As such, knowledge may be sold or purchased and is considered as a central pillar of national and transnational economic progress. In Muslim beliefs, knowledge does have a concrete role to play in economic life, but its ultimate value is not viewed in pure material terms. Its value is conceived in the extent to which it contributes to enhancing community moral standing and fostering good attitudes in tune with Islamic beliefs and norms. The saying by Prophet Muhammad (PBUH) that deeds of a Muslim who pass away are terminated except in three cases, one of them is his/her legacy of knowledge that community continues to make use of is quite instructional in this regard.
- **Existential-Transcendental Knowledge:** In Muslim beliefs, knowledge draws from revealed as well as existential sources and there are no conflicts between both. The scientific miracles of the glorious Quran have been discussed in scores of conferences and many books around the world to demonstrate that revealed knowledge is in tune with empirical realities about Man and the universe. The transfusion of transcendental and existential knowledge in Islamic beliefs is instrumental in creating a synthesized sociology of knowledge that brings together spiritual and material worlds to bear on how we create, diffuse and apply knowledge in our life. Muslims believe Allah created the laws of the universe and the quality and quantity of our innovations would be highly contingent on our comprehension of those laws.
- **Individual-Community Knowledge:** If knowledge in the West is a tool for asserting individualism as a defining concept of social life, in Muslim beliefs, knowledge is an instrument of collective social cohesion and

solidarity in the community. Muslims engage in knowledge processes to generate innovations that would be brought to bear on community life in its collective sense. Of course, individual innovations are recognized in Islam as representing the person's creative potential to which he/she has a claim within intellectual property rights. But when those innovations are applied in the community life, their goal should be to promote common good and sustain moral cohesion and standards. This suggests that as a resource, knowledge cannot be left to the whims of individuals to decide its social uses against the will of a collective community. It is here that Islamic morality is brought to bear on how knowledge can be addressed in the context of conflicting considerations.

- **Knowledge as Empirical/Revealed:** Muslims believe that the highest form of knowledge is the one revealed by Allah to His Prophet Muhammad (PBUH). It is true that this revealed knowledge, represented by the Holy Qur'an, is meant serve more as a moral guidance than a scientific handbook, but still it is viewed as a precious resource on our knowledge about Man and the Universe. As much as it is meant to enjoin Muslims in general to think about the complexity of the universe and of Man to deepen their faith, it also seeks to serve as a catalyst for scientists to explore various aspects of creation and harness their innovations to promote good and fight evil. This synthesis of the moral and the scientific was a defining feature of Arab-Muslim innovations in the golden ages of their civilization.

Conclusion

To conclude, the Islamic normative values pertaining to *ilm* or knowledge carry a significant promise for contemporary Arab societies to promote the establishment of knowledge societies. Knowledge is viewed as a virtue through which man would enhance his standing and ability to control his surrounding environment. However, the Arab World is never short of ideas that glorify knowledge acquisition and harnessing, but of the appropriate conditions for activating those values and bringing them to bear on community life. What is needed here is not mere prescriptions that reaffirm the substantial role of knowledge in the advancement of Arab societies, but rather of how to create the right political, economic and cultural conditions that make knowledge society a reality. In this case, the challenge facing Arab societies is how to synthesize the cherished values in our cultural heritage with the new trends in knowledge development and creation. In this context, the need for democratic, diverse, free, and just social systems is a must for the development of knowledge society in the Arab World. When combined with an advanced information technology system, the social, economic and political conditions would certainly generate knowledge that truly reflects the aspirations of communities for sustainable development.

Knowledge seeking and diffusion should be viewed as an integral part of worship (*Ibadah*) in its widest sense. Once Arab communities are mobilized to seek knowledge and harness it to their best benefits on the basis of religious convictions, then the building of knowledge societies would be carried out as an integral system of faith. In many Arab communities, knowledge seekers are estranged for some cultural or religious reasons, something that calls into question the inhibitive role of social values in the realization of knowledge societies. This vision requires that the concept of knowledge should be expanded to go beyond the traditional sources which have no practical value in contemporary life. This would require a more pragmatic approach to knowledge by basing it on the benefits gleaned by societies in their knowledge seeking and diffusion activities. This again would not be possible without strategic planning for the institution of knowledge through educational institutions, civil society groups, the business sectors, and above all government agencies. This again would require that knowledge should be viewed as a public domain with limitless access for all individuals. This step would require some economic and political planning to ensure community participation in creating, building and diffusing knowledge.

9

Emerging Patterns in the Era of E-governance: A Study of Users of 'Swedish Public Employment Service' on Internet

Ernesto Abalo, Martin Danielsson, Håkan Johansson, and Tobias Olsson

In the area of government to citizen information and services, digitalization has become a buzzword. Framed within the discourses on e-government or e-governance—or different mixtures of the two—various analyses have tried to point out, or even anticipate possible consequences of the appropriation of digital technologies, mainly the internet, in governmental services.

On the one hand, these analyses have pointed out a great deal of opportunities connected to the incorporation of the internet into governmental information and services. Policy makers have been quick to point to the increased accessibility as a great opportunity for the citizens; in Sweden this vision of accessibility has even been referred to as '24:7-governmental agencies'. Academics, among others, have also suggested that the digitalization of information and services opens up new possibilities for citizens' access to and control of governments.

On the other hand, a number of problems have also been identified. For instance, the digitalization of public registers holding personal information has been interpreted as a threat to the citizens' integrity: Will digitalization bring a new surveillance society? The most frequently debated problem, however, at least within research, has been the fear of digital divides. Will the internet create digital cleavages between different groups of citizens?

So far, however, neither the hopeful nor the dystopian analyses have made enough efforts to critically evaluate their claims. Such evaluations can start from different points of departure, and in this paper the starting point is the citizens as users of governmental information and services through the internet: What patterns of inclusion and exclusion emerge as a governmental agency digitalizes its information and services by making them increasingly internet based?

The initial analysis of data reveals interesting differences between social groups in terms of both perception and use of the internet—in general—and the resources offered by SPES in particular. For instance, the users' various degrees of education is a strong, determining factor when it comes to use of internet SPES' services.

The chapter starts from a conceptual elaboration of various notions of e-government and e-governance. Thereafter, the survey data is described and elaborated on before moving into a discussion of the wider significance of the findings: What does data suggest in terms of patterns of inclusion in and exclusion from a society in which governmental agencies, to an increasing extent, use the internet for their information and services?

SPES—A Swedish Governmental Agency on the Internet

During the last decade there has been a substantial drive towards digitalization of the services within Swedish governmental agencies. Among theses agencies the Swedish Public Employment Service (SPES) has come to rely specifically on internet based information and services. Its development of web based self service started already in 1995 and today the agency's digital information and services have become very important to both employers seeking people to employ and the potential employees looking for jobs (AMS 2003:7: 9). In short: internet services are to an increasing extent becoming a backbone of the Swedish Public Employment Service.

In this respect the Swedish Public Employment Service is an example of—or perhaps even a forerunner for—the general digitalization of Swedish governmental services. At the heart of the visions of digitalization lies the idea that contacts between governmental agencies and the citizens to an increasing extent ought to be digital. This process of course offers new possibilities to the citizens, to get information, to interact with officials, to make use of services, etc., but also places new demands on them; the citizens are not only invited to use digital services, they are also expected to do so. Hence, the digitalization is, arguably, also a matter of *reconfiguring* what it means to be and act as citizen vis-à-vis governmental agencies.

This reconfiguration poses a number of important questions, not least in terms of what patterns of inclusion and exclusion that emerges in a society in which governmental agencies, to an increasing extent, use the internet for their information and services. In this paper we will critically discuss such patterns through an analysis of use and perception of the internet services offered by the SPES. The statistical data are brought from a survey of 762 unemployed citizens using SPES's services on the internet (Abalo & Danielsson 2008): What social factors determine use and perception of the internet in general and SPES's internet services in particular among the unemployed users/non users? And what are the possible consequences of these patterns of inclusion and exclusion for the citizens' relationship with digitalizing governmental agencies?

SST, E-government, E-governance and the SPES—A Theoretical Contextualization

The digitalization of Swedish governmental agencies can of course be understood from various points of theoretical departure. This analysis is informed by the overarching perspective often referred to as SST, Social Shaping of Technologies (cf. McKenzie & Wajcman 1999; Latham & Sassen 2005), and specifically those studies focusing on the media and the internet within these traditions (Silverstone 1994; Slevin 2000; Miller & Slater 2001).

The label social shaping of technologies subsumes several different strands of social science research under the frame of technology, and specifically ICTs. The research tradition includes Brian Winston's (Winston 1998), and Partice Flichy's (Flichy 1995) studies of the dynamics of technological development, as well as ethnographic, close readings of the appropriation of new media among various groups of users (Silverstone & Hirsch 1992; Olsson 2006). Other strands of research within the tradition analyse the social shaping at the producer stage, which seek to answer what ideas and ideologies are encoded into specific applications of new media. Still other studies analyse the shaping of new ICTs through political regulation, and centre on the ideological battles surrounding them (Goodwin & Spittle 2002), or how the politics of market regulation shape the emergence of ICTs in society (Sussman 1997). These seemingly very different studies do, however, share an important assumption: That it is both possible and useful to "open up technologies" and analyse their social dimensions, often as an explicit criticism of technologically-deterministic propositions about ICTs' societal "effects" (Williams 1974). In this case, in analysing use and perception of the internet in general and the services offered by SPES in particular, the SST approach points to the importance of paying heed to the social and cultural contexts—and the material, social, discursive and digital resources connected to them (Murdock et al 1992; Warschauer 2003)—in which the users live and appropriate the internet and the specific information and services offered by SPES's website.

From this theoretical point of departure the study has situated itself within the field of research into *e-government* and *e-governance*—a field that so far has paid meagre (to say the least) attention to SST-issues such as users' differentiated access to the various resources used in shaping the use and perception of ICTs (Löfstedt 2005).

As *e-governance* points to changes in societal governance, *e-government* is best understood as a part of a contemporary change in governance regime, and this change in regimes is of course important for research to pay attention to: Who wins and who loses in the change of governance? So far, however, research in this area has predominantly been interested in discussing and analysing to what extent the application of e-services and e-information can enhance governmental services and make them more efficient (cf. Ho & Pardo 2004; Grönlund 2005; Zuurmond 2005; Sundberg 2006), or it has been preoccupied with analysing the specific benefits of certain governmental websites (cf. Morison & Newman 2001; Kuk 2002; Josefsson & Ranerup 2003; Seifert 2003; Torres et al. 2006). To a certain extent research has also paid attention to the citizens as users of these services, but most often these studies have tended to be either rather simplistic in their conceptualisation of the citizens as internet users (cf. Hogg et al. 2003; Thomas & Streib 2003; Reddick 2005; Carter & Bélanger 2004; Bélanger & Carter 2006), or they have been instrumental in their view of the citizens as users (cf. Carter & Bélanger 2004; Hägglund 2006; Horst et al 2007). Hence, this study aims to contribute to this field of research with a view of the citizens as socially and culturally contextualised users of governmental e-services and information drawing on their specific material, social and discursive resources in their encounters with digitalised governmental agencies.

Methodology

The paper presents statistical data from a survey of 762 unemployed citizens using the Swedish Public Employment Service, a governmental agency that has come to rely specifically heavy on internet based information and service. The data (a SRS of 762 unemployed Swedes, out of 1916 (response rate=40 %), brought from SPES's register of unemployed Swedes) was collected in April 2007. The sample is a national random selection. The response rate is rather low, but the analysis of the respondents falling off reveals that the respondents completing the postal survey make up a good representation of the group as a whole in terms of level of education and ethnicity. In terms of age, however, the older respondents seem to have been more likely to complete the survey than the younger respondents. There is also a similar tendency in terms of gender, where the female respondents have been more ambitious in completing the survey than the male respondents. Hence, when it comes to factors such as age and gender the data are somewhat less reliable as a representation of unemployed Swedes.

The Unemployed and the Internet

Our analyses make it obvious that the use of as well as the attitudes to the internet and the website *www.ams.se* (which is SPES's website) varies with several factors. The respondents' social class and especially their level of education are—not surprisingly referring to other similar studies—strong determining factors when it comes to use of and attitudes to the internet. On the other hand, other results are more surprising with reference to previous research; ethnicity and to some extent age seem to be of less importance among the unemployed respondents when it comes to determining use and perception of the internet.

On access to and experiences of the internet

The highly educated respondents have better access to the internet. Nine out of ten highly educated respondents have home access to the internet compared to 74 percent among the less educated. The highly educated have also usually had access to the internet for a longer period of time. One third of the highly educated have had home access to the internet for eight years or more compared to 19 percent among the least educated respondents. In terms of age the younger age groups have better home access to the internet than the older ones. On the other hand more than a third of the oldest age group has had home access to the internet for eight years or more.

When it comes to experience of internet use, the respondents level of education is of great importancc. Six out of ten highly educated have used the internet for eight years or more, compared with 25 percent of those with a lower level of education.

Table 1: Internet experience with respect to level of education, age and ethnicity. All results in percentages, frequencies within brackets

	Low	Middle	High	20-30 years	31-40 years	41-55 years	56 years ≤	Yes	No
None	11 (30)	3 (6)	1 (2)	1 (1)	2 (3)	7 (15)	12 (21)	4 (8)	6 (32)
0-3 years	32 (86)	19 (45)	12 (22)	10 (17)	23 (36)	27 (59)	26 (45)	29 (63)	19 (95)
4-7 years	32 (87)	36 (86)	27 (51)	37 (64)	32 (49)	31 (68)	28 (49)	33 (73)	31 (158)
8 years ≤	25 (69)	42 (101)	60 (114)	52 (89)	43 (66)	36 (79)	34 (60)	34 (75)	44 (221)
Total	100 (272)	100 (238)	100 (189)	100 (171)	100 (154)	101 (221)	100 (175)	100 (219)	100 (506)

Furthermore, the younger are more experienced internet-users than the older. Thus, both level of education and age have considerable impact on access to and experience of the internet, which however, ethnical background seem to have to a far lesser extent.

On Current Internet Use

The level of education also determines the current use of the internet among those in search for a job to a great extent. The highly educated respondents use the internet more often than those with a low level of education, and the highly educated also spend more time on the internet. A third of the highly educated respondents are very frequent internet users, whereas only 16 percent of those with a low level of education can be considered to be very frequent users.

Once again, the respondents' age is important to their usage, the younger use the internet more often than the older. The respondents' ethnical background does not seem to be of much importance in this respect. Considering the fact that the highly educated respondents as well as the younger ones seem to spend more time on the internet it is not at all surprising that these groups are also

Table 2: Internet use (time per week) related to level of education, age and ethnicity. All results in percentages, frequencies within brackets

	Low	Middle	High	20-30 years	31-40 years	41-55 years	56 years ≤	Yes	No
Low	33 (80)	17 (40)	13 (25)	11 (18)	21 (32)	28 (58)	30 (45)	24 (51)	22 (104)
Frequent	51 (125)	57 (132)	53 (99)	54 (91)	53 (80)	51 (106)	56 (84)	50 (105)	54 (256)
Very frequent	16 (40)	25 (58)	34 (63)	36 (61)	26 (39)	22 (46)	15 (22)	26 (55)	24 (114)
Total	100 (245)	99 (230)	100 (187)	101 (170)	100 (151)	101 (210)	101 (151)	100 (211)	100 (474)

more frequent users of a large number of internet services, such as e-mailing and the use of various public and banking services.

On the Attitudes to the Internet

The respondents' attitudes to the internet vary—just like their use of the internet—with respect to their levels of education. The highly educated have more positive attitudes to the internet than the respondents with less education. As large a part as 90 percent of the highly educated are positive to the internet (compared to 71 percent among those with a low level of education).

Table 3: Attitude to the internet related to level of education, age and ethnicity. All results in percentages, frequencies within brackets

	Low	Middle	High	20-30 years	31-40 years	41-55 years	56 years ≤	Yes	No
Positive	71 (198)	84 (201)	90 (169)	89 (154)	88 (135)	76 (171)	69 (123)	81 (178)	80 (408)
Neutral	15 (41)	12 (28)	9 (16)	7 (12)	8 (12)	16 (35)	17 (30)	11 (24)	13 (66)
Negative	5 (13)	2 (4)	1 (1)	2 (3)	2 (3)	5 (11)	1 (2)	4 (8)	2 (10)
No Opinion	10 (28)	3 (6)	1 (2)	2 (4)	2 (3)	4 (9)	13 (23)	5 (11)	6 (28)
Total	101 (280)	101 (239)	101 (188)	100 (173)	100 (153)	101 (226)	100 (178)	101 (221)	101 (512)

The younger age groups are more positive to the internet than the older ones; however none of the older age groups present a very negative attitude. Ethnicity does not seem to have any significant impact on the general internet attitudes, 80 percent of all groups have a mainly positive internet attitude.

The highly educated respondents' positive attitude to the internet becomes even more obvious as we look into how the various groups perceive the internet in terms of its qualities. The respondents with a high degree of education tend to perceive the internet as "easy to use", "fun", and "instructive" to a greater extent than the less educated groups, and they also generally value all specific internet functions (for instance e-mailing) higher than the less educated respondents. The perception of the internet also varies with age. In general, the younger respondents rate the internet higher than the older ones. With a few exceptions, the respondents' ethnical background has little impact on their perception of the internet.

Table 4: Internet self-confidence related to level of education, age and ethnicity. All results in percentages, frequencies within brackets

	Low	Middle	High	20-30 years	31-40 years	41-55 years	56 years ≤	Yes	No
Big	40 (98)	64 (148)	70 (128)	75 (128)	66 (99)	48 (98)	40 (60)	58 (118)	56 (267)
Neutral	32 (77)	25 (57)	22 (41)	19 (33)	19 (29)	36 (72)	33 (50)	22 (44)	30 (140)
Low	22 (54)	9 (21)	5 (9)	4 (7)	13 (19)	10 (21)	24 (36)	15 (30)	12 (55)
No opinion	6 (14)	2 (4)	3 (5)	2 (3)	3 (4)	6 (12)	3 (4)	5 (10)	3 (13)
Total	100 (243)	100 (230)	100 (183)	100 (171)	101 (151)	100 (203)	100 (150)	100 (202)	101 (475)

Also the younger respondents are very confident when it comes to using the internet, and—once again—the respondent's ethnicity does not seem to impact on their internet self-confidence.

Considering the abovementioned results it is reasonable to state that the highly educated respondents as well as the younger ones are well off in terms of digital resources, and that their opposite groups—the respondents with a low level of education and the older respondents—are weaker. The respondents' ethnical background, however, seems to be of minor importance.

The Unemployed and the SPES's Digital Information and Services

The unemployed respondents' view of as well as use of SPES's digital resources is constituted by a number of different factors, for instance their use of and attitude to the website *www.ams.se* and their actual and preferred modes of contact with SPES as a governmental agency. These factors will be paid extensive attention in this part of the paper, and they will mainly be related to the respondents' levels of education since the analysis above strongly indicates that this is the most important social factor to pay attention to. However, also other relevant social factors will be paid attention to, mostly in passing though.

General Patterns of Use of www.ams.se

The respondents' level of education is an important factor in determining their use of *www.ams.se.* Among other things, this is manifested in the fact that twenty percent of the respondents with a low level of education are non users of *www.ams.se,* compared to seven percent among the highly educated.

Table 5: Use of www.ams.se (frequency and time per week) related to level of education, age and ethnicity. All results in percentages, frequencies within brackets

	Low	Middle	High	20-30 years	31-40 years	41-55 years	56 years ≤	Yes	No
How often?									
Never	20 (56)	7 (16)	7 (14)	4 (6)	7 (11)	15 (35)	19 (35)	8 (18)	13 (69)
Low	26 (74)	34 (81)	30 (57)	38 (65)	32 (50)	28 (63)	25 (46)	27 (61)	32 (165)
Middle	34 (97)	37 (90)	35 (66)	36 (62)	36 (56)	34 (77)	34 (62)	36 (80)	34 (177)
High	20 (58)	23 (55)	27 (51)	23 (39)	25 (38)	23 (52)	22 (41)	29 (65)	21 (106)
Total	100 (285)	101 (242)	99 (188)	101 (172)	100 (155)	100 (227)	100 (184)	100 (224)	100 (517)
Time per week									
Low	51 (143)	43 (103)	40 (75)	44 (76)	47 (73)	45 (102)	46 (84)	42 (93)	47 (224)
Middle	42 (118)	51 (124)	51 (95)	51 (87)	48 (75)	46 (103)	45 (81)	53 (117)	45 (231)
High	7 (20)	6 (15)	10 (18)	5 (9)	5 (8)	9 (20)	9 (17)	6 (13)	8 (41)
Total	100 (281)	100 (242)	101 (188)	100 (172)	100 (156)	100 (225)	100 (182)	101 (223)	100 (516)

The highly educated respondents' better home access to the internet is also mirrored in the use of *www.ams.se.* 80 percent of the respondents with high or average ("middle") levels of education visit the website from their homes, compared to 68 percent among the respondents with a low level of education—also, almost 25 percent of them visit the website from the SPES's local offices. Similar patterns also appear in terms of age, where the younger respondents tend to access the website from their homes to a greater extent than the older ones.

The Use of Various Parts of www.ams.se

Also when it comes to the respondent's use of the various services offered on the website, the educational differences reappear. *Platsbanken,* the most popular service on the website (*Platsbanken* is a database holding data on vacant positions), is never used among more than 20 percent of the respondents with a low level of education. The pattern reappears when it comes to the service *Mitt CV*—a service that allows the users to put their CVs on *www.ams.se* for potential employers to see. Almost 50 percent of the respondents with a low level of education state that they never use that service.

Attitudes to www.ams.se

The unemployed respondents' level of education is also of relevance when it comes to their attitudes to the website *www.ams.se,* especially in terms of their views of a number of explicit statements about the website. To start with, the highly educated respondents are far more likely than others to agree on the statement: "*It is easy to find vacant positions through the website.*" The respondents with a low level of education, however, are more likely to agree on statements such as "*The language on the website is complicated*" or "*The website demands very much from the user.*"

Table 6: Attitudes to the statement *"The language is complicated"* related to level of education, age and ethnicity. All results in percentages, frequencies within brackets

	Level of education			Age				Foreign heritage?	
	Low	Middle	High	20-30 years	31-40 years	41-55 years	56 years ≤	Yes	No
Agree	18 (47)	11 (26)	9 (16)	10 (17)	15 (21)	15 (31)	14 (24)	20 (42)	11 (52)
Nor agree or disagree	28 (74)	34 (80)	17 (31)	24 (41)	21 (31)	30 (63)	30 (53)	26 (56)	27 (135)
Disagree	23 (61)	37 (87)	55 (102)	54 (91)	44 (64)	30 (64)	23 (41)	36 (76)	37 (183)
No opinion	31 (83)	17 (40)	20 (37)	12 (21)	20 (29)	26 (55)	33 (58)	18 (38)	25 (124)
Total	100 (265)	99 (233)	101 (186)	100 (170)	100 (145)	101 (213)	100 (176)	100 (212)	101 (475)

All together these data point to a digital divide between groups of unemployed citizens with reference to their different levels of education. The highly educated respondents seem to use the web as a resource in their search for jobs in just the way that the SPES wants them to do. The respondents with less education, however, obviously find the new situation more problematic. Internet use in itself is more problematic to them and they also perceive *www.ams.se* per se as problematic to use in several respects.

The Unemployed and the Digitalization of the Contacts with the Governmental Agency

Despite the fact that *www.ams.se,* in essence, is a digital extension of SPES as a physical, governmental agency, this is not necessarily how it is perceived. For instance, among the less educated respondents there is a tendency to rate SPES as a governmental agency much higher than they rate its digital extension into *www.ams.se.*

The difference between SPES as a physical, governmental agency and as a digital extension becomes salient when it comes to how the unemployed respondents get in touch with the governmental agency compared to how they prefer to get in touch with it. In the survey the respondents were asked to rank different channels of contact with SPES—e-mail, telephone and face-to-face meeting—in terms of (1) which of the channels they were mainly using, and (2) which of the channels they preferred using.

Table 7: Actual and preferred channels of contact with SPES related to level of education an age. All results in percentages, frequencies within brackets

	Level of education			Age			
	Low	Middle	High	20-30 years	31-40 years	41-55 years	56 years ≤
Actual channels							
E-mail	16	21	39	31	25	20	24
	(31)	(40)	(66)	(49)	(30)	(34)	(31)
Face-to-face visit	44	41	22	34	31	37	45
	(111)	(92)	(39)	(55)	(43)	(77)	(75)
Telephone	49	39	43	36	48	49	39
	(121)	(84)	(76)	(59)	(67)	(98)	(62)
Preferred channel							
E-mail	13	25	41	33	34	14	25
	(26)	(51)	(71)	(52)	(43)	(25)	(34)
Face-to-face visit	56	43	32	33	38	54	52
	(143)	(97)	(56)	(54)	(55)	(114)	(85)
Telephone	37	34	31	36	31	35	31
	(91)	(74)	(56)	(58)	(43)	(70)	(50)

Nearly 40 percent of the highly educated most regularly use e-mail for contacts with SPES compared to only 16 percent among the less educated. Furthermore, the respondents with higher education also much rather prefer e-mail contacts with their contact persons at SPES than the less educated respondents. On the other hand, the less educated are more frequent face-to-face visitors at their SPES offices than the other groups, and are also much more in favour of these contacts than the other groups.

Concluding Discussion

In his book from the year 2000, *Democracy in the Digital Age,* Anthony G. Wilhelm is looking for a more nuanced way of understanding patterns of inclusion and exclusion in the emerging "information society". Wilhelm argues that questions related to inclusion in and exclusion from the digitalizing society have been reduced to issues of physical access to the technology per se, within politics above all, but also within academic debates—and may we especially add the various debates on e-government and e-governance. As an alternative to this rather crude notion of access, he proposes a model which makes it possible to speak in terms of grades of exclusion. In his model Wilhelm (ibid.: 74) uses the metaphors *core* and *periphery* and relates them to class in the emerging "information society"; people with low socio economic status become situated in the periphery of the digitalized society, whereas socio economically well of groups move into its core.

Referring to the data presented here, we have on the one hand seen degrees of digital exclusion, where for instance people with low levels of education and older people seem to be on their way to the peripheral parts of the digitalizing society. On the other hand, we have also seen emerging patterns of rather strong inclusion, where mainly well educated people together with young people seem to be on their way to its core. The groups on their way to the core in the era of digitalized governmental services and information has—as it seems to our data—several years of experience of internet use. They also use the internet very often, for long hours of time, and for different reasons. From this they also develop good self-confidence when it comes to interne use; they seem to feel confident doing most things through the internet. The groups on their way to the peripheral parts make up the complete opposite (for instance people with low levels of education): they have less internet experience, spend fewer hours on the internet, do not feel confident in using it, and also find the internet itself difficult to use.

This situation calls for at least three separate but interrelated reflections. Firstly, with reference to the data collected within this specific study, the emerging patterns of digital inclusion and exclusion are not only a matter of participation within exclusively digital environments. As the SPES makes additional parts of its services and information internet based, the formation of core and peripheral groups also get "real world" consequences as the respondents' abilities to look for and actually get jobs will vary. The groups of internet savvy people looking for jobs can shape (Williams 1974; Murdock et al. 1992; Bakardjieva 2005) the internet into a useful tool for their needs of information and services, whereas unemployed respondents—on their way to the peripheral spheres of the digitalizing society—are at risk of also getting less job opportunities, at least by help of the governmental agency.

Secondly, our analyses might also serve as a more general example of what patterns of inclusion and exclusion that might emerge as a consequence of the digitalization of Swedish governmental services; some groups win while others lose. So far, however, such issues have hardly been on the agenda in the political and administrative discussions concerning the creation of the "24:7 governmental agencies". Instead, they have mainly been discussed in terms of making governmental information and services more "efficient" and more accessible to the interested users. Still, however, governmental service and information ought to be equally accessible to all citizens, and this might obviously not become the case as additional parts of governmental information and service become digitalized.

Finally, the presented analyses might hopefully inspire new takes within research on e-government and/or e-governance. Our study underscores the need for data and analyses on how citizens understand and make use of the new, digital possibilities offered to them. In this case we have seen how various social factors, notably level of education and to some extent age, impact on the use and perception of digital, governmental information and services, and such knowledge ought to be essential if the field of research aims to develop itself in a reflexive manner; e-government and e-governance do not mean the same thing for all citizens. Hopefully our study is just one out of many to come that aims at understanding what notions such as e-government and e-governance might mean to the actual citizens who make use (and/or do not make use) of the digital possibilities offered to them from various governmental agencies in their everyday lives.

10

Digital Divide in Contemporary Brazilian Society

Denize Correa Araujo

This chapter analyzes the complexity in the adoption of digital technology as well as the factors that frustrate its instrumental power to bring about classes inclusion in the globalized Brazilian contemporary scenario. Departing from a clip of a feature film that shows the arrival of computers in a poor suburb and the social, political and cultural implications of it, I intend to suggest the intricate chain of elements that can be considered responsible for the almost impossible attempt to create an egalitarian environment for the so called "digital excluded". My hypotheses are that political interests, cultural lack of support in education, and the huge gap between social classes have created barriers for any kind of inclusion.

Despite all these problems, I believe that digital inclusion is easier to be attained than social inclusion, as digital inclusion is not capital intensive while social inclusion is heavily based on the economic access to goods and services in a society. The clip I have selected to support my point of view is from the film "Quanto vale ou é por quilo" (2005), by the Brazilian filmmaker Sergio Bianchi, famous for his straightforward way to portray Brazilian misfortunes. The scene depicts children from low income families waiting for the arrival of computers in one of the Digital Centers supposedly created to correct the effects of digital divide among social classes. When the computers arrive, three problems are immediately detected: the promise to have new computers was not accomplished; the children are digitally illiterate; the unprepared social assistants cannot control the situation, which culminates in a pile of broken computers, a huge mass of children claiming for justice, and a generalized feeling of frustration and anger towards the coordinators of the NGO's (non-governmental organization) failed project.

The sequence of images presented above clearly shows the various stages of this process. In the first image, the President and the Vice-President of the NGO (non-governmental organization) are in the middle of the scene, surrounded by

Eu gostaria de agradecer a parceria
empreendedora da Stiner...

para abrigar o primeiro centro
desse projeto...

para a menor desigualdade
na distribuição de informação...

children and instructors. The beginning of the speech attracts their attention: "I would like to thank the enterprising partnership of Stiner". In the third image, the speech continues: "to open the first center of this project". The happy expression of the children encourages him to continue: "whose aim is to minimize digital divide in the information distribution". In the fifth image, the President cuts the ribbon as a symbol of the official opening of the center. As soon as he does it, the children run to the computers in a chaotic way. Knowing that the children and instructors will soon find out about the old computers (new computers were promised), the president tries to steal away from the place immediately. In the seventh image, there is a long moment of silence between the two men, immediately followed by the sarcastic comment: "what a success, no?" Inside, as expected, the children start checking the computers. One of the boys pushes a computer to the ground, followed by others in the crowd. One of the instructors shouts: "Are you crazy, moron? You stupid?" The behavior and the use of slang by the instructor clearly demonstrate the kind of attitude they have towards the deprived children. Simultaneously, the scene also shows the disrespectful attitude of the children towards the new space. This significant clip from the film sums up the depth of corruption among those who claim to be change agents in the Brazilian society.

Choosing arguments by Manuel Castells and Anthony Wilhelm about electronic democracy, concepts by Dominique Wolton and Pierre Lévy on the function of Internet and collective intelligence, and anthropological assumptions by Arjun Appadurai and Nestor Garcia Canclini on the late effects of colonialism, I suggest that political interference in Brazilian education prevents progress, that lack of social skills makes it difficult for lower classes to surpass barriers, and that cultural inheritance causes imbalance within a mass mediated society. However, I argue that digital inclusion is easier to be approached than social inclusion, which is a chronic feature of our double colonization process, initiated with the arrival of the European colonizers and continued with North American influence, together with the effects of globalization. Sérgio Amadeu da Silveira suggests that illiteracy and poverty "can be compared to the effects hunger produces in the first years in a child´s life, so it is not correct to classify digital exclusion as a mere consequence of social exclusion" (2001, p. 18).

If, in general, digital divide continues to exist in many areas in Brazil, there have been some success stories too. There have been two successful projects in my hometown, Curitiba, capital of Paraná: the "Lighthouses of Knowledge" and "The Streets of Citizenship". The second intends to promote digital inclusion and citizenship formation by creating electronic centers with specialized instructors to provide information on the use of computers as tools to facilitate procedures such as payment of debts, acquisition of goods for the house or office, as well as news information and opinion developer. The "Lighthouses of Knowledge Project" has built 45 libraries in many different city areas, providing not only books for children and teenagers but also computers for research and writing. Therefore, on the one hand, there are many problems associated with the concept of digital divide. On the other hand, some projects are worth considering. Not all the NPOs have negative connotations. I believe that, by analyzing Brazilian attempts to fight digital divide, I came across a complex net of challenges that intervene in constructive proposals, but also found some fruitful projects.

Digital divide seems to be more evident in underdeveloped countries, due to the social divide that is a feature of postcolonial cultures, or hybrid cultures, as Canclini suggests. In Brazil, while privileged social classes have access to the most sophisticated gadgets, lower classes suffer from the lack of adequate schooling and housing. Another problem is the lack of interest of government agencies in providing access to new technologies for lower classes, which results in the interference of private organizations that take advantage of the situation.

Together with the understanding of the technological device, knowledge of its implementation must be one of the main conditions. The simple fact of providing computers to the lower classes does not mean that they are going to be useful for citizens who cannot interact with them. This is the case illustrated in the film in analysis here, in which there is a representation of the arrival of many computers and their destruction, a few minutes later.

Some years ago, one of Rio de Janeiro´s governors, Leonel Brizola, created a series of schools for lower classes, the CIEPs, all of them equipped with computers. In a couple of years, the computers were abandoned because people could not use them. Not only students but also teachers had difficulty in working with them, in making them useful for their classes. Again, Castells' assertion can be applied to the situation: "the rise of informationalism in this end of the millennium is intertwined with rising inequality and social exclusion throughout the world." (1998, p. 70).

Although I believe that digital inclusion is easier to deal with than social inclusion, one important fact that cannot be underestimated is that of the debilitating role played by poverty and lack of skills in undermining all the expectations of equality. Considering that it is in the best interests of many politicians to keep people from being critical of the system, this situation remains unaltered. In Brazil, voting is compulsory and the number of almost completely illiterate people surpasses those of critical citizens. Having illiterate and non critical voters is convenient for governors, who are elected by the majority of votes.

In one of my articles, "O caráter pseudo da inclusão digital" ("The pseudo character of digital inclusion"), I question the meaning of "digital literacy". Can a person who uses the Internet only for receiving and sending e-mails be considered "digital literate"? (Araujo, 2007, p. 165). Even considering that people use the Internet for information, does it qualify him or her for a digital literate citizen? At the moment, the use of Internet is much more complex than acquisition of information and e-mails exchanging. Internet is a tool that can offer possibilities of interaction, of critical and cultural knowledge, and even of organizing political manifestations. Internet and its interfaces, especially mobile phones, wi-fis, lan houses and cibercaffes constitute what I call "digital hipertropolis", or a megametropolis in which virtuality is negotiating its space. Internet users interact in chats, virtual communities, blogs and photologs, create avatars, exchange ideas, buy and sell merchandise, pay bills, and use all kinds of advantages offered online. These are the "digital included". Unfortunately, they are only a segment of users (Araujo 2007 p. 166).

When social problems are of great extent such as in Brazil, which is a country that offers First World facilities and Third World drawbacks, it is easier to understand the following statistics produced by IBGE (Brazilian Institute of Geography and Statistics): 54% of Brazilians never used a computer, 14% have Internet access, 1.5 million children are out of school; of the 162.000 public schools in Brazil, 129.000 do not have Internet access, 40.000 do not have a library, 25.000 do not have electricity. (www.ibge.org.br/internet2008)

The use of technology is part of the world globalization. Arjun Appadurai, attempting to explain what he calls disjunctures, suggests five dimensions of global cultural flow which can be termed: (a) ethnoscapes; (b) mediascapes; (c) technoscapes; (d) finanscapes; and (e) ideoscapes. He uses terms with the common suffix "scape" to indicate, first of all, that these are not objectively given relations which look the same from every angle of vision, but rather that they are deeply perspectival constructs, inflected very much by the historical, linguistic and political situatedness of different sorts of actors: nation-states, multinationals, diasporic communities, as well as sub-national grouping and movements (whether religious, political or economic), and even intimate face-to-face groups, such as villages, neighborhoods and families. (1989)

For the sake of this research, the "scape' that better explains digital divide is the "technoscape", although all the terms work in conjunction and complement one another. Appadurai defines "technoscape" as

> the global configuration, also ever so fluid, of technology, and of the fact that technology, both high and low, both mechanical and informational, now moves at high speeds across various kinds of previously impervious boundaries ... the odd distribution of technologies, and thus the peculiarities of these technoscapes, are increasingly driven not by obvious economies of scale, of political control, or of market rationality, but of increasingly complex relationships between money flows, political possibilities and the availability of both low and highly-skilled labor. (1989)

On the other hand, the complementation of the "scapes" can more satisfactorily discusses the totality of the effects caused by disjunctures and differences among countries:

> States throughout the world are under siege, especially where contests over the ideoscapes of democracy are fierce and fundamental, and where there are radical disjunctures between ideoscapes and technoscapes (as in the case of very small countries that lack contemporary technologies of production and information); or between ideoscapes and finanscapes (as in countries, such

as Mexico or Brazil where international lending influences national politics to a very large degree); or between ideoscapes and ethnoscapes (as in Beirut, where diasporic, local and translocal filiations are suicidally at battle); or between ideoscapes and mediascapes (as in many countries in the Middle East and Asia) where the lifestyles represented on both national and international TV and cinema completely overwhelm and undermine the rhetoric of national politics: in the Indian case, the myth of the law-breaking hero has pieties and the realities of Indian politics, which has grown increasingly brutalized and corrupt. (1989)

Cultural hybridization appears to be best elaborated and summarized by Nestor Garcia Canclini as a type of societal restructuring and as a kind of transitory social movement (2005: 23-46). Canclini interprets cultural hybridization as "a useful interpretation of relations of meaning that are reconstructed through mixing". For the author, hybridization needs to be understood in the "context of ambivalences of the globalized mass diffusion and industrialization of symbolic processes, and of the power conflicts these provoke" (Idem: 29), and, further: "(...) cross-cultural thinking and practices are resources for acknowledging difference and elaborating on the tensions that arise there" (Idem: 31). Cultural hybridization therefore transcends processes of mestizaje, creolization *and the like, and re-opens the problems of "how to design forms of modern multicultural association" (Idem: 33)*.

Brazil is one of the countries in which hybridization is visible in social, economical, educational and technological spheres. From the colonization up to the moment, there has been a huge gap between social classes, which is reflected in all the other sectors of life. Poor people struggle to find jobs, to send their children to school and to be able to survive the continuous economic crises that jeopardize all kinds of efforts that intend to minimize their miseries. On the other hand, government corruption, inherited from the first colonizers, persists and impunity prevents efforts to make justice. Even with a supposedly "left" and "oppositional" government, the situation has not improved. Quite the contrary, only rhetorical discourses have tried to cover corruption and impunity. While the most privileged classes are completely "digital", purchasing the many electronic imported products offered in Brazil, the lower classes remain excluded.

Dominique Wolton raises another question that exemplifies the complexity of what is called digital inclusion:

Direct communication, without mediation, as a technical performance. That appeals for dreams of individual freedom, but it is illusory. The Net can give access to a mass of information, but nobody is a citizen of the world, wanting to know everything, about everything, in the whole world. The more information there is, the more we need middlemen—journalists, archivists, editors, etc.—that filter, organize, prioritise. No one wants to play the newspaper chief editor's role every morning. Equality of access to information doesn't create equality of use of information. To confuse equality of access with equality of use is techno-ideology". (1999c)

Therefore, it is difficult to predict the use of Internet and, even more difficult, to verify digital inclusion. In the midst of all these difficulties, however, what counts positively is the increasing number of initiatives from city inhabitants who want to improve their life quality. In Salvador, Bahia, there are many projects, such as Yellow Arrow, Undersound, Intersections, 230 Miles of Love, Geograffiti, MurMur, TwittAround, Wikicrimes, Citysense, Gamebody, Wikimap and Quickmaps. (http://andrelemos.info).

In Curitiba, PR, Brazil, there are two projects designed to promote digital inclusion: the "Lighthouses of Knowledge Project" and the "Streets of Citizenship Project". The city has a population of approximately 1,788,559 people, being the largest in the Southern Brazil (7th largest nationwide), and has the largest GDP in the Southern Region (ranking 4th nationwide) according to IBGE (2005).

In the eighties, the city began a project called the "Faróis do Saber" (Lighthouses of Knowledge), a segment of the "Master Plan" designed by Jaime Lerner, Curitiba's Mayor and State Governor for many years. Being an architect and urban planner, Lerner is responsible for the many improvements in the city, such as transportation system, pedestrian-only streets and decentralization. He is also responsible for the design of many touristic attractions such as the Botanical Garden, the Iron Opera, and the University of Environment. The idea of the Lighthouses of Knowledge, however, was Rafael Greca's, who had visited, with his wife Margarita Sansone, the Lighthouse of Alexandria (which was, three centuries before the Christian Era, the center of the world and one of the Seven Wonders of the Ancient World), that was the inspiration for the innovative and unprecedent educational project (Moacir Werneck de Castro).

Curitiba, capital of the State of Paraná, is considered an ecological city. It has a sensible income distribution, according to national standards, and well-guided community spirit favoring a fruitful empathy between the its administrators' creativity, and its people's cooperation.

The Lighthouses of Knowledge are free educational centers which include libraries, Internet access, and other cultural resources. Job training, social welfare and educational programs are coordinated, and often supply labor to improve the city's amenities or services, as well as education and income. Every Lighthouse of Knowledge is named after a writer, from Paraná or elsewhere, such as Emílio de Menezes, Rubem Braga or Manuel Bandeira.

These brightly coloured, 52ft-high, lighthouse-shaped libraries contain about 7,000 books and are the first public terminals to offer internet access in Brazil. On the top of each lighthouse there's a night-time watchtower with space for a light and a policeman, the idea being to keep the neighbourhood safe for children. The aim is to have a Lighthouse of Knowledge within walking distance of every child's home or school. These community libraries work in partnership with municipal schools, have a collection of approximately 5000 books, provide cultural reference and leisure for the community, and are designed to diversify

the opportunities of access to knowledge, expanding the area of formal education. In each quarter of the city these "Lighthouses of Knowledge" have been implanted with a library and room of computer science, to public use, mainly by students.

Among the Brazilian capitals, Curitiba has the lowest rate of illiteracy and is also number 1 in education in comparison with other Brazilian capitals. Curitiba is divided into nine regional governments (equivalent to subprefecture), which manage the 75 districts of the municipality.

The *Ruas da Cidadania* ("Streets of Citizenship") are the symbol of administrative decentralization; it is a reference point and meeting place for the users of municipal utilities, in a regional context, taking into account the needs and rights of the citizen in trade, leisure and services, facilitating the access of the population for different services in the areas of health, justice, policing, education, sport, housing, environment, urban planning, social service and supply, and so on. Several units work annexed to the terminals of public transport in Curitiba. Their nuclei offer services in the local, state and federal areas.

A decentralized and accessible government has been a cornerstone of Curitiba's planning philosophy since the "Master Plan' was approved in the 1960s. Curitiba's "Streets of Citizenship"—mini-malls of government branch offices located throughout the city—are perhaps the best example of bringing city hall down to size. The first "Street of Citizenship", in Boqueirão, opened in 1995, in conjunction with Curitiba's hosting the United Nations' Habitat World Day. This was the first time the international event had been held in a Latin American country. Five additional malls have been constructed since then, at major bus terminals throughout the city. Curitiba's "Streets of Citizenship" were funded in part by the InterAmerican Development Bank to fulfill its mission of better integrating communities with government (www.pbs.org/frontline world/fellows/brasil1203/citizenship.html).

Each "Street of Citizenship" houses a regional branch of the various city offices. Nearby residents and commuters can access municipal departments, banking offices, state and federal agencies, and special courts all in one location. People pay their property taxes; register their children for local schools, file for discounted transit passes and sign up for military service.

In conclusion, I can say that, although digital inclusion is a complex issue in Brazil, some activities are worth mentioning, such as the two initiatives in Curitiba: "The Lighthouses of Knowledge" and the "Streets of Citizenship", which are attempts to offer less privileged people opportunities to interact electronically, following the digital advances that are providing global information. I believe that Digital Divide is still a problem to be solved in hybrid countries, but the many opportunities brought up by the advances in technology can offer possibilities for people interventions and projects that can minimize its negative effects.

11

WSIS, Turkey and Information Society

Babacan Taşdemir and Funda Başaran Özdemir

It is not possible to understand the central dynamics of contemporary society without understanding the role of media from the conventional newspapers through to television and radio, and the Internet in the society. While there are various ways of classifying the roles and functions of media in society, it is a general held view that much of the modern culture has been transmitted by the media as stated by Stevenson (2002:3). While recognizing the great importance of media in contemporary societies, the rapid and radical changes in media sector in recent years should be considered. Dan Schiller defines these changes in media as the redefinition of "social purposes and institutional functions of world communication" according to the demands of global capital (2001, 51).

Beginning with the late 1980s, neoliberal policies—that is, the policies that maximize the role of markets and profit-making and minimize the role of non-market institutions through deregulation and privatization (Friedman, 1982:2–3)—began to be implemented fully or partially in many countries. The information technology sector did not remain untouched by these structural changes in national economies. New technologies reduced the cost of information transmission and processing and enabled the liberalization of telecommunication networks. Across the world, governments have adopted neoliberal policies by reducing government intervention in product markets, opening the domestic market and privatizing the financial and public sectors, including communication industries. The changing political-economic environment in the world and technological developments caused rapid and radical transformation of the communication landscape. The initial steps of neoliberal policies in the communication sector were the divestiture of AT&T in the US telecommunication market and privatization of British Telecom in the UK in 1984 (Yong Jin, 2008:357).

The introduction of neoliberal economic policy in communication sectors has resulted in the break-up of public monopolies over broadcasting and telecommunication industries and deregulation of communication markets. WTO has played an important role in this process. The global institutions like IMF and World Bank have directed the economic policies and forced governments to adopt neoliberal policies in developing countries.

The effects of neoliberal policies on the media were the privatization of previously government-owned media, concentration of ownership within media markets; conglomeration of media industries across media and non-media industries and internationalization of markets (Boyd-Barret, 2006:23). Kaya stated this process as a completion of fusion between the media and big business (2009, 233). Critical political economists argue that neoliberalism has resulted in the concentration of ownership among a few mega-media giants. The nature of this concentration points out the political nature of neoliberalism which is supportive of business domination of all social affairs as Robert McChesney argues (2001:2). According to McChesney, "*adherents of 'deregulation' claim that, regardless of the facts, the turn to private domination is necessary and beneficial for society as a whole*" (2003:129) and this claim disregards that the media system is not simply an economic category, it is responsible for transmitting culture. Transformations in the media and communication environment under neoliberal policies in Turkey have proved all these critiques of political economists. In accordance with the global developments, concentration of media ownership, the trend of commercialization in the communication sector, emergence of oligopolistic structure in telecommunication sector as well have been striking facts of communication environment of Turkey since the beginning of 1990s. As has been the fact of other developing countries, the information society project is the next step in Turkey.

According to many scholars, the information society project was a substitution of modernization project and the further step of delivering the communication markets to multinational corporations (Bhuiyan, 2008:106, Schech, 2002, Schiller, 1999) Actually, Information Society has material and ideological roots in 1960's debates on post-industrialism when everyone was mourning the death of the modernization project. Machlup, Porat and Bell conceptualized the idea and it gained momentum in the 1980's as American capitalists and state managers sought an effective reply to the growing competitiveness of their European and East Asian rivals. The Information society discourse has taken centre stage position on the global political agenda since the early 1990s with Al Gore's call for a Global Information Infrastructure (GII). The discourse of UN and developed countries in 1960's which included elimination of poverty and building of modern society in the under-developed countries was replaced the information society discourse in 1980's. During this period, utopian works of some scholars like Bell were moved to the policy domain. In parallel with the privatization and liberalization of communication sector, the "information society" discourse became hegemonic in 1990's.

According to Geray, there is a basic difference between the first theoretical approaches developed around the concept of information society and resulting political documents. Although theoretical approaches proposed the concept of an information society within the context of balancing and improving the capitalist system, political documents have attempted to create the framework for contemporary capitalism (2002:132). However, despite these differences, a series of judgments, which has reached the level of claiming that humanity in general has been living through one of the deepest transformations of its existence (Kumar, 1995), has been both implicitly and explicitly accepted. These claims inclining towards the quite different levels of the life have gained further strength from the development of new information and communications technologies. According to many scholars, the "revolutionary" development in information and communication technologies has created a "new" form of society, economy, culture and policy, and the people of the 21st century have been living in a "new era". Development in information and communication technologies is also the starting point of the analysis of "new economic, social and cultural unity" "because of its special feature of spreading to all areas of the human activity" (Castells, 1996:5). More modest assessments suggested that information and communication technologies are important in three special areas: national development, the emergence of transnational society (global civil society) and regional economic unification.

There are many powerful criticisms of information society theory (Garnham, 2001; D. Schiller, 1988, 1999; Webster, 1995). Therefore, the purpose of this study is not to develop an extensive critique of information society theory here, but to explore the contradictions of the information society discourse it is intended to analyze the discourse of Turkey's "Information Society Strategy (2006-10)" in comparison with the discourse of the information society at the WSIS where information society was made a goal for every country in this study.

Research Design and Methods

We focused on WSIS official texts and "Information Society Strategy (2006-10)" document prepared by State Planning Organization of Turkey for a better understanding of the overall social processes and structures which have been reflected or represented and also constructed or constituted by Information Society discourse. Another important focus of this study is historical changes which answer the question of "what and how have different discourses combined to produce Information Society discourse?" In this respect, Critical Discourse Analysis (CDA) which describes discourse as a 'social practice' with a dialectical relationship: "the discursive event is shaped by situations, institutions and social structures, but it also shapes them" (Fairclough and Wodak, 1997:259) is the most appropriate way of analyzing constructed interrelations between policy documents.

Discourse has been conceptualized as action in CDA. This means that it is a "form of social practice" (Wodak, 1996:14, 16). As the discourse is a form of social practice, it cannot be analyzed without taking into account the context in CDA. This necessitates giving importance to the past and the present discourses which have been articulated before the discourse historically. Fairclough states that CDA "entails working in a 'transdisciplinary' way through dialogue with other disciplines and theories which are addressing contemporary processes of social change" (Critical Discourse analysis). The emphasis on 'transdisciplinarity' of CDA means that "the theoretical and methodological development of CDA and the disciplines/theories it is in dialogue with is informed through that dialogue, a matter of working with the 'logic' and categories of the other in developing one's own theory and methodology" (2005:53). In this sense, CDA analyzes the particular features of texts by integrating textual analysis into multi-disciplinary research on change. The methodological framework of this study derived from CDA, because of the critical realistic premises of it and the focuses of political issues like social inequalities and power relations which are signifying, constructing, justifying or supporting by language use. But the 'transdisciplinarity' of CDA gives chance of using not a static and single method.

CDA doesn't concern language as the only object of study, but concern to the linguistic aspects of social processes and structures. Main interest of CDA is the question as to how power is exercised by language use in speech and writing. This requires considering ideology. According to Fairclough, ideologies are "significations/constructions of reality which are built into various dimensions of the forms/meanings of discursive practices, and which contribute to the production, reproduction or transformation of relations of domination" (1992, 87). This conception of ideology is useful to answer the key question that is whether ideology is a property of structures or a property of events (88). The answer of CDA to this question is both. In a sense, ideology is conceptualized in CDA as in the balance between Althusserian subject that is ideologically constituted and the subject with the capacity of act individually and collectively as agent. This answer also implies the location of ideology. Fairclough states that "ideology is located both in the structures which constitute the outcome of past events and the conditions for current events, and in events themselves as they reproduce and transform their conditioning structures" (1992:89). Even so the ideologies become naturalized as "common sense" in discursive practices, there always be an emancipation possibility in this conceptualization by means of hegemonic struggle. Hegemony is derived from Gramsci's analysis of western capitalism and revolutionary strategy in Western Europe. Gramsci used the term hegemony to indicate the way of domination of one class over others. This implies not only political and economic control, but also the ability of the dominant class to project its own way of seeing the world so that those who are subordinated by it accept it as 'common sense' and 'natural' (Forgacs, 1988, p. 343). According to Gramsci, there are three dimensions of hegemony: intellectual, moral and political. Intellectual and moral dimension of hegemony refers to consent and political dimension refers to domination, subjugation, force and coercion. But economically dominant class provides social consent by means of allies from other social classes. Hegemonic struggle takes place in "constructing alliances" process. In this process, hegemonic struggle in terms of the articulation, disarticulation and rearticulation of elements is in harmony with Fairclough's conception of discourse. It is related to the concept of "orders of discourse" which is used to link discourse to society by Fairclough. "An order of discourse can be seen as the discursive facet of the contradictory and unstable equilibrium which constitutes hegemony, and the articulation and rearticulation of orders of discourse is correspondingly one stake in hegemonic struggle" (93).

Since the order of discourse is defined as "the totality of discursive practices within an institution or society, and the relationships between them" (Fairclough, 1992, 43), the discourse analysis have to be carried out along the text, the production and interpretation of texts and social practice at the same time. The formation of text, the content of text and the context in which the texts are described, understood and interpreted becomes important with these three dimensions of order of discourse. To analyze the formation of text, the way of framing the problem, the way of solving the problem, discussion strategies, proof strategies and the support devices for arguments have to be taken into consideration. To analyze the content, the questions of "what is apparently said?" or "what sorts of representations of the world are provided?" have to be asked to the text. But the analysis of context is most crucial one. In CDA, "all discourses are historical and can therefore only be understood with reference to their context" (Meyer, 2001, 15).

In this study, contexts and texts are taken as interconnected and the intertextual and interdiscursive relationship among WSIS documents and policy report from Turkey have been analysed historically in the broader sociopolitical context by exploring the contradictions of the hegemonic Information Society discourse. The analysis draws attention to the themes on which the discourse of the documents concentrates. The evaluation particularly focuses on two framing themes: Why people need the Information Society and the problems that the Information Society will resolve. These two themes are also the categories of the analysis, which includes basic definitions, conceptualizations, assumptions and arguments that are designed to legitimate all these sub-categories in accordance with the nature of the CDA.

Analysis of WSIS Documents

The World Summit on the Information Society (WSIS) was held in Geneva and Tunis, in 2003 and 2005, respectively. Four core documents were published including the Declaration of Principles and Plan of Action of that Principles declared at Geneva Summit, the Tunis Agenda for Information Society and the Tunis Commitment Documents were declared in the second phase (WSIS, 2003a, 2003b, 2005a, 2005b).

These documents are closely interconnected and thus together are a common effort to create a global and hegemonic view of the Information Society. First, from the first article at first summit, documents begin in the name of the whole world. . .

> 1. We, the representatives of the peoples of the world, assembled in Geneva from 10-12 December 2003 for the first phase of the World Summit on the Information Society… (WSIS, 2003a)

However, these global representatives are unable to truly define the concept of the Information Society. In the article below, the Information Society is a new society of new era whose primary benefit is 'expanded human communication':

> 67. **We are firmly convinced** that we are collectively entering a new era of enormous potential, that of the Information Society and expanded human communication. In this emerging society, information and knowledge can be produced, exchanged, shared and communicated through all the networks of the world. All individuals can soon, if we take the necessary actions, together build a **new Information Society** based on **shared knowledge and founded on global solidarity** and a better mutual understanding between peoples and nations. We trust that these measures will open the way to the future development of a **true knowledge society.** (WSIS, 2003a)

What is inferred by 'expanded human communication' is revealed in the second sentence beginning with "In this emerging society…" It is said that 'multiplication' of the information and facilitating distribution process is inherently related to the expansion of human communication and thus to the new society. Nevertheless, the documents say nothing about the content/messages of the Information/Knowledge to be shared. The first problem here is that the distinction between information and knowledge is not clear and second problem is to assume that facilitating the exchanging/sharing of information/knowledge would create a 'mutual understanding between [the] peoples' of the world. Here, it is ridiculous to assume that misunderstandings between people stems from 'entropy'.

Moreover, it is also assumed that the Information Society is a process at the end of which a 'true knowledge society' would emanate. It appears that the writers of the documents are confused about the concept of society. Another indicator of this argument, given in the extract below, is that the Information Society is said to be an 'evolving' concept, reminding us of the idea of the 'linear development' of the 'Modernization Discourse'.

> 2. The Information Society is an **evolving concept** that has reached different levels across the world, reflecting the different stages of development. Technological and other change is rapidly transforming the environment in which the Information Society is developed… (WSIS, 2003b)

The optimism stemming from the technological determinist stance is a striking element of documents. Article 8 states;

> 8. **We recognize** that education, knowledge, information and communication are at the core of human progress, endeavor and well-being. Further,

> Information and Communication Technologies (ICTs) have an immense impact on virtually all aspects of our lives. The rapid progress of these technologies opens completely new opportunities to attain higher levels of development. The capacity of these technologies to reduce many traditional obstacles, especially those of time and distance, for the first time in history makes it possible to use the potential of these technologies for the benefit of millions of people in all corners of the world. (WSIS, 2003a).

Another article, writes that,

> 5. The Tunis Summit represents a unique opportunity to raise awareness of the benefits that Information and Communication Technologies (ICTs) can bring to humanity and the manner in which they can transform people's activities, interaction and lives, and thus increase confidence in the future. (WSIS, 2005a)

The WSIS discourse has also a serious problem in the sense that it excludes some important international agreements from its conceptualization of Information Society. The article below states that,

> 18. Nothing in this Declaration shall be construed as impairing, contradicting, restricting or derogating from the provisions of the Charter of the United Nations and the Universal Declaration of Human Rights, any other international instrument or national laws adopted in furtherance of these instruments. (WSIS, 2003a)

The critique presented by Hamelink's (2004) article seems crucial for the issue. Hamelink (2004) argues that as the WSIS discourse mentions the commitment to all relevant international agreements, the absence of the World Telecommunications Agreement and the TRIPS Agreement among the referenced texts is really remarkable. The former agreement demands that nations liberalize their markets and has far-reaching implications for the governance of the basic infrastructures of telecommunications. For Hamelink, this agreement restricts social policy to the limits defined by "commercial players" and as a result "trade interests rather than socio-cultural aspirations determine national telecommunication policy" (Hamelink 2004:285). As for the TRIPS Agreement, like the World Telecommunications Agreement demonstrates the thrust from the major industrial IPR (Intellectual Property Rights) holders. Hamelink advocates that in the current battle against content piracy the key protagonists are more concerned about the protection of investments than the public interests in producing creative work. Hamelink proposes that the current international IPR protection regulations from which small individual and communal content producers hardly benefit are the best proof of this argument.

Thus, Hamelink draws attention to the conflicting nature of the WSIS discourse: while the WSIS official texts refer to international agreements mentioning the equality of human beings and the like, international regulations such as the TRIPs agreement give priority to the interests of international media conglomerates. A further supporting argument can be extracted by focusing on the agents and the role of the agents of the Information Society as defined by the WSIS discourse, for example, various social agents in the process are defined as follows:

> 20. **Governments, as well as private sector, civil society** and the **United Nations and other international organizations** have an important role and responsibility in the development of the Information Society and, as appropriate, in decision-making processes. Building a people-centred Information Society is a joint effort which requires cooperation and partnership among all stakeholders. (WSIS, 2003a)

The United Nations and other international organizations are seen as facilitators of the process. Meanwhile, civil society, governments and especially private sector are seen vital to the process. Among them, the private sector is seen as the most critical agent and the leader of the process. Accordingly private investment is seen as superior.

Here are examples from the Tunis documents:

> 13. **In the past**, financing of ICT infrastructure in most developing countries has been based on **public investment. Lately**, a significant influx of investment has taken place where **private-sector** participation has been encouraged, based on a **sound regulatory framework**, and where public policies aimed at **bridging** the digital divide have been implemented. (WSIS, 2005b)
>
> 26. **We acknowledge** the following prerequisites for equitable and universal accessibility to, and better utilization of, financial mechanisms:
>
> a) Creating policy and regulatory incentives aimed at universal access and the attraction of **private-sector investment.** (WSIS, 2005b)
>
> 55. **We recognize** that the existing arrangements for Internet governance have worked effectively to make the Internet the highly robust, dynamic and geographically diverse medium that it is today, with the private sector taking the lead in day-to-day operations, and with innovation and value creation at the edges. (WSIS, 2005b)

Thus, the WSIS discourse acknowledges that it is the private sector which would essentially invest into and operate/direct the process of the Information Society. Governments are also seen as critical in building an enabling environment for the Information Society their role being to facilitate the operation of the free market. Section 6 of the document of Declaration of Principles is a good example:

> **6) Enabling environment, and regulating the market**
>
> 39. The rule of law, accompanied by a supportive, transparent, pro-competitive, technologically neutral and predictable policy and regulatory framework reflecting national realities, is essential for building a people-centred Information Society. Governments should intervene, as appropriate, **to correct market failures, to maintain fair competition, to attract investment, to enhance the development of the ICT infrastructure and applications**, to maximize economic and social benefits, and to serve national priorities. (WSIS, 2003a)

The concept of the 'enabling environment' is one of the most recurrent elements in the WSIS documents and this concept has much to do with deepening and globalizing industrial capitalism. Facilitating 'international trade' (global flow of capital) is one central themes of the concept:

> 40. A dynamic and enabling international environment, supportive of **foreign direct investment**, transfer of technology, and international cooperation, particularly in the areas of **finance, debt and trade**, as well as full and effective participation of developing countries in global decision-making, are vital complements to national development efforts related to ICTs. Improving global **affordable connectivity** would contribute significantly to the effectiveness of these development efforts. (WSIS, 2003a)

That is to say, national efforts related to ICTs should be complemented by integration into a global market economy. In comparison to the roles of governments and the private sector, the task assigned to civil society is not clear.

Why do People need the Information Society?

Having underlined some critical issues concerning the WSIS discourse, now it is possible to begin the main parts of the analysis starting with the rationalization of the Information Society initiative. According the WSIS Tunis agreement the 'Social and economic divisions' between and within societies seems to be the most important rationale behind the initiative.

> **13. We also recognize** that the ICT revolution can have a tremendous positive impact as an instrument of sustainable development. In addition, an appropriate enabling environment at national and international levels could prevent increasing **social and economic divisions**, and the widening of the gap between rich and poor countries, regions, and individuals—including between men and women. (WSIS, 2005a)

As an extension of the purpose of narrowing 'divisions', the 'digital divide' is one of recurrent themes of the Geneva document:

> 1. 10. **We are also fully aware** that the benefits of the information technology revolution are today unevenly distributed between the developed and developing countries and within societies. We are fully committed to turning this **digital divide** into a digital opportunity for all, particularly for those who risk being left behind and being further marginalized. (WSIS, 2003a)

What is striking is the shallowness of the conceptualization of the concept 'digital divide'. In the WSIS documents, it is argued that 'access' to ICTs is the solution and a whole section in the Declaration of Principles is allocated to the issue of access.

> 3) Access to information and knowledge
>
> 24. The **ability** for all to access and contribute information, ideas and knowledge is essential in an inclusive Information Society. (WSIS, 2003a)

The article above mentions the term 'ability', however, there is nothing about how to improve this ability and it seems to assume that 'access' will automatically solve problems of the users of ICTs, problems of the citizens to participate the political life, and problems for the economic agents of the countries. Other important articles related to the issue of 'access' are as follows:

> 25. The sharing and strengthening of global knowledge for development can be enhanced by **removing barriers to equitable access** to information for economic, social, political, health, cultural, educational, and scientific activities and by facilitating access to public domain information, including by universal design and the use of assistive technologies. (WSIS, 2003a)
>
> 27. **Access to information and knowledge** can be promoted by increasing awareness among all stakeholders of the possibilities offered by different software models, including proprietary, open-source and free software, **in order to increase competition**, **access by users**, diversity of choice, and to enable all users to develop solutions which best meet their requirements. Affordable access to software should be considered as an important component of a truly inclusive Information Society. (WSIS, 2003a)

Thus, connecting everyone to the Internet and other communication technologies is deemed 'sufficient' there is nothing said about the 'quality' of the messages to be diffused through the new technologies. Other assumptions here are that 'market competition is good and it is necessary to attract private investment to develop access to information and knowledge.

The last rationalization theme to be mentioned here is the stress on 'benefits for governments and private sector', 'administrative and commercial concerns' are reiterated many times through the text. Below is one example:

> 7. ICT applications: benefits in all aspects of life
>
> 51. The usage and deployment of ICTs should seek to create benefits in all aspects of our daily life. ICT applications are potentially important in government operations and services, health care and health information, education and training, **employment**, **job creation**, **business**, agriculture, transport, protection of environment and management of natural resources, disaster prevention, and culture, and to promote eradication of poverty and other agreed development goals. ICTs should also contribute to sustainable production and consumption patterns and reduce traditional barriers, **providing an opportunity for all to access local and global markets** in a more equitable manner. Applications should be user-friendly, accessible to all, affordable, adapted to local needs in languages and cultures, and support sustainable development. To this effect, local authorities should play a major role in the provision of ICT services for the benefit of their populations. (WSIS, 2003a)

As is seen again, after stating that ICTs will create benefits in all aspects of daily life, the document largely focuses on trade-related issues and on administrative concerns of governments. In contrast, the document fails to mention the political rights of the public or enhancing the democratic structure of the society.

What Problems will the Information Society Resolve?

The role of administrative and commercial concerns in shaping the WSIS discourse is more salient when it comes to the promises of the ideal of the Information Society. Kumar (1995) states that proponents of the ideal of the Information Society adopts an almost utopian view of the new ICTs and thus, the advocates argue that the whole dimensions of peoples lives have undergone or will undergo a radical transformation, focusing on the beneficial aspects. In this argument, it can be contended that the WSIS discourse is an obvious continuation of this utopian academic view, as seen in the extract below:

1. We, the representatives of the peoples of the world, assembled in Geneva from 10-12 December 2003 for the first phase of the World Summit on the Information Society, declare our common desire and commitment to build a people-centred, inclusive and development-oriented Information Society, where everyone can create, access, utilize and share information and knowledge, enabling individuals, communities and peoples to achieve **their full potential** in promoting their sustainable development and improving their quality of life, premised on the purposes and principles of the Charter of the United Nations and respecting fully and upholding the Universal Declaration of Human Rights. (WSIS, 2003a)
2. **Our challenge** is to harness the potential of information and communication technology to promote the development goals of the Millennium Declaration, **namely the eradication of extreme poverty and hunger; achievement of universal primary education; promotion of gender equality and empowerment of women; reduction of child mortality; improvement of maternal health; to combat HIV/AIDS, malaria and other diseases; ensuring environmental sustainability; and development of global partnerships for development for the attainment of a more peaceful, just and prosperous world.** We also reiterate our commitment to the achievement of sustainable development and agreed development goals, as contained in the Johannesburg Declaration and Plan of Implementation and the Monterrey Consensus, and other outcomes of relevant United Nations Summits. (WSIS, 2003a)

Here, ICTs are attributed some sort of magical power and this is clearly a discursive strategy to attach that kind of public interest to the real orientation which is commercial or trade-related. For example, in the Declaration of Principles referred to above, also includes this article,

> 9. **We are aware** that ICTs should be regarded as tools and not as an end in themselves. Under favourable conditions, these technologies can be a **powerful instrument, increasing productivity, generating economic growth, job creation and employability** and improving the quality of life of all... (WSIS, 2003a)

In relation to commercial orientation, the emphasis on entrepreneurship and competitiveness in accordance with the neo-liberal discourse are other striking themes reiterated many times in the documents. Fostering entrepreneurship and competition which are the main motives of free market economies thus, become main purposes of the commercial orientation.

> 90.b) *developing and implementing enabling policies* that reflect national realities and that promote a supportive international environment, **foreign direct investment** as well as the mobilization of domestic resources, in order to promote and **foster entrepreneurship**, particularly Small, Medium and Micro Enterprises (SMMEs), taking into account the relevant market and cultural contexts. These policies should be reflected in a transparent, equitable regulatory framework to create **a competitive environment** to support these goals and strengthen **economic growth**. (WSIS, 2005b)
>
> 33. To achieve a **sustainable development** of the Information Society, national capability in ICT research and development should be enhanced. Furthermore, partnerships, in particular between and among developed and developing countries, including countries with economies in transition, in research and development, technology transfer, manufacturing and utilization of ICT products and services are crucial for promoting capacity building and global participation in the Information Society. The manufacture of ICTs presents a significant opportunity for **creation of wealth**. (WSIS, 2003a)
>
> 31.Continuous and adult education, re-training, life-long learning, distance-learning and other special services, such as telemedicine, can make an essential contribution to **employability** and help people benefit from the new opportunities offered by ICTs for **traditional jobs, self-employment** and **new professions**. Awareness and literacy in ICTs are an essential foundation in this regard. (WSIS, 2003a)

Foreign Direct Investment (FDI), entrepreneurship, competitiveness, sustainable development, job creation and economic growth are used together to show the main purpose of the document. They are seen as the ways of providing equitable access to Information and this is presented as the way of alleviating a varied range of social problems. Thus, it is clear that the WSIS discourse assumes an identification between the terms of the hegemonic, dominant economic view and deep social problems as the solution and problem, respectively. As for the ICTs, the technology is represented as the mediation between the solution and the problem. As a result, this kind of rationalization is technologically determinist, economically reductionist, utopian, shallow, and thus optimistic.

Not surprisingly an extension of this view is related to the international order of the world. Taming the National Economies for Global Capitalism thus becomes another theme of the WSIS discourse.

> 34. The attainment of our shared aspirations, in particular for **developing countries and countries** with economies in transition, to become fully-fledged members of the Information Society, and their **positive integration** into the **knowledge economy**, depends largely on increased capacity building in the

> areas of education, technology know-how and access to information, which are major factors in determining development and competitiveness. (WSIS, 2003a)
>
> 14. **We are greatly encouraged** by the fact that advances in communication technology, and high-speed data networks are continuously **increasing the possibilities for developing countries**, and countries with economies in transition, **to participate in the global market** for ICT-enabled services on the basis of their comparative advantage. These emerging opportunities provide a powerful **commercial basis** for ICT infrastructural investment in these countries. Therefore, **governments should take action**, in the framework of national development policies, in order to support an enabling and **competitive** environment for the necessary investment in ICT infrastructure and for the development of new services. At the same time, countries should pursue policies and measures that would not discourage, impede or prevent the continued participation of these countries in the global market for ICT-enabled services. (WSIS, 2005b)

Among these specifications on the administrative and related economic concerns, in the article reproduced above, 'content' is given a very limited space in the documents. The whole passage quoted from Declaration of Principles concerning the 'content' diffused via the ICTs is shown by the quotation below (section 8 in the Declaration of Principles). It is worth noting that there many more articles about the 'administrative and economic concerns' and here only the most striking examples are presented. As can be seen, the references to 'cultural differences' are merely clichés and nothing substantial is mentioned about this important area:

> 8) Cultural diversity and identity, linguistic diversity and local content
>
> 52. Cultural diversity is the common heritage of humankind. The Information Society should be founded on and stimulate respect for cultural identity, **cultural and linguistic diversity**, traditions and religions, and foster dialogue among cultures and civilizations. The promotion, affirmation and preservation of diverse cultural identities and languages as reflected in relevant agreed United Nations documents including UNESCO's Universal Declaration on Cultural Diversity, will further enrich the Information Society. (WSIS, 2003a)
>
> 53. The creation, dissemination and preservation of content in diverse languages and formats must be accorded high priority in building an inclusive Information Society, paying particular attention to the **diversity of supply of creative work** and due recognition of the rights of authors and artists. It is essential to promote the **production of and accessibility to all content**—educational, scientific, cultural or recreational—in diverse languages and formats. The development of local content suited to domestic or regional needs will encourage social and economic development and will stimulate participation of all stakeholders, including people living in rural, remote and marginal areas. (WSIS, 2003a)
>
> 54. The preservation of cultural heritage is a crucial component of identity and self–understanding of individuals that links a community to its past. The Information Society should harness and preserve cultural heritage for the future by all appropriate methods, including digitisation. (WSIS, 2003a)

Analysis of Information Society Strategy (2006-10)

As will be revealed in the analysis below, the discourse of the Turkey's Information Society Strategy 2006-10 document (TISS) is inherently connected to the WSIS discourse. It can even be argued that TISS discourse is largely shaped by the WSIS discourse. Even so, it is noticeable that in the process of preparing the TISS, various policy papers written by Turkish public authorities included some certain counter-arguments vis a vis the hegemonic stance of the WSIS discourse. These counter arguments concentrate on the issue of the free-flow of information connected the issue of Intellectual Property Rights (IPRs).

Again clichés are used to define the issue of IPRs in the WSIS documents taken from the perspective of advanced capitalist countries. The article that follows illustrates this point;

> 42. Intellectual Property protection is important to encourage innovation and creativity in the Information Society; similarly, the wide dissemination, diffusion, and sharing of knowledge is important to encourage innovation and creativity. Facilitating meaningful participation by all in intellectual property issues and knowledge sharing through full awareness and capacity building is a fundamental part of an inclusive Information Society. (WSIS, 2003a)

In contrast, a Turkish policy paper, The Contribution of Turkey to the WSIS (bilgitoplumu, 2003) deals with the issue from the view of a country which is disadvantaged in the current global world order. For example, in comparison to the WSIS documents focusing on the 'mere access' to ICTs, it is stated that "To achieve the goal of transforming into an information society thoroughly, the opportunity of **access and use** of ICTs should be provided to all" (stress is the authors'). In accordance with this emphasis on the combination of 'access and use', the policy paper deals with the issue of IPRs:

> 4.The intellectual property rights should be subject to the regulations of **WIPO** rather than IMF, WB and WTO.
>
> 5.The protection period of products and works of art which are assessed within the scope of intellectual property should be shortened by taking into consideration the rapid technological and economic developments.
>
> 6.Due to high costs of copyright and patents, developing and least developed countries are not able to have some specific ICTs. By considering this point, deterrent mechanisms and rules should be set up in order to change the policies of **multinational corporations** on copyright and patent that are to be applied to the developing and least developed countries. (Bilgitoplumu, 2003)

This policy argues that the emerging Information Society should not be built on the old order of the world in terms of the international flow of information. Nevertheless, the WSIS discourse creates a disclosure about the newness of the emerging society without discussing the continuation of an existing unequal order for, at least, the IPRs. Even so, despite the fact that 'The Contribution of Turkey to the WSIS'—policy paper has some substantial counter-arguments against the WSIS discourse, this alternative stance was rendered practically invisible in the Turkey's Information Society Strategy 2006-10 prepared by another policy authority, the State Planning Organization. It is known that an international consultancy group 'Peppers and Rogers' (http://www.peppersandrogersgroup.com) has played a great role in the preparation of this final policy document. Above all, this document, accompanied by an Action Plan, is a product of a political initiative. Hence, it is an appropriate subject for a discourse analysis through which this paper aims to reveal the discursive as well as ideological similarities between the WSIS discourse and Turkey's Information Society discourse.

Why do People need the Information Society?

In the introductory chapter of the document (SPO 2006), the relationship between ICTs and society is defined within the technological determinist view. It is argued that "Innovations in Information and Communication Technologies (ICT) have an important affect on the development of globalization and influence all areas of economic and social life, all segments society." In other words, these innovations **cause** a social transformation. (SPO 2006:1). Furthermore, in the following chapters in the document the term "**holistic**" is also used to refer to social transformation: "Transformation into an information society is a **holistic** phenomenon which involves not only a change in traditional mechanisms of the economy but also social and cultural change." (SPO 2006:21).

After presenting the Information Society as an irresistible and irreversible outcome of the technological advancements, the rationalization of the existing policy process is based on two salient legimating discursive elements; opportunities and risks. For example, in the chapter "The Information Society Opportunities of Turkey", it is argued that "although ICT and the globalization of the world economy provide great **opportunities** to countries in the race for development and international competition; they also pose new **threats**."(SPO 2006:3). The stress put on the "technological revolution" seems to be another important discursive element. In accordance with the theoretical base provided by technological determinist and optimist studies, it is claimed that in an environment of the "ICTs revolution" undeveloped countries have the opportunity to narrowing the gap between them and developed countries.

A related "risk" theme is the "digital divide" which is one of the main themes of the WSIS texts. After classifying the mission of "eliminating the digital divide" (SPO 2006:6) as one of primary areas of the initiative in accordance with the WSIS, it is said that Turkey "faces a digital divide both in the national and international context." (SPO 2006:8).

The presentation of the Information Society initiative as an international dominant trend shows that this initiative is taken as given and thus, is not subject to reasoning. Shortly, it is asserted that in environment created by the new ICTs, economic organization in respect to global competition, productivity and new commodities, is changing and hence, it is mandatory to follow the given prescriptions.

What Problems will the Information Society Solve?

It is a salient fact that economic orientation and the corresponding jargon is dominant in the discourse of the strategy document: "The **ultimate** goal of transformation into an Information Society is to get a bigger share from the **world production** and to raise the level of social welfare by increasing **competitive** power" (SPO 2006:3). In accordance, some concepts such as "competitiveness", "productivity/effectiveness", and "sustainable economic growth" are among most frequently used concepts of the report.

A series of assumptions play a significant role in arguing the economy and trade related projection about the Information Society. The "network effect" idea based on the claim that the adoption of ICTs would have a triggering effect on other sectors of the economy is the most salient one:

> Hence, Turkey will be able to realize **sustainable economic growth** by increasing her global **competitiveness and productivity** as a result of the network effect, which will be created by constructing the relationship between and within the government, the citizens and the businesses based on the ICT. Thus, Turkey will be able to reinforce its position within the economic and social networks emerging on a global scale.
>
> The Information Society Strategy will be a fundamental instrument in coordinating all actors of the economy with an integrated approach, in directing all efforts and resources towards the same objective, thus attaining the set targets in order to achieve the transformation summarized above. (SPO 2006:4-5)

Furthermore, the economic expectations based on the principles of the free capitalistic market, administrative expectations are also revealed in the strategy report. It is important to note that the neo-liberal bias of the strategy report becomes clear in presenting administrative expectations. The apparent expectation from the "holistic" social transformation is merely eliminating and shortening excessive bureaucratic applications which are 'burden' on the citizens and companies. In this respect, it is not clear how the Information society will contribute to democracy and citizenship. The section 2.1 on Citizens states that,

> Usage of ICT by individuals in the society not only fundamentally affects their own lives but is also closely related to the transformation of the **government** and the **businesses** which provide products and services based on these technologies, and to the development of the ICT sector... Such a development will also trigger and accelerate the transformation of other elements that offer goods and services to meet the demands of the citizens. (SPO 2006:7).

In the first sentence it is argued that three main areas would benefit from ICTs: individuals, governments and businesses. **Individuals**' (as apolitical social elements) are assumed to be independent of commodities created by **governments** and **businesses**; and government services and businesses products and services. Then the second sentence mentions that citizens have needs for goods and services that are produced by government (services) and by businesses (commodities). It is clear that here citizens are in fact **customers**. As is seen what is stressed here are e-state and e-commerce applications. However, there is no discussion on how simplifying bureaucratic applications will qualitatively transform citizens' lives.

So it becomes clear that administrative expectations are mainly related to facilitating trade-related activities via the adoption of ICTs. Creating an 'enabling environment for entrepreneurs and companies' (private sector) is one of the main themes of the strategy report as it is in the WSIS documents. Both the WSIS documents and the strategy report assign the government some key tasks to create an environment for free capitalistic market operations as a neo-liberal leitmotif. First, it is advocated that citizens should be customers for the new ICTs: "it is important to **ensure** that citizens adopt ICT speedily and make these technologies a part of their daily lives in the process of transformation into an information society." (SPO 2006:7).

In regard to the 'enabling environment' some clichés are repeated in the document. For example, after describing the transformation as 'holistic', it is stated that,

> With her young and dynamic demographic structure, **growing economy**, and experienced **entrepreneurs** who can take the advantage of the globalizing world economy in an ever-improving way, the process of transformation into information society, implying a holistic social and economic transformation, offers great opportunities for Turkey. (SPO 2006:19).

Furthermore, there are some erroneous comments on societal development: "By leveraging these opportunities effectively, **a holistic transformation strategy** should be followed until 2010 in order to achieve a **sustainable economic** and social development through improved **international competitiveness** based on knowledge and increase social welfare." (SPO 2006:19). This latter sentence is also a neo-liberal cliché: 'holistic transformation' is not a phenomenon that can be explained by sustainable economic growth or international competitiveness. Moreover, holistic transformation/social transformation is itself an ultimate purpose rather than being a prerequisite for economic growth.

Content as an issue related to the qualitative dimension of transformation is not even a prior issue in the strategy, as it is not contained in the WSIS texts. The space allocated to the issue of content is very limited and only directly related to decreasing the bureaucratic applications:

> In higher education, interactions such as enrolment, dormitory and scholarship applications among others will be transferred onto electronic channels. An integrated data bank will be established for primary and

> secondary education to support the process of achieving information-based education policies. e-Testing applications will be made more widespread. Library services, catalogue scanning and content access services will be made available on electronic media.(SPO 2006:30)

Conclusion

It is worth the note that WSIS documents and "Information Society Strategy (2006-10)" of Turkey has belonged to historically same period, the first half of 2000s. In accordance with Turkey's economic, political and cultural commitments to global capitalist system, the discourse of "Information Society Strategy" document strongly depends on the hegemonic discourses of World Bank and the European Union. Accordingly and naturally, the discourses of WSIS documents and TISS are strongly interconnected.

The most important ideological and discursive interconnection between these texts is the assumption that the only positive social interaction is the market-driven economic relations, which originates from the neoliberal ideologies. Both discourses share the optimist and technological determinist views rooted in commercial concerns. As well as commercial ones, bureaucratic concerns have the same pressure on the utopic expectations from the ideal of information society. Both discourses exclude the complex content of the concept of information (Capurro and Hjørland, 2003). That is to say they do not theorize or discuss the concept of information itself: is it a bit of information or equal to a completed opinion about the world we live in. In fact these interconnections between WSIS and TISS discourses are parts of a social and material entity which is in turn reproduced by these discourses as dependency relations. These dependencies caused the Turkey's information society discourse to be a reproduction of hegemonic global discourse of information society. As stated by Geray, the outcome of this hegemonic discourse as desktop colonialism in which a few hegemonic blocs come into being and market tangible and intangible goods and services of the information economy starting from elite and businesses of the periphery, taking advantage of globally built information networks (2005:186-188).

In Turkish information society discourse, information society is under construction as stated by Hamelink for WSIS discourse (2004:288). According to Hamelink, this society can be characterized by violation of free speech rights through forms of political and commercial censorship, extension of the corporate ownership on public information, the consolidation of corporate power on communication markets, decreasing public inequalities and the access to information dependent upon purchasing power (2004, 289). These problems are true for communication environment in Turkey. However, WSIS official discourse and Turkey's information society discourse have not included cultural and social issues together with the media.

Section C

MEDIA AND DEVELOPMENT

12

Opening up the Black Box of Participation: A Reception Study of Mediated Participatory Practices

Nico Carpentier

Within the Web 2.0 hype, participation (again) became a key signifier, promising the fulfilment of our democratic fantasies. Looking at the history of mediated participation, we can distinguish a number of these upsurges, like the 1970s debates about the New World Information and Communication Order (NWICO), combined with the rise of the Community (and Alternative) Media Movement. On a positive note, these increased forms of participation within the sphere of the media can be seen as part of what Mouffe has called the democratic revolution, which affects all societal spheres (and not just politics): "*... the effects of the democratic revolution can be analysed in the arts, theory, and all aspects of culture in general ...*" (Mouffe, 1997: 11). Slowly but surely the impact of this 200-year democratic revolution has generated a more egalitarian society, and has facilitated (in the case of mediated participation) citizens to exert the communication rights. On the downside, the democratisation of democracy is a slow process that has not undone (and will not undo) all societal power imbalances. This also affects the nature of participation itself, as its definition (and its intensity) is part of the societal-political struggle between minimalist and maximalist versions of democracy. Quite often the contemporary celebratory uses of participation (implicitly) subscribe to a more minimalist ideological-democratic position, black boxing participation's diversities of meanings and intensities, and ignoring its role within the democratic revolution. Through these logics, participation risks becoming an object of celebration, trapped in a reductionist discourse of novelty, detached from the reception of its audiences and decontextualised from its political-ideological, communicative-cultural and communicative-structural contexts.

This chapter aims to add to the debates on the democratic revolution and the political-ideological significance of mediated participation by comparing the reception of two North Belgian participatory media products. One of these case studies is based on the "new" world of a *YouTube*-like online platform called *16plus*, the second case study is based on the "old" concept of access television in a 2002 TV programme called *Barometer*. In both cases, the reception study shows little enthusiasm or downright rejection from the part of their audiences, although the focus group members still use a maximalist (and almost contradictory) discourse of media democracy, and fiercely critique the mainstream media and their professionals. Through an analysis of these multi-layered audience receptions, this chapter will show that participatory practices are not unconditionally appreciated by audience members, but subject to specific conditions of possibility. Albeit in different degrees, these case studies show the importance of quality and social relevance for the evaluation of participatory practices.

The Key Concept of Participation

The key concept of participation has been used in a variety of ways and domains, and its success has not necessarily been to its advantage. Already in 1970 Carole Pateman (1970: 1) wrote that *"the widespread use of the term [...] has tended to mean that any precise, meaningful content has almost disappeared."* There are two ways to deal with this contingency of the notion of participation. A first strategy is based on the expression of regret for the significatory chaos, combined with the attempts to undo it by (almost archeologically) unravelling the authentic meaning of the concept of participation. This strategy is relatively old: already in 1969, Arnstein published her ladder of participation, which had the following 8 steps: manipulation, therapy, informing, consultation, placation, partnership, delegated power, and citizen control. From a slightly different angle, the OECD (2001) developed a three-stage model (information distribution, consultation and active participation), which nevertheless structurally resembled Arnstein's ladder.

Considerably less critical and radical than Arnstein's model—as the bottom and top steps of the ladder were eliminated—we are offered the following definition of participation, which is "*a relation based on partnership with government, in which citizens actively engage in the decision- and policy-making process. It acknowledges a role for citizens in proposing policy options and shaping the policy dialogue - although the responsibility for the final decision or policy formulation rests with government*" (OECD, 2001: 16). This definition carries with it the echoes of one of the classic definitions of participation, developed by Pateman in her 1970 book *Democratic Theory and Participation*. Here, Pateman distinguishes between partial an full participation, where partial participation is defined as "*a process in which two or more parties influence each other in the making of decisions but the final power to decide rests with one party only*" (Pateman, 1970: 70). Full participation is seen as "*a process where each individual member of a decision-making body has equal power to determine the outcome of decisions.*" (Pateman, 1970: 71).

All these definitions and approaches have a common—almost messianistic—

concern towards the concept of participation: they want to protect and rescue it. The tactics used are relatively similar, because they all consist of creating a difference with "other" practices which are only nominally participatory, and which can then be unmasked as forms of "pseudo-participation". The second strategy to deal with this significatory diversity distances itself (at least in a first instance) from the question of differentiating between authentic participation and pseudo-participation, but focuses on the significatory process that lies behind the articulation of participation as part of a political-ideological struggle. From this perspective, the definition of participation is one of the many societal fields where a political struggle is waged between the minimalist and the maximalist variations of democracy and politics. It is a struggle between two political-ideological, archetypical models, where on the one hand - in the minimalist model - democracy is confined to processes of representation, where participation is limited to elite selection through elections, and the political to the domain where political elites organise their decision-making processes. On the other hand, in the maximalist model, democracy is seen as a more balanced combination of representation and participation, and the political is articulated as a dimension of the social (Mouffe, 1997; 2000), which can play a role in the sphere of political decision-making, but also in other societal spheres (such as the economy, culture, and media, to name but a few).

The second strategy to deal with the significatory diversity of the concept of participation is not as disconnected from the first strategy (looking for authentic participation) as might appear at first sight. There are namely three components from the first strategy which are worth salvaging. First, taking a closer look at the definitions used in the first strategy, it becomes reasonably easy to distil the core issue in this participation debate (and the political-ideological struggle that lies behind this debate). The concept that features repeatedly in these definitions—in many different forms—is power, and more specifically the way that power is distributed in society. Some prudence is in place here, though, as power is often reduced to the possession of a specific societal group. Authors like Foucault (1978) have argued against this position, claiming that power is an always-present characteristic of social relations. In contemporary societies, the narrations of power are always complex narrations of power strategies, counter-powers and resistance.

These power struggles are never limited to one specific societal field (e.g., "the" economy), but are present on all societal fields and levels. Despite (or because) this nuance, the debates on participation can be seen as a struggle for political power (in the broadest sense possible), or better, as a power struggle on who can take on which roles in society. In the minimalist models, power is centralised as much as possible, whilst in the maximalist models the decentralisation of power is preferred. Revisiting the first strategy (based on authenticity) allows us to see the participation debate as a latent conflict (which is sometimes rendered manifest) on who can become involved in societal decision-making processes, in the definition and resolution of societal problems, in the choices regarding which procedures should be followed, and in the societal debates about these definitions, procedures and resolutions. Who is empowered and granted the opportunity (and "the" power) to speak thus becomes an integrated part of the debates about participation and the underlying political-ideological struggle.

Second, from the first strategy we can also derive the need to delineate the concept of participation, whilst still maintaining its contingency and structural openness. The above-mentioned debate about participation requires some form of discursive fixity, which obliges us to return to the first approach and the core concepts that are used in this approach. These core concepts are articulated in contingent ways, but also their mere existence is of importance here. This argument might seem superfluous at first sight, would it not be for the involvement of two other notions—namely access and interaction - in the participation debate. As the relationship between both notions and power is much less stronger and explicit, their inclusion also becomes part of the struggle for the minimalist or maximalist articulation of participation. Although the differences between access, interaction and participation have been dealt with more extensively in other texts (see Carpentier, 2007), it remains crucial to distinguish between these concepts. It suffices here to refer to one example, where the difference between two of these concepts was established, namely the Unesco-debates on access and participation (from a communicative perspective, within the framework of the development of a New World Information and Communication Order—NWICO). In the Unesco-debates, access was defined as "*the use of media for public service. It may be defined in terms of the opportunities available to the public to choose varied and relevant programs and to have a means of feedback to transmit its reactions and demands to production organisations. Participation implies a higher level of public involvement in communication systems. It includes the involvement of the public in the production process and also in the management and planning of communication systems. Participation may be no more than representation and consultation of the public in decision-making.*" (Quoted in Servaes, 1999: 85) Especially when the internet gained its momentum, concepts like access and interaction saw their importance increase. As both concepts are "only" necessary conditions for participation, the increased importance of access and interaction caused an implicit downgrading of the more radical and maximalist component of the meaning of participation. Exactly the implicit nature of this downgrading complicates the analysis of the political-ideological struggle behind participation, and simultaneously legitimates the delineation of the notions of access, interaction and participation.

Finally, a third component that needs to be highlighted is the unavoidability of the positioning of any author that intervenes in these debates. Ideology does not stop at the edges of analyses, but it is an integrated part of it. This does not ignore the fact that the debate on the "correct" definition of participation is too simple: for this exact reason we need the second strategy. But a mere description of the dynamics of power in participatory processes is also too simple. This is yet another area where the first strategy proves to be helpful. This means more specifically that I subscribe to the call of a number of authors (Mouffe (1997), but also Giddens (2002), to name but two) to continue deepening democracy, and to include all societal fields (including the media) in this democratisation process. This does not imply that all expert systems should be annihilated mercilessly—this might be a bit of a difficult position for an academic to take—but this does mean that the power equilibriums and the participatory potential in every domain of the social should be analysed carefully, and ways should be discovered to maximise both of them. This plea for an increase of societal power balances has a clearly utopian dimension. Situations of full-participation—as described by Pateman—are utopian non-places (or better: "never-to-be-places") which will always remain unattainable and empty, but which simultaneously remain to play a key role as ultimate anchoring points and horizons for our analyses. Despite the impossibility to fully realise these situations in the social praxis, their fantasmatic realisations serve as breeding grounds for democratic renewal. As the French writer of Irish descent, Samuel Beckett, once put it eloquently[1] : "*Ever tried. Ever failed. Never mind. Try again. Fail better.*"

What about the 21st Century (Mass) Media?

Given the ubiquity of contemporary (mass) media and their societal roles, media organisations also become relevant in the discussion about participation. Of course, this diversity is again structured by the above-mentioned minimalist-maximalist debate on democracy and participation. From a minimalist perspective more emphasis is placed on the ritual and symbolic forms of participation, where the media are seen to be contributing to communality. Citizens frequently participate in (semi-)collective mediated rituals and surround themselves with (carriers of) meaning which construct their imagined communities. These meanings are not just communicated through the more obvious examples (like news (papers) and documentaries) but also through literature, soaps, reality TV, cartoons, etc. In most cases, the participatory nature of these receptions (however active they may be) is relatively limited, and one may wonder whether the term (mediated or symbolic) interaction, or even mediated quasi-interaction (Thompson, 1995) is not more appropriate. From a more maximalist perspective, the attention is focused on the more intense forms of media participation, where non-professionals are effectively involved in the mediated production of meaning (content-related participation) or even in the management and policy-development of content producing organisations (structural participation).

In the history of mediated communication we can find many variations. If we travel back into the early years of communication history, it is not even that farfetched to consider the many pamphlets as forms of media participation. But also the start-up phase of radio knew many examples of non-professional broadcasters. Not surprisingly, it was Bertolt Brecht's radio theory (see Marc Silberman's (2001) collection of Brecht's essays) that provided us with the foundations of the dream of the transformation of radio as a tool of distribution into a tool of communication. But especially from the nineties (of the 20th century)—and in some cases earlier, like for instance in the case of Hakim Bey's *TAZ* (1985)—the focus of participatory theoreticians shifted towards the so-called new media. The development of the internet, and especially the web would not only render all information available to all, but would also create a whole new world of communication, with in its slipstream the promise of a structural increase of the level of (media) participation. In the meanwhile, this dream seems to have come true, at least at first sight: while at first people still had to do the effort of constructing their own webpages, the web 2.0 technologies now provide popular and accessible ways to publish texts, images, and audio and video material.

But the discourse of novelty that accompanies these evolutions, brings along a number of substantial problems. Our attention has become focused on the participatory potential of new media, which brings us to ignore the capacities of "old" media. Suddenly, the newspaper, the radio and the television appear to be media from the past century, not relevant enough to be incorporated in the debates on participation. This causes three crucial mistakes to be made. First, the cultural importance of the old media is tremendously underestimated. These old media still play an important role in the everyday lives of many people. Blinded by the futurist megalomania, and by the hope for a better future, the taken-for-granted presence of the old media is often forgotten. Secondly, the institutional nature of the present-day media worlds is equally often ignored. A vast number of media products are still produced by media companies, which are old top-down systems based on capitalist logics and not always in favour of the maximalist approaches towards participation and democracy. In this dazzling techno-optimism, it is often forgotten that the routines, identities, practices, conventions and representations that circulate in the old media system have not been lost, but still co-structure the "new" media system. Thirdly, the discourse of novelty feeds into the technological-determinist model, assuming that specific media technologies are per definition more participatory than others. Without wanting to underestimate the specificity of technologies, or without positioning them as "*determined technologies*" (Williams, 1974: 7), the participatory potential of media technologies remains dependant on the way that they are used. In practice, this means that web 2.0 technologies can perfectly be used in top-down non-participatory ways.

The caution expressed in the previous paragraph does not bear witness of my blindness for the participatory potential of old and new media (technologies), nor for the increased diversity of these participatory practices. It would be hard not to mention blogging, vlogging, webzines, internet radio (and television), podcasting, digital storytelling and wikis here. But even in this enumeration, it is difficult to escape the technological angle, as all labels refer to specific technologies. Because of this focus, we tend to decrease the importance of media producers and consumers. Ultimately, networks consist of humans and non-humans, of organisms, humans and machines. To put this differently, for every cyberspace there is a cyberplace inhabited by media users that work and live in these places. In their own daily lives, within specific social contexts, they make use of specific media technologies. Secondly, these participatory processes (as mentioned before) are not guaranteed by these specific technologies. Each technology can be used in a wide variety of ways, and its participatory nature is often (still) dependant of the power (im)balance between a professional media elite and the non-professionals that become involved, and not by the technology as such. Thirdly, the use of these technologies, and their participatory potential cannot be detached from their organisational component. Participation is organised, and is in many cases produced by the operations of formal (or sometimes informal) organisations. Even in the blogosphere, the existence of the individual writer-publisher (the Author as Barthes (1984) would call him or her) is a romantic illusion, because the blog-infrastructure is provided by a variety of organisations and companies. This organisational context is to a high degree—as Henry Jenkins (2006) argues in *Convergence Culture*—a commercial and commodified context, which results in a combination of top-down business processes with bottom-up consumption and production processes. The existence of YouTube, with Google as its owner—is a case in point here.

The discourse of novelty, and the privileging of new media, is not the only key problem in participatory media theory. As mentioned above, the importance attached to participation, to the maximalist versions of democracy and to the broad approaches towards the political is intrinsically ideological and normative. As such, this has to be considered unavoidable, but at the same time things are complicated by the rarity of the more radical-maximalist versions in social praxis. The least one can say is that these radical-maximalist versions do not have the advantage of the taken-for-grantedness that is generated through (semi-)hegemonous practices and discourses. In his analysis of participatory development theory, Sparks (2007: 59) points to this dilemma (albeit in a specific theoretical context) by stating rather harshly that participatory development theory is based on "*very contentious claims*", because of the following paradox: "*the dominant paradigm passed in theory, but retained a very extensive appeal in practice; the participatory paradigm, on the other hand triumphed in development theory, but has failed to command any substantial support in practice.*" Although Sparks' focus on social systems brings him to ignore the perspectives of a (rather crucial) actor, namely the people-to-be-developed—a reduction which also limits the transposition of this critique to the broad field of participatory media theory-his argument does allow emphasising that the reluctance of specific social systems (like the mainstream media system) to engage in the more radical-maximalist versions of participation is limiting the actual appearance of these versions in social praxis. Because of this structural absence (or limited presence), one cannot but permanently question the relevance of these (radical) participatory models, and point to the need to legitimise the (academic) attention for the exceptional.

At the same time Sparks' omission of the people (or the public) as a relevant actor raises questions about their perspectives on these participatory practices, including mediated participatory practices, when the peoples or publics are confronted with them. This brings us to a second core problem: within the field of mediated participation, their perspectives and receptions have only rarely been researched (see Livingstone and Lunt, 1994; Huesca, 2008, for exceptions in the respective fields of audience discussion programmes and youth-produced radio), which paradoxically renders their voices relatively absent in the theories that aim to increase their voices in society[2]. In the case of new media, it is important to stress that the conflation of producer and audience is not total, and that participatory media products still have audiences that are not involved in the participatory process. We can here refer to alternative media studies, where a similar problem has been established: "*It is a paradox, however, that so little attention has been dedicated to the user dimension, given that alternative-media activists represent in a sense the most active segment of the so-called 'active audience*" (Downing, 2003: 625). This argument legitimises the need for introducing more reception studies (see e.g. Staiger, 2005) into the area of participatory (online) media, focussing on how audiences interpret and evaluate the outcomes of other people's participatory activities, at the level of content and process.

Thirdly, participatory media theory has the tendency to isolate the concept of participation, and to ignore the conditions of possibility of its relevance, appreciation and significance. The often made (implicit) assumption is that participation is necessarily beneficial, and that if it is only enabled, it will also be appreciated by all those involved, who will nothing but gain from them. This assumption is problematic because it decontextualises the participatory practices, and disconnects them from a very necessary articulation with democracy, empowerment, equality and a number of other crucial concepts. This decontextualisation also leads to the belief that the societal appreciation for and impact of participatory practices will not be affected by the political-ideological, communicative-cultural and communicative-structural context. As participatory media practices are not situated in a vacuum, one can for instance safely assume that these practices will be interpreted (and gain signification) through already circulating discourses on the societal roles of media organisations, their media professionals, and their audiences. Similarly, also the expectations on what is to be considered personal, private, public and political, and on who has the right to express what, affect these interpretations and evaluations. Although these discourses are not necessarily stable and rigid, they also cannot be considered hyper-fluid, as they have a certain degree of inertia. Moreover, however heterogeneously articulated these discourses on the media sometimes may be, they are often imbedded in hegemonic processes that again fixate them.

Two Case Studies on the Reception of Participatory Media Products

Given the importance of the audiences' reception and the discursive (and other) contexts in which participatory processes are situated, there is a strong need to incorporate both components in the study of participatory media. In this article, two case studies are developed, both related to the North Belgian public broadcaster VRT, which allows me to incorporate an institutional angle, focussing on the role of media professionals within these participatory processes. The case studies differ in the type of technology they use: One of them is using an "old" technology and the other one is using a "new" technology to facilitate participation. At the same time, both case studies are similar, as they both generate (reasonably) intense forms of participation, where the power relationship between the media professionals and the participants are (or seem to be) fairly balanced, allowing the participants to produce audiovisual material themselves, and to enter into a production process which is more than "mere" access or interaction.

The first case study deals with the online platform *16plus.be*. Given the abundance of choice of available material and the angle of this article, a case study was developed based on material that was produced by clearly inexperienced non-professionals, who for the very first time experimented with the participatory opportunities offered to them. Nine films were selected, based on the work of nine groups of youngsters, who received a video training at the *7th Flemish Science Week*[3] (which took place from 23 to 27 October 2006) as a small project of the Institute for Broadband Technology (IBBT), in collaboration with *16plus*, one of the North Belgian public broadcasters' (VRT) online platforms. The format used in these films is fairly similar and based on a collage of interviews on the streets and in shops with a diversity of people. The sound of the films is in many cases rather difficult to understand, and it as least one film the raindrops on the lens of the camera are clearly visible. The films do not always have an introduction, or a clear storyline, and the relationships between the different parts are not always explained. The films allow the viewer to look at the "normal" scenes of everyday life, without adding a layer of aesthetisation or narrative structure, which is more typical for professionally produced media products. Instead we get to see the raw data of the everyday, without much decoration. In this sense, the cameras become little flâneurs that observe (with some distance and detachment) what de Certeau (1984) called the discreteness or the singularities of everyday life.

The case study analysis is based on a combination of interviews with media professionals,[4] and a qualitative content analysis of the nine films and 15 focus group discussions. These 15 focus group discussions[5] were organised at the end of 2007 and analysed also using discourse-theoretical analysis.[6] In each of the focus groups, two or three of the nine films were screened, and then discussed by a total of 131 respondents. Internal homogeneity was based on educational level and age, while an equal distribution (across the focus groups) on the basis of sex and region was implemented. The following table gives an overview of the four clusters of focus group discussions, where in each of the clusters (except cluster three) four focus groups were organised based on an young/old (Y/O) and lower education/higher education (L/H) matrix.

Table 1: The 16plus Focus Groups

Cluster 1 (FG1-4)	Cluster 2 (FG5-8)	Cluster 3 (FG9-11)	Cluster 4 (FG12-15)
Y/L|Y/H|O/L|O/H	Y/L|Y/H|O/L|O/H	Y/L|Y/H|O/L	Y/L|Y/H|O/L|O/H
Everyday Life in Ghent	Ways of Eating	The Shopping Ladies	The Commandments of Nonsense
Multicultural Ledeberg	Drinking	Colourful Ledeberg	Buttocks in Belgium
The Commandments of Nonsense		Fashion	

The second case study is based on the access TV programme *Barometer*, which was broadcast in 2002 on the TV1 channel of the VRT. *Barometer* is an access TV programme inspired by BBC's *Video Nation*,[7] produced by Kanakna, and broadcast on the TV1 channel of the VRT. There have only been two series as the VRT decided to discontinue the programme at the end of 2002, because of a too small market share (interview Wendel Goossens, VRT's *Barometer* producer). A first series of five episodes was broadcast between April 30, 2002 and May 28, 2002, and a second series of eight episodes between September 5, 2002 and October 22, 2002. Each 20 minute episode of *Barometer* was based on six two and a half to three and half minute "video letters", produced by "ordinary" viewers, but edited by the members of the production team. The programme and the films are introduced by Michiel Hendryckx, a (press) photographer. The topics of these films varied widely, but the programme remained focused on human-interest stories. These stories could consist of a report of an event, a statement or a call for action. Some other stories used an emotional approach, while others were based on pranks. Quite often the films showed the representation of the self, sometimes in relation to other societal groups and to society.

Again a combination of interviews with media professionals,[8] and a qualitative content analysis of Barometer episodes and focus group discussions was used. For the focus groups, a selection (based on thematic diversity) of four episodes from the first series was made. These four episodes were broadcast on April 30, May 7, May 14 and May 28, 2002. 14 focus group discussions were organised, with in total 122 respondents. Similarly as in the *16plus* case, internal homogeneity was based on educational level and age, in combination with an equal distribution (across the focus groups) on the basis of sex and region. Again a discourse-theoretical analysis was used as a methodological tool. The following table gives an overview of the four clusters of focus group discussions, again based on a young/old and lower education/higher education matrix, in combination with the topics of the *Barometer* episode that was screened to them.

Focus Group Critiques on 16plus

The *16plus* focus group respondents argue extensively and continuously why they dislike the nine films, using the concept of the banal in a number of cases. For instance, Yvette (F, 60, H, 16plusFG3[9]) summarises her critique on the interviewing as follows: "*there was actually no single important question. These are all banal things. They are banal things.*" Watching the films sometimes provokes crude reactions, as exemplified by the statement of Alain (M, 52, H, 16plusFG7): "*The main advantage of these films is that they are short.*" Some even doubt the authenticity of the films: "*They are so amateurish. I even got the impression that they did that on purpose, it was so much beyond ... That's my impression*" (Danielle, F, 50, H, 16plusFG7). The negative evaluation of the focus group respondents focus on three components of the films: the level of the content, the reasons for making the films, and (especially) the formal qualities of the nine films.

At the level of the content of the films (focussing on everyday life), the respondents point to the lack of relevance and usefulness. Shari (F, 17, H, 16plusFG2) for instance says: "*yeah, I really don't understand what the use is.*" The lack of relevance is explained by the low educational and informational level of the films that the respondents were screened, as can been seen in the (again ironic) fragment of one of the focus group discussions.

> Hendrik (M, 20, L, 16plusFG1): *It wasn't that educational. I didn't really learn something from it, I think.*
> Jan (M, 17, L, 16plusFG1): *Well, I do know a new joke now.*
> Dries (M, 17, L, 16plusFG1): *Yes, maybe so.*
> Joran (M, 18, L, 16plusFG1): *Which one? I've already forgotten it.*

Similarly, the focus of the films on everyday life provokes comparisons with holiday pictures which firmly positions these films in the realm of the private, and can again considered symptomatic for the perceived low social utility of the films.

Table 2: The *Barometer* Focus Groups

Cluster 1 (FG1-4) Y/L|Y/H|O/L|O/H April 30, 2002	Cluster 2 (FG5-6) Y/L|Y/H May 7, 2002	Cluster 3 (FG7-10) Y/L|Y/H|O/L|O/H May 14, 2002	Cluster 4 (FG11-14) Y/L|Y/H|O/L|O/H May 28, 2002
• Practising firemen • A 16 year old happy mom • A practical joke involving a traffic light • A mucoviscidoses patient receiving a pair of new lungs • A complaint against rack renters• Elderly skydivers	• Ode to the potato • A reaction to the "complaint against rack renters" film • Enjoy life, with measure • 5 generations of women • Physically challenged on horseback • Love in a home for the elderly	• Women in the restaurant and café business • Children playing music with garbage • Baby with slow growing right hand • Farmer has his cow consecrated • A reaction to the "physically challenged on horseback" film .• UFO experiences	• Breast amputation • Clean streets • Women's football • The Lets system • A reaction to the "cutting trees" film • The elderly back to school

The second component for critiquing the films is based on the (perceived) motives attributed to the producers. Here the banality of the films is argued on the basis of the producers being bored and having nothing else to do, or their ambition to make themselves noticed, as is illustrated by Dries (M, 17, L, 16plusFG1): "*These are people that want to be noticed and put something on the internet.*" The killing time argument is used by Anneke (F, 34, H, 16plusFG2), when she says: "*It's difficult to have an opinion about it, because there is really no contribution. There was nothing in it, there was no content. There was ... it was just killing time.*"

The formal quality of the film is the third component that attracts fierce critiques from the respondents. The respondents not only argue that there are no real topics or content, or that the topics are treated in a superficial way. At the same time they formulate a lethal avalanche of formal critiques. The films are described as poorly filmed (with the rain drops on the lens mentioned frequently), the framing and editing are seen as problematic, and the sound quality is poor. In general, there is a lack of aesthetic quality. The respondents also refer to the lack of narrative structure and focus, and to the poor preparation and research of the producers ("*They are just improvising*" (An, F, 23, H, 16plusFG6)). This is strengthened even more by the critiques on the usage of dialects and the slobby clothes of the producers. It brings one of the respondents to the conclusion that they are not even trying: "*But it is apparently not even their ambition to deliver something good, because they are not doing their best*" (Dorien, F, 21, L, 16plusFG1).

On many occasions, the perceived lack of aesthetic, narrative and technical quality is juxtaposed to the quality of professional media productions. Here, media professional act as a constitutive outside which provides the discursive framework to criticise the amateur productions. Max (M, 20, L, 16plusFG10) for instance describes what would be necessary improve the quality of the films: "*Everything* [needs to change]. *The sound and the images ... It needs to be recorded by a decent camera, and the sound should be recorded by a sound engineer, and the editing should be done by an editor. Somebody specialised.*"

Focus Group Discourses that Legitimise *16plus*

Despite the unanimous critiques on the formal and content-related qualities of the nine films, a number of discourses emerge that legitimise the existence of the films. However banal the films are perceived to be, the respondents quickly agree to the democratic right of ordinary producers to create and publish films like these. They also point to the importance of the learning process for the producers, and to the pleasure it generates (for the producers—not necessarily for their audiences). These legitimising discourses again use the professional media as a constitutive outside, but this time critiquing the mainstream media as manipulated and unreal(istic).

The discourses of pedagogics and pleasure are reasonably straightforward legitimisations of the films. On the one hand the respondents refer to the learning process and the ability of the producers to improve their skills (as part of a learning-by-doing process, or through the feedback they receive). As Fabio (M, 26, H, 16plusFG6) puts it: "*Who knows, they might put together a perfect one and a half hour film in 10 years time.*" The respondents also speculate about the possibility of these films being the result of a school assignment, and a more institutionalised learning process. Interestingly, some of the older focus group respondents refer to their own learning process as "film amateurs" (using 8 millimetre cameras). On the other hand, the respondents point to the pleasure that the producers derive from making these films, and the ability of the producers to be creative. Jos (M, 49, H, 16plusFG7) formulates this as follows: "*The question also is whether we should always strive for the high arts ... My first impression also was: they are just messing about, but these people have actually been quite creative. They weren't just consuming, they were having fun.*" Another element of this discourse is the pleasure generated by showing these films to your own social networks.

The respondents also refer to a discourse of democracy, freedom and empowerment to legitimise the existence of these films. The producers are deemed to be free to exert their democratic right to publish the material, and an infringement on that right is often immediately depicted as censorship and rejected. The democratic rights discourse is combined with an emphasis on ordinary people, as these films are seen as ways to provide media access to ordinary people for both the youngsters who produced the films, as for the people who featured in them. Despite the debates caused by the complexities of the concept "ordinary people" the respondents point to the authenticity and spontaneity of the films, which in turn is seen as a way to "really" represent reality. The access of ordinary people to the media then becomes a privileged way to achieve a realist portrayal of everyday life, as is summarised by Jos (M, 49, H, 16plusFG7): "*but I also think that ... at the beginning it looks like nothing, but now, by talking and thinking about it ... it is a very realist image.*"

The discourses of pedagogics, pleasure and democracy are complemented by a fourth discourse that legitimises the existence of these films by reverting to the outside identity of media professionals and mainstream media organisations. In contrast to the professional quality argument discussed above (which discredits amateur producers), the discourse of professionalisation is a critique launched at media professionals and mainstream media organisations, through which the nine films gain importance and legitimacy. The nine films are not only deemed different but also more real and authentic because they are subjective (whilst professional journalists are seen as having to be neutral), because the ordinary people featured in the films gain unmediated access, without "*being put words in their mouths*" by "*professional journalists*" (Tiny, F, 83, L, 16plusFG11), and because they are not part of a commercialised media system focused on the spectacular, which is fiercely critiqued in the focus groups. Through these differences, the authenticity and realism of the non-professional films becomes valued. In the professional media system, ordinary people are seen as victims of media professionals: "*Even if they show ordinary people in the media, on television, they can do with them what they want to*" (Muriel, 17, F, L, 16plusFG5).

Focus Group Critiques on Barometer

In contrast to the reception focus groups of *16plus*, the *Barometer* respondents put in their critiques less emphasis on the quality problems and on the problems related to the motives of the makers. Although the respondents express their appreciation for the programme, there is little enthusiasm to be found for *Barometer*, as the relevance of the programme is repeatedly questioned. Respondents take a neutral or indifferent stance towards *Barometer*, or claim in other cases that it is a useless, silly, light-weight and insignificant programme. Stijn (M, 21, BaroFG6) for instance describes the *Barometer* participants as "*very subjective, very small people that … have something to tell. And it isn't extremely convincing.*" Other participants refer to the lack of informational and educational value, as for instance in the following fragment:

> Jesse (M, 23, H, BaroFG8): *The educational value wasn't that high, I think.*
>
> Menno (M, 19, H, BaroFG8): *I think there have been worse programmes on television.*
>
> Jesse (M, 23, H, BaroFG8): *Yes, that's true, yes, yes.*
>
> Kristel (V, 24, H, BaroFG8): *[Programmes] that really make them look ridiculous.*
>
> Jesse (M, 23, H, BaroFG8): *They keep their dignity somehow …*

In their evaluation of *Barometer*, the focus group respondents often refer to the genre of human-interest in general and to a number of specific North Belgian human-interest programmes. There is almost complete unanimity that *Barometer* belongs to the human-interest genre cluster, because of its focus on everyday life stories, on personal and individual experiences, and on emotions, and because of its positive approach of the social. Although the authenticity of the ordinary participants is seen as the main strength of the programme (see below), the lack of relevance critique on *Barometer* becomes intertwined with the similar but more general critique on human-interest. Ria (F, 55, H, BaroFG10) for instance remarks: "*But if they are going to film somebody of us (ordinary people), than nobody is going to watch it. That is too boring, that is too monotonous.*" A few seconds later, Monique (F, 52, H, BaroFG10) continues: "*That is something we're experiencing on a daily basis, we don't need to get to see that on television.*" In another focus group, we'll find a similar example:

> The idea that "everybody has to appear on television, and everybody has something that is of interest to them and you should be able to share that with the world" … I absolutely disagree. I shouldn't bother people with what I am doing. That isn't interesting for other people. And that is also the case the other way around [laughs]. (*Greet, F, 21, H, BaroFG6*)

The critique on the lack of relevance of the mediated representation of everyday life is strengthened by the perceived need to have a stronger professional intervention, in order to contextualise the personal experiences and narrations provided by the *Barometer* participants. The strong presence of the lack of relevance critique in the focus groups does not imply that the critiques on the motivation of the *Barometer* participants are not mentioned in the focus group discussions. But they again interlock with the lack of relevance critique, as the focus group respondents detach themselves from the *Barometer* participants and from the potential audience members that might be interested (in contrast to the focus group respondents). This process of detachment first of all consists of emphasising that the films produced by the *Barometer* participants are mainly relevant for the makers themselves, as it allows them to get on television, to have their voices heard, to express themselves, to tell their stories, but also to get something off their chest, to voice their frustration or desperation, and to call for attention or for help. This distancing from the participants is further strengthened by their articulation as strange, abnormal or marginal -or through a more spatial logics- as rural. The second way focus group respondents disconnect themselves from the audience of *Barometer* is by pointing to the existence of audiences that might *be* interested in the programme, because they (but not the focus group respondents) can identify with the people on the programme or with the situation in which they find themselves, or because it might help or inspire them.

Finally, the focus group respondents also use a critical discourse on the quality of the produced material. But as indicated before, the respondents are much less critical than was the case with the *16plus* films. In the *Barometer* focus groups the participants are repeatedly positioned as amateurs, but at the same time the focus groups respondents explain that they do not mind that much, because the technical problems (like an instable camera) are not considered dominant and are not deemed to structurally affect the content. As one focus group respondent puts it, the technical problems gave the *Barometer* films their "charm":

> Siska (V, 47, H, BaroFG14): *It's absolutely not bad for amateurs.*
> Moderator: *And what does make this a good film, and what makes it bad?*
> Valérie (V, 37, H, BaroFG8): *They managed to communicate their message, eventually. If though it wasn't professionally recorded, they still managed to show what they were engaged in and what they wanted to tell. If they succeeded in doing that, then the film was successful too.*
> Siska (V, 47, H, BaroFG14): *It wasn't good technically speaking, but maybe this was the charm of it ...*

Also the juxtaposition with media professionals persists, as respondents repeatedly explain that a more intense involvement of professionals would improve the technical quality of the films. For instance TJ (M, 20, L, BaroFG11) puts it as follows: "*Your camera perspective will always be better if you have a professional crew doing it.*" However dominant and taken-for-granted these professional aesthetic and technical quality criteria are in the focus groups, the respondents accept the more amateurish films and express the need to avoid a too strong professional interference in the production process of the films. Even the presence of the host is often extensively debated, and the editing and selection of the *Barometer* video films is frequently regretted (but still deemed necessary).

Focus Group Discourses that Legitimise Barometer

In the case of the reception of *Barometer*, the programme becomes mainly legitimised through its capacity to offer a forum or a podium to ordinary people to narrate and represent their personal stories, opinions and experiences. This "*very early form of User Generated Content*" (Ellen, V, 21, H, BaroFG6) as one participant called it, is linked to "*the democratisation of television*" (Bert, V, 21, H, BaroFG6), where "*it is no longer the large production companies or casting firms that decide who gets on (television). Everybody can have a go, John Doe. But I think that this is still more interesting for people who have the urge to say something.*" This discourse is combined with a (communication) rights discourse that emphasises the right of ordinary people to communicate and represent themselves on television, and which values their presence in one of the key public spaces. Their presence is also articulated as authentic: Despite some remarks about the nervousness and over-preparation, the respondents consider them natural, spontaneous, real and honest.

This also explains why the respondents are sceptical towards the idea of adding experts to the programme, as this would alter the power balance of the programme, and potentially create a situation that is "*patronizing if you would have an expert look over their shoulders.*" (Luc, M, 54, L, BaroFG6) But it is mainly the media professionals and the mainstream media system that become (like in *16plus*) a constitutive outside. The work of the participants is defined as authentic and spontaneous because the intervention of media professionals remains limited. Moreover, media professionals are articulated as restrictive towards the democratic capacity of the media, partially because of their media-centeredness. Pascal (M, 49, H, BaroFG14) provides us with this critical analysis: "*Television is and remains organised deceit. And you should take into account that if that make a programme it is of course with just one intention, and that is to make sure that people are sitting in front of the TV and that they have their ratings.*" This generates an interesting paradox, where the mainstream media are seen to offer a poor perspective on reality and are deemed manipulative, but they are accepted because they master the aesthetic and narrative professional standards. On the other hand, the "amateur" films have only limited aesthetic and narrative qualities, but offer a more realist and authentic perspective on everyday life.

The discussions on the motives of the makers and the discourse of pleasure are in the focus groups very much embedded in the democracy and rights discourse. Although the focus group respondents remain largely indifferent about the produced content, and the lack of relevance critique remains—"*Everybody has the right to be on television. But I would to keep it for more useful things.*" (Isabel, V, 16, L, BaroFG1), they do recognise the communicational need (and rights) that motivated the makers to participate in the production of *Barometer*, the authenticity it generates and the pleasure that arises from being part of these participatory practices. Also the audience becomes articulated within this discourse, as the symbolic power of these self-representations is valued,[10] following a line of argument which is characteristic for the evaluation of the democratic capacity of human-interest programming. As Sarah (V, 25, H, BaroFG6) puts it: "*Simply the ordinary person that gets to see ordinary people on television, instead of news about—I don't know- whatever has happened.*"

At the same time, the respondents do recognize the limits of the participatory practices, especially when referring to the media professionals' interventions at the level of selection and editing. As the host of *Barometer* explicitly mentions in his introduction that he has selected the contributions that were actually broadcast in the programme, the respondents identify this as one of the major interventions of the production team. In some cases the respondents refer to censorship, in other cases the respondents talk about the consequences for those who were not selected.

The second professional intervention that is discussed is the editing. Here things are much less clear, as the respondents have little factual information about the production practices of the production team. This results in much speculation, where some respondents express their belief that it is "*100% uncut*" (Jan, M, 24, L, BaroFG7), others talk about "*minimal editing*" (Hugo, M, 24, L, BaroFG5) and yet others frame it as manipulation: "*So it is manipulated a bit by the television (professionals)*". Although this is not problematised by the respondents, they do regret that the participants lose control over the end product, and that the participatory process is limited.

In some cases the respondents distrust the (professional) production team and take their speculation (without being invited by the moderators) to another level. During one conversation, the respondents discuss the possibility that the production team assists during the filming [because it is "*too organised*" (Carl, M, 24, L, BaroFG7)] or prepares the shoot beforehand.

> Koen (M, 27, H, BaroFG6): *I think that they visit the participants beforehand.*
> Kristel (V, 24, H, BaroFG6): *Yes, they first discuss it, I think so.*
> Koen (M, 27, H, BaroFG6): *Giving them guidelines, "do this, do that, …"*

In one other conversation the respondents discuss the possibility that the production team did not wait for the videotapes to come in, but actively recruited participants. In this discussion, one of the respondents (Tim, M, 25, L, BaroFG6) states that it might all be "*fake*", as he "*can't imagine that an elderly couple says, hey, let's make a movie when we are going to our mobile phone class.*" He later adds that *Barometer* "*makes it appear that these people have send in the names on their own initiative*", to which another respondent replies: "*Nothing gets on television by somebody's own initiative.*" (Phille, M, 21, L, BaroFG6) Regretfully, the interviews with the *Barometer* media professional showed that these critical voices were quite accurate. The media professionals intervened in order to plan and structure the actual filming, to select and edit the "raw" material (excluding the host from playing a role in this (part of the) process), but also to scout for participants,[11] even if the host explicitly said in his introductions of the programmes that he selected the films, and that the participants had reacted to his call to send their material to the VRT.

Conclusion

Participation is a concept which is often deemed socially and politically beneficial, although we often see the preference for more gentle, minimalist, on interactiveness-based participatory practices, which black box the core of the power relations of the social systems that might be organising or facilitating these participatory practices. Many social systems remain sealed off from the more radical versions of participation, where an equal division of power is strived for. Given this socio-political constellation and societal organisation, it might come a bit as a surprise to see how negative the focus group respondents react to the two case studies which do offer (at least at first sight) these more intense and maximalist forms of participation. There is one complication: At the theoretical level, the respondents do express their appreciation for the participatory practices they get to see, and frame these practices on the online forum and on television in a discourse on democracy, freedom and empowerment. They strongly feel that "ordinary people" have the right to perform online and on television, and that the access to these realms of representation should not be reserved to media professionals and elite members. They moreover repeatedly criticise the mainstream media system on a diversity of levels, as for instance its ways of representing our realities, the abuse of the power it is claimed to have, the abuse of (ordinary) people that are involved, and the media-centeredness and commodified nature of its objectives.

However, this does not imply that the focus group respondents can be considered enthusiast fans of the two programmes they get to see. The participatory nature of the production process (and its outcome) may be theoretically applauded in the focus groups, but the actual materialisations are met with fierce critiques or with indifference. In the case of *16plus*, the use of the "new" online technology does not protect the films from being severely critiqued. Especially the perceived lack of aesthetic, narrative and technical quality forms the basis of a series of harsh critiques that almost completely discredit the films. In the case of *Barometer*, the televised programme, the respondents are less harsh in their critiques, but they still fail to see the social relevance of what is being screened to them, and remain indifferent and disconnected. They do accept the personal relevance for the makers, but consider that to be insufficient to legitimise distribution on prime-time public television.

The reactions of the focus group respondents show that mediated participation is not enough for a programme to be positively valued. In order to be appreciated, there are a number of necessary conditions that have to be met. The (rather extreme) case of *16plus* shows that the basic conventions about aesthetic, narrative and technical quality, as defined by the professionalised mainstream media system are deeply rooted within the taste cultures of these (North Belgian) audience members, and that a radical (almost avant-garde) rejection of these conventions is considered unacceptable. The *Barometer* case exemplifies at the same time that these quality conventions are not that rigid, and that there is some space for "amateurs" to diverge from these quality conventions. But more importantly, the *Barometer* case also shows us (together with the *16plus* case) that the respondents use social relevance as a key principle for evaluating media output. They critique *Barometer* for falling into the human-interest trap of privileging the private and the personal without transcending it. Both case studies show that the respondents experience a strong need for media to be magical, to use (aesthetic, narrative and technical) languages that are exceptional, and to narrate stories which are socially relevant. Just showing everyday life, or just organising participation, is simply not enough.

NOTES

1. In order to do history not too much injustice: Samuel Beckett wrote these often quoted words in relationship to the impossibility of art, and not in relationship to democracy.
2. Again, there are exceptions. See for instance Mody's (1991) work on participatory research methodologies.
3. http://www.vlaamsewetenschapsweek.be/
4. These interviews were with Filip Fastenaekels (new media team VRT and *16plus*), Lode Nachtergaele (IBBT collaborator *16plus*) and Tine Deboosere (VRT moderator *16plus*). All interview and programme citations are translations from Dutch by the author.
5. A 16th focus group discussion was not used in the analysis because of quality problems.
6. Discourse-theoretical analysis (DTA—see Carpentier & De Cleen (2007)) builds on a combination between Laclau and Mouffe's (1985) discourse theory and critical discourse analysis. Methodologically speaking, it is based on the general principles and methods of qualitative research (Wester, 1987), but uses the discourse theoretical and critical discourse analytical instruments as sensitising concepts.
7. http://www.bbc.co.uk/videonation/history/. See also Carpentier (2003).
8. Interviews were held with Michiel Hendryckx (Presenter *Barometer*), Isabel Dierckx (Kanakna *Barometer* Producer), Wendel Goossens (VRT Producer *Barometer*), Noel Swinnen (Manager Kanakna), Frank Symoens (Production Manager TV1 VRT), Jean-Philip De Tender (Channel Adviser TV1 VRT), Eva Willems and Joke Blommaerts (*Barometer* researchers).
9. The first three codes refer to the sex (Female/Male), age and educational level (High/Low) of the focus group respondents. The 16plusFG or BarometerFG code refers to the number of the focus group.
10. In this context, also the discourse of pedagogics is used, but (in contrast to the 16plus case) only for referring to the opportunity for the audience to learn from these self-representations.
11. Not only did the host of the programme explain uneasiness with the situation he was (unknowingly) placed in, but in a 2008 *Facebook* exchange, also Isabel Dierckx (*Barometer* Kanakna producer) confirmed that there were four researchers involved. In subsequent interviews, Joke Blommaert and Eva Willems then confirmed the role they played in scouting for potential participants.

13

Encapsulating a Freirean Logic of Empowerment

Examining the Sonagachi Project, a community-oriented peer outreach initiative among sex workers in Calcutta, India

Satarupa Dasgupta

The *Sonagachi Project* is a HIV/AIDS intervention program undertaken in a red light district of Calcutta, India. The initiative is referred to as the *Sonagachi Project*, owing to its origin and location in the district by the same name. The project in question started in 1991 to ascertain and arrest the incidence of sexually transmitted diseases (STDs) and HIV/AIDS among sex workers in and around the *Sonagachi* district in Calcutta (Jana, Basu, Rotheram-Borus, & Newman, 2004). The project was funded by a national healthcare research institute and later by the state-based West Bengal AIDS prevention council (Jana et al., 2004). The said project was initiated by a group that comprised a local physician, an Ethiopian public health worker, and healthcare and social service professionals of Calcutta. But later, the project was spearheaded by he sex workers themselves who acted as peer outreach workers (Jana et al., 2004). The *Sonagachi Project* is still going on in Calcutta as a peer outreach and participation based program, under the guidance of the sex workers. Statistics from UNAIDS and NACO show a significant drop in the incidence of HIV infection and a significant increase in condom usage in Sonagachi after the project was implemented. The original aim of the project was to disseminate awareness information about STDs and HIV/AIDS among sex workers, and arrest the infection incidence among the latter population. However in addition to the targeted outcomes project achieved outcomes like unionization of the sex workers and establishing micro-credit societies and vocational training centers for the sex workers (Jana, Banerjee, Saha & Dutta, 1999).

Health intervention projects among sex workers in red light areas usually entail dissemination of health services, promotion of condom adoption and emphasis on individual behavior adjustments. Recent World Health Organization guidelines indicate that in order to achieve success HIV/AIDS intervention project among sex workers "must also aim for increased sex worker involvement and control over working and social conditions" (WHO guidelines, 2005, p.7) "Peer education community mobilization and 'structural interventions' are proposed as potential program strategies to be adopted by community-based projects in which sex workers' participation is promoted as a central feature. The evidence for this approach comes from a rather small group of 'successful' projects" (Evans & Lambert, 200, p. 468). An example of such a successful project is the *Sonagachi* STD/HIV Prevention Project in Kolkata, India. Implementing community mobilization through peer outreach techniques the *Sonagachi* Project is an instance of an initiative that is noted to incorporate "best practice" methods in accordance to UNAIDS guidelines of 2002 (Jana et al., 2004).

This chapter analyzes the strategies of the peer outreach model of the *Sonagachi Project* from a Freirean perspective. Paulo Freire, an educationist, postulates a vision of emancipating marginalized groups from socio-economic and political mechanisms of oppression, and facilitating agency among disenfranchised populations. Such empowerment of marginalized groups is visualized by Freire through education and communicative action. Freire rearticulates the scope and function of education by foreseeing an interchangeable role among educators and their adult pupils. Such education—which takes the form of mutual interaction among knowledge seekers and propagators—entails the dissemination of information on collective rights and discerning the sources of oppression (Freire, 1970). Such a process of knowledge dissemination is postulated by Freire as an effective mechanism of questioning and subverting institutionalized authoritarian structures (Freire, 1970). Freire also emphasizes the importance of involvement of the marginalized groups themselves in the process of education and empowerment. The objective of the current paper is to explore the methodology adopted by the *Sonagachi Project* in accordance to Freirean logic of empowerment and emancipation. The paper tries to analyze whether the participation oriented development action undertaken by the *Sonagachi Project* conforms to the Freirean paradigm. The paper also discusses whether Freire's notion of critical pedagogy and transformative social action is reflected in the peer outreach program undertaken by the *Sonagachi Project*. The project's strategy of negotiating with the stake-holders is also examined in context of Friere's idea of problematization of restrictive social order and stigmatization of the marginalized. Finally, the paper explores the attributes of empowerment communication in a Freirean context and whether the *Sonagachi Project* conforms to the variety of empowerment communication.

Discussion

Paulo Friere, a Brazilian born educationist is internationally acclaimed for his ideas on adult education and empowerment. Freire conceptualized the notion of critical pedagogy, "a term associated with teaching strategies sensitive to the effects of relation based on race, class, gender, ethnicity, and so forth on learning and consciousness formation" (Morrow & Torres, 2002, p.1). Freire offers a vision of bypassing oppressive structures and facilitating social and political engagement among disenfranchized groups. Are the postulations of Freire relevant for the analysis of the intervention process executed by the *Sonagachi Project*? Before examining the *Sonagachi Project* in Freirean terms I would like to analyze the notion of participation in context of development communication. It needs to be examined how the idea of participation evolves from the Freirean paradigm and whether participation based development communication forms the framework of the *Sonagachi Project*.

Development communication is noted to be a client-oriented strategy, contributing a powerful set of tools for the success of development initiatives. (Michelle & Chaman-Ruiz, 2003, p. 1). The participatory approach in development communication emphasizes community, interpersonal interaction, and understanding based on mutual regard. The concept of participation is noted to generate a discourse that "evolves from people serving as a mirror of their aspirations and needs rather than being imposed upon by others. It allows people to become subject of their own development and not simply objects of technology or processes" (Thomas, 1994, p. 475). Development communication program based on participation has to possess a comprehensive understanding of the needs and perspectives of the client/target population (Michelle & Chaman-Ruiz, 2003). While participation based communication programs can be aimed at the individual for social or behavior change, the collective involvement of a community for facilitating health and welfare is also quite common.

As Figueroa et al. (2002) observe, "there is a wide-spread belief in the field of development communication, that community participation is a valuable end in itself as well as means to a better life" (p. iii). The basic tenets of participation entail the generation of unhindered dialogue and active social engagement; also "it requires that individuals have a voice in the decisions that affect them" (Stiglitz, 2002, p. 165). Importantly, such participation based development action finds their theoretical assumptions corroborated by Frerian postulates. Freire emphasizes dialogue as the means of empowering disenfranchized groups—as Morrow and Torres (2002) note, the general principle of Freirean pedagogy lies in underlying "subject-subject dialogue" (p. 130). Such interpersonal dialogue among the teacher and student is noted to be one of the means of disseminating knowledge, precipitating active social involvement and participatory action, thereby effectuating the dissolution of oppressive and restrictive power structures.

Now let us look at the *Sonagachi Project*. The latter involves participation based communication intervention that was undertaken at three concurrent levels—community, group and individual. At the community level, the STDs and HIV/AIDS incidence was defined as a problem for the entire local community and its mitigation was articulated as the responsibility of all members. At the group intervention level, the sex workers were mobilized as peer outreach workers. The latter were given requisite training to serve as sources of preventive health information and knowledge of safe sexual practices among their colleagues. At the individual level, the intervention entailed the empowerment of the individual sex worker in multiple ways. For instance, "outreach workers served as models for their sex worker peers that it was possible to gain literacy, respect, employment, and self-confidence" (Jana et al., 2004, p. 410).

One of the characteristics of the *Sonagachi Project* was that the target population i.e. the sex workers were not considered to be passive recipients of information lacking in choice or agency, but instead they were treated as change agents themselves. (Jana et al., 1999, & Blankenship, Friedman, Dworkin and Mantell, 2006). As noted previously, the peer education program generated by the *Sonagachi Project* succeeded in achieving outcomes beyond its immediate objectives of controlling transmission of HIV/AIDS and STDs. The community outreach programs brought sex workers together and facilitated sense of camaraderie among the latter. Training of the sex workers by the program management as outreach workers, and subsequent dialogue within the sex workers themselves, helped in decreasing the perceived powerlessness of a heavily marginalized community (Bandopadhyay, Ray, Banerjee, Jana, Saha, Kerrigan, & Mahendra, 2002). Such action undertaken by the sex workers themselves can be said to in concurrence with Friere's observation that "the oppressed must intervene critically in the situation which surrounds them and whose mark they bear...while conviction of the necessity of the struggle is indispensible to the leadership, it is also necessary for the oppressed" (Freire, 1970, p. 54).

Importantly, Freire does not emphasize mass media for achieving effective communication but focused on interpersonal interaction in a revitalized public sphere. The *Sonagachi Project* also did not utilize the mass media tools but rather focused on "face-to face interactivity" that Freire considered at the center of a communication process (Downing, 2001, p. 834). The dialogue initiated by the sex workers with their peers effectively helped in disseminating awareness information about sexually transmitted diseases and safe sex behavior. Also it increased social participation by resulting in the formation of a sex workers' self-governed organization that looked after the needs and rights of its members. Perhaps the guiding principles of the *Sonagachi Project* can find a resonance in Freire's idea of a humanizing pedagogy "in which the leadership establishes a permanent relationship of dialogue with the oppressed..the method ceases to be an instrument by which the teachers can manipulate the students, because it expresses the consciousness of the students themselves" (Freire, 1970, pp. 55-56). Such a case as the *Sonagachi Project* in which the mantle of leadership is assumed by the oppressed themselves can propose a unique case-study especially when analyzed in context of Freirean ideology of emancipation and empowerment.

Notions of Critical Pedagogy and Transformative Social Action in the Sonagachi Project

Freire's notion of a critical pedagogy lies at the heart of his notion of empowering marginalized groups. The critical pedagogy intends to "facilitate a transition from a 'magical consciousness' to 'critical consciousness' ... such facilitation requires three components: a critical and dialogical method, a changed curriculum content, and specific techniques to 'codify' and 'decodify' messages" (Morrow & Torres, 2002, pp. 120-121). Magical consciousness encapsulates the internalized code of dominance and submission that perpetuates the marginalization of subordinated groups, whereas critical consciousness refers to the awareness that questions the asymmetrical power equations. This is achieved through an active and empathetic process of dialogue and by revitalizing traditional learning systems. Codification is intended to "stimulate people 'submerged' in the culture of silence to 'emerge' as conscious makers of their own 'culture' " (Freire, 1970, p.11). Decodification is "signified by a 'culture circle' under the self-effacing stimulus of a coordinator who is no 'teacher' in the conventional sense, but who has become educator-educatee—in dialogue with educate—educators too often treated by formal educators as passive recipients of knowledge" (Freire, 1970, p 11). Thus the process of critical pedagogy as propounded by Freire not only involves the stimulation of a critical awareness that questions he established statusquo but facilitates the process of transformation of the traditional learning process by generating participatory social action.

Can Freirean notion of a critical pedagogy have relevance for the methodology adopted by the *Sonagachi project*? Did the project undertake measures to change the internalized code of marginalization of the sex workers? As discussed earlier the project facilitated an active process of dialogue among sex workers. But did such a dialogic method revitalize traditional means of dissemination of knowledge and redefine functional roles of teachers and students? These questions may be answered if we look at some of the strategies adopted by the *Sonagachi project*.

It appears that one of the vital strategies of the *Sonagachi project* was the definition of a common problem at the community, group and individual level. The identification of such a common problem was done to facilitate the process of community dialogue and collective action. This in turn was intended to accelerate the dissemination of awareness and collective rights information among the sex workers. As Jana et al. (1999) note, efforts were made to identify and appreciate a broad array of issues that determine the priorities of the sex workers and to localize these issues in their general environment. "Whatever the objective of the program may be, it has to take into account and build on what the targeted community perceives as their immediate and urgent needs" (Jana et al., 1999, p. 3). In case of the *Sonagachi Project*, adoption of condom usage and safe sexual practices were not the initial priority of the sex workers. Rather obtaining healthcare facilities for themselves and for their children were noted to receive greater attention. The *Sonagachi Project* sought to prioritize meeting the personal needs of the sex workers instead of gearing the campaign towards an occupational health initiative. Such an approach conforms to the client-oriented strategies of participation based communication techniques. It also conforms to Freirean postulation of a political identity of the subjugated themselves. The negotiation of the priorities of the marginalized population through a dialogic process facilitates the struggle against agents of disempowerment. Such a perception of common needs can facilitate a collective way among the marginalized "to seek out true avenues of communion with them, ways of helping the people to help themselves to critically perceive the reality which oppresses them" (Freire, 1970, p. 166).

One of the important aspects of the *Sonagachi Project* was its initiative of re-articulation of issues related to sex work—including the status of sex work itself—and stressing the right of sex workers to avail material resources and opportunities. Jana et al. (1999) emphasize that there was no endeavor to rehabilitate the sex workers, rather the latter "were accepted for what they were" (p. 2). Sex work was reconceived as a valid form of employment and the rights of the sex workers—to demand benefits such as healthcare for themselves and educational opportunities for their children—were emphasized. Can such a process of re-articulation of sex work serve as the means of fostering a critical consciousness that facilitates empowerment from oppressive power structures? It appears to be so in case of the *Sonagachi Project.* As Jana et al. (2004) observe, "by engaging sex workers in roles of power and decision making within the program, a set of principles emerged that assisted in reframing the problem of HIV from an issue of individual motivation, will, or behavioral commitment to a problem of community disenfranchisement" (p. 407). By refusing to generate alternative professions for the sex workers, the project succeeded in creating a respectable status for the target population, besides mitigating the stigmatization of the latter's profession. The project thus created a public space that facilitated community dialogue and public action. This is concurrent with Freirean logic of democratized public domain in which "members of a community take action as a group to solve a common problem ... this leads to..social change that increases the collective capacity to solve new problems" (Figueroa et al., 2002, p. 6).

As noted before, the Freirean notion of dialogue leading to education is a dialogic one in which the "educator learns from the educatees in the same way that the latter learns from her or him, the roles of educator and learner becomes almost interchangeable" (Mayo, 1999, p. 65). In the *Sonagachi Project* the educators and the educatees were the sex workers themselves. Based on a community based peer outreach procedure, the project thrived on the dissemination of knowledge from the outreach worker to her colleagues and the exchange of information among the sex workers. The project offers a unique instance in which the exchange of information among the educators and educatees made their roles mutually interchangeable, as Freire postulates. Importantly, no formal trainers like healthcare providers or teachers were employed to spearhead the project. It appears that in the *Sonagachi Project* the social status of educators and educatees were identical. It has been noted that participation based development communication programs often involve the employment of opinion leaders who mobilize public opinion. These opinion leaders can be public figures such as politicians, media celebrities, religious leaders or civil society representatives (Michelle & Chaman-Ruiz, 2003). Opinion leaders are sought because "societies listen best to their opinion leaders" who "can become a third voice ... this voice is particularly effective if the initiative's key champion has low credibility or if the initiative is not favored by public opinion" (Michelle & Chaman-Ruiz, 2003, p. 22). Interestingly the *Sonagachi Project* did not use public figures as opinion leaders. Rather the sex workers themselves, instead of acting as passive recipients of knowledge from formal information sources, sought to mobilize opinion by peer outreach projects. As Downing (2001) notes,

> Freire's pedagogy can serve as the core philosophy to think through the nature of the activist producer-active audience relationship ... it proposes a democracy of the communication process, once more acknowledging the audience as joint-architects with the media producers, radically unlike the 'they watch it, so we must be giving them what they need' ideology of commercial media (p. 834).

The *Sonagachi Project* may be said to be a relevant example of Freirean notion of critical pedagogy in which the passive and the marginalized facilitate transformative social change through a dialogic process.

Negotiation with stakeholders in Sonagachi: Validating the potential of Freirean notion of collective action against institutionalized oppression?

Freire's notion of problematization of the social hierarchy and marginalization seeks to explain the institutionalized oppression of disadvantaged groups and the maintenance of the statusquo. As Montenegro (2002) elaborates on Freire's postulates,

> Under repressive social conditions such as colonialism or dictatorship, Freire suggests material oppression which denies people opportunities for agency, and symbolic oppression which denies them positive or active definitions of self leads to fatalism. If these forms of oppression are exerted with sufficient force or duration, people may come to consider their hardships as inevitable and unassailable, so that the appropriate response seems to be adaptation rather than resistance (p. 520).

Freire's notion of problematization is a process through which the established unequal social order is questioned and disrupted. As Cornish (2006) notes,

> The social order is problematized when subjects can conceive of alternative social arrangements to those that currently exist. Stigma is problematized when those who are stigmatized do not accept their stigmatized status as the 'way things are' but believe that things could be different, and they may legitimately demand and expect better. According to Freire, such problematization is the condition of transformative collective action" (p. 463)

Does the marginalized population in the *Sonagachi Project* manage to dismantle oppressive structures or dislodge the history of material or symbolic exclusion? One of the key features of the *Sonagachi Project* is the identification of stakeholders within the sex work industry. The latter includes individuals both within and outside the realm of sex work such as landowners of sex workers, pimps, clients, law enforcement agencies and members of political parties. The stake-holders represent powerful groups that have traditionally marginalized, oppressed and stigmatized the sex workers. *Sonagachi Project* tries to emphasize the status of sex work as a labor industry and focuses on the losses of the stakeholders in case of a high incidence of HIV/AIDS infection among the work force. As Jana et al. (1999) observe, such an initiative also help in forming public opinion against harassment of sex workers by powerful agencies such as police and pimps. Such identification and mobilization of stake-holders appear to be a concrete step in countering the forces of material oppression and a materialization of the Freirean notion of "problematization" of stigma and social order.

The *Sonagachi Project* facilitates relationships between the sex workers and the stakeholders; the project frames sex work in a way that it is deemed useful in maintaining the financial interests of the latter. The program is useful to sex workers for a variety of reasons such as reduction of HIV and STD incidence, free healthcare, credit opportunities, vocational training facilities etc. It is useful for the stakeholders by maintaining a viable and healthy workforce (Jana et al., 2004). An integration of the interests of the stakeholders and the target population facilitates an understanding of issues relevant to successful community interventions—this is identified by Michelle and Chaman-Ruiz, and Figueroa et. al, as one of the characteristics for facilitating transformative social action as Freire visualizes.

Freire's pedagogy is based on the notion that asymmetrical power relationships that obstruct free exchange of communication and dissemination of knowledge among disempowered groups. However, as Shor (1992), Long (1995) and Morrow and Torres (2002) note, Freire does not suggest a complete repudiation of authoritarian structures to overcome the latter. Instead, the way to surmount inequality and oppression is to "stimulate doubt, criticism, curiosity, questioning a taste for risk-taking, the adventure of creating"(Freire, 1993, p.50). As Shor (1992) and Morrow & Torres (2002) note, Freire emphasizes almost a reciprocal relationship between authority and freedom. While emphasizing the need to dissipate marginalization and disempowered groups, Freire does not exclude the role of authoritarian groups in shaping a critical pedagogy that aspires to liberate disempowered masses. "Relations of domination and marginality provide the basis of shared existential experience that has a universal dimension" (Morrow & Torres, 2002, p. 130).

Empowerment communication has its theoretical framework based in participation oriented development communication but is specifically geared towards fostering research agendas that facilitate social transformation and justice. As Mefalopulos (2002) observes, communication for development is motivated towards generating participation, dialogue and dissemination of vital knowledge—"Communication can assist development by advocating and adopting models that genuinely require dialogue as a form of collaboration among all stakeholders and that genuinely require sharing knowledge as the best form of mutual education" (Mefalopulos, 2002, p. 836). Such forms of participation oriented communication appear to reflect Freirean ideology of empowerment-oriented research that seeks to mitigate the impact of institutionalized power differentials. In fact, Freire's approach has found application in diverse fields such as "participatory action research, community development, health promotion, social work, and liberation psychology" (Morrow & Torres, 2002, p. 1)

Yet empowerment of the target population often remains a desired but not achieved result in development communication initiatives. Empowerment communication, with its emphasis on power differentials, potentially offers analytical means of addressing structural inequalities in groups that historically have been marginalized. As White (2004) observes, empowerment needs to be based within the universal principles of social justice—"one framework of public responsibility that has broad cultural and political acceptance is the language of human and collective rights" (White, 2004, p. 830). Perhaps the following observation of Mefalopulos offers a description of empowerment communication in the most succinct way—

> Empowerment communication intends to be a step further towards its development that gives control over their own lives to the very people who have traditionally been made passive, or partially active, recipients of those efforts by those in charge of development policies. While still within the boundaries of the current paradigm, empowerment communication also advocates its demolition, basing it on the genuine application of democratic ideals, which should by now pay more attention to the universal human rights regardless of other factors, e.g. nationality, religion and socio-economic status (Mefalopulos, 2002, p. 836).

Sex workers in India are vulnerable to HIV/AIDS infection due to reasons not restricted to unprotected sex alone. Their marginalized position in a social hierarchy results from a combination of factors like gender, class and social stigmatization and ostracization. Their social exclusion compounds their marginalized status and enhances material deprivation. More than often they are rendered powerless to take decisions about their own health and welfare, and hence often do not respond favorably to behavior change intervention techniques (Jana et al., 2004). Consequently, conventional intervention methods, that are aimed towards generating behavior change, may prove to be inadequate towards achieving the desired goal of adoption and implementation of safer sexual practices among the sex workers.

While it can be postulated that the application of empowerment communication may be appropriate among sex workers in India, can the *Sonagachi Project* fall in the ranks of the said variety of communication? Evidently, the *Sonagachi Project* incorporates activities that were not included in the agenda of the initiative originally. The project succeeded in achieving its targeted outcomes i.e. significant increase in condom usage and significant decrease in HIV/AIDS infection incidence. But in addition the project also generated literacy programs directed towards the sex workers and their kin, loan services, microcredit initiatives and provident funds for the sex workers, and finally caused the trade unionization of the sex workers. The *Sonagachi Project* undertook efforts to prevent harassment of sex workers by the police, local anti-social elements and pimps. The project also managed to incorporate the sex workers' children in mainstream schools Out-of-school education and vocational training were also imparted to these children. Hence, the *Sonagachi Project* endeavored to mitigate the stigmatization of targeted women both within and outside the realm of sex work.

In order to effectuate the peer outreach program, the sex workers were also given "on-the-job training and special capacity-building sessions" (Jana et al, 1999, p. 4). Jana et al. (1999) note that such interactive training sessions increased the sex workers' self-confidence and paved the path for initiatives such as forming their own micro-credit society. The said sessions also inspired the sex workers to combine and form an exclusive platform for the sex workers. Referred to as the *Durbar Mohila Samnwaya Committee* (DMSC) the sex workers' collective evolved out of the *Sonagachi Project* and offered them an opportunity to assert their collective voices. "The DMSC furthered in-group recognition among sex workers, and the articulation and demand for their rights as workers" (Jana et al., 2004, p. 411). Importantly DMSC now actively participates in AIDS and sex workers conferences across the world and involves itself in issues pertaining to sex workers internationally (Nath, 2000 & Hogg, Cahn, Katabira, Lange, Samuel, O'Shaughnessy, Vella, Wainberg, & Montaner, 2002).

Evidently the *Sonagachi Project* obtained outcomes that were not anticipated by the project initially. As Jana et al. notes, "even as the *Sonagachi Project* began with a vision of occupational health, it was not foreseen that over the course of a decade the sex workers would become a quasi-trade union" (Jana et al., 2004, p. 411). Additionally the *Sonagachi Project* generated vocational training and financial programs for the sex workers and their kin. It is evident that initiatives like *Sonagachi Project* can ultimately transcend their primary agenda and facilitate greater outcomes. Perhaps it will be right to refer to such a mode of participatory communication and intervention as evidenced by the *Sonagachi Project* as empowerment communication. As Mefalopulos (2002) notes, "participatory communication, and even more, empowerment communication, is not just about decision making in the development context, but it affects every aspect of social, economic and political sphere of life" (p. 836). The *Sonagachi Project* not only impacted the health behavior of the targeted population but facilitated empowerment in the social, cultural, political and economic sectors. Such a mode of empowerment communication as executed by the *Sonagachi Project* appears to encapsulate the essence of Freirean ideology of dissipitating power differentials in a praxis-oriented fashion. Freire's idea of generating agency for the disempowered rests on a democratization process of the latter by facilitating collective transformative action. Empowerment communication—as exemplified by the *Sonagachi Project*—can offer the means of facilitating such transformative communicatory action that democratizes the public and socio-political spheres of heavily marginalized groups like the sex workers of Calcutta.

Conclusion

Freire posits a process of education centering around the concept of praxis, an educational process though which the adult learner is encouraged through critical 'authentic' dialogue, to unveil some of the social contradictions in existence within one's community and beyond ... the process of education that Freire advocates is a democratic one, which also has a collective learning dimension. His is a pedagogy in which the learners' voices are valorized and are engaged with critically throughout the learning process. (Mayo, 1999, p 74).

The *Sonagachi Project* offers one of the unique case-studies that reflect the essence of Freirean notion of empowerment among a heavily marginalized group. The project facilitated a unique process of learning among the sex workers by mobilizing the latter as peer educators. The communicative action undertaken by the peer outreach program of the *Sonagachi Project* embodies Freirean postulates of dialogic action. The project reflects Freire's notions of redefining the roles of the educator and the student. The project strategies also mirror Freire's idea of involving the marginalized in the process of their empowerment and emancipation. An active process of problematization of restrictive social order and stigma—as postulated by Freire—is undertaken in the project.

The *Sonagachi Project* managed to provide social, economic and political agency to the sex workers. By rearticulating the trade of prostitution the project endeavored to de-stigmatize sex work and mitigate social powerlessness of the sex workers. By forming credit societies the project aimed to provide financial self-sufficiency to the sex workers. And by offering the opportunity of forming a union the project facilitated political visibility of the sex workers. Notwithstanding its initial objective of being a health behavior change endeavor, the project started to operate within the framework of public responsibility and the universalist discourse of human rights which encapsulates the essence of Freirean logic of empowerment and emancipation. A future study can further explore such participatory communication frameworks in the light of Habermasian theory of communicative action. The creation of a discursive space by the project for dialogue and collective intervention can be analyzed in context of Habermas' conceptualization of "public sphere" in conjunction with the Freirean notion of democratization of communicative action.

One of the drawbacks of the *Sonagachi Project* is the lack of data verifying the effectiveness of the project. The researchers cite statistics from UNAIDS and NACO which show a significant drop in the incidence of HIV infection and a significant increase in condom usage in *Sonagachi* after the project was implemented. But the researchers themselves admit that no studies were undertaken that specifically measured the efficacy of the *Sonagachi Project*. As the authors emphasize, "A randomized controlled trial has yet to demonstrate the efficacy of the intervention model" (Jana et al., 2004, p. 406). Basu, Jana, Rotheram-Borus, Swedeman, Lee, Newman and Weiss (2004) note that the *Sonagachi Project* was replicated among a group of sex workers in North-Eastern

India. The latter study results show the efficacy of a community based intervention process in increasing safe sex practices and decreasing HIV/AIDS incidence. However the said study does not mention whether the intervention in the North-Eastern India managed to replicate the multiple outcomes of the *Sonagachi Project* that included empowerment of the sex workers within social, political and economic realms. Bandopadhyay et al, (2002) also conducted in-depth focus group interviews that demonstrated the efficacy of the participation based community development approach adopted by the *Sonagachi Project*. Notwithstanding the lack of concrete data ascertaining the effectiveness of the *Sonagachi Project*, one may observe that the unique methodology adopted by the initiative and its multiple outcomes emphasize the importance of a sustainable participation based community intervention program. On a concluding note, the *Sonagachi Project* may be noted to represent the potential of collective action interventions encapsulating Freirean ideology. The project may serve as a relevant case-study for planning sustainable interventions—within the framework of the Freirean model of empowerment and emancipation—among disempowered groups across the world.

14

Internet and Political Communication Dynamics in India

Navneet Anand

In a country which is dubbed as the software powerhouse of the world, it's only logical to assume that a media tool such as Internet will play a significant role in as important an institution as politics. In fact, there has been a quantum shift in the way technology has been adapted into the domain of political communication in India in the new Millennium as compared to 1990s. Political parties, leaders, party activists and voters in urban India have all been re-oriented to a new milieu in which technology including the Internet plays a crucial role.

The political discourses and dissemination in the Indian society, however, still largely remain in the realm of traditional media. But slowly a small group of initiators are pushing the boundaries of mediation leading to the adaptation of new media such as the Internet into political strategy framework. Also the advent of new Millennium which brought about host of changes such as rapid diffusion of technology, emergence of new framework of political strategy and rise of a class of political leaders more alert to compelling global trends, aided in this process.

Though the General Elections of 2004 did not see any critical use of the Internet for propaganda, campaign or influencing political opinions, use of other technologies such as Short Messaging Service did hint at the disposition of stakeholders towards adaptation of technology in political processes. Things have moved at even faster pace in the last five years and Internet has acquired a significant presence in the dynamics of politics, especially in the urban areas.

Today it's not uncommon to find political activists spending some time out of their busy schedule in sending bulk e-mails either to journalists or party officials. They and their leaders are also aware of the infinite amount of information on the Internet and use it whenever they need to dig out tricky information. The trend may largely be urban now but in future with diminution of digital disparities it could replicate in smaller towns and even villages.

Grassroots workers in these areas soon may start looking at Internet favorably, following what psychologists call, demonstration effect.

That's about future. Presently, stunted spread of information infrastructure, low literacy and geographical and gender barriers are among the many access gaps in non-urban areas, preventing masses to get *wired* into political processes. But with a host of new government and private sector initiatives, things are likely to change sooner than we expect. India has a good telecom revolution model to imitate.

Having set the tone, the study argues that while Internet does impact and alter the world-view of the literate urban Indians, including their political attitudes, it has not as yet become a significant tool of the political class in their communication strategy. And even as some tiny initiatives are underway to exploit the potential of the medium, traditional media such as newsstudys and television continue to hold sway and swing political opinions and attitudes.

However, there is no denying the fact that, even though only marginally, but Internet has acquired some of the time earlier consumed by the traditional media. It has apparently induced a small community of early adapters to seek out time from their social and professional engagements for this medium. Another factor that makes the medium important is its effective use in tandem with newspapers and television.

The Internet today is being placed decisively along with conventional media tool in the political communication space—posting of the press release on a party's website or bulk mail of the same are few pointers. The dual usage pattern has given some political communication strategists a distinct edge in articulating their viewpoints as we shall illustrate subsequently.

For the user community, the Internet is becoming a handy tool for cross verification of conflicting political and ideological claims. Other than enlarging their perspectives, Internet is also enabling a process of information empowerment.

The methodology in the study has used a mix of primary and secondary sources of data collection. Other than review of literature in the area, the study has used interviews using structured and unstructured questionnaires, content analysis of newspaper reports, and data published by government and private agencies. The author has also been a participant observer of many relevant processes and this study seeks to draw from such experiences.

The study has been divided into five sections. Section 1 seeks to address the evolution and growth of the Internet in India. It attempts to show how the Internet has been able to democratize information generation and dissemination. It also looks at how Internet has been empowering people in a variety of ways. The growth of this medium and factors which are fuelling this have also been probed. Section 2 looks at the interplay of political communication and the positioning of the Internet in it. It discusses some live examples of how political class is using Internet in articulating their agenda. It also investigates how, even though only marginally, Internet enables changes in attitudes and behaviors of people. Section 3 looks at the causes such as digital disparities and literacy barriers that may actually be impeding the natural growth of Internet as a medium of mass communication. Section 4 sets out the predominance of traditional media in India. It also highlights how the use of the Internet decisively with traditional media has been giving political class and users' groups an edge in their communication paradigm. Section 5 attempts to summarize the main arguments and also look at future.

Internet: The Great Enabler

Internet is a vast network of computers where flow of information is seamless. It contains an infinite amount of information that is often open to access by millions across the globe. Internet has also helped establish a whole new pattern of communication among individuals, institutions and agencies — a pattern that is cheaper, faster, transparent and less intrusive. Internet has thrown open innumerable opportunities for people living in different parts of the globe to connect and communicate with each other giving rise to a variety of new business avenues. India has especially been at the forefront of this IT revolution and according to Nasscom total IT-BPO industry reached USD 71.7 billion accounting for 5.8% of India's GDP.

What does the Internet signify? Among others, the Internet heralds the death of distance. This in fact was the title of an interesting book by F Cairncross of *The Economist* (Cairncross, 1997). Cairncross argued how the modern communication technologies including Internet have given a new dimension to our personal and professional lives. Their impact is felt both at the micro level (interpersonal communication) and macro level (global business).

Others have pointed out the factors that make Internet different from all past media that bring the outside into the home. First, because it is digital it implies that parents, children and outsiders can send, retrieve, transform, and store the material that moves across it. Second, the web's two-way, interactive nature means that members of family and outsiders can respond to one another in a seamless manner. Third, Internet's ability to function through sophisticated computer software and hardware means that people's activities can be tracked, stored and predicted through analysis and projections (Turow et al., 2003).

It's also important to note that Internet transgresses the print and broadcasting models by (1) enabling many-to-many conversations; (2) enabling the simultaneous reception, alteration and redistribution of cultural objects; (3) dislocating communicative action from the posts of the nation, from the territorialized spatial relation of modernity; (4) providing instantaneous global contact; and (5) inserting the modern/later modern subject into a machine apparatus that is networked (Poster, M 1999).

Internet is also seen as an "enabling technology." When its introduction is sensitive to local values and committed to local capacity-building, it offers important opportunities to such as facilitating open dialogue, improve governance, reducing poverty and improving economic opportunities. In other words, access to the Internet can enable people in all kinds of ways (Jhunjhunwala, 2000).

Like in many other societies, in India also, the Internet as a media of communication has helped enlarge knowledge frontiers. For social and scientific researchers, it has provided a ready reference source whereas for many professionals Internet has provided vistas of learning new practices and processes. Today, in many premier Indian universities such as Jawaharlal Nehru University and Annamalai University, professors do not hesitate to ask their research students to "refer" to the Web. The first love of many journalism trainees today is the net and most of the newsrooms have net connections in place. Normally lost in their initial assignments, they take refuge in the net and treat it as a companion that potentially carries an answer to many of their information woes. Many pregnant women in urban India seek answers to many of their anxieties on the Internet. Cyber cafes in Indian cities are full of youngsters who are constantly seeking to knit a web of relationship through the World Wide Web. Doctors, architects and chartered accountants are constantly Googling on the Internet to locate novel reference case. Insurance firms and their agents are relentlessly bombarding "feeler" emails to unknown customers, much like many other small and big businesses. In a nutshell, the web has been weaving a curious net of expectations around people and has been altering their worldviews and behaviors in many ways.

All this has led observers to note that,

> "while the original purpose of the Internet was to facilitate the electronic exchange of research, programming, mail and other information among educators and researchers, it evolved in ways no one planned or expected once the military relinquished Internet development and funding responsibilities to civilians organisations in the early 1980s" (Filder, 1997).

Important scientific data and scholarly thoughts have continued to account for much of the traffic, but it is the relationships among people that have shaped the medium. What has mattered most to Internet users is the free exchange of ideas and discussion of values. Over the years this rather anarchistic network of networks has become a haven for uncensored, free-wheeling discussions on everything from sexual fantasies to religious teachings *(Ibid).*

Such trends have led a group of skeptics to believe that Internet may be an "unreal universe, a soluble tissue of nothingness. While the Internet beckons brightly, seductively flashing an icon of knowledge-as-power, this non-place lures us to surrender our time on earth. A poor substitute it is, this virtual reality where frustration is legion and where—in the holy names of Education and Progress—important aspects of human interactions are relentlessly devalued" (Stoll, 1995).

While the thesis may have its own reasoning and could be subjected to debate, in the Indian context it would be naïve if we start glorifying the glaring psychological deviations that this medium may bring about. India, like many other Asian countries, is as yet very new to this medium. The Internet services in India were launched on August 15, 1995 by Videsh Sanchar Nigam Limited (VSNL) (TRAI, 2006). During the first three years of VSNL operation, the Internet subscriber base grew slowly. By the end of March 1998, it had barely reached 140,000 subscribers. But subsequently, it spread rapidly.

The growth of Internet has also been fuelled by the economics of it. According to an estimate by the Internet and Mobile Association of India (IAMAI), online advertising was likely to hit US $ 49 million in 2006-07, which is a substantial jump from US $ 9 million in 2003-04 and US $ 24 million in 2004-05. Travel portals are today selling an average 3,780 air tickets per day as compared to 22,580 tickets by carriers. *(Business Standard, Sep. 26, 2006).*

The number of Internet users too has been rising rapidly. According to a survey by IAMAI and marketing research group IMRB International, the number of Internet users in India has grown to 37 million in September 2006 up from 33 million in March 2006. (Internet and Mobile Association of India, Mumbai, September 2006). The survey also found that the number of "active users" has risen from 21.1 Million in March 2006 to 25 Million in September 2006. The latest figures for 2010 by Internet World Statistics puts India as the fourth largest country in terms of number of users at 81 million in 2010. "Active User" is an internationally accepted and widely used category to define users who have used the Internet at least one in the last 30 days.

The survey also found that while the youths below 35 led the growth, smaller cities and towns recorded a whopping 142 percent year-on-year growth. In fact 25 percent of all the users belong to the smaller towns. Another survey conducted by US based research and consulting firm *eTForecasts* says that India has emerged as the fourth largest user of the Internet in the world. The firm contended that "The developing countries have room to grow and wireless web usage will account for much of future Internet user growth." *(www.hindustantimes.com, January 10, 2006).* According to RNCOS, an industry intelligence firm, Internet subscribers in India are likely to grow at a CAGR of around 56 percent in 2010-11 to 2013-14.

Such growth has not taken place in a vacuum. It has been supported actively by a host of government initiatives including investments in creating information infrastructure or infostructure. In November 1998, for instance, the Government recognized need for encouraging spread of Internet in the country and opened the sector for provisioning of Internet Services by private operators. Government has approved a scheme for the establishment of State Wide Areas Networks (SWANs) at a total outlay of US$ 745 million over a period of five years. According to the government, these SWANs would extend data connectivity of 2 Mega bits per second up to the block level in all states and Union Territories. *(Ministry of Communications & Information Technology, 2005-06)*

What has been especially noteworthy are the serious reforms being triggered by various state governments. This coupled with a push from the Central government is creating the right environment for the proliferation of Internet infrastructure and subsequently its use.[1] In fact, a southern state, Andhra Pradesh became so proactive in initiating IT reforms that its capital Hyderabad came to be known as Cyberabad.

At the central level the policy and programmes for the Information Technology sector are guided by the Department of Information Technology which falls under the Ministry of Communications & Information Technology of the Government of India. The former minister, 40-year-old Dayanidhi Maran, an economics graduate has attended a prestigious management programme at the Harvard Business School at Boston in USA and has spent a decade managing affairs of his family business in print and television media. On June 24, 2006 Maran declared a Ten Point agenda stating the vision for telecom and IT sectors. Along with an emphasis on telephony network expansion and rural telephony, Maran has also reiterated the need for better broadband coverage. He has laid out a vision which seeks to ensure broadband coverage for all secondary and higher secondary schools by 2007; broadband coverage of all public health care centers by 2007; and broadband coverage for all *Grampanchayats* (village governing units) by 2010. *(dmaran.nic.in/initiative2006.htm).* The plan also seeks to create one lac Community Service Centers spread over 6000 blocks.

The Government of India has also approved a National e-governance Plan to lay the foundation and provide the impetus for long-term growth of e-governance in the country. The plan seeks to create the right governance and institutional mechanisms, set up the core infrastructure and policies and implement a number of Mission Mode Projects (MMPs) at the center, state and integrated service levels to create a citizen-centric and business-centric environment for governance. Some of the MMPs include Income Tax, Pensions, Insurance, Banking, Passport Visa and Immigration, Land Records, Transport, E procurement etc.

A few encouraging trends emerge from the above findings. One, the political class forming core of the government which is at the centrestage of spearheading an IT revolution is receptive to the need of enlarging access of Internet. Especially, in the recent past India has seen emergence of a liberal, global political class which is more in sync with the international trends and are fast embracing newer ideas and values. They also value the contribution such enabling technologies could play in changing world-views of people and in ensuring transparency in governance. Two, given the pace at which technologies such as the Internet are being replicated in a variety of activities is indicative of the fact that in times to come it would find a preeminent positioning in the political domain as well. Three, preceding discussion has also indicated the pace at which people are using the Internet for negotiating a variety of life opportunities including knowledge upgradation. In this backdrop it's only logical to assume that in near future the Internet will become a tenacious guide of people's political choices also.

In a nutshell, this is a critical juncture before a take-off point of the marriage of Internet and political communication.

Internet in Indian Political Communication

The vastness of the country makes the use of the Internet as a tool of political articulation and negotiation quite relevant. India is a huge country with complex political and social networks. Among others, elections in the country manifest the magnitude of effort require to connect to people. In fact, elections in India are events involving political mobilization and organizational complexity on an amazing scale.

According to the Election Commission of India, in the 2004 election to Lok Sabha (lower house of the Indian Parliament) there were 1351 candidates from 6 national parties, 801 candidates from 36 state parties, 898 candidates from officially recognized parties and 2385 independent candidates. A total number of 38,99,48,330 people voted out of total electorate size of 67,14,87,930. The Election Commission employed almost 4 million people to manage the election. In 2009 elections, the number grew further.

Given the large number of people engaged in political process, it's only natural that political class took recourse to all the possible means of communicating with them. While the predominant mode for this has been a mix of traditional media including print and television—latter too is a new import in Indian political communication milieu—recognition of newer technologies is at the heart of the impending sweeping changes. During the 2004 General Elections the use of SMS by the Bhartiya Janata Party (BJP) was much talked about.[2]

At a workshop of Indian Youth Congress workers on Communication Management in July 2006, a spokesperson of the Indian National Congress Jayanthi Natarajan urged young party workers to get Internet savvy and recognize the inherent potential of the medium in establishing contacts with people. The Internet, along with the traditional media of communication, would give workers a dual edge in reaching out to maximum number of people. President of Bhartiya Janata Yuva Morcha, the youth wing of right-wing BJP, Anurag Thakur who is also a Member of Parliament, uses Internet "not only to reach out to large number of party men and women but also common people who are keen on our activities." In a popular Rashtriya Ekta Yatra, a journey through 12 Indian states in early 2011, led by Thakur, there were constant updates on the party's website and his personal Facebook account of the many activities.

Political scientists too have noted the changing communication paradigm of political parties in the new contexts. In the Information Age, writes John K White of the Catholic University political parties aren't what they used to be. At once, the Internet has leveled the playing field, as information becomes instantaneously available to party producers and consumers. Parties are no longer the primary filter of political information. Instead, they are just one provider-among many-of several different types of information that are available on the World Wide Web (White, 2006). As parties adapt to these new conditions, new definitions-replete with new assumptions about their functions-are likely to shape the ongoing debate about their roles and functions in the 21st century. And some have noted that even though the "Internet's collective audience is still relatively small and fragmented compared to the established forms of mainstream media, its potential power to influence opinion makers and young affluent voters has not been overlooked by politicians and special interest groups" (Fidler, 1997).

In the US and UK the Internet as a medium of political articulation and dialogue is growing in popularity and user groups are positively responding to the appeals and arguments sent to them through the net.

In the Indian context also, as argued above, the situation is gradually changing. Today political parties and user groups are both aware of the potential of the medium and are beginning to use it to their advantage, albeit a very small percentage of people. Three of the six national political parties, BJP, INC and Nationalist Congress Party (NCP) have strong presence on the Internet. Their websites bjp.org and aicc.org in carry information about the philosophy and principles on which the parties have been established. True to the Indian tradition of eulogy, the website are eloquent in their depiction of leaders besides carrying a host of information relevant for a wide array of audience—from a casual researcher to someone keen on joining the party to a journalist and even the grassroots political workers.

This democratization of information is quite a shift from earlier days when to find out even the basic relevant details about the parties, one had to spend days. In fact BJP was one of the early movers as far as a web presence is concerned. The workers in the media cell at the party headquarters at New Delhi had initiated the process of incorporation of the Web in their activities way back in 1998. From sending press invites to journalists to sharing major media clippings and their analysis with the state units, the workers used the Internet effectively.[3]

The WWW presence of parties is symptomatic of the realization that an *audience* conducive to the Internet exists, and there is a need to serve it. Randeep Singh Surjewala, a minister in the Haryana Cabinet and a leader of the Congress Party with mass appeal, argues that there is surely a small but significant audience that political workers are increasingly taking notice of. Calling the Internet a wonderful medium of communication and political articulation, Surjewala also informs how his government in Haryana has been making sincere efforts to ensure the best possible use of the Internet. "Thirty nine out of 90 legislators in Haryana assembly are Internet savvy and we are also suggesting all our bureaucrats to become Internet proficient to better serve our people," says Surjewala, minister in-charge of Transport, Public Health and Parliamentary Affairs. The young minister is also aware of the great leveling effect created by the Internet. "It's not only a powerful political tool not only for dissemination of information but also of enlightenment of people," he said while adding that he filters a great deal of information from the Internet for his personal and political use (Personal Communication).

Another political outfit, the Indian Youth Congress (IYC) too is using the Internet on a reasonably larger scale along with newsstudy and television media.

Ashok Tanwar, former President of the outfit and now a Member of Parliament, who holds a doctoral degree from New Delhi's prestigious Jawaharlal Nehru University (JNU), attempted to keep in touch with all his state units through an email. One of the reasons for the large-scale use of Internet, both internally and externally, have been the profile of both the leaders and their target groups or even the cadres[4] (Personal Communication). They are all young and more predisposed to modern values and technologies. In fact in Delhi the outfit and its students' wing the National Students Union of India (NSUI) used the medium of the Internet to connect with the potential voters during the Delhi University students' union elections in September 2006.

The significant point to note here is the profile of the users' group. Most of the students enrolled in over 80 colleges of Delhi University who constitute the major vote bank are people who belong to the well-off socio-economic strata of the society. For a majority access to the net is not a major problem. They would access either at home or are found to be frequenting cyber cafes to check their e-mails or chat. In the process they are likely to get exposed to the political messages and ideas as well.

Problems of Access and Bias

This observation brings us to the critical question of access to those in the far flung areas. In India, access is still a problem and most of the Internet users are confined to large parts of urban areas. Rural areas which still comprise large parts of the country have access gaps not only in terms of infrastructure but also literacy and this becomes a major hurdle in filtering of political information through the Internet. Though the Government of India has been making efforts to bridge the disparities by addressing issue of infrastructure, the problem is a complex one and requires an integrated approach.

Based on his studies in India, Brazil and US, Mark Warschauer argues that promotion of ICT and literacy access requires an integrated effort at enabling (1) Physical resources, (2) Digital resources, (3) Human resources, and (4) Social resources. (Warschauer, 2005). Physical resources encompass access to computers and telecommunication connections. Digital resources refer to digital material that is made available online. Human resources revolve around issues such as literacy and education (including the particular types of literacy practices that are required for computer use and online communication). Social resources refer to the community, institutional and societal structures that support access to ICT.

Both the government and the political class, say experts, do not as yet take such a comprehensive view of this issue. Primarily for the political class, it's argued, the Internet may not seem to be yielding any direct results, at least anything that they could perceive of. This results in a lukewarm response to the idea of the Internet as a tool of articulation of political ideas especially vis-à-vis people in the rural areas[5] (Sahay, 2006).

Little surprise then that out of the six national political parties, only three have a web presence whereas majority of the 40 odd regional parties have not as yet felt the need for a presence on the net barring few of their media cell office bearers carrying a Gmail or Hotmail e-mail account. Even the BJP which was an early mover in using the Internet has its website only in English language limiting its use for many of its own party workers at the grassroots levels.

Even some state agencies such as the Election Commission of India, it seems, have not as yet taken note of the potential of the medium even if limited. Thus while it had allowed free access by all recognized National and State parties to the state owned electronic media-AIR and Doordarshan- on an extensive scale for their campaigns during elections, there has not as yet been any provision for allotting some bandwidth on the Internet. In fact, the total free time allocated during 2004 General Elections extended over 122 hours on the state owned Television and Radio channels. If we compare the cost of buying airspace versus the web space, the latter would be much cheaper in comparison. While it's true that mere web space would not suffice, allocating a web domain to parties would surely induce them to recognize the potential of the medium. However, the parties and other agencies involved cannot ignore the medium for long especially given the pace at which the number of people using it is growing.

The Predominance of Traditional Media

All said, it can't be disputed that in India like in many other Asian countries print and television continue to attract the maximum attention of the media consuming population. Some of the statistics in fact serve as an eye opener. According to the Registrar of Newspapers of India office, every morning a staggering 15,67,19,209 copies of 60,413 registered newspapers roll out reaching millions. At over 150 million, this number is five times higher than the Internet users.

The overwhelming presence of the print media and television—there are a whopping 80 million cable & satellite homes in the country—coupled with their long history and tradition of playing a predominant role in political discourses in the Indian context make the political class more conducive to this media. It is this media, sociologists have argued for long that has helped deconstruct many of the complex notions of society and also in forming a "social construction of reality." In fact, sociologists studying the mass media of communication have said that traditional media such as newspapers and television are akin to the "air we breathe" (Croteau, et al., 2006). "The media have become the dominant social institution in contemporary society, supplanting the influence of older institutions such as the educational system and religion" (*Ibid*, p. 5)

It had its flip side too. In fact the heavy dependence on traditional media by the public across societies has led to few interesting conceptual positions. The worry that the new public was defined increasingly by its vulnerable condition of isolation and spectatorship became a long-term concern of academics worried about the civic life (Ewen, 1996). In 1948, two leading sociologists Paul Lazarsfeld and Rober Merton coined the term "narcotizing dysfunction" to refer to a phenomenon where citizens' immersion in media stories about politics short-circuited their desire to get personally involved in issues (Lazarsfeld, et al., 1948). Fifty years later, a political scientist found evidence for the hypothesis and argued that increased addiction to television in the United States discouraged people from going out into their communities and contributing to social life.

In India also such a perception is beginning to emerge though there has not been much research to unveil the psychological dimension of this phenomenon. The urban pockets of the Indian society which have been on an upswing after liberalization and excessive commercialization may also be reaching a similar state. For some civic optimists Internet may turn into a tool to reverse this alleged decline in social participation. "They contend that the new digital technology combines an ability to learn about a huge range of topics with a facility to get actively involved in that topic by immediately writing or talking back to the posters of the material" (Turow, et al. 2003). This, according to optimists, leads to a true area of social and even civic engagement. This is disputed by the pessimists who say that public engagements through the web take place for small segments of the public. Most of the people, they argue, spend virtually all of their web time in the commercialized area of the web which is merely a more targeted version of traditional mass media.

Then there is problem of acceptability as compared to the other media tools which have had long histories. A media sociologist argues that Internet is still struggling to gain respectability amongst its users and will continue to do so in terms of the following: (i) Source: What is the source of the information? Is the author known? On what authority does the author write and what are his or her credentials? (ii) Bias: What is the intent or purpose of the website? Is it dissemination of news or a propaganda or merely scholarly information? Is it fairly objective? (iii) Reliability: How reliable is the information which has been posted on a website? How is it generated? (iv) Currency: How current is the information and how often is the website updated?[6]

Perhaps it's this disjoint, some say, that turn off the political class against the potential of the medium. Little surprise that out of the six mainstream national political parties and over 40 regional recognized parties with many having strong presence in the central government, just about 10 percent have a presence on the web. For the users' groups also, surveys have shown that it's mostly entertainment, academic research and e-commerce that pull them to the Internet. While there is no known survey as yet to gauge how much political information people draw from the Internet, it can be safely concluded that it's close to miniscule.

However, what's important to note is that most of those who are net savvy and inclined politically, do at one time or the other use the medium for doing some quick research on a host of political topics. It ranges from finding out about the vote percentage of a party or the profile of the leader and even its compelling ideologies.[7] In an informal discussion conducted in the form of a random survey, it was interesting to note that all those who were asked to spell out their Internet adaptability and comfort level informed that they were prompted to the medium after having read or seen a news item on a newsstudy or a television channel.

Even though it indicates the obvious domination of mediums which have been in existence for decades—while television may only be over four decades old, the history of print in India is over 225 years old—the finding also confirms the dual use patterns of users groups. That a small group of early adapters and users are beginning to figure Internet in matters of political knowledge and behavior patterns is an indication of the shape of things to come.

With growing political competitiveness and an ever increasing preponderance of new media tools, it may not be a distant possibility that a substantial chunk of political discourses are equally carried out in the domain of Internet also. Also, with the likelihood of a majority of literate youngsters in urban cities and smaller towns getting wired, political parties may soon start looking at a strategy of indoctrination using this medium, which often has the capability of striking a personal rapport with the user.

The combination of the two and their use in tandem is a new phenomenon that will have important consequences for both the users groups and political communication strategists. One media tool like newsstudy can be used to reinforce the views of the other viz Internet and vice versa. The dual use also enables seamless access of media content for users groups and simultaneously throws a new challenge to those in charge of encoding of messages, for they constantly need to upgrade the flow of information. The combination is especially fruitful for political strategists. The continuum of media vehicles—newsstudy, television, internet—besides providing an opportunity of targeting audience of all hues, also means moderation of opinions and feeding of propaganda in gradations.

An interesting case in point is the politics of petition being pushed into the domain of the Internet. Right to Information (RTI) activists used the online petition mode to stall some objectionable proposals to amend the Act. Similarly, there have been instances when people have collected online signatures in support of their social causes. Websites such as petitiononline.com and petitionthem.com have turned into a rallying point for the people. "Internet signature campaign may not be sufficient to make a campaign successful but can be a valuable value-add" (Ghosh, 2006). The story goes on to argue that undeniably, the politics of petitioning is fast recasting itself as New Age shorthand for democratic activism. And it is here to stay.

However, to broad base various advantages of the Internet, we'll require displacement of digital and social disparities. Issues of literacy, access to hardware, conducive to social disposition towards use of technology and provision of content which is in sync with people's aspirations besides its language will have to be addressed. Interestingly, one of the key facilitators in all this is the political class itself. If they are able to do replicate small success stories in large parts of the country, political class would possibly be the best beneficiary of it.

Summing up

The present is pregnant with possibilities for the future. This aptly sums up the

Internet and political communication interplay in India today. India has been an exception of certain global trends in media consumption. Globally, circulation of newspapers and magazines has been on a decline but India has witnessed a reverse trend. Similarly, India has seen some unprecedented growth of Internet connections and users and we have seen emergence of cyber pockets in many parts of the country. Small information kiosks with photocopiers, outstation dialing system, cell phone accessories and at times a PC with a dial-up facility at every nook and corner of small towns of India is altering the communication dynamics of people like never before. There is an ever-growing desire among people to seamlessly connect, communicate and explore.

A small yet formidable group of politicians are beginning to push the agenda for a networked society which is also finding reflection in new policies of the government. This group is also using Internet as a medium of articulation and mediation with people, their constituency. Similarly, a small users' group is also getting adept at using the Internet for a variety of purposes. And even though the new medium can not possibly supplant time occupied by newspapers and television, their use in tandem is a new-age occurrence with important implications for both users groups and political communication strategists. Even as the future looks bright for the interplay of these two, society will have to collectively address the critical issue of bridging the gaps between the digital haves and have nots. Only then the country shall stand to gain substantially.

NOTES

1. India is a federal country, and the Constitution gives the states and union territories significant control over their own government. The legislative assemblies are directly elected bodies set up to carrying out the administration of the government in the 28 States of India. In some states there is a bicameral organisation of legislatures, with both an Upper and Lower House. Two of the seven Union Territories viz., the National Capital Territory of Delhi and Pondicherry, also have legislative assemblies.
2. BJP, a leading national political party with pan-Indian presence, led a coalition of parties to form the Central government known as NDA or National Democratic Alliance from 1999 to 2004. Its aggressive campaign including the use of new media tools were widely discussed among user groups and even political class
3. Dina Nath Mishra, a former Member of Parliament belonging to the BJP and who also led the media cell of the party from 1998 to 2003 informs this in a conversation with the author. Pardeep Kumar, Spokesperson, Indian Youth Congress & Shiv Bhatia, member, All India Congress Committee
4. Pardeep Kumar, Spokesperson, Indian Youth Congress & Shiv Bhatia, member, All India Congress Committee
5. Sahay is serving as the Director, Information & Publicity, Delhi Government, Delhi India
6. Dr Md. Firoz, Associate Professor and Chairperson, Department of Media and Communications, Manipal Academy of Higher Education (MAHE)—Dubai Campus Dubai, United Arab Emirates opined this in response to an email questionnaire
7. The author found this when he did a random survey to check the efficacy of Internet vis-a-vis people's political information. The people spoken to here included bureaucrats, journalists, civil society activists and management professionals in New Delhi and Mumbai

15

Women Empowerment and Poverty Reduction in Bangladesh

A Study of the Village Pay Phone Program

Linda Hultberg

The Village Pay Phone (VPP) program is one ICT development program, initiated in 1997 in Bangladesh by Grameen Telecom. It aims to diffuse the advantages of the mobile phone to rural people that have no other access to telecommunication services and thus include them to combat their poverty. The program targets women that live in rural areas, and encourages them to become owners of a mobile phone and start a small enterprise by renting it to others. The program is projected to alter the power relations among men and women in the male-dominated Bangladesh.

Women in rural Bangladesh are hard working. Foremost, they perform heavy household work and child caring throughout the days. Women's contribution to the family income is not recognized to the same extent as men's, even though they are involved in many such activities also (Islam, undated).A woman seldom earns money on her own, but is dependent on her father, then husband and thereafter her son for economic security (Hartman, Boyce, 1998). Hence, women constitute a vulnerable group in Bangladesh society (Landguiden, 2008). Even if the constitution promotes equal rights to women, women still suffer from discrimination and violence that occurs in the home, at the workplace and on other levels of society as well (Ministry of Women and Children Affairs, 2008; SIDA, 2007). Two thirds of the women in Bangladesh are illiterate because of the families' reluctance to pay for their daughter's education (Landguiden, 2008).

This study will investigate how the VPP might have altered the lives of sixteen female owners of such a mobile phone. It will aim for an understanding of its impact on power relations between men and women as well as poverty reduction.

Telecommunication and the Village Pay Phone Program in Bangladesh

Bangladesh has developed rapidly the past ten years, but is still one of the world's least developed countries. About 82% of the population lives under 2 dollar a day and 75% lives in rural areas of Bangladesh (Landguiden, 2008). Bangladesh is also one of the world's densest populated countries (SIDA, 2007). In 1990 just 0, 21% of the population had a fixed line telephone (United Nations Statistics, 2007), and the process of getting a one was costly and could take years (Yusuf, A.M., & Alam, Q., 2007). As the mobile phone services developed in the world the Bangladesh government opened up the mobile service sector for private sector competition. The mobile phone soon came to replace the fixed line telephone since it enabled interconnection in various parts of Bangladesh where fixed line networks had been impossible to establish. As Grameen Phone Ltd, Aktel, Citycell and Banglalink entered the market the cost of the mobile phone services decreased immensely during 1997 and 2007 (Yusuf & Alam, 2007). In Bangladesh the number of cellular subscribers increased from 0.06% in 1998 to 13.25% in 2006 (United Nations Statistics, 2007).

The Village Pay Phones (VPP) are owned by women living in rural areas of Bangladesh. The owner receives a loan from the Grameen Bank to purchase a mobile phone from Grameen Telecom and rents it to other villagers. As a result, rural people in Bangladesh will also have access to telephone services and achieve new opportunities to combat their poverty, by being connected to the rest of the world. Meanwhile, the women's businesses will generate an additional source of income. The idea of the VPP program was introduced to the Grameen Bank in 1994 by Iqbal Quadir (Cohen, 2001). The Grameen Bank was initiated by Professor Muhammad Yunus and gives women micro-loans which they can use to incept a small business. The Grameen Bank is unique as they focus on women's participation and access for loans; 97% of the loan recipients are women (Grameen Bank, 2008). Hence, the great focus on women as owners and operators of the VPP. Professor Yunus was rewarded the Nobel Peace Prize in 2006 for combating poverty through the micro-credit program. In 2007, the Village Pay Phones have been established in 61 of 64 districts of Bangladesh and the total number of VPPs had exceeded 297,079 (Grameen Bank, 2007). Iqubal Quadir says that sustainable economic development is "*of the people by the people and for the people*" (Quadir, 2006). He also include that "*[a] woman with a mobile phone becomes important in a village. It changes power distribution*" (Twist, 2005).

The Village Pay Phone project that started in 1997 is today somewhat outdated. Today mobile phone is diffused widely among poor people also in Bangladesh. Since other mobile phone companies has entered the market the mobile phone have became less costly. Mobile phone service from other companies than Grameen Telecom is rented out as well.

Purpose and Research Questions

Quadir's intention of the VPP program was to ensure the rural people's access to the VPP, but studies show that the female VPP owners have limited possibilities to operate the business. Therefore, it is important to find out what have influenced the women's tendency to hand the VPP over to a male operator and what role the female owners play. Moreover, the studies showed various ratios of male and female operators in the sample. They are conducted during the same period but cover different areas of Bangladesh. There is need for a study that covers a greater variety of districts in Bangladesh to find a range of situations in which the VPP is operated. Furthermore, earlier studies indicate that the VPP operators have become empowered by the program and agree upon many aspects (Bayes, 2001; Aminuzzaman et al., 2002). But in spite of the findings Aminuzzaman et al. concludes that the VPP generally does not alter the operator's life drastically. These studies were conducted around the year 2000. Since then the mobile phone has become highly diffused among the people in rural areas, aspects of women empowerment might have changed. Finally, the studies put little focus on female owners of the VPP as individuals in different contexts. Therefore, this paper approaches the field from a different angle than earlier studies in accordance to Kabeer's advices (2001). In this way focus is on empowerment among individuals and is describing empowerment while referring to its context and letting the women's experiences prevail the paper.

The purpose of the paper is to outline what is influencing the way the VPP is implemented in the women's everyday life, and how the VPP alters the life of the women concerning empowerment. Empowerment will be studied as a relational and motivational construct that includes both power redistribution in relationships and achieving the motivation to influence. This study will approach the field following Kabeer's advice of how to study women empowerment, and aims for an understanding of how female owners of the VPP have experienced this program and what meaning they put in the VPP. Two questions were framed:

- What aspects of the women's everyday life and the mobile phone affect the women's access and use of the mobile phone and the VPP?
- What benefits and restraint have the women experienced from the VPP and the mobile phone?

The first question aims to find out the women's use and access of the mobile phone and the VPP. They refer to how the mobile phone is implemented in the women's everyday life and aim to describe how the characteristics of the mobile phone, VPP and the female owners influence the women's use of and access to it. The third question aims to determine the latent meanings of the mobile phone and the VPP among these women. By finding out what opportunities and restraints it brought, one can understand what it means to the women to have a mobile phone and VPP. It will also determine if women have become empowered by the VPP, by relating their experiences of benefits and restraints with theories of empowerment.

Theory of Empowerment

Empowerment is constructed on the basis that there is an unequal distribution of power among people that results in people's experiences of power or powerlessness. There are different sources of power: personality, organizational strength, property, wealth, and class (Lord & Hutchison, 1993). This chapter is based on the following two definitions of empowerment. The first considers power over someone: *empowerment as a relational construct.* This creates a dependency or interdependency relationship between people and is relationally constructed. When a person's performance outcome is dependent on others' actions or responses, he or she is subordinated to others. People in power are able to make decisions or take actions that favor their own need and/or desire. Empowerment is effected when the diversity of power is redistributed and decreased. In this sense, to empower is to delegate sources of power to people (Conger & Kanungo, 1988). On the other hand, one must not take for granted that empowerment is the same as delegation, participation and resource sharing. Conger and Kanungo (1988) give the second definition of empowerment: *empowerment as motivational construct,* which argues for an urge among people for power and the ability to influence and control other people. The need for power is met when the person perceives that she has power over, can cope with, situations, events or people and experience a feeling of self-determination. Such feelings stem from the sense of self-worth or personal usefulness. Powerlessness is sensed, Lord and Hutchison (1993) write, when a person does not think that his/her actions will have any influence on their own or others' decision. From this perspective, empowerment is to enable or motivate people.

Research Design and Methods

The study takes a qualitative approach, and does not aim for generalization to measure empowerment or find causal relations between access/use and empowerment, but aims to bring to light some women's experiences of the VPP. The underlying philosophy of this study is that of a hermeneutic phenomenology (Bjurwill, C., 1995). An understanding of the women's experiences of the VPP and what meaning it bore was achieved by open survey questions. Sixteen female VPP owners, who may or may not be the operator of the VPP, constituted the sample. The sample included women that have owned the mobile phone for a long period of time as well as women who had recently obtained it. Women who once operated a VPP from the Grameen Telecom but do not any longer are also included in order to picture how the meaning of the VPP might have changed the past years. Women of various ages, religion, family situations, locations, occupations and NGO experiences were included. A purposive cluster sampling was made to choose villages that represent various parts of Bangladesh: Chittagong, Feni, Brahmanbaria, Gazipur, Rajshahi, Dinajpur and Bagerhat. In each village a "snowball method" was used to find the female VPP owners.

Women's Access and Use of the VPP and the Mobile Phone

The study revealed that out of sixteen VPPs, fourteen mobile phones were handed over to the owner's husbands or male relative, and that in seven of these cases the female owner assisted the man to operate it. One VPP was mainly operated by the owner and one was operated by the owner only. Most of the women were pleased to let their husbands operate the VPP and the most frequently given reason was seclusion. As women are not allowed to stride outside their home, go to the market or invite unknown men to their house, they cannot operate the VPP. In the evenings, when the husband has finished his work at the shop, or when he comes home for lunch and rest the female owner take care of the VPP, but send their children to deliver it to users. One woman, Dipti, believes that women in general do not wish to operate the VPP because their families do not want their female family members to work outside home because it could cause them a bad reputation. "*If steps are taken against these restrictions, women will be able to start a business*", Dipti says. Six of the owners said that they did not want to operate the VPP because their domestic work is too time consuming for them to go out.

> I am a very hardworking woman and have many children and grand children and I am rearing cows and ducks and grow vegetables. Because of so much work at home I would not be able to run a business from outside the home. Just give me some work in home within two hours I will have it completed. (Rubia Begum)

She understands that men and women have equal rights but she thinks that it is their culture and social norms not to share responsibility for domestic work. Dipti says that she could not operate the VPP side by side her work at BRAC (Bangladesh Rural Advancement Committee), which include traveling around villages to collect loan-repayments. Women with different levels of education, though still low, said that they possessed too low skills to operate the VPP successfully.

> "I never thought I would operate the VPP. As I am an illiterate one, and can't even count the money; I think it would be a problem for me to run the business. Rather my son and my nephew can do it." (Rubia Begum)

Three women bought the VPP because a husband son or male relative needed an employment. Accordingly, it was decided on beforehand that the husband would operate the VPP. Three of the respondents believe that business is not for women and therefore handed the VPP over to their husbands. Shamrina says: "*He* [her husband] *decided that business is not a matter of women, so it is not for me. It is rather for my husband to operate it.*" Tahmina Begum thinks that it is her husband's duty to run a business as he is the "*guardian of the family*".

However, there are two women that take the main responsibility to operate the VPP. Papiya Begum decided together with her husband to buy the VPP from Grameen Phone, but she decided herself that she needed a mobile phone to keep contact with her family when she moved to her husband's house. She started to operate the VPP from her shop to gain an extra income. The shop constitutes a part of her house, which is located near the central part of the village and its school. Majeda Begum operates the VPP herself from 8 AM until 2 PM and then goes home to do her domestic chores. At 4 PM she goes back to the shop and stays there until sunset. After sunset her son continues her VPP work. Her relatives are also her neighbors so she considers that she can leave her children safe at home while working in the shop. She incepted the VPP business to earn money.

> I have three sons and one married daughter. In 1999 only one of my sons was old enough to work, and he has a farm to spend some time for. So there was no one else in my home that could operate the VPP but me. Also, I feel secure operating the mobile phone as all businesses around my shop are run by my relatives. (Majeda Begum)

Women and men use the mobile phone for different personal purposes. In almost all cases women used the mobile phone to call relatives and family in distant places. Men used it to enhance their businesses efficiency. Dipti is the only woman in the sample that uses a mobile phone in her work: to keep close contact to office staff at BRAC and her husband while she is traveling between villages. Five women did not know how to use the mobile phone, but let other family members dial the number for them, or send greetings forward to the woman. They were either not interested in using/learning how to use it or incapable to because of illiteracy. Three women had not used the mobile phone.

> I never use the mobile phone. I do not even know the number. I hand it over to my son to dial the number so I can talk to my relatives. My son discourages me to learn the mobile phone as he will always be available to help me when I need the mobile phone. (Safali)

Some respondents discussed whether the mobile phone and the VPP are for men only or not. Taposhi believes that the mobile phone is both for men and women, but that its business is for men only.

> Though I cannot operate the mobile phone because of my illiteracy, my daughter can. It proves that it is for both men and women. [...] But operating the VPP in the village is a male task, because women cannot go there. (Taposhi)

Some women think that the VPP and the mobile phone are for both men and women. "*We are all equal in my family. So it is not a matter of male business only. I can also operate this one*", Dipti says. Majeda, who operates the VPP herself, rather believes that *"it depends on the borrower's mentality"* if a woman will become an operator.

Searching for Empowerment

To begin with, this study shows that the 'Phone Ladies' have experienced various economical benefits and restraints from the VPP. Many of the operators and owners of the VPP experienced an increased income when initiating the VPP, but two operators had not experienced any economical profit from the VPP, but gotten poorer. One claims that the profit is foremost made by the Grameen Phone, not by the operators. The income was often spent on the family rather than on individuals of the family. In three families the VPP gave the husband an employment. Majeda Begum supported her family financially, while Papiya Begum uses the income to increase the family's living standard. Men that operated the VPP from their shops used it to enhance their businesses. Two families could send one or two of their male family members abroad for work and two respondents used the money to initiate other businesses that are still prosperous. Two families spent the money on their daughters' dowry and weddings. None of the women uses the money from the VPP for personal benefits; rather they see the increased income as beneficial for the family and thus also them. "*I never bothered about my personal profits. If my son earns some money it would probably benefit my family too*", Rubia Begum says. Families that have experienced an income from the VPP also experienced that the VPPs have fell into decline. Rubia Begum says: "*Now the mobile phone is so common that even the rickshaw pullers have one. [...]Even the fishermen, who barely have any clothes, have one also.*" Some say that the call rate is too high so they had to hand the VPP back to the Grameen Bank, and buy a mobile phone from Banglalink, which cost less. Most of the respondents had problems now and then to collect payments, but it did not put them in economic crises.

All but two women experienced social gains from the VPP. One woman said that people did not perceive her differently. Most of the women experienced a positive change in their social relations after receiving the mobile phone even though they did not operate it. They became somewhat prestigious and received attention and respect from others, particularly from women. For some, their social network increased, although three women experienced quarrels with friends, who could not pay for their calls, or parents, who have teenagers that use the VPP. The owners of the VPP are still well known by name among the villagers in the surrounding areas but is not in focus in the same was as before.

> At the beginning many people gathered in my house. As the mobile phone is available everywhere now they do not come to my house anymore, but if I meet them when I go shopping they soon recognize me. However, I believe that the mobile phone has given me the opportunity to meet more people, which I enjoy very much when I go to the market. So I feel better. (Jostana Akhter)

To Taposhi Rani Das, a Hindu woman, even Muslims come to use the mobile phone. Such inter-belief relationships are not common, but still they have a very good relationship with the Muslim families living nearby.

The women had also experienced some changes in the family atmosphere since they bought the VPP. Six women said that family members respected them more as an owner of an income generating source. Two women felt that their family had become more prestigious and one experienced that the introduction of the VPP as an income generating source lessened the quarrels between the family members and that her husband started to treat her better a few felt that they were important for their families, since they could provide the family an income and a mobile phone. Parveen Akhter says that after getting the mobile phone she feels proud of being able to generate some income, and now she also feel that she is an important person in the area. Dipti Roy says:

> When I had no mobile phone I felt inferior to other people, but when I got the mobile phone I felt that it made me less inferior. Before I considered myself a weak woman because I had no mobile phone and felt shy in front of other people.

Some women, however, did not notice any changes in the family because of the VPP. Parveen Akhtar once asked her husband to hand the phone back to Grameen Phone but he did not as he needed it in his shop. She had no power to make a decision about the mobile phone as she has in other income generating activities. *"I am just the manager of the house. As a woman I have to sacrifice a lot, they never hear my voice."* But she finds it okay as they are a typical Bengali family. Safali Begum explains that the VPP was a reason for many quarrels in the family, since the family lost much money from that business.

> We have experienced a lot of conflict within the family because of the Village Pay Phone. I have to pay the bill, meanwhile my son or husband claims that they will not continue the business, and by that time I have to pay the bill to Grameen Bank. (Safali Begum)

From these experiences she has got the courage to quarrel with her son, who is the operator, and the power to put the responsibility for paying the bills to the Grameen Bank in her son's hands.

None of the women experienced any individual restraints coming with the VPP. In its place they were now able to maintain regular contact with family members and relatives living in distant places by using the mobile phone. Most of the women, however, do not know how to use the mobile phone, and ask a family member to dial the number for them. Other received news about their relatives from their husbands, daughters or sons.

Jostana learned from Grameen Telecom how to operate the VPP. She operated the VPP when her husband came back from his work and was responsible for paying the bill to the bank. She thinks that the VPP has made her rely on her own capabilities as she managed to operate the VPP successfully, and she would like to incept a similar business again. But as the VPP is not income generating anymore her self-esteem has decreased concerning the business, but when it comes to social relationships it increased.

> From getting the VPP I learned about the mobile phone system, I also learnt about overseas countries which I had no knowledge of before. I know some overseas countries' capitals, people living there and the country code for calling someone in that country.

> I also learned to contact strangers. Before, I never opened the door for strangers. But now I invite you. I have knowledge of how to socialize with people I do not know. Also I can travel by myself to the city (Chittagong) since I know how to take help from other people. I f you ask me to go to Dhaka I could. And I can use the mobile phone if I need to contact people or find out the address.
>
> Now women are more conscious about their rights. About one third of all women of our village feels shy and is concerned about other's criticisms. The rest in our village hardly bother about the criticisms. But it is not a result of Grameen Bank or Grameen phone only, it depends on many things. (Jostana Akhter)

Discussion

This study supports earlier findings on women's limited access to the mobile phone. In the study made by Bayes (2001), in the very beginning of the program in 1998, women constituted 45% of the operators, while Richardson et al. in 2000 came across 23% female operators. The study by Aminuzzaman et al. in 2002 included only 4% female operators, and this study depict only two out of sixteen. Accordingly, the number of female operators has decreased during program, taking the location of sample under consideration also. There are several aspects of the women's everyday life that hampers them to operate the VPP. The ones depicted here are: purdah, heavy domestic work, illiteracy, men's advantage in business activities in public places, and the general assumption of men being the guardian of the family.

Firstly, most women are limited to operate the VPP because they are restricted to move about in public places or to invite unknown people to their house. To avoid breaking the norms of seclusion they operated the mobile phone from their house in the evenings when their husband was at home, and send their children to deliver the mobile phone when needed. It shows that the VPP is employed by the women in such a way it does not impede with the norms of seclusion. Important to mentions is that none of the women said that they can move around more freely now than before as a result of the VPP. One woman though, find it easier to travel to the city as she has the mobile phone, but without the self-esteem to disregard others' criticisms it would still have been impossible. It shows that this aspect of empowerment, supported by Bayes (2001), is not supported here. Rather the VPP is similar to the micro-credit enterprises that he mentions, which confine women to conduct business at home. The two women who operated the VPP themselves, did so from their house in the central part of the village, or received the family's support to work at the market place. The VPP alone is not a trigger for women to start entering public spheres. In this way the traditional gender roles are maintained as the women keep their work in the house while men retain business in the public sphere. Secondly, many women cannot manage the VPP business since they have heavy domestic work throughout the days. Since too heavy domestic chores and child caring are not handed over to men, there is little time and strength left for women to go to the market place and operate the VPP from there. Also, everyone agreed upon that the business would not generate a good income if operated from home distant to the central part of the village. Therefore, women that answered for the VPP business were able to combine both domestic chores as well as the VPP business. As a result, the VPP do not change norms of job division either. Thirdly, some women were unable to operate the VPP or use the mobile phone because of their illiteracy or inability to count. In Bangladesh boys are more often sent to school than girls and acquire an early advantage to do such business. Here, gender norms decline women's access to the VPP. The VPP does not encourage the women to learn how to read, count or do business. Since, a few educated women chose to not operate the VPP, education alone may not be sufficient for women to use it. However, it is indispensable knowledge in order to operate the VPP business. The women's reluctance to use the mobile phone will be discussed further down. Finally, men traditionally support the family financially in Bangladesh and are often handed the VPP to enhance their previous businesses, to operate it side by side with their shop at the market or to become employed. Sometimes, the men take the initiative to get a VPP through their wife. Obviously, the VPP appears to fulfill its purpose better in the hands of the men than women, which is supported by the fact that the decision to hand it over to the husband is mostly made on advance, and is not impeded by the Grameen Phone officials. Some women would not think of being involved in such income generating activities. The fact that some women were not motivated to learn how to use it, indicate that the mobile phone has not been adopted by women to the same extent, although everyone mentioned they had access to the phone when they needed. Their access can be questioned as many are dependent on others to use it. This implies that the VPP does not encourage the women to enter the public sphere of business and that they do not find much use of learning the mobile phone but rather stays dependent on others in that matter. The need of a mobile phone does not come with the mobile phone, nor does it seem to alter existing gender patterns and ideas of labor division. The mobile phone has been placed in a male dominated area, public business, which limits its usefulness for women; instead of encouraging them to enter the public business domain. The VPP delegates the woman a choice to do business, but it does not motivate her or give her the self-esteem needed to operate the VPP. Support is needed from, family members and Grameen Phone officials and education centers.

Almost all women experienced an increased number of social relations from which they gained respect and honor, even though they did not operate the VPP themselves; their house constituted a place for social gatherings and gossiping. By meeting strangers more frequently and learning how to act the situation, they have become less shy and gained self-esteem, which seem to mean much to them. Aminuzzaman (2002) and Bayes (2001) do notice that women experience a greater social capital but they do not point out that the women feel more comfortable in such situation because they have experienced them frequently. Today, however, the women are not renowned as someone who owns a mobile phone, but as someone who once brought it to the village and their house is not a meeting point any to the same extent as before. Still, they are known by name. What is not mentioned in earlier studies is that a few women of the sample perceived themselves in a more positive way now than before they gained prestige. However, their fame as owners of a mobile phone is not protruding, supporting what Aminuzzaman et al. (2002) stated. The study cannot state, however, whether this prestige had made them sense that they have a greater influence over situations and people. Power distributions do not seem to have changed as Quadir anticipated in his speech in October 2006. Only a few women experienced that they had got some voice by owning the device and many women in the sample do not think that they have a greater possibility to influence others after getting the mobile phone. The fact that several women did not mention any changes in the family atmosphere at all shows that the VPP had little to do with it. It also indicates that women might find themselves empowered when they receive respect from others and when they feel recognized and not when given power over someone or something. They also find meaning in meeting people.

From the initiation of the program the VPP generated a good extra income until the mobile phone became more affordable, which lowered the demand and so also the profit. As a result, some operators subscribed to Banglalink or Aktel that offer lower prices. Also men could buy a mobile phone from these companies, which made them independent from the women to buy it, and use it as an extra source of income. In the long run, the VPP has not been a very successful business, though it still generates some extra financial income. Also, women's power, as a result of them being the only ones getting hold of a desired devise, has been somewhat diminished. When it comes to financial independency the VPP did not empower the women in the majority of the cases. The women rarely mentioned any personal access to the income. No women mentioned any personal economical benefits from the VPP and none of them took a percentage from it. Instead, the profit was generally invested in public businesses or spent on the family, or the daughters' dowry and wedding, which is not considered a tradition that favors women. Important though is that, families became less dependent on others since they no longer need to borrow money from more wealthy villagers. The dependency relation between families, that has been a result of poverty, has become somewhat redistributed. Such findings do not go in line with Bayes (2001) study that stresses women's financial independency from other villagers. The paper, however, does not reveal if decisions about the family's economy are made jointly or not, but it does not support that the VPP makes women financially independent from male relatives.

As the VPP and the mobile phone were introduced into the women's everyday life, they experienced new capabilities and abilities. Foremost, all women said that the mobile phone enabled them to contact their families and relatives more easily. Since women move in to the husband's house after marriage, and might therefore live in areas far from her relatives sometimes, it can be difficult to contact them. Almost all women of the sample had relatives in other areas. Previous studies show that female users of a mobile phone tend to use it to call family and relatives but do not consider it empowerment. However, the women are now more able to determine themselves when to contact their families according to their needs and wishes. As all women pointed out this new ability it seems to be one of the most prevailing ways in which the mobile phone has empowered them. Only few women noticed other knowledge and capabilities that they did not think they had before. There were only a few women that experienced new knowledge about other places and people. The finding tends to correspond with earlier studies about women empowerment, but was not prevalent throughout these interviews.

Conclusion

The VPP program has made the mobile phone accessible to poor rural people. It has enabled them to share vital market information, contact family and social services, as well as enhancing their existing businesses. However, the mobile phone, as well as its benefits, mostly falls into the hands of men who wanted a job, or who already had access to the public sphere in which business is made.

The mobile phone did not give women power over people, nor did it give them sources of power such as financial means. It did not boost their sense of being able to influence their surrounding either. But, it enabled a very few of them, who had family support, to enter the public sphere to do business and take part of the information flow there. Mostly the VPP gave the women prestige, opportunity to meet strangers and feel somewhat comfortable, as well as the possibility to call their family. Here, women consider empowerment as being important to someone, rather than being in power of someone.

This study shows that empowerment is neither a linear process, similar to all women, nor a direct cause of something. It is important to mention that empowerment did not occur to many women and for some women the change was barely noticeable. The mobile phone does not ensure empowerment of the female owner as anticipated by Iqubal Quadir, nor have they been empowered in the same way. It is shown that the VPP program is no more than one source of women empowerment that needs to cooperate with many others to reach out to all women.

ICT do not alone have a great impact on entrenched social and cultural norms in ICT development programs. Instead social and cultural norms play a very outstanding role in how technological devises will be employed. In this study, Purdah, domestic work, illiteracy, and the idea of men as the "guardian of the family" kept the women aside from the VPP. Furthermore, the Grameen Telecom officials did not support the women's ownership of the VPP, but encouraged them to hand it over to their husbands. Grameen Telecom needs a thorough monitoring and supporting strategies in order to help women to employ the business into their everyday life. Although they are given a source of power they need motivation and self-esteem to operate it. They also need to need the mobile phone.

Since, technology is partly a social construct in which men takes an active part also, it is therefore valuable to conduct a study on men's experiences and thoughts about such a program. It would be helpful to compare and contrast the women and men's experiences to find out how the different sexes participates and benefits from the program as well as how they might influence each other's opportunities to become empowered.

To take programs for women empowerment in Bangladesh further it is important to continue to outline power relations among men and women and their possibilities to participate and benefit from such programs. One need to outline what possible pitfalls and to do so one must understand the women's lifeworlds so that the change in power distribution and the motivation to influence is accepted by and convenient to the women. What aspects of her lifeworld influence her possibilities to participate and benefit from the program, and what are the needs of the program's target group? Also, one must follow up the programs as the conditions, under which it is implemented and developed, changes. That is, short term as well as long term benefits and restraints must be considered and followed up.

16

Possibility of Applying Universal Service Policy Principle on Mobile Phone Service in the case of South Korea

Hyunwoo Lee

Most countries of the world have carried out the universal service policy so far in order that their people can have access to the essential telecommunication service, i.e., telephone service, at affordable and equal costs, regardless of incomes and geographic locations. Telecommunication carriers had been obligated to provide universal service by the 1970s when telecommunication service was given by national governments and public enterprises monopolistically. However, universal service has been guaranteed by public policies as liberalization and privatization put its responsibility on the telecommunication service providers since the 1980s, and in recent times, universal service has drawn public attention all the more as telecommunication technology has been remarkably advanced.

In order to provide universal service, each country has built up nationwide telecommunication networks with common carriers, has given subsidies to the residents of rural communities and remote islands who have used telecommunication service at high costs, and has given subsidies to the disabled and the low-income bracket. To be specific, ultimately universal service aims at improving social exclusion and divide caused by the market economy, on the principle that the essential telecommunication service should be given to everybody at affordable costs.

The Korean government impliedly provided universal service in the form of internal cross subsidy and the connection fee-addition system. In 1998, the universal service system was expressly stipulated in Telecommunications Business Act (Gwon O-Sung, 2004, p.32). Relevant laws had been continuously revised since then, and so universal service policy has been carried out with local calls, pay phones and telecommunication service for remote islands. But as telecommunication technology has remarkably advanced since 1998, there has been a need to review and revise the universal service policy (Gwak Jung-Ho,

2005; Jo Joo-Eun, 2006; Jung Yin-Sook, 2006; Korea Information Society Development Institute (KISDI), 2002, 2003, 2005).

In particular, the nation's telecommunication market has undergone rapid changes in terms of the keen competition between the telecommunication carriers, the advancement of their technologies, and the appearance of alternative telecommunication means such as the ubiquitous mobile phone. In the past, the emphasis was on the advancement of wired telecommunication services, but recently wired communication has been rapidly substituted by wireless telecommunication. The change has been so rapid that the market of mobile telephony has already attained maturity. Consequently, mobile phone service has come to be recognized as an alternative to wire phone service and an indispensable means of telecommunication (Gruber, 2001; Gruber & Verboven, 2001; Noguchi & Takashima, 2000; Moon Sang-Deok, 2003; Sung Nak-Yil, 2004; KISDI, 2004). A recent survey shows that 82 percent of Korean people recognize mobile phones as one of the necessities of life (KISDI, 2004, p.15).

Though mobile phone service has become an indispensable means of telecommunication in Korea, yet those, who have difficulty in having access to its services due to geographical, economic and physical difficulties (the underprivileged), account for above 10 percent of the whole nation. Given the fact that 76.1 percent of Koreans use mobile phones as of 2004, its growth rate has stagnated as the market has been almost saturated (KISDI, 2005, p.5). However, it seems difficult to give mobile phone service even to the underprivileged, within market function. In fact, a survey of the underprivileged found that 72.4 percent of them can not use mobile phone service due to expensive handsets and high tolls (Kim Jung-Yop, 2005, p.43). It means that social exclusion and divide is caused by market function even in mobile phone service.

As mobile phone service has been the indispensable means of social communication, it is natural that the few who have difficulty in using mobile phones feel a sense of alienation universally (universal alienation). On that score, exclusion and divide, for those who are in the blind spot of market function, needs to be resolved in some way.

In line with this scenario, this study aims at examining the possibility of applying universal service policy principle on mobile phone service under an environment where telecommunication technology has been highly advanced.

The Present Status and Characteristics of Nation's Mobile Phone Service

In this chapter, have been present state of nation's mobile phone service and its characteristics dealt with in order to ascertain whether the service answers the foregoing three questions raised to investigate the applicability to the universal service policy. First, the penetration rate of mobile phone service and the present status of social exclusion were investigated to review the necessity of mobile phones. Second, the characteristics of nation's mobile service market were reviewed to ascertain whether consumer welfare can be improved by introducing universal service.

The Present Status of Mobile Phone Service

Table 1: Sectors to which Various Mobile Services are Applicable

Sector	Function	Using
Economy	Banking	• mobile banking - inquiry(savings, exchange rate, transaction) - transfer, credit card, cashing service
	Commerce	• mobile commerce - commercial transaction - information service(e-ticket, discount coupon)
	Job seeking	• SMS service - job seeking support center - qualification/disqualification noticing service
Society and Culture	Maintaining social network	• voice call, SMS service • mobile chat, mini homepage - mobile nate-on, cyworld
	Public politics	• mobile e-government • service toward civilians (civil petition, escrow service, e-voting) - mobile administration • SMS service - social participation
	Education	• mobile learning - providing educational contents • mobile educational administration - class registration, issue identifications/certifications
	Entertainment	• mobile game/video - game service - video service • DMB(digital mobile broadcasting)

Source: KISDI, 2005, p. 7.

The Table 1 well shows that mobile phone service is closely related to daily life. Currently, mobile phone service is given throughout all sectors including economy, society and culture. In the economic sector, banking and commercial transactions are performed by the medium of mobile phones, and ward offices and portal internet sites transmit help-wanted ads through SMS (Short Message Service). In the social and cultural sectors, a social network is operated by telephone call, messenger service, SMS and mini homepage, and the nation participates in politics on the electronic government, and education service is expanded by mobile education contents and school administration, and users enjoy electronic games, and besides, various mobile services are given. Furthermore, mobile phone service is expected to be applied even to special sectors like medical service though it is still in germ like 'Diabetic Phone' and 'Emergency Phone'. In future, mobile phone service is expected to be more expanded concurrently with the distribution of RFID (Radio Frequency Identification) technology.

In the case of Korea, mobile phones have been remarkably substituted for wired phones. As shown in the Figure 1, the number of mobile phone subscribers has remarkably increased since 1996 and had exceeded 4 million in 2006, and so the diffusion rate account for about 83 percent (the Ministry of Information and Communication, 2006). In particular, the gap between subscribers has been continuously widened since mobile phone subscribers got more than wired phone subscribers in September 1999. Likewise, the demand for telecommunication service has been shifted from wired service to mobile service. As shown in the Figure 2, traffic between wired phones (LL) has decreased every year but traffic between mobile phones (MM) has continuously increased since mobile phone service was introduced.

The gap between the two has been remarkably widened since traffic between mobile phones exceeded traffic between wired phones in 2001, and actually, KISDI and the Ministry of Information and Communication analyzed that traffic between wired phones has decreased 10 percent every year but traffic between mobile phones had increased at least 10 percent in the recent three years and such a phenomenon will be more prominent from this year (*Electronic Times*, Oct. 18, 2006). The phenomenon suggests that mobile phone service is not a complement to wired service but is a substitute for it. Also, the fact that the national demand for mobile phone service and wired phone service account for 62.8 percent and 36.5 percent respectively (the statistical data of the Ministry of Information and Communication, as of Sep. 2006) shows that the indispensable means of telecommunication is shifted from wired phones to mobile phones. Now mobile phone service has been one of the necessities of life formally, and actually, a study found that 82 percent of the whole nation recognizes mobile phones as one of the necessities of life (KISDI, 2004, p.15).

The Gap between Social Groups in Mobile Phone Service

Table 2: The Use Rate of Mobile Phones in Demographic Variables

		Using	Not-using
	Total	76.6	23.4
Sex	Male	81.4	18.6
	Female	71.8	28.2
Age	6-19	43.3	56.7
	20's	97.6	2.4
	30's	95.7	4.3
	40's	91.6	8.4
	50's	93.2	16.8
	over 60	49.9	50.1

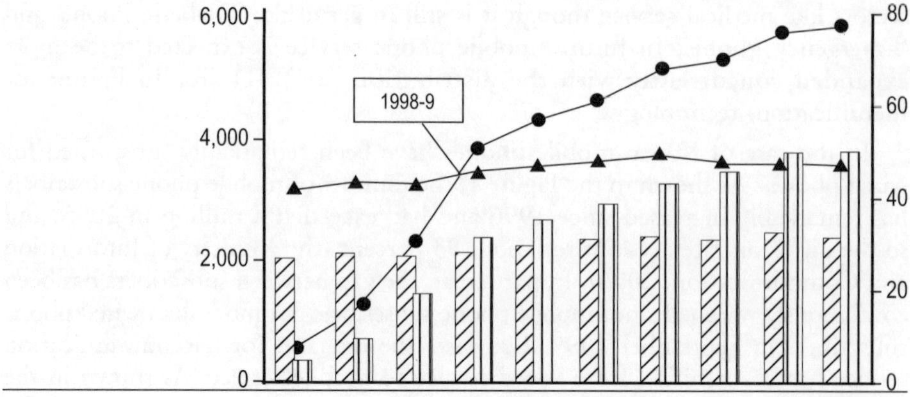

	1996	1997	1998	1999	2000	2001	2002	2003	2004	2005-6
subscribers (fixed)	1,560	2,042	2,005	2,125	2,155	2,272	2,349	2,285	2,357	2,294
subscribers (mobile)	318	683	1,358	2,344	2,682	2,965	3,234	3,385	3,659	3,741
penetration (fixed, %)	41.7	43.5	43.1	45.0	40.7	43.0	43.3	47.2	47.3	47.5
penetration (mobile, %)	6.1	14.7	30.0	45.0	50.3	57.1	61.3	70.2	76.1	77.5

Figure 1: The Change of the Number of Telephone and Mobile Phone Subscribers

Source: KISDI, 2006, p.5.

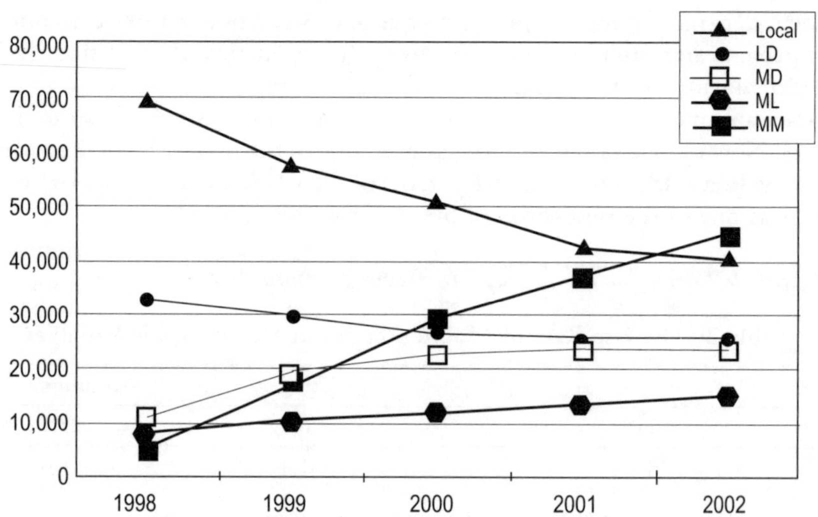

Figure 2: The Increase of Phone Traffic in Each Type

Source: KISDI, 2004.

		Using	Not-using
Sex × age	Male 6-19	40.6	59.4
	Male 20's	97.5	2.5
	Male 30's	98.4	1.6
	Male 40's	96.4	3.6
	Male 50's	92.7	7.3
	Male over 60	69.0	31.0
	Female 16-19	48.3	53.7
	Female 20's	97.7	2.3
	Female 30's	92.9	7.1
	Female 40's	86.7	13.3
	Female 50's	73.8	28.2
	Female over 60	35.5	64.5
Education	Uneducated/primary school graduates	33.7	66.3
	Middle school graduates	78.5	21.5
	High school graduates	92.5	7.5
	University graduates	97.6	2.4
	No response	61.5	38.5
Occupation	Professionals/administrators	98.1	1.9
	Office workers	98.4	1.6
	Selling	91.6	8.4
	Production	79.3	20.7
	Agricultural/fishery	62.0	38.0
	Unemployed	64.4	35.6
	Students	56.2	43.8
	Housewives	77.4	22.6
	No response	97.1	12.9
Income(won)	under 1 million	52.4	47.6
	1 million-2 million	75.0	25.0
	2 million-3 million	78.8	21.2
	3 million-4million	82.5	17.5
	over 4 million	86.4	13.6
	No response	76.9	23.1
Province	Seoul	84.3	15.7
	Pusan	77.1	22.9
	Taegu	74.4	25.6
	Inchon	79.7	20.3
	Kwangju	74.7	25.3
	Taejeon	75.4	24.6
	Ulsan	77.9	22.1
	Kyunggi	81.3	18.7
	Kangwon	70.5	29.5
	Chungcheong	68.4	31.6
	Jeonra	64.2	35.8
	Kyungsang	69.5	30.5
	Jeju	65.3	34.7

Source: NIDA, 2006, p. 214.

As shown in the Table 2, the use rate of mobile phone service was different according to demographic variables such as gender, age, academic career, occupation, income and location the same as other information services including internet. In point of gender, males who use mobile phones accounted for 81.4 percent, while females account for 71.8 percent; the rate of males who use mobile phones was about 10 percent higher than that of females. In point of age, the people in their twenties and thirties who use mobile phones accounted for 97.6 percent and 95.7 percent respectively. In a word, almost all of the age range uses mobile phones. On the other hand, people aged sixty and upward accounted for just 49.9 percent. Also, the difference between males and females was analyzed in each age range. Males and females in their twenties and thirties did not show a significant difference, but people aged 40 and upward showed significant differences. In the case of those who are in their forties, male users and female ones accounted for 96.4 percent and 86.7 percent respectively, and in the case of those who are in their sixties, males and females accounted for 69.0 percent and 35.5 percent respectively. The result suggests that the use of mobile phone service is different even in the underprivileged, and so the order of priority needs to be arranged in the underprivileged so that the preferential group can be backed up politically.

In point of academic career, the uneducated and primary school graduates, middle school graduates, high school graduates, and university graduates and the more highly-educated accounted for 33.7 percent, 78.5 percent, 92.5 percent and 97.6 percent respectively, especially, the rate of primary school graduates who use mobile phones was about 45 percent lower than middle school graduates. In point of occupation, professionals and administrators, and office workers accounted for 98.1 percent and 98.4 percent respectively, but on the other hand, production workers, and agricultural and fishery workers accounted for 79.2 percent and 62.0 percent respectively. Namely, the rate of the blue-collar was lower relatively to the white-collar. And in point of monthly income, those whose monthly income is less than one-million won (about one-thousand dollar), less than two-million won, less than three-million won, and four-million won and upward accounted for 52.4 percent, 75.0 percent, 78.8 percent and 86.4 percent respectively. Also in point of location, the rate of metropolitan areas such as Seoul, Gyeonggi, Incheon and Busan was 12 or 13 percent higher than that of the provinces such as Gangwon, Chungcheong, Jeolla, Gyeongsang and Jesu. In result, it was found that demographic variables such as gender, age, academic career, income, location and occupation are the cause of the gap between social groups in mobile phone service.

As shown in the Table 3, the usage of mobile service was different according to demographic variables such as age, academic career, occupation and income. In point of gender and location, significant differences were not observed in internet access, text message transmission and receipt, picture transmission and receipt, download service and payment service, differently than the use rate of mobile phones. Instead, significant differences were observed in point of age, academic career, occupation and income the same as the use rate of mobile

Table 3: The Usage of Mobile Service in Demographic Variables

		Internet access	SMS	Image	Music/ VOD	Payment for goods
	Total	43.8	78.5	18.7	34.8	27.8
Sex	Male	43.7	77.2	17.4	34.0	29.4
	Female	43.9	80.1	20.0	35.7	26.0
Age	6-19	69.6	96.5	38.6	69.0	42.6
	20's	68.2	97.9	34.8	68.6	53.9
	30's	43.6	93.3	20.0	35.7	32.6
	40's	32.6	76.7	7.8	18.8	14.5
	50's	21.6	48.0	3.7	6.0	5.6
	over 60	18.4	25.1	2.0	3.4	2.6
Sex×age	Male 6-19	68.2	96.3	35.9	67.1	43.1
	Male 20's	69.9	97.3	32.3	67.3	56.7
	Male 30's	43.1	92.6	19.9	35.9	36.4
	Male 40's	31.7	75.5	8.0	18.5	16.4
	Male 50's	25.5	48.4	4.0	7.1	7.6
	Male over 60	17.8	26.8	2.4	4.4	3.0
	Female 16-19	70.1	96.6	41.3	70.9	42.2
	Female 20's	66.3	99.5	37.5	65.7	50.8
	Female 30's	44.1	94.1	2.2	35.5	28.3
	Female 40's	33.5	78.2	7.5	17.2	12.2
	Female 50's	16.6	47.5	3.2	4.5	3.1
	Female over 60	14.5	22.6	1.5	2.0	1.9
Education	Uneducated/primary school graduates	33.7	54.5	14.5	27.7	16.5
	Middle school graduates	42.1	84.3	17.7	31.5	19.1
	High school graduates	44.6	80.7	17.6	34.1	26.8
	University graduates	48.9	99.8	22.2	39.6	36.9
	No response	77.1	77.1	55.0	55.0	39.8
Occupation	Professionals and administrators	47.0	96.3	22.8	37.1	40.6
	Office workers	50.7	99.3	22.7	43.1	37.4
	Selling	37.0	72.9	11.2	24.7	19.4
	Production	28.6	62.7	7.1	14.6	13.8
	Agricultural/fishery	17.9	45.4	1.9	5.4	3.7
	Unemployed	47.8	80.2	22.8	41.1	29.8
	Students	71.9	97.3	39.3	71.4	48.1
	Housewives	33.6	74.8	12.4	21.3	16.7
	No response	33.7	72.0	21.1	29.4	22.8
Income (won)	Under 1 million	23.6	50.7	9.5	19.0	1.4
	1 million-2 million	39.2	76.5	16.4	29.3	25.2
	2 million-3 million	45.1	82.2	18.4	29.3	25.2
	3 million-4 million	49.0	82.8	22.2	41.3	30.0
	over 4 million	49.5	81.6	21.9	41.2	33.8
	No response	53.7	81.7	10.7	41.5	40.4

		Internet access	SMS	Image	Music/ VOD	Payment for goods
Province	Seoul	39.2	77.5	24.9	41.2	29.6
	Pusan	43.0	74.4	11.5	29.2	26.3
	Taegu	37.5	81.3	13.0	28.8	27.6
	Inchon	52.8	85.5	27.0	42.5	41.5
	Kwangju	48.9	86.0	16.6	37.8	42.7
	Taejeon	42.3	81.8	3.7	30.2	5.8
	Ulsan	30.0	72.2	4.1	14.6	13.5
	Kyunggi	52.0	77.7	24.8	41.3	31.7
	Kangwon	48.3	72.1	29.1	35.6	32.9
	Chungcheong	40.6	75.5	4.3	28.6	10.0
	Jeonra	43.7	86.7	15.1	28.0	34.1
	Kyungsang	38.3	77.5	10.5	23.5	22.7
	Jeju	55.8	82.0	17.8	37.6	22.0

Source: NIDA, 2006, p. 219.

phones. In point of age, the usage of internet access, text message service, picture service, download service and payment service was in inverse proportion to age range. And in point of academic career, the usage of five services was remarkably low in the ill-educated and it increased proportionally. In point of occupation, the application of professionals and administrators was 2 to 2.5 times higher than that of production, agricultural and fishery workers. In point of income, the usage of such services was higher in the high-income bracket.

The Structure of the Mobile Phone Service Market

As shown in the Table 4, the market share of the top mobile carriers of OECD member countries was 59.2 percent in 1998 on the average, but decreased by about 10 percent, 49.9 percent, in 2003. Such a phenomenon was observed in most member countries, especially in the case of Swiss, Turkey, the Netherlands, Austria and Italy, their market share decreased by 20 to 30 percent. Nevertheless, the market share of the top mobile carriers of Korean and Mexico increased by 11.9 percent and 16.2 percent respectively, compared to 1998. Korea's top mobile carrier recorded 54.5 percent of market share as of 2003 and the value was ranked tenth in OECD member countries.

Table 4: The Market Share of the Top Mobile Carriers of OECD Member Countries

Rank	Country	Carrier	1998	1999	2000	2001	2002	2003
1	U.S.	Verizon	30.3	27.9	24.5	22.9	23.1	23.7
2	U.K.	Vodafone	37.5	33.2	29.1	27.9	26.1	25.6
3	Poland	PTC	40.6	44.3	41.5	37.5	34.6	35.7
4	Canada	Bell Mobility	37.6	35.5	36.1	36.4	36.8	36.8
5	Greece	Cosmote	51.9	42.7	37.5	37.0	37.6	37.4
6	Netherlands	KPN	65.1	51.6	44.9	43.4	41.9	38.5

Rank	Country	Carrier	1998	1999	2000	2001	2002	2003
7	Germany	T-Mobile	47.4	41.0	40.1	41.1	41.6	40.6
8	Austria	Mobilkom	65.2	53.3	46.0	43.7	44.6	43.2
9	Czech	Eurotel	61.2	55.1	50.2	46.6	45.5	43.4
10	Australia	Telstra	58.9	49.9	47.1	47.4	45.7	45.2
11	Sweden	Telia	52.9	51.5	51.4	49.7	46.1	45.6
12	Italy	TIM	70.4	61.0	51.5	46.9	47.7	45.8
13	Portugal	TMN	47.0	45.3	44.1	45.4	46.2	46.4
14	Hungary	Westel	60.4	58.0	57.1	52.7	49.8	47.5
15	France	Orange	49.7	48.7	48.2	48.2	49.8	48.8
16	Denmark	TDC	45.0	43.9	45.3	49.3	46.9	49.4
17	Spain	Telefonica	64.8	60.3	55.8	56.6	54.9	52.4
18	Belgium	Belgacom	71.0	64.8	58.2	52.9	54.2	52.9
19	New Zealand	Vodafone	78.5	68.4	60.5	56.9	50.2	54.0
20	S. Korea	SKT	42.6	43.0	40.8	40.9	53.2	54.5
21	Ireland	Vodafone	n/a	62.4	58.8	57.6	56.3	54.7
22	Finland	Sonera	67.8	63.2	62.9	58.8	55.6	54.8
23	Slovakia	Globtel	n/a	53.5	55.6	56.1	59.5	56.1
24	Japan	NTT DoCoMo	57.3	57.0	59.0	59.1	58.3	56.9
25	Switzerland	Swisscom	100.0	74.9	68.9	66.9	63.2	61.9
26	Luxemburg	P&T	n/a	62.9	60.8	60.5	61.8	63.6
27	Turkey	Turkcell	100.0	69.1	68.9	64.3	67.4	67.6
28	Iceland	Iceland Telecom	n/a	78.6	74.8	70.2	67.3	67.6
29	Norway	Telenor	75.0	72.4	72.1	69.4	69.5	68.9
30	Mexico	Telcel	61.7	67.7	69.8	74.4	76.7	77.9
	OECD average		59.2	54.7	52.0	50.7	50.4	49.9

Source: Merrill Lynch (2004). Global Wireless Matrix.

As shown in the Table 5, HHI of OECD member countries was 4,765 on the average in 1998 but decreased by 4,013 in 2003. Such a phenomenon has been observed in most member countries. In the case of the Netherlands, Austria, Portugal, Italy and Swiss, HHI remarkably decreased by 2000 to 4000. It means that market concentration rate remarkably decreased. As opposed to the trend, HHI of Korea and Mexico conspicuously went up by 1,584 and 1,966 respectively. Although HHI somewhat felt, it accounts up to 1800 and upward in most member countries excluding the United States, namely, the concentration ratio of the mobile service market is considered to be very high on the authority of the foregoing fact. Also given the fact that the diffusion rate of mobile phone service had been over 80 percent in OECD member countries including Korea and the mobile service market had come to maturity already and new carriers have difficulty in entering the market, HHI may not decrease heavily anymore.

The nation's mobile service market is noncompetitive due to high concentration rate and tipping effect. It seems that the high concentration rate of the nation's mobile service market restricts people's use and access to mobile phone service in that the concentration rate of the mobile service market is positively correlated to tolls and profits but is negatively correlated to the diffusion rate of mobile phones (Merill Lynch, 2005).

Table 5: HHI of OECD Member Countries

Rank	Country	1998	1999	2000	2001	2002	2003
1	U.S.	2323	2063	1847	1742	1672	1655
2	U.K.	2868	2666	2535	2521	2505	2501
3	Netherlands	5458	3797	3109	2898	2821	2568
4	Canada	3106	2921	2841	2825	2879	2890
5	Austria	5463	4220	3597	3362	3334	3131
6	Greece	4033	3472	3384	3397	3340	3244
7	Germany	3833	3474	3400	3435	3414	3336
8	Poland	3609	3737	3536	3377	3336	3342
9	Denmark	3960	3432	3229	3479	3366	3501
10	Australia	4362	3855	3666	3676	3582	3562
11	Portugal	4332	3742	3600	3602	3627	3638
12	Italy	5836	4913	4051	3612	3834	3756
13	Czech	5252	5053	4406	4000	3936	3791
14	Sweden	4019	3951	3979	3915	3802	3795
15	Hungary	5215	5128	5046	4448	4078	3815
16	France	4052	3888	3805	3792	3940	3879
17	Spain	5061	4769	4184	4180	4053	3888
18	Belgium	5880	5274	4508	4116	4105	4047
19	Finland	5618	5279	5070	4508	4081	4104
20	S. Korea	2662	2622	2592	2889	4075	4146
21	Japan	n/a	3767	3966	4347	4285	4182
22	Switzerland	10000	5939	5244	5031	4678	4564
23	Ireland	n/a	5308	5155	4876	4811	4620
24	New Zealand	6621	5675	5218	5096	5000	5032
25	Slovakia	n/a	5024	5062	5075	5182	5075
26	Turkey	n/a	5717	5718	5232	5201	5097
27	Luxemburg	n/a	5334	5234	5221	5278	5373
28	Iceland	n/a	6631	6227	5540	5191	5621
29	Norway	6245	6005	5979	5755	5763	5717
30	Mexico	4558	5106	5434	5966	6295	6524
	OECD average	4765	4425	4187	4064	4049	4013

Source: Merrill Lynch (2004). Global Wireless Matrix.

Actually in the case of Korea, the rate of telecommunication expenses to household consumption expenditures, and real household telecommunication expenses ranked top in OECD member countries (iNews 24, Oct. 18, 2007). It is considered that nation's mobile phone service causes the burden of high tolls in that mobile phone service accounts for 75 percent of nation's household telecommunication expenses (National Internet Development Agency (NIDA), 2006). A survey of the underprivileged found that 72.4 percent of them does not mobile phone service due to expensive handsets and high tolls (Kim Jung-Yop, 2005, p.43). The result well shows that they are blocked to mobile phone service, the indispensable means of telecommunication, due to the barrier of cost.

Conclusion

Most countries of the world have recognized wired phone service as the baseline-level telecommunication service, and have been making efforts to enable their people to have access to wired phone service through the universal service system. However, the advancement of communication technology has substituted wired phone service by mobile phone service as an indispensable means of telecommunications. So, universal service needs to include mobile phone service to take into cognizance changes in the telecommunication environment. Accordingly, this study was carried out to ascertain whether mobile phone service can be brought within the ambit of universal service obligation, in an environment where telecommunication technology has been constantly changing.

In the matter of 'the significance of the universal service policy and its ultimate goal', it was found that the concept of universal service has been historically reestablished according to changes of telecommunication environment as well as the question of whether universal service can be expanded beyond wired phone service was based on various theories such as the discrimination principle, the consumption standard, network externality and informational gap. Also given the concept that the universal service policy aims at making the whole nation have access to the baseline-level telecommunication service and use the service at affordable costs irrespective of geographic, physical and economic discriminations, the applicability of a specific telecommunication service to universal service should be investigated on the basis of the question of whether:

Market function and consumer welfare can be improved by introducing the universal service policy into the market on the premise that market concentration ratio and competitive ratio should be analyzed by the relevant country.

In point of 'the present state of characteristics of nation's mobile phone service', it was judged that it is possible to apply nation's mobile phone service to universal service on the basis of the above-mentioned three conditions such as necessity, social exclusion and divide, and market concentration and competition. Above all, in the aspect of necessity, it was found that mobile phone service has been the core means of social communication in that the diffusion rate of mobile phones counts up to 83 percent and they account for 70 percent of the demand for nation's telecommunication. Next in the aspect of social exclusion and divide, it was found that mobile phone service cannot be sufficiently provided to remote islands and mountainous areas as well as the use rate of mobile phone service was different according to demographic variables such as gender, age, academic career, occupation, income and location. Lastly, in the aspect of market concentration and competition, nation's mobile service market is noncompetitive and high concentration rate, tipping effect, restricted rate competition and earnings over normal profits are observed. Thus, it may be certain that market function should be complemented by the universal service policy to the end that the gap between social groups in the use of mobile phone service that has been one of social necessities may be narrowed as well as the demand for social communication may not be distorted by high tolls.

Lastly, the cases of foreign countries were reviewed to judge the possibility of bringing mobile phone service within the ambit of universal service. It was found that the expansion of universal service has a legal basis. In the case of Korea, Enforcement Decree of Universal Service Act stipulated that the base rate of mobile phone service shall be reduced by 30 percent to the disabled and the low-income bracket. It well shows that the social necessity of mobile phone service is well reflected in the existing system. Also, in process of executing the universal service policy, each country has recently considered the universal design of handsets, software and contents, teaching how to use, and the restriction of tolls, not to mention accessibility. Given the fact that the gap between social groups in telecommunication service has been segmented to accessibility, usage, availability, usability and level, multidimensional access is judged to be effective to increase the availability of the underprivileged and to be significant in discussing nation's advanced universal service in future. The United Kingdom and Japan has considered the question of whether high-speed internet and mobile phone service can be included in universal service focused on wired phone service, in order to cope with changes of users' needs. Also, the Unites States and Australia has already carried out advanced universal service. But in the case of Korea, detailed schemes for the institutionalization of advanced universal service have not been worked out systemically though 'Information Gap Solution Act' and 'Framework Act on Informatization Promotion'stipulate that advanced telecommunication service including high-speed internet service shall be provided as universal service. But now, the question of whether mobile phone service is applied to universal service should be discussed in that nation's mobile phone service has recently satisfied requirements for the introduction of universal service to a certain extent.

Section D

MEDIA & THE NEGOTIATION OF IDENTITY

17

Being Cultural Citizen: Role of Media

Shan-Shan Li

In the age of globalization, the physical movement of people across national boundaries has become rapid and phenomenal. Even when people are not physically mobile, media have made it possible for them to achieve a virtual mobility across national boundaries (Appadurai 1990, 1996). Media also have the power to facilitate cultural understanding and to forge new cultural identities (e.g. Cottle 2000; de Leeuw and Rydin 2007; Ginsburg et al. 2002; Gillespie 1995; Ross 2000). Encountering both 'home' and 'host' country media in the host country, the displaced people negotiate cultural differences and develop a new/hybrid cultural identity. Scholars in media ethnographic research generally agree that media from a home country help the displaced people maintain their home culture and 'past' identity, while their new/hybrid identity is forged by consuming media in the host society (e.g. de Leeuw and Rydin 2007). The former, to some extent, hinders their cultural integration, while the latter enhances such processes (de Leeuw and Rydin 2007; Fazal 2007), although host country's media can also reinforce social separation and marginalisation (Sjoberg and Rydin 2008; Jakubowicz et al. 1994), as well as cause a 'split' identity (Gillespie 1995).

However, previous research mostly focuses on migrants, diaspora and other kinds of sojourners, such as guest workers, while studies focusing on international students are sparse (Li 2009). This is surprising since international students have also been major border-crossers since the 1980s. From 1990 to 2001, cross-border students studying in OECD (Organisation for Economic Co-operation and Development) area rose from 1.01m to 1.58m (Deumert et al. 2005). In the Chinese context, mostly influenced by the 1997 Opening-up Policy under Xiao-Ping Deng's national economic reform, *chu guo re* (leaving China fever) and *liu xue re* (overseas study fever) became a trend in China (Zhao 2007; Yunnan Daily 2002). In 2008, 179, 800 Chinese students went overseas to seek foreign education (161,600 at their own expenses) (MoE 2009). China has become one of the biggest source countries for cross-border students on tertiary-level (OECD 2009). In Australia, up till 2007, Australia has achieved to be the fifth most popular country (the third among English-speaking countries), which provides international education (AEI 2003, 2006). August 2009 saw 29.347 Chinese international students studying in Australia (AEI 2009). That is to say, despite the large number of Chinese students studying in Australia, these students' media and cultural experiences remain unknown. This represents a serious gap in the knowledge of these students' cultural life and transformation. In this light, this article tends to investigate the media experiences of Chinese (Beijingese and Shanghaiese) who study in Sydney. It mostly focuses on these students' Internet usage and television consumption, given that these are the two main forms of media consumption for this group.

Research Design and Methods

Participants involve 13 current Chinese students (Beijingese and Shanghaiese) who study in 5 universities in Sydney. Three one-on-one interviews have been arranged with each of them. The first one was a general interview about their everyday life in Australia and media usage. The interview is intended to seek background information about their life. The second and the third interviews were Australian soap opera viewing and discussion sessions. The programmes shown were *Neighbours* and *Kick*. Since the soap opera has been regarded as the most realistic fictional media genre, and a soap opera programme reflects the culture of the region where it is based (Allen 1985, 1995; Buckingham 1997; Dyer et al. 1981; Kilborn 1992; Crofts 1995; Cunningham and Jacka 1997; Hobson 2003; Wober and Fazal 1994; Geraghty 1991); it is expected that Chinese students' reactions to the shows will reflect their understanding of Australian society and culture. Australian soap opera *Neighbours* tells stories of domestic lives of a group of Anglo-background people living in a rural residential area in Melbourne. *Kick*, launched by SBS in July 2007, involves characters from a variety of cultural backgrounds, such as Greece, Vietnam, Russia and Lebanon, and the programme focuses on representing multicultural issues. Therefore, it is expected that Chinese students' interpretations of *Neighbours* will reveal their understanding of Australian mainstream (Anglo) culture, while their reactions to *Kick* will show their feelings of living in Australian multicultural society.

Background—Everyday Life and Cultural Experiences

Unless the cultural experiences of other types of the displaced people, Chinese young intellectuals have better cultural understanding of the host society, better language skills and more cultural flexibility. Influenced by Western media productions, such as films, television serials and music (mostly from America or UK), which are available in China, these students have a good understanding about Western culture and understand some cultural differences between the East and the West before they leave China. However, they tend to generalise Australia as one of the 'Western countries'—just like America or European countries. Apart from those who have families or close friends in Australia, their understanding of Australia mostly came from intermediate companies, university prospectus or travel brochures. Their imagined Australia is a Western country but with a nicer sky, beautiful beaches and rural sceneries (Also see Forth 1994). Nevertheless, better cultural understanding did not help much in making Chinese students integrate into Australian life quickly when they arrived. They have a variety of difficulties in communicating with either local Australians or people from other cultural backgrounds.Firstly, although Western culture did not bring Chinese students much cultural shock, the cultural shock was generated from the fact that Australian society is multicultural, and the universities they attend have 'too' many *Chinese* students:

> "I found there are so many Chinese here. That surprised me. And I felt that Australia is not a very Europeanised country ... Australian culture is quite different from that of other European countries." (male) "[In our classes,] the lectures are Chinese, and almost all of the students are Chinese. It seems that we spent millions of yuans simply to borrow a classroom from Sydney University! ..." (female)

Participants felt disappointed when they found that Australia is not 'Western enough' when they arrived. One of the participants defines her university as "a Chinese university simply with more 'foreigners'" (female). One of the participants studies Chinese-English translation; therefore, all of the students (except one who is from Singapore) are Chinese. This fact hinders her from getting to know non-Chinese friends. Some other courses, especially business-related courses, are also mostly occupied by Chinese students. Such 'surprising' fact even makes some students suspect that Australian universities' intention of offering such courses is simply to grab students' money. Anyway, no matter how Chinese students perceive Australian society or universities, it is obvious that high percentage of Chinese students in classes hinders them from having more interaction with non-Chinese students at their universities.Secondly, Chinese students have difficulty in making non-Chinese friends due to 'cultural differences'. They revealed that they feel lack of topic when they chat with non-Chinese students, and they cannot get each other's humour. Thirdly, Chinese students have less opportunity of communicating with local Australian people (also see Chalmers and Volet 1997). Most of them live in shared properties with other Chinese students and do not have much communication with people living in the neighbourhood either. They do not involve much in social life, such as going to pubs or attending recreation progrmmes. Due to the above reasons, they make few local friends.In her study of Chinese in Australia, Ang (2000) suggests two types of overseas Chinese. One type of them wish to assimilate into the mainstream. But because they are refused by the dominant culture, they have to Sinicise as non-assimilated Chinese. Another type try to de-Sinicise. But because of the influence of multiculturalism, they become faithful to their Chineseness. Both of the features can also be found in the case of Chinese international students' cultural experiences. Having less opportunity of mixing with people from the mainstream, they have to group up with peer Chinese students and keep Chinese way of living in their daily life. Also, their realisation of living in a cosmopolitan city reinforces their sense of being *Chinese* students.As a consequence, Chinese students have a strong sense of their Chinese identity. In the mean time, however, they also understand Anglo culture and the multicultural society of Sydney. But such understanding can hardly be 'up-dated' in their everyday life, due to their less interaction with non-Chinese. They are flexible in understanding others, but such cultural competence does not weaken their sense of Chineseness. They feel comfortable with living within their Chinese student circles as well as keeping Chinese lifestyles in Sydney. With the above background, the rest of the article will discuss how such life condition will influence Chinese international students' media usage, and how their media experiences can influence their cultural and identity transformation.

Media Usage Patterns

The InternetChinese students have heavy usage of the Internet. This phenomenon can come from three main reasons. Firstly, these Chinese young people, with good Internet skills, such as visiting websites and using e-mails and IMS, prefer new media to traditional media. They agree that the Internet is more convenient, efficient, interactive, personalised, and has larger volume of contents. Secondly, nearly all of the participants (except one PhD student who can get a computer from the university) brought a laptop from China, and have Internet access at home. This is in contrast to the fact that they do not own many other media. Some of them do not have a television set at home or do not have a TV good enough to allow them accessing all of the free-to-air channels. One of the participants reported that apart from a laptop, the only medium he owns is a radio, which was found from the street. Therefore, the Internet became the most convenient and the cheapest medium that Chinese students can access. Thirdly, the Internet is used as a tool to kill the time that these students might spend to have some other entertainment activities if they were in China. Coming from 'more modernised' and 'busier' city (Beijing or Shanghai), participants are used to the variety of entertainments, such as Karaoke, night restaurants and shopping, which are available at night in their home city. So, for them, the quiet Australian street with all of the shops closed after 5:00 pm is 'boring'. As a consequence, they rely on the Internet to make up 'the lost entertainments'.Except for the time spent on the Internet, Chinese students' Internet usage does not have much difference with that of when they were in China. They visit both Chinese and English websites for both information and entertainment purposes. They read news and seek information from both kinds of the websites. For more entertainment-based websites, Youtube, Tianya and Sina etc. are reported being regularly visited. Some Chinese forum websites such as Tianya and Tiexue, which contain a variety of topics ranging from news, gossips to on-line novels are also popular among these students. They show multi-loyalty in visiting websites. The websites that they visit enable them to be virtually connected with China, Australia and the rest of the world. In this sense, the Internet provides Chinese students with a virtually internationalized world so that they can be culturally mobile/flexible in their on-line life.It is true that Chinese students' on-line life can facilitate their cultural adaptation; however, using the Internet also turns them away from Australian society in reality. Firstly, as has been addressed formerly, the Internet is used as an alternative for Chinese students to fill in their spare times, the increasing amount of on-line time spent inside thc room leads to reduction of interpersonal communication—especially with non-Chinese—in reality. Secondly, considering that they are reluctant to give voices on-line, such as posting messages in forums, and have little discussion with non-Chinese about the contents that they have viewed, the virtually internationalised world reversely keeps them in-door and away from Australian society off-line. Television ConsumptionAs to the case of those who do have a television set at home, factual programmes such as news and current affairs are vastly viewed. They consume contents about both China and Australia, as well as big issues in the rest of the world.They realise that factual programmes are useful for them to understand Australia:

> "When I see things [on the television], I can know things happening around me. I can know places and situations in Australia. It is very good ..." (female)

Issues about China on the television will especially be brought to these students' attention. These issues become the topics when they contact friends and families in China. Such contents help strengthen their sense of connection with home and Chinese identity:

> "When the Tibet issue raised, we [with her boyfriend] used to watch news everyday … like [Beijing] Olympic Games, of course I watch … If I find anything about China, I will especially chase it. …"
>
> "... For example, on the day when the [Beijing] Olympics closed, I even did not know ... I did not pay much attention to the exact date. [I then called my mum.] I said: "mum, I slept in that day." The worst is the day on which all Chinese mourn [for the casualties in the Sichuan earthquake] ... three minutes' mourn. Then I called my mum, I said: "Mum, I feel guilty. I will seriously stand for three minutes tonight as the penalty." Look, it's such a big issue, which is known by the whole world. But I did not know just because I did not switch on the TV that day! ..." (female)

Issues about China will arouse this participant's great attention. She will actively continue to seek more information about these issues from other sources such as the Internet or her families at home. She also uses these materials as topics to communicate with home. In this sense, contents about China in factual programmes enhance Chinese students' emotional connection with China and strengthen their sense of 'extended home' (de Leeuw and Rydin 2007; also see Cunningham et al. 2000). For them, anything about China is a thing related to self. News, which is mostly addressed in the public sphere, has been brought to their personal life (Sjoberg and Rydin 2008). In short, factual programmes on Australian television, on the one hand, facilitate Chinese international students to understand Australia and integrate into its society. Knowledge about the host society helps them settle down in Australia more comfortably. On the other, these programmes can also reinforce their emotional feeling of connection with home and Chineseness. By consuming this kind of programme, they are flexible in living in between the two worlds, and it is their contents which enhance their cultural mobility. However, considering that issues about Australia are mostly used for 'surviving' in the host society, only issues about China can arouse their emotional attachment; factual programmes do not play a significant role in reducing these students' sense of their Chinese identity.In contrast, Chinese students seldom consume Australian-made fictional programmes. If factual programmes can provide them with information about Australian public life, fiction, such as soap operas, can offer a peep into Australians' more private everyday life. Chinese students use factual programmes to understand Australia's places and people. But they do not take advantage of using Australian fictions to have a look at what Australian people do everyday domestically. None of the participants reported that they had watched or even knew about Australian soap operas. Apart from bad media access, they reported that it is not easy for them to find many Australian fictional programmes on the television. By zip-zapping the channels, they found American programmes occupying most of the time slots, and they are more entertaining because of their better production quality and more dramatic scenarios. Also, American programmes such as *Sex and the City* and *Friends* are available on DVDs in China. They like them and are 'used to' these programmes. Therefore, they do not intentionally make an effort for searching Australian programmes when they watch television. As has been addressed earlier, the research uses soap opera viewing and discussion sessions to investigate to what extent Chinese international students have integrated into Australian society. Such method was proved to be useful, given that all of the participants agreed that the shows 'truly' reflect Australian social reality. Characters' behaviours did not bring much surprise to the participants. Earlier, we addressed Chinese students understand 'Western' culture even before they arrived in Australia, and they do not have much communication with local Australians when they are in Sydney. Therefore, they tended to interpret the fiction by their imagination of 'Western people' when they were asked if the fiction reflects reality:

> "They [the characters] are not like us, but I am not surprised about it. For example, their complicated love life … It is like common sense … I saw them on the television when I was in China." (female)

This participant perceives the show as true through her 'common sense', which she generated from her television viewing experiences in China. Her reaction to the programme reflects her good cultural flexibility which she had already had before she arrived in the host society.However, although participants are culturally flexible in understanding the stories, the shows reinforce their sense of being 'otherness', and their interpretations of the programmes reflect their less assimilation into either Australian mainstream (Anglo) or the multicultural society of Sydney. When *Neighbours* was shown to the participants:

> "[By watching this programme], we can see local Australians' lives …" …"…When I was watching this programme, I felt that I was watching a group of foreigners. It has nothing to do with me. Our lives are completely different …" (male)

This participant believes that the show can let people know about local Australians' everyday life. However, he identifies the difference between his life and lives in the fiction such as teenagers' study load and social phenomenon of divorced family. His responses to the show reflect his less assimilation into the Australian mainstream lifestyle. Watching the programme aroused his sense of being different.The social reality of multicultural Australia represented in *Kick* is also rejected by Chinese students. *Kick* reflects SBS's representation rationale in terms of handling migrants since the 1990s. Rather than treating migrants as 'others', SBS handles them and cultural diversity as existing in Australian society on daily basis. (Ang et al. 2008) The programme is seen as a "real *Neighbours*" (Ang et al. 2008:157). However, such social reality has contradiction with what Chinese students experience in their daily life:

> Interviewer: "Did this programme remind you anything about yourself?"Participant (female): "No. It totally has nothing to do with me … When I was watching this, I felt that I was watching someone else … Nothing in the show has similarity with my culture. They [the characters] are already localised. They don't have problems like what I am encountering—I am new in Australia, so I don't know much in here, I don't understand things in here, and I don't feel fit in this society. I just feel that the characters in the show are locals, whose lives are completely different from that of mine."…"I heard local people's comments. They don't think multiculturalism is good enough. Multiculturalism does not mean that people from different cultural backgrounds can mix harmoniously. When people [from different cultural backgrounds] find out that they cannot mix together, they will break up into groups. For example, this group is Chinese, that group is Korean, and that group is local. Then these groups will not have any communication with each others for good … The society then becomes a group made up of a lot of sub-groups … The only difference is that they used to live in different countries, and now they live in the same country—actually no difference."Interviewer: "Do you think people in the show are in separated groups?"Participant: "They have already mixed well. They are not in sub-groups. They have already been in the sub-group of 'locals'. The show did not choose anybody from other sub-groups."

This participant identifies the difference between migrants who were brought up in Australia and sojourners such as international students who came at their later age and are relatively new in the host society. In her real study life in Sydney, her close communication circles are made up of Chinese students only. So she believes that people from different cultural backgrounds live in separated sub-groups. The cosmopolitan society that she perceives through her university life experiences follows a "container model" (Beck 2006:27) involving national boundaries. She believes that the show reflects Australian social reality. However, the contradiction between her pluralistic view in understanding the fiction and essentialistic description of Australian social reality interestingly reflects the contrast between her culturally pluralistic mediated life and more culturally fixed real life in Australia.However, Chinese students do have wish for being integrated into the multicultural community in the way that the characters do:

> "Australia is a hot-pot, having people from a variety of nations. They are mixed harmoniously. It is very nice." ..."I am afraid that I cannot fit in this community [in the fiction]. But if I were brought up here, I would be able to fit in. I came here when I had already grown up ... [therefore,] surely I cannot have much interaction [with them] ..." (female)

This participant likes the harmonious multicultural community in the fiction. However, similar to the participant addressed above, she realised that her sojourner status makes it difficult for her to be an insider of such a community.In short, less consumption of Australian fictional programmes has the effect of leading to Chinese students' less knowledge about Australians' domestic life. They can imagine how Australians' everyday life looks like thanks to their good understanding of Western culture. However, there is a contradiction between their flexibility in understanding the media world and relatively essentialistic Chinese-styled life in reality. Their interpretations of the Australian soap operas reflect their status of less integration into either Australian mainstream (Anglo) or multicultural Sydney society, and the programmes reinforce their sense of being social outsiders.Only one of the participants have satellite TV at home, because she lives with her extended families who are immigrants. Most of the students have difficulty in accessing home media productions. It is true that some Chinese television programmes are available on SBS from time to time. However, most of the participants do not take advantage of accessing home productions. They have the habit of zip-zapping when they watch TV. So, some of them do not have much knowledge about the characteristics of SBS. Nevertheless, they do not have the strong desire of accessing Chinese programmes through Australian television, although sometimes a sudden spot of a Chinese show will make them a bit excited and feel 'being at home'. It seems that they can be comfortable for consuming media at the host society, rather than desperately looking back for home productions; although financial status could be an influencing factor as well.

Discussion

Mediated life and real life are different for Chinese international students. From the study of their Internet usage and television consumption, we can see that they are more culturally flexible in mediated life whereas less culturally cosmopolitan in real study life. Wrench and Solomos (1993) identify the phenomenon of privatisation of migrants' pluralistic cultural life. For Wrench and Solomos (1993), cultural flexibility is practiced by migrants in their private sphere; whereas, their voices are still silenced in the public sphere of the host society. Husband (2000) applies Wrench and Solomos' (1993) theory on studies of media practice, and suggests that due to the limitation of media's practices of reflecting and providing cultural diversity, migrants can only experience cultural pluralism in their private space, whereas their cultures are still invisible in the mediascapes—the public space—of the host society. The phenomenon that Husband (2000) suggests suits to the case of media experiences of Chinese international students who study in Sydney as well. The students lead a culturally pluralistic life in the media world in their domestic space—home or virtual transnational communities with families and friends in China; however, they are less, if not none, visible in the Australian public sphere. For one example, as has been addressed earlier, the Internet keeps these students remaining inside their private residences but away from the Australian public society. Also, they are reluctant to give their say on the Internet. Therefore, their voices are rarely heard by the Australian general public either on-line or off-line. For another, factual programmes on television which they enjoy consuming, and heavily consume, functions more about facilitating their maintaining Chinese (transnational) communities in their personal life, but less about being involved in Australian public democracy. With the lack of consumption of more 'domestic' programmes, such as Australian fictions, these students bring news issues in the public sphere into their private sphere so as to get emotional connection with their homeland. As a consequence, in both Australian mediascapes and real society, these young sojourners still remain marginalised, if not invisible.The reverse process—the publitisation of Chinese international students' personal life in Australian media does not really happen. In her study of Hong Kong Chinese in America, Ong (1999) suggests that globalisation is a competition for global visibility. Hong Kongese strategically use Chinese transnational media to make Chinese image and cultures globally visible so as to accumulate cultural capital and cultural power for living in the globalised American society. It is obvious that with weak financial competence, Chinese youth cannot take advantage of supporting media institution to make their images visible in Australian mediascapes. However, a participant revealed her realisation of the importance and power of such mediated visibility: This participant has a Chinese boyfriend who belongs to a Chinese minority. The boyfriend experiences Chinese media's marginalisation of national minorities. The participant is influenced by her boyfriend, and agrees that media should make every culture equally visible:

> "My boyfriend always complains: "Why there is not a channel for minority communities in here [Australia]?" ... He said that media should distribute time slots to different nationalities ... and introduce their cultures ... He said that if media do not function as recording, guiding and informing [cultures] ... if they do not show [minority cultures], nobody will know [those minority cultures] ..." (female)

In this conversation, although this participant did not directly talk about Chinese's visibility in Australian media, she has the realisation that media should bear responsibility of making social minorities visible. However, when she was asked how media should make minority cultures visible in Australian media, she could only offer documentaries or travel programmes. Probably because of her strong sense of her Chinese identity, she still attributes herself to a general Chinese national group, while her more personal life might still remain invisible according to her design.Some participants do wish overseas Chinese's more private lives to be shown in media. They express that such topics can arouse their interests. But such programmes are not found on Australian television:

> "I haven't found any programme which is very close to my life [in Australia]. If there were any, surely I would be interested in watching it ... Should they make something about overseas students' life in Sydney, surely I would pay attention to it ... A couple of years ago, Chinese television showed a programme talking about stories of Chinese students in Sydney, and I paid attention to it ..." (male)

This participant anticipates programmes can be more relevant to his personal life. However, such kinds of programmes are not found on Australian television. Nevertheless, some participants do not mind too much whether or not their personal lives will be reflected in media:

> "Should they show Chinese international students' life in Australia, it would be close to my life. But the life in this show [*Kick*] is different [from that of mine]. It is impossible for every television programme to reflect a particular audience's life, otherwise it is not interesting to watch ... We watch TV to experience others' lives, which makes watching TV interesting ..." (female)

For this participant, the value of media is to provide access to others' lives, so she does not complain if she cannot see her life reflected in media. In this sense, flexibility of understanding media and their operations can also make Chinese students be tolerant for being invisible in Australian mediascapes.All in all, different individuals have different opinions about media's operation of cultural diversity. More or less tolerant for media's practices, it is obvious that the media that Chinese students encounter in Australia makes them lead a pluralistic life within media world in their domestic sphere while marginalised, if not say invisible, in the public sphere of Australian mediascapes.

Conclusion

Influenced by the effect of globalisation and transnational mediascapes, Chinese international students obtained certain cultural knowledge about the host society even before they entered it physically. Such experience can help them understand the host society with less culture shock when they arrived. However, 'container-styled' (Beck 2006) university life and limited media access make it difficult for them to become Australian social insiders. The Internet and Australian television —the two main media that they consume in Australia—do not play a significant role in either facilitating them integrating into Australian society or weakening their sense of Chinese identity. The problem of media access and media's representation alienate these students into the social margin. There is a distinctive contrast between Chinese international students' mediated life and real life in Australia. Their mediated life involves good cultural flexibility and transnational mobility; whereas, in reality, they are more stable of living within Chinese sub-group and Chinese transnational communities, keeping their Chinese lifestyle and remaining a strong sense of their Chineseness. They show multi-loyalty in their on-line life, but the Internet to some extent hinders them from having more interaction with people from diversified cultural backgrounds (including locals) off-line. By consuming factual television programmes, they live as informed 'global citizen'; however, only issues about China can arouse their emotional loyalty, and such issues strengthen their sense of being Chinese and living at 'extended home' (de Leeuw and Rydin 2007). Being comfortable with consuming globally-popular American fictional television and zip-zapping viewing behaviour somewhat hinder them from watching Australian fiction, which might give them more idea about Australians' everyday life in private sphere. The above facts reflect the phenomenon of privatisation of migrants' pluralistic life suggested by Wrench and Solomos (1993) and developed by Husband (2000)—although these students are able to practice cultural plurality in their domestic space in media world, they still remain less visible in either real Australian society or Australian mediascapes. Meanwhile, the reverse process—publishing these Chinese young sojourners' life in the media world—has not been achieved; although, because of a better understanding of media operation and acceptance of what are on offer by media, such limitation can also be tolerated by (some of the) Chinese students.Nevertheless, this study also has its limitations. Firstly, as the participants have been in Australia on average for less than three years, the media's influence on their cultural transformation in a longer period cannot be revealed. Secondly, the limited number of participants brings danger of generalising the experiences of the vast number of Chinese students studying in Sydney. Thirdly, the study did not tend to investigate the relation between participants' Internet usage and television consumption, so as to reveal how different medium experiences can be combined to influence participants' cultural life. Finally, given that soap operas are generally regarded as females' genre (Geraphty 1991; Hobson 1982, 2003; Mumford 1995), it is possible that participants' interpretations of the programmes may be gender-based rather than culturally based. Therefore, further research is needed to explore whether or to what extent media institution in general or individual medium in particular, may better facilitate these international students living either a more culturally pluralistic life or an assimilated life, in both mediated and real world, during both a shorter and a longer period.

18

Virtual Diasporas

Notion of 'Home' and Identity Formation in Cyberspace

Elitsa Ivanova

In social sciences, there is a relatively long tradition in examining different forms of human mobility, particularly migration. In this field a significant body of research has been devoted to different aspects of migrant and refugee settlements in 'host' societies. Especially the studies on diaspora have attracted considerable attention from the academic sphere; since the 1980's a steadily growing interest in this issue can be witnessed. Also, the events on 9/11 and its aftermath led to a revitalizing of the concept of diaspora and gave rise to renewed public and scientific discussions about migration and diversity. The complex process of thinking and re-thinking through this concept generated a great bulk of scientific literature on this issue and new notions of diaspora identities and experiences (e.g. Diamandaki 2003; Tsagarousianou 2004) emerged. At the same time, the growth of new claims to the diasporic status gives us a reason to look back at the various articulations of this category, to scrutinize them and to consider their analytical value.

Thus, one aim of this article is to provide a brief overview of the recent academic debate on diaspora; it also attempts to elucidate the development of the concept within social sciences; it selectively focuses on different aspects of the discussions among theorists and hopes to make a critical evaluation of these. In addition, it presents some preliminary thoughts on the significance of the notion of home for contemporary (virtual) diasporas. In so doing, it draws special attention to research which focuses on and discusses the 'nature' of diasporic communities and the processes of a diasporic identity formation. In the field of migration studies a substantial literature has been devoted to the meaning and definition of 'diaspora'; a considerable number of studies assume the relationship with its erstwhile homeland to be the primary factor for any a diasporic group. Moreover, the symbolic and material significance of the notion of home has been strongly accentuated.

However, there are also examples of recent research which questions this view on diaspora (e.g. Hanafi 2005; Tsagarousianou 2004). Instead of seeing them as backward looking, as previous research tended to do, the relationship of diasporic groups with multiple locations through both geographical and cultural boundaries is emphasised as well as their ability to construct and negotiate their identities. Moreover, it is argued that an increasing detachment from the place of origin is a characteristic feature of modern dispersed communities, i.e., they are not only connected to the centre but also to each other (Hanafi 2005; Georgiou 2006). While recognizing and joining the critique of approaches focused mainly on the dynamics of nostalgia and memory of diasporic communities with an ancestral territory and appreciating the view of diasporas as forward-looking and actively engaging in activities on both local and transnational level, on a theoretical level this paper suggests that the notion of home has not lost its significance; though the primacy given to it by previous research should be tuned down, it is still highly relevant for the formation of diasporic identity. It is argued that for contemporary diasporas the place of origin is rather a point of reference, and the attachment to the former 'homeland' is experienced as more symbolic in nature. In this context, modern technologies and especially new electronic media become highly relevant since they deeply affect the cultural processes in which migrants engage. Internet in particular becomes a crucial factor for the process of a diaspora's identity formation, and it also creates new ways of experiencing immigration and of engaging in cultural practices, including those concerning the original homeland. Here, the relationship with the latter is seen as a source not only of remembrance, but of cultural creativeness and inspiration which affects the ways a diaspora reconfirms and positions itself. Without overemphasizing the notion of home in relation to diasporas, it is argued that it is of equal significance as the opportunities given by processes of deterritorialization, reterritorialization and delocalization.

The article hopes to make a contribution to the ongoing debate on media and diaspora. It is a continuation and not a break from existing studies in the filed of media and migration.

A Need for Theorisation

In academic discourse, the usage of the term 'diaspora', despite its ancient roots and history[1], is a relatively recent phenomenon. Before the 1980's there are few occasional quotations of the concept which was mainly used to describe migrant groups: migrants maintaining their ethnic tradition, a strong feeling of collectiveness (see also Anteby-Yemini & Berthomière 2005). Despite the fascination with the notion of diaspora in the 1980's the term was often used casually and in an untheorised way, usually just to describe phenomena characterised only by the dispersion of a population originated from one nation-state in several 'host countries'. Authors such as Clifford (1994) and Cohen (1997) were critical of this tendency and underlined the need for more theorisation. The call for approaching and studying diasporic phenomena resulted in a variety of efforts to delineate the concept of diaspora; the research carried out during this period reveals different kinds of theoretical positions and multiple inclusions of the notion. Moreover, the past thirty years could be characterised as a period of expansion of the concept, in academic and policy discourses one can witness a significant grow in its usage, importance and centrality. As a result, the literature on diaspora has grown voluminous and a variety of typologies were presented which all try to describe the concept and make it more comprehensible. Even a casual acquaintance with the recent research on diaspora reveals that this is one of the most difficult and slippery terms in casual usage today. Moreover, the classifications of diaspora presented so far are indicative of the different nuances the term itself bears on. Now we are speaking of "religious diasporas" (Bruneau 1995 in Anteby-Yemini & Berthomière 2005), "cultural diasporas" (Cohen), "virtual diasporas" (Diamandaki), "fear diasporas" (Appadurai), etc. The historical association of diaspora with exile, isolation and loss, with dispersion and displacement from the ancestral homeland as a traumatic experience indicates the deeply emotional and political connotations of the term. However, the variety of literature on this subject also reveals the difficulty of managing the concept; the considerable number of definitions and typologies make the risk of confusion more and more apparent. Obviously, there is a need to evaluate this notion, to consider the ramifications of what it denotes.

Conceptualising Diaspora

Tracing the study of diasporic formations in the late 20th century and the beginning of 21st century, one can witness a gradual shift of perspectives from focusing on immigration, emigration and their regulation towards attempts to broaden the study of diasporic experience while integrating it with contexts of citizenship, culture and identity, and processes of globalisation. As pointed out by Fazal and Tsagarousianou (2002), today the concept of diaspora is inseparable from the process of maintaining and negotiating and in some cases reinventing cultural identities.

The idea of diaspora varies greatly and the recent interest from the side of the academic sphere has generated many efforts to conceptualise this notion. William Safran (1991) for example, proposed a way of constructing an ideal type of diaspora. Displaced populations are identified as a diaspora when they fulfil the following conditions: they are communities that are dispersed from a centre to a periphery or foreign nation, that retain collective memory or vision of homeland, that are committed to restoring their ancestral homeland, and that believe they cannot be accepted by the host society and therefore remain separate from it (see also Nagel 1999:249). As this description indicates, here the symbolic and material significance of the homeland are emphasized. However, this attempt to list a working definition of diaspora has also its limitations and constraints: it puts too strong an emphasis on the nexus of diasporas with the 'homeland' and does not comprise other relationships and linkages a diaspora community can have (see also Fazal & Tsagarousianou 2002; Tsagarousianou 2004). Trying to expand the concept, Cohen (1997) proposes some additional criteria to those suggested by Safran. According to him, a definition of 'diaspora' should include those groups who scatter voluntarily or after fleeing aggression, persecution or extreme hardship. Moreover, Cohen states that a sufficient time period has to pass before any community can be described as a diaspora. In his view, there should be indications of a transnational community's strong links to the past that thwart assimilation in the present as well as the future. Further, the concept needs to recognise more positive aspects of diasporic communities. For instance, the tensions between ethnic, national and transnational identities can lead to creative formulations. Finally, it should acknowledge that diasporic communities not only form a collective identity in the place of settlement or with their homeland, but also share a common identity with members of the same ethnic communities in other countries (Cohen 1997:25).

In addition, Cohen (1997) constructs another typology that lists five different forms of diasporic community. According to origin, he distinguishes between victim (Jews, African and Armenians), labour (e.g. Indians), imperial (e.g. British), trade (Chinese, Lebanese), and cultural diasporas (the Carribeans abroad). Especially the latter type of diaspora lays emphasis on the creativity and innovation possibilities a diasporic community can have. However, the typology suggested is rather descriptive and still relies on the origin and the strong relationship to the past (see also Anthias 1998, Tsagarousianou 2004); moreover, it does not tell us much about the role of contemporary diasporas in a globalizing world. As pointed out by Werbner, viewed historically, it is evident that, whatever their origins, there can be a convergence in the experiences of different diasporic communities (2005:473).

The great popularity of the term 'diaspora' is also related to the substantial influence of postcolonial theorists like Stuart Hall (1990) and Paul Gilroy (1993) who focused on the positive dimensions of transnational experience. In their writings the cultural significance of diasporic experience has been emphasized and the artistic work and representations of diasporic intellectuals on the margins have been praised. However, recent research has critiqued the aestheticisation of the diaspora concept and has questioned the view on diaspora as always enlightened, progressive, or anti-nationalist, proposed by postcolonial authors. Werbner for example argues for "a recognition that the imagination of diaspora is constituted by a compelling sense of *moral co-responsibility* embodied in material performance which is extended through and across space" (2005:129, author's emphasis; see also Werbner 2002).

Recent research (Tsagarousianou 2004) on migration studies suggests that diasporas should not be seen so much in the light of displacement; it is their connectivity and the various relationships that scholars should focus on. Moreover, diasporas should not be defined on the ground of ethnic origins and only seen as an extension of an ethnic or national group, but as imagined communities, continuously reconstructed and reinvented (Brah 1996; Tsagarousianou 2004; Werbner 2002). Diasporas' self-mobilization around their awareness of themselves as a diaspora, their ability to imagine themselves as such and to construct the appropriate discourses are those fundamental elements that make the concept meaningful and legitimate (Tsagarousianou 2004). As indicated above, one response to the contemporary revival of the term is related to the problematising of the empirical definition of diaspora. However, the bulk of the literature in this field (see e.g. Safran and Cohen) has been concerned with attempts to define the limits of the concept. The efforts to create typologies over diaspora imply at the same time a wish to create order in the variety of definitions. As pointed out by Werbner, the aim of this categorizing activity is not so much to interrogate the current organisation or cultural location of diasporas, but to look to historic origins and try to determine some fundamental features of diaspora (2005:473). The attempts to identify some set of key characteristics would constrain the field of investigation; moreover, they are indicative of a desire to universalise, a search to find structural similarity and simplicity, and to homogenise a plurality of human experience, often denominated by various researchers as 'diasporic experience'. There is also a risk that there is a discrepancy between diaspora as a theoretical concept and distinct historical 'experiences' of diaspora (Clifford 1994), a slippage which is hard to avoid.

Part of the difficulties also comes from the production of various analyses from very different disciplinary vantage points. Nowadays, the study of diasporic phenomena is an interdisciplinary filed of research (which, of course, makes it more vulnerable to critique from different academic positions). That explains why some researchers define a group as diaspora when referring to their history of exile, while other focus on their religion or a memory of the homeland. Some other scholars (e.g. Brah 1996) suggest that the study of diasporas should call for a concept in which historical and contemporary elements are understood in their diachronic relationality. At the same time, all these intellectual traditions indicate a field that is "constantly open to new explorations, both in terms of theoretical orientation and empirical conduct" (Georgiou 2007:6).

The Question of 'home'

A considerable part of the attempts to present a typology of diaspora has a common feature: they place particular emphasis on the perceived strong nostalgic links diasporas have with the homeland or the place of origin. However, the concept of home is much more complex than this research suggests. In fact, notions of 'home' and 'memory' are always problematic and contestable in that they are involved in a wider set of politics about exclusion and belonging. Brah's discussion of this notion gives a hint of how intricate and problematic it could be:

Where is home? On the one hand, 'home' is a mythic place of desire in the diasporic imagination. In this sense it is a place of no return, even if it is possible to visit the geographical territory that is seen as the place of 'origin'. On the other hand, home is also a lived experience of a locality. Its sounds and smells, its heat and dust, balmy summer evenings, sombre grey skies in the middle of the day…all this, as mediated by the historically specific of everyday social relations (Brah 1996:192) Moreover, the notion of home has a strong connection with the materiality of everyday life and experience. Also, it is "intrinsically linked with the way in which processes of inclusion and exclusion operate and are subjectively experienced under given circumstances. It relates to the complex political and personal struggles over the social regulation of 'belonging'" (ibid.:192). It has references to another notion, that of the people who are presumed to be indigenous to a territory (Brah 1996:190), but also to multiplicity of locations through geographical and cultural boundaries (Fazal & Tsagarousianou 2002:11).

Brah further argues that the problematic of 'home' and belonging is specific to the history of a particular diaspora even if it is constitutive of the diasporic condition. When, how and in what forms these aspects become apparent and how they are handled vary between different diasporic formations. What is really important to many individuals is not so much the need for a concrete homeland or the homing desire as such. Not all diasporas uphold an ideology of 'return' to a place of 'origin'; some diasporic formations place a particular emphasis on cultural identification (Brah 1996:193). The diasporic imagination often involves the search for routes as well as roots (Gilroy 1993); moreover, it also includes the need to constantly negotiate and understand the state of being in-between the place of origin and the place of destination and settlement. Another perspective is introduced by Stuart Hall (1993) who sees diasporas as products of the cultures of hybridity. Similarly to previous research (e.g. Safran), he claims that these hybrid communities maintain strong links and identification with the traditions of their 'homelands'. However, in contrast to more traditional understandings of diaspora, Hall suggests that these hybrid communities will not return to the past or if they do, the place called homeland will be transformed beyond recognition as a consequence of modernisation. In that sense there is no going 'home'. Diasporas themselves articulate elements and traces of histories and traditions, languages and systems of beliefs of both the countries of settlement and the countries of origin. They belong at the same time to several 'homes'—and thus to no particular home. What is more, they are the product of a diasporic consciousness where identity is always "an open, complex, unfinished game—always under construction" (Hall 1993:362).

However, there are also examples of recent research which questions those more traditional approaches to diaspora that strongly emphasise the power of nostalgia (Hanafi 2005, Georgiou 2002, Tsagarousianou 2004). Here, the notion of home within contemporary diasporas is understood as comparatively weaker in relevance. Tsagarousianou (2004) for example suggests that diasporic identities can often draw much more on the experience of migration and settlement, on 'making' one's home than on a fixation to a 'homeland'. Moreover, giving prominence on the relationship between diasporas and their erstwhile countries hides the risk of essentialising the origins and reifying what is supposed to be found at the origin (e.g. tradition, language, etc). The insistence on the constitutive role of a 'place of origin' draws attention away from the potentialities of diasporas (Tsagarousianou 2004:58). Instead of seeing them as backward looking, as previous research tended to do, here, the relationship of diasporic groups with multiple locations through both geographical and cultural boundaries is emphasised as well as their ability to construct and negotiate their identities. Recent explorations also highlight the great impact new electronic media have for the increasing detachment of the periphery—diaspora—from the centre (the homeland) (Hanafi 2005; Georgiou 2006). Georgiou, with reference to HRNet (Hellenic Resources Network; http://www.hri.org/info/hrnet-info.html), shows that it can offer services and influence the centre, in this case Greece, but at the same time it can exist in its own right. Georgiou sees this as a new diasporic condition, that is "increasingly decentralised, autonomous and it challenges old meanings of belonging to a diaspora" (2006:12). In contrast, Werbner argues that diasporas are relatively autonomous of any centre, but, paradoxically, they show recognition to the place of origin and acknowledge at least some obligations and responsibilities to it and to the larger whole (2002:123). According to her, many modern diasporic formations are still characterized by their imagined attachments to a place of origin and/or collective historical trauma. Thus, diasporas can be seen as both ethnic parochial *and* cosmopolitan (Werbner 2002:120; 2005:471; author's emphasis).

Recent studies on diaspora (e.g. Tsagarousianou 2004) also emphasise the frequent involvement of diasporic formations in complex processes of cultural and political action on both local and transnational level. In so doing, they articulate elements from different countries and engage in negotiations that often overcome the constraints of 'ethnicity'. That assumption stands near to Hall's (1990) suggestion that diaspora mainly refers not to displaced 'cultural groups' but to the construction of shared cultural codes and memories, in which we all are involved. The engagement in diasporic cultural politics, he claims, opens up for various creative possibilities. Hall (1993) and Cohen (1997) underline the diasporas' potential for cultural creativity, their ability to reconfigure cultural features from the home and host country and to take advantage of the economic and cultural opportunities on offer. As Tsagarousianou writes, it is important to recognize the 'opportunity structures' that the combination of migration and connectivity that the diasporic condition entails give rise to (2004:59), to see them as forward-looking, as symbols for empowerment and enrichment.

Mediation of Community and Identity

Between media and diaspora there is an intimate relation; indeed, diasporas are highly depended on media and communication technologies for sustaining relations between different locations, groups and individuals. Within the context of diaspora, Internet in particular acquires considerable importance for at least some theoretical and practical reasons. In many cases, it becomes an important part of the daily life of migrants; moreover, it has the capacity to help them transform their social and material world (Smith 2002). By enhancing the possibilities for simultaneity, it improves their ability to stay connected with their erstwhile as well as host countries, and with each other. In order to maintain these relations diasporic groups rely very much on networks which expand from the currant locale to the transnational and global (e.g. Georgiou 2006). At the same time, the flexibility and openness of the Internet make possible the reconstruction of both community and place (Diamandaki 2003). By providing a sense of contemporaneity and synchronicity, the Internet, and on-line communication in general, also further communal feelings and action among migrants. What is more, they contribute to the creation of novel contexts of social interaction and provide new terms and conditions for membership and belonging. Internet can also encourage bringing about new processes of personal and collective identity formation and it offers new possibilities for the negotiation of, inter alia, national and ethnic identity.

Internet has a particular value for migrant populations since it gives them the possibility to expand the scope of community communication, self-expression and self-representation, to challenge boundaries and restrictions around and within community public communication (Georgiou 2006). It also provides diasporic/minority groups a space where they can express and/or obtain access to alternative images, values and perspectives often unavailable in mainstream media (see also Georgiou 2006). Novel phenomena such as digital nations or digital diasporas not only gain visibility in cyberspace but they also challenge traditional notions of home, togetherness, community and identity in various ways. However, even if Internet opens up for variations and new opportunities, and makes it easier to overcome traditional identifications, what we should be aware of is that it does not alter the social bases of identity or the conventional constraints on social interaction discourse (see also Diamanadaki 2003). Moreover, the research on Internet and diaspora cannot go further without also looking at the off-line world, without including a social dimension. Advances in communication technologies cannot be equalled with new forms of human communication (Hanafi 2005). As recent research (Georgiou 2006:13; Hanafi 2005) has shown, on-line communication has a particular value for diasporas in the context of their everyday life and it is highly related with their off-line (and other on-line) cultural experiences and practices. Face-to-face relationships are still of great importance and factors of traditional physical contact remain highly significant (Hanafi 2005). Thus, Internet cannot be studied and understood without also including the social context of diasporic experience.

As indicated earlier, in the context of diasporic populations, on-line communication not only strengthens identity, but it contributes to a qualitative change in the experience of migration. However, the access and use of the Internet by migrant groups are still connected to other factors such as social and economical conditions and cultural capital. In some cases poverty and social exclusion as well as existing inequalities in e.g. technology competence still remain powerful restraints.

Virtual Diasporas

From the side of media and communication studies much research has been done on media and diaspora. A considerable number of studies are devoted to diasporic and migrant uses of media and communication technologies. Here, the focus lies primarily on the questions of identity and belonging (e.g. Georgiou 2002, 2006; Gillespie 1995). At the same time a significant amount of work is related to the new technologies and to the Internet in particular. In this area, research has been primarily directed at the significance of networking across boundaries. The role of new media, particularly in advancing (or restricting) participation in a political and/or cultural public sphere has also been many researchers' (e.g. Siapera 2005) object of study (Georgiou 2007). As indicated above, a great part of the research on media and diaspora is devoted to online communities. However, to talk about online formations and cyberspace in general as if they were a homogeneous group or a single and uniform type is somehow inaccurate. Online communities, virtual diasporas[2] included, are very diverse in their composition, their goals and their evolution, and cyberspace is "a pluralistic, multi-tasking and distributed environment made up of very different sub-contexts of communication" (Diamandaki 2003). Therefore, if digital communities and online identities are to be understood, their uniqueness must be considered (ibid.). Besides a common goal, symbolic capital as some shared history, language and culture is often presumed to be a prerequisite for the reproduction of a community in cyberspace. The socialisation process the participants engage in when joining a community entails some key factors: norms and rules have to be adopted, cultural codes and hierarchies need to be followed. Through these meaning-making practices online communities become a new arena for the articulation of social experience and identity (see also Diamandaki 2003).

As implied earlier, the cyber communities are not naturalised communities; neither should they be seen as 'given communities': they have not existed forever or in any essential way. A possible way of understanding online collective formations, virtual diasporas included, is as "imagined communities". Although the original usage of Anderson's concept refers to the study of nations, it could also be applicable in the context of online diasporas. Even in this case we can talk about deterritorialised groups which think of themselves, despite their dispersal, as a community, as sharing a collective past and common destiny and hence also a simultaneity in time.[3] The valuable in using Anderson's notion is that it emphasises the constant imaginary construction of identity, of its reinvention and reconstruction and draws attention away from the presumed authenticity or falsehood of online communities (comp. Diamandaki 2003).

One of the recent projects examining diasporas as a virtual phenomenon is that of Katerina Diamandaki (2003). More precisely, she studies how ethnic groups and diasporic communities use the Internet to create identity and gain visibility and recognition in the public sphere. The flexibility and openness of Internet, she argues, not only gives the opportunity of constructing community and place anew, but it is another archive, mirror and laboratory for the negotiation of national and ethnic identity. Depending on the communities they represent, the practices they enact and the goals they seek to attain Diamandaki distinguishes between diasporic and nondiasporic ethnicities and nationalities. Here, I will just bring up the classification of online diasporic communities which includes: *nations or national groups without a state* (e.g. the Jews, the Kurds, the Palestinians, etc), *expatriate/immigrant communities of existing nation-states* exemplified by the Greek and Iranian expatriates, the overseas Chinese, crossover communities such as African-American or European-Americans, etc., and *communities of dissidents who have fled totalitarian regimes.*[4]

However, even though Internet opens up for the reconstruction of ethnic or national identities, in the end it is not totally different from its non-virtual expressions. According to Diamandaki, these digital formations function as "spaces for the re-articulation of the same "social dialogues" that usually preexisted in the offline worlds and around which issues of national determination were produced and reproduced. The online does not erase the offline, she suggests, but changes its meaning, its modus operandi as well as its sociological implications. However, the online communities and identities discussed by Diamandaki are structured on the basis of commonalities that do not go beyond those of ethnicity and nationhood."

Virtual diasporas, likewise their real counterpart, are not a monolithic phenomenon. As implied above, most diasporic groups have the propensity to generate a plurality of virtual diasporas around areas of interest such as religion, politics, gender, professions and the like. Since the membership comes from the same pool, these virtual diasporas tend to be made up of intersecting circuits that crisscross one another while maintaining their distinct focuses (Laguerre 2002).

Virtual Diasporas and the Notion of Home

As already mentioned, Diamandaki (2003) identifies three categories of online diasporic communities: nations or national groups without a state, communities of dissidents who have fled totalitarian regimes and expatriate communities of existing nation-states. The first two types (whether online or offline), even if they have different purposes, are characterised by strong links to their ancestral countries. Whether the main discourses refer to uprooting, displacement and suffering or to "resistance" and "democracy", in both cases the symbolic and material importance of the homeland and a vision to return to it are emphasised, thus revealing a traditional notion of 'home' which is somehow irrelevant for the line of argument here.[5] That is why for my discussion I will take the latter category—expatriate communities of existing nation-states—as a point of departure. These diasporic groups (migrants and expatriates) make use of the cyberspace when seeking all possible ways for resolving the dilemmas of immigration and handling the innumerable problems affecting their everyday lives. According to Diamandaki (2003), this type of digital communities may have no clear-cut political causes; usually their main purposes are to maintain links between members scattered all around the globe and to promote their general well-being. Most of them, the Chinese expatriates' Huaren.Org for instance, although their main objective is to create a sense of commonality and togetherness and to raise consciousness among their dispersed members, are also actively engaged in the politics of identity. In so doing they create a new space for intra-diasporic communication, convergence zones where they can meet and engage in cultural activities, or discus issues of common interest, issues concerning the nature of migratory experience and—through this—the relationship to the country of origin. Here, the debate is continuously centred mainly on the search for identity, on answering the question of"who they are" and "what home is, or has been" (see also Danforth in Tsagarousianou, 2004:59), which also implies positioning themselves towards the place of origin. As Hall writes: "identities are the names we give to the different ways we are positioned by, and position ourselves within, the narratives of the past" (1990/1997:52). That is, the homeland is a point of departure, a point of identification in the process of diasporic identity formation, a significant aspect which should not be overlooked or underestimated. However, the process of positioning oneself towards the homeland can imply but is not necessarily constrained to a nostalgic effort of sustaining one's identity. Moreover, it could be further argued that today a diaspora's attachment to a homeland is more symbolic in nature, i.e., the original 'home' is experienced symbolically; while remaining highly evocative it has become de-linked from territory (see also Kennedy & Roudometof 2001:35, 37).

However, in the context of virtual diasporas, recent research (Mallapragada 2000, in Diamandaki 2003) has also shown how the Internet allows the constant imaginary construction in direct and everyday practices such as reading newspapers from home, discussing issues of common concern by sharing cultural codes, meeting people, all online. Engaging in these activities, they offer a set of symbols and terminology which attempt to reproduce familiar settings and terms of discourse in locations far remote from those in which they were originally embedded (Mandaville 2001:183f). It is thus inevitable when the homeland is reimagined in diasporic contexts that various processes of cultural translation are set in motion. This way, online communities reframe the experience of immigration, reframe their relations with home and with the rest of the diaspora around the globe. Even if the notion of home makes itself felt in all these activities, it does not necessarily mean that it automatically refers to nostalgic desires of, and their idealisations of an original country. It could be assumed that it is rather a process of cultural identification, which could be more important than a homing desire through a wish to return. Recent research (Fogt & Sandvik 2008) also shows that the Internet can help to unite people who live in exile, and may reduce the feeling of loss as a result of being so far from the rest of the family. At the same time it can function as a tool for establishing and maintaining social networks. Moreover, the relationship with the erstwhile homeland, be it actual or imagined, should not be seen as necessarily reducing the potentialities of diasporas. On the contrary, engaging in cultural activities on the web can be considered a potential for cultural creativity, offering similar possibilities as the interaction with other locations and societies within and beyond the boundaries of the country of settlement.

We have recently witnessed the launch on the net of new techniques and programs which, it could be assumed, have the capacity to greatly enhance and facilitate the contacts diasporic groups have with their erstwhile countries. It could be argued that the introduction of web-radio, web-television, video-calls creates new ways of experiencing immigration. Today, members of any a diasporic group have the opportunity to listen to radio programs from home in real time, and to experience the intimacy of face-to-face interaction when calling home (via Internet), which not only creates an impression of shrinking time and place, of contemporaneity and simultaneity, but also makes the experience itself more direct and 'real', more intense and brings up an impression of simultaneity *with* an almost physical co-presence. Thus, the original home is experienced in a more direct, even emotionally charged way, something, which, in effect, can reinforce the sense of belonging to the country of origin and strengthen cultural distinctiveness (as well as attenuate them depending on the feelings and associations the contact creates). One possible effect is also the strengthening of the moral responsibility diasporic members show to the place of origin and their acknowledgement of at least some obligations and responsibilities to it (see also Werbner 2002). However, how such innovations as the above-mentioned affect the process of a diaspora's identity formation in reality should be an object of further investigations.[6] Moreover, the age aspect plays also a significant role; for many members of the new generations of diasporic populations, their presence on the Internet allows the construction of diasporic identities which differ from those of their parents and those of people living in the original 'homeland' (see also Georgiou 2006). Thus, their experience of and relationships with the place of origin could take quite different forms. At the same time, we should also consider that diasporic communities are also actively engaged in developing contacts and networks not only with the ancestral countries or the places of settlement, but with each other as well. Thus, the original home is just one, though significant, point of reference and identification among many others.

The above examples are all important aspects in another process in which online diasporas engage: the creation of a home away from home (see also Diamandaki 2003). The new home can be seen as an imagined or symbolic unity build around shared meanings, the product of active engagement in "cultural and political action that articulates elements from different cultures and different frames of action and experience in one, more or less coherent whole" (Fazal & Tsagarousianou 2002; Tsagarousianou 2004). Thus it consists of and integrates components from both the country of origin and the country of settlement, as well as other places around the globe, of constructed cultural codes and memories, something that releases a potential of cultural creativity and innovation, and is precisely the quality which enables diasporic communities to remain viable for its members (see also Kennedy & Roudometof 2001). The new 'home' becomes a symbolic construct self-consciously used in order to represent a space of cultural distinctiveness rather than geographical entity.

Conclusion

More than anything else the Internet provides spaces where dispersed members of a diaspora can go in order to find others 'like them'. It is in this sense that we can speak of the Internet as allowing dispersed diasporic communities to create a new form of imagined community. Consciously constructed in order to function as meeting-points of dialogic encounter, as places understood through memory, history and constructed cultural sites, these virtual communities have a potential life-enhancing quality for those who participate in them. Whether they consist of expatriates who left a distinct country, are an exiled people, or belong to a stateless ethnic group, they have found a way through the Internet to create a home away from home (see also Diamandaki 2003). In the constructing process they articulate elements and traces of histories and traditions, languages and systems of beliefs of the countries of settlement and, inevitably, the countries of origin. The homeland is always there in the diasporic consciousness and imagination; it is a mental construction, and more than anything else, a point of identification; it is in relation to it that a diaspora (online as well as offline) negotiates and articulates its identity. In regard to identities online, what we should be aware of is their ephemeral character. How durable and coherent can the digital image of a diaspora be in the ever-changing nature of cyberspace? In a way, it is doomed to be always in process, fleeting and evanescent, permanently open to reproduction and change. Internet, like any other frontier of human experience reconfigures the way we form and project our identities. It may help us construct virtual ethnicities through crossing multiple borders, as in the examples above, but it has also potential to create new identities online, identities that go beyond the limitations of ethnicity and nationhood.

NOTES

1. We find its etymology in the Greek language; initially, it was used to refer to Greek settlements scattered around the ancient Mediterranean, and later to dispersed Jewish communities (Nagel 1999:249). At that point the notion of diaspora was associated with migration and colonisation, with processes and experiences of displacement, dislocation and mobility.
2. Perhaps here is the moment to define what I mean by virtual diaspora. Here, I take on Michel Laguerre's conception of the term, who defines it as follows: "the use of cyberspace by immigrants or descendants of an immigrant group for the purpose of participating or engaging in online interactional transactions". Such virtual interaction can be with members of the diasporic community living in the same country of settlement or in other countries, with individuals or entities in the homeland, or with non-members of the group in the host country or elsewhere. Virtual diaspora can also be seen as a cyberextension of a real diaspora. According to Laguerre (2002), no virtual diaspora can be sustained without real life diaspora and in this sense it is not a separate entity, but rather a pole of a continuum.
3. On the simultaneity in time of imagined communities see Anderson 1983.
4. For an overview of non-diasporic online communities see Diamandaki 2003.
5. These types of (virtual) diasporas are constructed mainly on the base of ethnicity and nationhood. However, other categories of diaspora, e.g. the religious one, have religion as primary point of identification (see e.g. Mandaville 2001).
6. Yet, recent research (Fogt & Sandvik 2008) has shown that through the Internet minority groups can both strengthen their diaspora identity and their attachment to the country of settlement).

19

Identities and Media of Brazilian Diaspora

Fernando Kuhn

Around 1.5 million Brazilians live abroad. This is the official statistic given on the web site of the Ministry of External Relations (MRE)[1] . But the real number is supposed to be very much higher. Data from the same Ministry quoted by Fusco (2006) and Patarra (2005) show a total of 1,887,895 in 2001. Another estimation attributed to the Brazilian Institute of Geography and Statistic (IBGE) indicates that 2 million Brazilians have left the country (De Azevedo, 2004), that is almost the same number—1,964,498—revealed in a compilation prepared in 2002 by Brazilian embassies and consulates, known as "RCN2002", that is also available on the MRE web site[2] . According to a report prepared in 2003 by the Brazilian Association of Anthropology, as referred to by Sasaki (2006), the number has reached 3 million, while as per the estimate of the Brazilian representative in the United Nations Population Fund (UNFPA), announced in 2006, it is between 3 and 4 million (Andrade, 2006; Dominguez Ávila, 2007). However, the fact that the major part of the Brazilian emigration in recent years has occurred illegally does not help in counting the correct numbers of emigrants (Carvalho & Campos, 2006).

Brazil has for long been a nation with low rates of emigration until the last quarter of the previous century. More than that, it is "accustomed" to see itself as a "land of opportunities" (Póvoa Neto, 2006, p. 1). The Portuguese colonisation and the settlement of African slaves brought from Cape Verde, Guinea Bissau, Angola and Nigeria (Santos, 2005; Gomes, 2003), along with with the diverse indigenous peoples living in the country at the time of the arrival of the discoverers, completed the "tripod" of Brazilian ethnic composition until the second half of the 19th century. Since then, it has received waves of immigrants from different countries like Italy, Germany, Spain, Portugal, Lebanon, Poland, Russia, Ukraine and Japan.

Recent immigration comes mainly from bordering countries (Patarra, 2000; Patarra & Baeninger, 2001; Gomes, 2003) like Bolivia (Poma Ulo, 2001; Sprandel, 2005; Cafardo, 2005; Da Silva, 2006)—1,500 per month, according to Roli & Fernandes (2007)—Argentina, Chile and Peru (Patarra & Baeninger, 2001), Colombia (De Oliveira, 2006; Rodrigues, 2006) and Uruguay (Patarra, 2000; Patarra & Baeninger, 2001), but also from Korea (Galetti, 1996; Cavalcanti, 1999; Patarra & Baeninger, 2001; Mera, 2005; Sprandel, 2005), China (Patarra & Baeninger, 2001; Gomes, 2003; Giannini, 2005), Japan and Angola (Patarra & Baeninger, 2001; Bógus, 2007), Lebanon (Gomes, 2003), and Nigeria (Calixto, 2007). After signing an agreement with the United Nations High Commissioner for Refugees (UNHCR) in 1999, Brazil also took part in the international efforts to shelter Afghan, Liberian, Serbian (Kim, 2005) and Palestinian/Iraqi (Kim, 2005; Jardim, 2006) families who had left their countries due to war and civil strife. According to Giannini (2005) Brazil has about 1.5 million of immigrants living illegally.

Brazilian emigration was, therefore, something rare, a fact that used to be restricted to a few students and professionals of advanced areas (Patarra, 2005). Only during the military dictatorship period, when refugees left the country, a (small) flux could be observed (Sarrible, 2004; Patarra, 2005; Schiltz, 2007). But due to a combination of factors, during the 1970 decade Paraguay started to attract many Brazilians in search of land to cultivate. Its "March to the East" governmental policy, that stimulated the exodus from the central zone of Paraguay to the eastern border region (Hanratty & Meditz, 1998; Haesbaert & Santa Bárbara, 2001; Zaar, 2001), the removal in 1967 of a Paraguayan law that prohibited the acquisition of lands by foreigners (Sprandel, 2006), the consolidation of Brazilian agricultural frontier in the Southern states of the country, culminating with the convergence of internal migratory flows into the state of Paraná, in the frontier with Paraguay (Marques & Máximo, 2008), the displacement of Brazilian small farmers and farm workers, caused by the modernisation of agricultural techniques and the expropriation of lands for the building of the Itaipu hydro-electric power station and its reservoir, affecting about 42,000 people (Marques & Máximo, 2008; Zaar, 2001), and even the decision of workers who had been engaged in the dam's construction of settling in the region (Domínguez Ávila, 2007).

Brazilian emigrants found cheap and fertile lands in Paraguay, and lots of them became prosperous farmers. Even now many Brazilians remain unregistered, as Paraguayan government alleges, which does not have enough money and technical resources to regularise their situation. According to Dantas & Seligman (2008), while Brazilian Ministry of Foreign Relations estimates 150 thousand Brazilians live in Paraguay, the Ministry of Justice estimates the figure to have touched 400 thousand.

Reflections involving Brazilian emigration and related processes began to appear in the late 1980s, and since then the issue has increasingly attracted the attention of Brazilian press (Póvoa Neto, 2006), disseminating the idea that "the country had transformed itself from a traditional immigrant society to an expelling country. The amount of around 1,5 million Brazilian living abroad[3] became the starting point to the perception that the international migration would come to continue; the emigration tendency, besides, started being considering an important demographic question" (Patarra & Baeninger, 2001, p. 7).

Thus, to employ the classification suggested by Cohen 1994 (Georgiou, 2003, p. 30), if in a first moment Brazilian emigration could be considered as a kind of political diaspora, soon it acquired a labour nature, that is still being expressed even by the more symbolical than quantitatively relevant (Patarra, 2005) transference of Brazilian football players to non traditional football markets, like Moldova, Kazakhstan, Haiti, Cyprus, Estonia, Oman and Malta ("Brasil exportou", 2006) and the Russian republic of Chechnya (Ferrari, 2008).

So, in the middle of the 1980s, a huge and prolonged economic crisis, also known as "lost decade", impelled lots of Brazilians to search for employment and better conditions of life abroad (Margolis, 1994; Goza, 1994; Patarra & Baeninger, 2001; Sarrible, 2004; De Azevedo, 2004; Higuchi, 2006; Salles, 2003 (Siqueira & De Lourenço, 2006, p. 187)), a decision that, in Schiltz (2007) analysis, was caused more by a feeling of frustration and lack of perspective than by economic factors. In a country that had received so many immigrants along its history, the opportunity of obtaining a foreign citizenship appeared as a natural and legal alternative available for many descendants of Portuguese, Italian, German and Japanese families.

With low-paying jobs being refused by Japan's younger population during the prosperous years of the 1980s, the solution found by many small factories for the recruitment of unskilled labour was to bring illegal workers from Pakistan, Bangladesh and other regions of Asia, thus raising, the challenge of integrating heterogeneous groups of people, with the already existing cultures in the Brazilian society (Linger, 2001).

In 1990, Japanese authorities revised the immigration law and a new status of permanence called 'long-term resident" was created, encouraging the immigration of third-generation Japanese and of non-Japanese spouses of second- and third-generation Japanese (Higuchi, 2006, p. 4), "a low cost means of helping to resolve the shortage of manpower, with the additional advantage that the immigrants who descend from Japanese ancestors are not seen to disturb the mythical ethnic homogeneity of the country" (Cornelius, 1995, p. 396 (Sasaki, 2002, p. 117)), and "would be capable of being assimilated into Japanese society without considerations of nationality" (Yamanaka, 1992, p. 7; Sasaki, 2002, p. 118), since they were "supposedly preadapted to Japanese language and customs" (Linger, 2001).

This sudden acceptance for working and living in the country of their ancestors, combined with well-established transnational labour recruitment networks between Japan and Brazil (Tsuda, 2000), triggered a huge influx of Brazilians—the largest population of Japanese descendants in the world, about 1.5 million (Linger, 2001)—into Japan, soon becoming the second largest population of foreigners in the country, estimated at 230,000 (Tsuda, 2000). The intensity of Brazilian immigration to Japan declined in the recession years experienced by the island since 1993, but Brazilians, with a registered population around 254,000, still are the third foreign group next to Koreans (what includes both South Korea and North Korea) and Chinese (Higuchi, 2006).

While Brazilian emigration to Paraguay and Japan occurred legally and in response to an official appeal (Schiltz, 2007), and blood ties (Bógus, 2007), historical and cultural factors played a role in the decision of leaving towards Europe (Patarra, 2005), the United States, due to its excellent economic conditions and the possibilities of social and economic mobility that it offered to its citizens (Marques & Máximo, 2008), became the obvious choice for those who did not have the same perspectives; young, white and middle-class people that penetrated illegally in the country and achieved unqualified jobs that were refused by white Americans and many times were not accessible for the black ones (Patarra, 2005), like waiters, shop assistants, babysitters, and other domestic services, jobs that in Brazil would have been incompatible with their social status, but that in the new country give them conditions of living a more comfortable life. According to De Azevedo (2004), and Patarra (2005), more than 7.00 thousand Brazilians live in the United States.

After 11th September 2001, when the country made the entrance of unqualified immigrants more difficult, Europe soon became a new alternative (Bógus, 2007; Schiltz, 2007). In 2007, 9,410 Brazilians were denied entry in European airports and 17 thousand were found living irregularly in the European Union (Rocha, 2008). Incidents involving the treatment given to Brazilians by Spain's immigration authorities came to light in 2008, with large repercussion in Brazilian media, and were received with indignation by the Brazilian government—and some Spaniards were refused entry in the country due to reciprocity procedures (Capriglione, 2008). Again according to data provided by the MRE, in 2003 there were 70 thousand Brazilians in Portugal, 35 thousand in Italy and 32 thousand in Spain (Patarra, 2005).

The Negotiation of Identities

The adaptation to a new country and its different culture, habits and rules is not usually an easy process. And it was not for most of Brazilian emigrants. Besides not finding a tropical weather and familiar food in their main destinations, specific circumstances have contributed to rise the feeling of strangeness.

Emigration to Japan had very peculiar implications. Even being born in Brazil and facing no problems of acceptance in Brazilian society, Japanese descendants—"nikkeis" (second generation, children of Japanese) and "sankkeis" (third generation)—are frequently seen as "Japanese" (Linger, 2001), because of their phenotype (Sasaki, 2002). "Often even they think they're Japanese" (Linger, 2001) and cultivate their "Japanese-ness" (Sasaki, 2002, p. 124-125; Suzuki, 2008), because of "their status as 'positive minorities' who are respected for their distinctive cultural qualities and social position", a pride that comes "from their affiliation and identification with the highly regarded First World country of Japan" (Tsuda, 2000, p. 20). Some even have a prejudice against Brazilians, as it was admitted by 44 percent of the people interviewed in a research carried out by Brazil's Datafolha Institute in June 2008 among Japanese and Japanese descendants living in São Paulo (Sakate, 2008).

But once in Japan, they found out that their idea about the country, its people and habits was very different from reality. According to Sasaki (2002, p. 124-125),

> "The Brazilian with Japanese features does not have the same spirit, values and socio-cultural conduct as the Japanese of Japan (...). Thus, their faces, that bore such a strong resemblance to the Japanese, ended up being the source of many misunderstandings. Sometimes the Japanese would demand that the Brazilian *Nikkei* behave like them, in accordance with the social and moral codes of conduct that were prevalent in Japan (because, given that they were descendants, it was presumed that they were culturally similar) (...) In this regard, very often, one heard accounts of how the non-descendant *Dekassegui* was treated better than the descendant, because the former was very visibly an outsider, a foreigner who had no Japanese features that disconcerted the Japanese".

In response to such exclusion, Brazilians adopted a defensive position, isolating themselves and gradually reconceptualising their country of birth as the true homeland instead of the country of their ethnic origin (Tsuda, 2000). Assuming the feeling of being Brazilians in Japan after being Japanese in Brazil (Linger, 2001; Sasaki, 2002), they join *samba* bands, wave Brazilian flags (Roth, 2002), promote Brazilian festivals, eat Brazilian food at ethnic restaurants, wear Brazilian clothes, and consuming Brazilian media products available in Japan, engaging "more actively in Brazilian cultural activities (...) than they ever did in Brazil" (Tsuda, 2000, p. 28).

The adaptation to the United States presented another kind of challenge. Marrow (2003) observes that "US natives are not usually familiar with the local and national origins of new immigrants, nor are they familiar with much of Latin American (not to mention Brazilian) history, geography, and culture (Margolis, 1994, 1998). Therefore, they often identify Brazilians according to dominant US ethno-racial categories, usually the same ones the US census utilises and publicises on forms throughout the country: white, black, Asian, Hispanic/Latino, and Native American.

On this purpose, Beserra (2005) argues that "in the racialised and racialising context of US society, all Brazilians have to go through a profound questioning of their racial identities because of their transformation into Latinos (...) For this society racialises arriving Latin American immigrants such that what you look like will impact on both the integration of individual Brazilians into US society and Brazilians' own definitions of Brazilianness". Although the term "Hispanic" is a category that may include anyone with a Spanish-derived surname, including those who emigrated directly from Spain itself, or even the Philippines (Levinson, Everitt, & Johnson, 2007), which is not usually the situation of Brazilians, it has become the preferential option for an ethnical classification of Brazilian population (Martes, 2003 (Jouët-Pastré, 2004)).

As speakers of a Latin language, Portuguese, and being originated from a Latin American country, it might be expected that Brazilians felt comfortable under the "Latino" classification. But, for several reasons, this is not what happens: the stigma of an identification normally "associated with low socioeconomic status, racial discrimination and, on the heels of massive new immigration from Latin America, disempowered immigrant status" (Marrow, 2003); the feeling of a "change of colours" (Martes, 2003 (Jouët-Pastré, 2004)), since Latino/Hispanic are considered as "non-white" and "non-black" and many Brazilians look 'white" or "black" (or even "Asian", as in the case of Korean-Brazilian immigrants described by Oh, 2002) enough to escape such external categorisation (Marrow, 2003)—Ramos-Zayas (2007) shows how, also for Brazilians, "'blackness' (...) has become a more valued benchmark of belongingness among Latin American migrants than 'whiteness'"; the political and cultural distance that still prevails between Brazil and Hispanic American countries, "a powerful image of stability" that was cultivated in a country that "has flourished as a great and solid empire surrounded by small and conflictive republics" against a perception of an arrogant posture combined to a linguistic barrier given by the fact that Portuguese language represents more difficulties to Spanish speakers than Spanish to Portuguese speakers (Crespo, 2006). For Siqueira & De Lourenço (2006),

> "The non-adoption of Latino, Hispanic, and even Latin American ethnic identity by most Brazilian immigrants in the U.S. imply that Brazilians feel different from the rest of Latin America. We assume that the rationale used by average Brazilians to consider themselves as an unique ethnic group is based on language—Brazilians are the only Portuguese speakers in the Americas; colonial history—the only country colonised by Portuguese in the Americas, and strong Brazilian nationalism. In addition, historical elite-led aspirations for Brazil to become a regional economic power, encouraged by military dictatorships and nationalistic economic development strategies, combined with a large territory rich in mineral resources to consolidate popular notions of uniqueness and distinction".

Although, as Marrow (2003) highlights, "Brazilians work to 'convince' US natives that the differences between themselves and Hispanics/Latinos are more important than their commonalities in lack of English language ability, immigrant status, foreign country of birth, and physical features—similarities usually more evident to US natives", in some situations—like claiming for rights and representation—it is very convenient for them to take part in the Latino community, once they alone form a too small community, as noted by Beserra, 2003 (Galli, 2005). It is also important to bear in mind that "Brazilian community", if there is one (Resende, 2003 (Jouët-Pastré, 2004) recommends the use of this term in the plural), is not homogenous—divisions by class, place of origin in Brazil and destination in the United States may influence the way Brazilians deal with the identity issue. The idea of belonging to the influent Hispanic/Latino group in Florida is not so disagreeable as it may seem in Boston (Jouët-Pastré, 2004), where "Black" appears to be a better option (Marrow, 2003). According to Martes, 2003 (Jouët-Pastré, 2004), the question of Brazilian identity is to be decided by the second generation of Brazilian immigrants—more capable, according to Menezes (2003 (Jouët-Pastré, 2004)), of perceiving the advantages of adhering to the Latino community.

Apart from the census categorisation, another option for many Brazilians has been the integration with the Portuguese community, not only in the United States (as described by Mulcahy, 2003) but in other countries where immigrants from Portugal have a consolidated presence, like Canada (Goza, 1994; Pacheco, 2004) and the United Kingdom (Evans et al, 2007). As Mulcahy (2003) notes, such integration is favoured by the fact that many times Portuguese immigrants are connected to Brazil due to familial ties—not to mention the common language, which also can be an attractive factor for people from Cape Verde, Mozambique, Angola, East Timor, São Tomé and Príncipe, Guinea-Bissau, Equatorial Guinea and Macau.

Even in Portugal, Brazilians immigration involves multiple identities, as pointed out by Machado (2006), determined by questions such as class, temporality of immigration, gender/sexuality, levels of Portuguese ascendance, colour/race, jobs/positions, regional origin and religion.

Mapping Brazilian Diasporic Media

If bordering countries like Paraguay are easily reached by Brazilian media (Sprandel, 2006; Albuquerque, 2006), what for immigrants reduces the appeal for the creation of their own ones, although even so some local radio stations broadcast in Portuguese at determined hours (Haesbaert & Santa Bárbara, 2001), in distant countries Brazilian Diaspora has engendered an increasing number of media vehicles during these decades. According to journalist Carlos Borges, founder of several Brazilian newspapers in the United States and creator of a series of events designed to promote Brazilian culture and people in the country, the total investment in Brazilian media jumped from less than 250 thousand dollars per year in 1992 to 12 million dollars in 2005. If in 1992 there were, in the whole country, only nine newspapers, one magazine and half a dozen of television programmes with a very limited local reach, Borges says, 14 years later Brazilian print media in the United States counted 120 publications, two Brazilian television networks covered the country and 76 web sites dedicated to Brazilian diaspora were active (Araújo, 2006).

According to Borges, Mendes, & Lima (2008), the first Brazilian publication in the United States was "Brazil News", that appeared in New York in July 1970 with 12 pages and one thousand copies. It did not last long, but in 1972 another newspaper was created in New York, "The Brazilians", that later became "The Brasilians" ("Brazil" is written with "s" in Portuguese). In the end of the 1980 decade, other four publications were founded: "Brazil Today", in San Francisco; "Brazilian Times", in Boston; "Brazilian Voice", in New Jersey; and "Florida Review", in Miami, which became a magazine in 2006—all of them are still in operation (Borges et al., 2008).

A few years later, the arrival of thousands of Brazilians workers to Miami, New York, Boston, Danbury (Connecticut) and Newark (New Jersey) coincided with the appearance of 20 newspapers, two magazines and some television and radio programmes, as reported by Borges et al. (2008). Brazilian media continued to grow, and in 1999 Brazil's "TV Globo Internacional" began to be distributed in the country by Dish Network. It was followed by "TV Record" and "TV Bandeirantes". In Canada, Brazilian community is served by monthly publications as "Etc & Tal Magazine", "Gazeta Brasil" and "Jornal da Mulher", quarterly "Brazilian Wave", and two weekly "BrazilNews" (Rodrigues, 2008).

In Japan, the first publication oriented to the Brazilian community appeared in Tokyo in the early 1990s (August 1991, as referred by Watanabe (2004); 1992, according to Ishi (2003)). "International Press" is a weekly newspaper, edited by IPC World, a big communication group that also includes a television channel, and has a circulation of 55 thousand copies a week (Borges et al., 2008). In 2003, the total number of Brazilian ethnic media was around 50, including free papers, small newsletters, and pornographic magazines (Ishi, 2003). Regarding press media, Ishi (2003), Shiramizu (2004) and Watanabe (2004) point out newspapers "Tudo Bem" (also from Tokyo, founded in 1993), "Folha Mundial", and "Nova Visão" (both from Hamamatsu, founded respectively in 1992 and 1995; Watanabe, 2004) as the most important ones—Shiramizu (2004) also highlights small communities newspapers in Aichi and Gunma prefectures, like "Aichi Popular" and "Ria de Rojipuro via Dori". But according to Borges et al. (2008), only the referred Tokyo newspapers remain active.

Portuguese-language TV channels are also available (IPC World is an affiliated of Brazilian "Rede Globo", but also has a channel that retransmits Brazilian "Record Internacional"; "Rede Globo Internacional" is broadcast in a SKYPerfectTV Channel—Borges et al., 2008) and radio programmes as well—Watanabe (2004) counts 11 of them, transmitted only in specific regions of the country. About 30 free magazines—two-weekly and Tokyo based Vitrine (owned by IPC World group) and Alternativa are the most important, with 250 page average and circulation around 55 thousand copies (Borges et al., 2008) complete Brazilian ethnic media, that in Ishi (2003, p. 484)'s view,

> "... is not bringing a solution just for a language literacy problem (providing news in Portuguese for people who do not understand Japanese). More than the so-called hard news, ethnic media has been a space of hot debates and artistic expressions by migrants (including attempts in literature, music, language and such), giving origin to a kind of *dekassegui's* culture".

Borges et al. (2008) observe that as many Brazilian television channels and programmes are available in Portugal, there is not a great demand for the appearing of diasporic media in the country. "Sabiá", that was created as a newsletter in 1992 and became a tabloid in 2003, is the most known. Maintained by an association of Brazilian immigrants in Lisbon, the paper has 12 pages, 7,500 copies and an undefined periodicity.

Even in countries of relatively recent Brazilian immigration, it is already possible to find publications directed to this segment: in the United Kingdom, Evans et al (2007) mention "half a dozen free publications produced in Portuguese that circulate awidely amongst Brazilians and other Portuguese-speaking communities in London", case of the magazines "Leros" and "Jungle Drums", and the weekly newspaper "Brazilian News", created in December 2001, that circulates in London with eight thousand copies; in France, Antunes da Cunha (2002) describes "Le Petit Journal" as an organ of the Association for the Development of the Portuguese and Brazilian Studies, of Portuguese-speaking Africa and Asia; in Spain, the Ministry of Work and Social Affairs reports the existence of one Brazilian magazine and one newspaper ("Los inmigrantes", 2007). Belgium and Germany have bilingual publications—that is the case of "Brazine Berlin"—that are supported by institutions dedicated to the promotion of Brazilian culture (Borges et al., 2008), while at least two magazines—"Brazil etc" and "Real" can be found in Ireland.

Brazilian media abroad tend to reflect the conditions and identities of the different communities they are related to. Different places of origin in Brazil, different destinations (in the United States, Brazilian are spread by states like Massachusetts, New Jersey, Florida, California, Georgia and Connecticut), different races, different classes, religion, alliances, interactions. Immigration issues are probably the only common point among such publications, but even so focusing in the specific implications to the community in question.

The Role of the Internet

But new ties are being established since the coming of the Internet, as it amplifies the means and opportunities for remaining "physically abroad but virtually at home" (Ros, Gonzáles, Marin, & Sow, 2007)—in what Christensen, 2003 (Fogt & Sandvik, 2008), referring to watching TV news from the original homeland, has characterised as a "transnational practice". Besides, it enables migrants to read in their own language, to keep up to date with events in their homeland and in the host country, to access information on regularisation, administrative procedures, job offers, training, housing and to find support against discrimination, (Ros et al, 2007), to listen to radio or downloading music from the home country (Rydin & Sjöberg, 2005 (De Leeuw & Rydin, 2007)), among other advantages.

As Karim (1998, p. 1) observes,

> "Global migration trends have produced transnational groups related by culture, ethnicity, language, and religion. Whereas members of some of these groups had generally operated small media (weekly newspapers, magazines, radio and television programming) to meet the information and entertainment needs of their communities, the emergence of digital technologies is enabling them to expand such communication activities to a global scale".

In this new context of construction of "transnational and local diasporic spaces" (Tsagarousianou, 2008), where "on-line diasporic communication has been developing extensively" (Georgiou, 2003), Dahan & Scheffer (2001, p. 91) identify three levels on which such means can be employed: "intrastate", for communication between the members of the various local 'communities', and with other ethnic groups; "trans-state national", for communication with the homeland and other communities living in other host states; and "global", for communication with other diasporas and global intergovernmental organisations and non governmental organisations.

Brazilian diaspora also benefits from all this new context. If in a first moment the trend was the transformation of bulletins into newspapers or magazines, now these can be transformed into web sites, aggregating recourses as audio, video, photos, links and message boards. Portals are created and rapidly become an important communicative reference in a given community, while blogs like "Mundo Pequeno" and "Brazilians abroad" connect different groups in different countries. "Mundo Pequeno" (<www.mundopequeno.com>), for example, compiles blogs of Brazilians living in 37 countries of all continents, from Uganda to New Zealand, from Iceland to Malaysia.

Due to the volatile nature blogs can assume, since most of them result of personal efforts subjected to different conditions, it does not seem recommendable to take specific blogs so seriously as long-term topics of research—their authors may return to Brazil, move to another city or country, or be forced to interrupt the postings for a number of other personal reasons. But meanwhile, lots of similar new initiatives can appear in diverse places, not to mention that, in many cases, inactive blogs still can continue to be accessed and prove their utility for an extended time.

An example involving former "Brazzil" magazine, currently "Brazzil.com" web portal, illustrates the opportunities brought by Internet to diasporic media. Da Silva-2 (2006) transcribes an institutional text where the portal, whose content is 90 percent in English, affirms that it is regularly accessed from more than 140 countries, including the United States (53 percent of the visits, Brazil (16 percent), Canada (5 percent), United Kingdom (4 percent), Germany, Australia and Portugal (2 percent), France, Italy and the Netherlands (1 percent), and declares its intention of connecting Brazil and all those—Brazilians or not—who have an interest about Brazilian way of life, its politics, economy and culture".

Operating on the levels described by Dahan & Scheffer (2001), or the spaces perceived by Georgiou (2003) and Tsagarousianou (2008), or simply, in what Diamandaki (2003) understands as the real consequence—instead of cultural homogenisation—of globalisation, carrying out a "cultural navigation between different localities", the media of Brazilian diaspora reserves a crescent role for multidimensional interactions.

NOTES

1. Retrieved February 15, 2008 from http://www.mre.gov.br/index.php?option=com_content&task=view&id=1411.
2. Retrieved March 10, 2008 from http://www.mre.gov.br/portugues/questoes/download/rcn2002.xls.
3. The authors quote data of the Consular Census (1996) and projections carried out by Carvalho (1996).

20

New Media and Oromo Diaspora Quest for Democracy and Self-determination

Habtamu Dugo

This chapter examines how the Oromo Diasporic communities make use of the new media for establishing and maintaining communication with people in Oromia and with one another around the globe in a wider national quest for democracy and self-determination. Writing about the Indian Diaspora, Bhat and Sahoo (N.D.) link the historical origin of the concept of diaspora to the Jewish context of disporic formation, that later acquired significance as an approach applied to the study of all immigrants and settlers outside the countries of their origin. Today, the term is used to describe any population that is 'deterritorialized' or 'transinational'[1] (Vertovec, 1997:277). Karim (1998:12) in his paper aimed at examining the communication links among members of diasporic communities stretching over several continents, argues that diasporic groups make extensive use of on-line services like the Internet, Usenet, Listserv, and the World Wide Web.

Embracing the optimist views of the role of the digital media in contributing to democracy from the side of the dissenting voices, Pippa Norris says:

> ... Dissident organisations traditionally have fewer political assets, fewer traditional advantages, but also fewer inhibitions about adapting flexibly to the opportunities of information and communication via the internet. If this account is essentially correct, digital politics can be expected to have most impact in levelling the playing field...for the diverse range of insurgent movements and challengers such as transnational advocacy networks, alternative social movements, protest organisations...(2004:281).

Two of the most prominent Oromo websites, oromoliberationfront.org and gadaa.com, which I have observed over years, are consistent with Norris' digital technology purposes of 'transnational advocacy' and 'alternative social movements', be it in their news, entertainments (music webcasts), or information sections.

Having written the above on the purposes of this paper and the significance of the topic, I will move on to the social, cultural, political and economic contextualisation of the problem.

General Context of the Oromo People and Oromo Diasporic Formations

"The Oromo make up over 30 million out of the present 55 million of the Ethiopian Empire" Gadaa Melbaa (1988 quoted in Oromia Online). Oromiffa (also Oromo or Afaan Oromoo) is considered one of the five most widely spoken languages from among approximately 100 languages of Africa, making it the third major language spoken in Africa after Arabic and Hausa (Gragg, 1982). Presently, the population is situated in Oromia Regional State of Ethiopia. And it is from there that a great number of this population is immigrating to countries all across the globe. I will shortly turn to the causes of the immigration in this section.

The Oromo have the most diversified culture fostered by a large population, large land area and diversified climactic conditions (Melba, 1988 quoted in Oromia). According to Melbaa, the most conspicuous aspect of Oromo Culture is the Gada System, the traditional democratic system, which organises the Oromo Society into 7-11 groups or sets that take leadership responsibilities for an eight year term of office. In his own words, Melba says, "The Gada System has guided the religious, social, political and economic life of the Oromo for many years, and also their philosophy, art, history and methods of time-keeping." Within this context, the economy of 90 % of the people is mainly based on traditional agriculture. The Oromo Diasporas share a great deal of the social, cultural and political ways of life with the mainstream Oromo population although it is different in economic activities, as it is not based on agriculture.

But the most relevant point to this article is that the reasons which have contributed to the formation of Oromo Diaspora across the globe have also been instrumental in the development of online alternative media. The history of the formation of Oromo Diaspora goes as far back as the 1880s when some European colonial powers such as Italy, France, Belgium and Britain were scrambling for Africa, and parallel with that Abyssinians, Semitic groups that constitute Northern Ethiopia today, conquered Oromia with the assistance of weapons from the former [European colonial powers especially France] (Baxter, 1994:169). He explains the nature of the conquest as,

> The incorporation of the different [sic] Oromo peoples [sic] took a series of bloody and brutal conquest, which could not have taken place if Menelik had not been able to get arms from other competing colonial powers …and if the area of conquest had not been ravaged by severe pestilence and famine (*ibid*).

Political scholars on the Horn of Africa, Holcombe and Ibssa (1990 quoted in Baxter 1994:169) further explain the colonial issue and its consequences as, "The Oromo were colonized: many were sold into slavery, others were reduced to near serfdom, and much of their land was expropriated." Thus, the act of being sold into slavery indicates the earliest formation of Oromo Diaspora in different parts of the world. For the sake of clarity, it is important to note that the colonisers of Oromian State of the Horn of Africa were not Europeans; it was rather a colonisation of one black people by another black power assisted by European arms; thus, perhaps, Oromia is the only state under black colonial rule to date.

In connection with this, one might expect the necessity of transnational communication between Oromo Diaspora and mainstream Oromo population and among Diasporas within a country, among Diasporas in different countries and among Diasporas on different continents. In fact, it is true that because of work opportunities related to globalisation, different peoples form different parts of the world are leaving their birth places and are forming some kind of Diasporic communities overseas of their own accord. However, what mainly drives the formation of Oromo Diaspora and partly makes it typical is its being the product of the exodus of political elites to exile to escape persecution because of political dissent at home. Zitelmann (1990 quoted in ibid) indicates the wider distribution of the Oromo Diaspora:

> It has been reliably estimated that at least half a million Oromo, especially the best educated and most politically aware, have become émigrés. Almost all have the sorts of skills that are so needed in Ethiopia. They live scattered in cities of Africa, the Middle East, the United States and Canada and in London, Melbourne, Stockholm, Amsterdam, Berlin, Hamburg and Rome

The figure of 'almost half a million' Oromo in Diaspora dates back to a time before an important event in the history of Ethiopia in 1991. In effect, more than two decades later, it is reasonable to expect at least the tripling of the number of Oromo population in Diaspora. The year 1991 was a year when different rebel groups overthrew the Marxist Mengistu regime. In the same year Oromo Liberation Front leaders, supporters and members were declared illegal and forcefully driven out of the country by the transitional government of Ethiopia led by Priminister Males Zenawi, (Human Rights Watch Report). That year is a turning point as formation of new waves of Oromo Diaspora began on a larger scale. Thus, it is worth illuminating what has been happening following the new wave of Oromo Diaspora.

Furthermore, in describing the political rivalry in Oromia after the overthrow of the Mengistu military junta in 1991, the 2005 Human Rights Watch report gives us a brief account of how Oromo Liberation Front and its leaders and supporters were forced into exile and a viable opposition representing the Oromo people is lacking as a consequence for the May 2005 "Elections":

> National Elections were scheduled for June 1992...OLF candidates were intimidated and prevented from campaigning effectively in most of Oromia...after the OLF became convinced that it would not be allowed to compete fairly in the election, it withdrew from the race (Human Rights Watch, May 2005).

The ruling Ethiopian Peoples Revolutionary Front (EPRDF) has been squashing dissent before and after the May 2005 "Elections" in the same way it did in 1991-92. As a result, the number of people fleeing from persecution to join Oromo Diaspora has been increasing at an alarming rate. It is impossible for me to give an exact figure of the people joining diaspora because there are no official statistics on that. Most of the migrants do not go through the Ethiopian government immigration department. They rather cross the borders with the neighbouring countries and live in refugee camps operated by UNHCR and from there gradually go to different continents and seek political asylum.

The digital media used by the Oromo Diaspora then is of the kind that has close connections with political disruptions. New media are used to air voices of dissent in order to counteract the ideologies and information manufactured by the government-controlled press in Ethiopia. Indicating the state monopoly over technologies and resources such as media, Marx and Engels (ND: quoted in Durham and Kellner 2001) maintain, "The ideas of the ruling class are in every epoch the ruling ideas: i.e., *the class which is the ruling material force of society is at the same time its ruling intellectual force"* (italics mine).

Quest for Freedom and Democracy

To refresh your memory, I have argued in the opening part of this paper that I am interested in examining how the Oromo Diasporic communities use the new media for communication and political activism that aims at promoting democratisation in their home country. In this connection, this section focuses on some of the literature on media and democracy regardless of the various types of democracies and shortcomings inherent in them. Writing on the application of democracy to online communities, Schuler argues that the term 'democracy' is difficult to define and that there is no consensus among scholars over it (2001:283). In spite of that, he identifies five elements of democracy: the first attribute is 'inclusivity' which means equal opportunity for participation for everybody. Second, it is a way that enables the citizens to place their issues on the public agenda; this view rejects the monopoly over media by power wielders and media owners. Third, democracy depends on a deliberative process; that is, it allows discussion on a wide range of views in order to reach some decision or consensus. The fourth attribute is concerned with 'equality at the decision stage' where every one is allowed to vote to influence the course of events. Fifth, 'representation' as an attribute of democracy solves the impracticality of involving all citizens in decision-making.

In essence, Schuler's five elements relate to democracy that is practiced in cyberspace. The important point Shuler makes is that he envisages the extraordinary opportunities that the Internet offers as a platform or infrastructure for modern democracy. This opportunity also characterises the Internet use by the Oromo Diaspora.

Human rights are inextricably linked to the bandwagon of democracy. In practising the latter, there is a need to make sure that information and communication in the media are bound to operate within the framework of the principles that are provided by People's Communication Charter formulated and ratified worldwide in the early 1990s. The principles are namely (1) media should respect human rights, (2) resources needed for communication such as frequencies of airwave and electricity have to be common, (3) information and communication in any society can not be monopolised, (4) the public should be empowered to participate in the communication process, and (5) communicators are obliged to be accountable for their shareholders and the public (Hamelink 2001:23-24).

Overview of New Media Theories

Carefully exploring the concept of 'bitsphere' and the 'public sphere' is indispensable to examine the role of media in democracy in general and the role of digital media used by the Oromo Diaspora for political activism in search for solutions to longstanding injustices in the Ethiopian State of the Horn of Africa. As the concept of 'public sphere comes' prior in time to 'bitsphere', it would be good to start off with the idea of the public sphere and then look at the 'bitshere' from an evolutionary perspective.

The work of Habarmas (1989) is perhaps seminal in areas of examining the democratic role of media. His basic argument is that the early development of modern capitalism created independent fora of public debate. Among the elements of this arena are "economic independence provided by private property, critical reflection fostered by letters and novels, the flowering of discussions in coffee houses and salon, and … emergence of independent market based press" (1989 in Curran 1991:83). These have been settings for the public to engage in critical political discussions. The Habermasian concept still holds true with a great majority of people living in towns and cities of Oromia where people gather in coffee houses, cafes, 'daadhii' houses (name for local beer houses) and engage in critical political discussions as they have their drinks- forced to get informal and non-fearful.

Nonetheless, Oromo Diaspora's public sphere cannot work in the same way as the participant émigrés are found scattered over different parts of the globe. Then what can be the substitute or complement to the public sphere in terms of diasporas? To answer this question I had to take the Internet, the World Wide Web, online discussion forums, listservs and so on in a parallel with Habermas' lists of arena for public debate. Thus, they are the arenas for public debate. I would adopt and adapt a word from Michell (1995:167 in Werry & Mowbray 2001:xviii) to refer to these arenas of digital media as 'bitsphere':

> For designers and planners the task of twenty-first century will be to build the bitsphere-a worldwide electronically mediated environment in which networks are everywhere…. This unprecedented, hyper extended habitat will transcend national boundaries; the increasingly dense and widespread connectivity that it supplies will quickly create opportunities…for planning and designing truly worldwide communities.

Restricting Press Freedom by Law

Before analysing the emergence of Oromo Diaspora's adoption of the new media as an alternative media, it is important to assess restrictive laws and government actions which have been responsible for the extinction of all forms of Oromo media in Ethiopia.

World Press Freedom Committee (WPFC) (2006: 151) reports that Ethiopia's press law criminalizes defamation, publishing 'false news' and insulting the Ethiopian government or security forces. The 1992 draft press law was inspired by more than half a century old and unrevised Ethiopia's penal code, not the constitution. Article 480 of the penal code states this:

> Spreading false rumours, suspicion, or false charges against the government or public authorities or their activities, thereby distributing or inflaming public opinion or creating dangers is punishable (WPFC, 2006:152).

In 1992, one year after the Tigrian Peoples Liberation Front (TPLF) ascended to power by the barrel of the gun, the regime further modified the provisions in the penal code by expanding them and writing them into the 1992 draft press law. The procedures and methods by which these laws were drafted were never clear and never involved all stakeholders. It was immediately done after the regime observed the necessity of banning the emerging Oromo press inside the country, which was followed by the banning/outlawing of the major opposition representing the Oromo people, Oromo Liberation Front (OLF).

This was the first turning point in the gradual erosion of Oromo press freedom in Ethiopia. Most reports from media watchdog groups tend to ignore this and take only the second turning point, the 2005 post election crackdown of the government on press freedom and journalist as a reference point. This was virtually the point at which the Oromo press came to a total standstill but the rest of Ethiopian press abuses most reported about was/is the Amhara press that represent/ed the interests of the opposing Amhara elites under the umbrella of Coalition for Unity and Democracy (CUD), before it was infiltrated and destroyed.

In terms of criminalizing journalists and media, the content of the 1992 draft press law was essentially similar to article 480 of the penal code. It included further restrictive clauses on capital physical and financial punishments. Article 10 of the 1992 press law states the following:

> Publication of a) any criminal offense against the safety of the state or of the administration…or the national defence force; b) any defamation or false accusation against any individual, nation/nationality, people or organization; c) any criminal instigation of one nationality against another or incitement of conflict between peoples; d) any agitation for war" is punishable by three years of imprisonment and/or a fine of up to the equivalent of $ 7,700 (WPFC, 2006:152).[2]

It is important to indicate that this law, which was drafted in 1992 and which came to significantly influence subsequent draft press laws of 2003 and 2004, was ratified and passed as the media and information law in July 2008, despite serious criticism and disapprovals from media watchdog groups, opposition parties, journalists, critics and academics. Many critics, however, fail to see the missing link between the current press law and the provisions of press freedom in the Federal Constitution of the country. The missing link is that this law was not inspired by the constitution which was adopted in 1994 and enforced in August 1995, three years later. Therefore, it is possible to argue that this law is not constitutional and that it is a brainchild of the prime minister and his former minster of information and current high advisor.

Article 29 of the Ethiopian constitution and its various clauses provide citizens the right to any opinion, thought, and free expression. This article has hardly been implemented as much as article 39 of the constitution which provides for self-determination. Article 29 (3, 4) of the constitution states this:

> (3) Freedom of the press and mass media as well as freedom of artistic creation is guaranteed. Press freedom shall, in particular, include the rights enumerated hereunder: a) that censorship in any form is prohibited. b) the opportunity to have access to information of interest to the public. (4) The press shall be granted institutional independence and legal protection to enable it to accommodate different opinions and ensure the free flow of information, ideas and opinions that are necessary in a democratic society.

Does the current law reflect provisions in article 29? No. Were any of the sub-articles ever implemented since 1995? No! Important to note here is that although the sub-article 4 states the need for institutional independence of media and communications, the methods by which this can be determined and who would grant them have not been clearly stated.

With the prevalence of one-party politics, it is hard to find solutions to Ethiopia's restrictive press laws for the non-existing independent press. Finding solution to that must involve first finding answers to the long-standing political domination by a minority regime. One cannot imagine the setting up of "an Independent Media and Communications/Regulator of Ethiopia", free from the Ethiopian Ministry of Information, which is a government arm. The realization for the institutional independence of media and communications will obviously be impossible with the current EPRDF/TPLF domination of the Ethiopian political scene in the narrow and selfish interest of barely one ethnic group.

Although most reports have not argued the point I have, they have begun a through appraisal of the bountifully serious deficiencies in the current media and information laws. For instance, Article 19, the London-based Global Campaign for Free Expression, carried out rigorous reviews and criticisms of the 2003 and the 2004 Ethiopia's press laws. In the laws' draft as well as final versions, the organisation found the following notable problems: its excessively broad scope; restrictions on who may practice journalism; government-controlled registration and certification systems; excessively broad exceptions to the right to access information held by public authorities; the granting of a right to reply remedy that undermines the principle of editorial independence; the establishment of a government-controlled Press Council with powers to prepare and enforce a Code of Ethics; powers vested in the courts to engage in prior-censorship; powers vested in the prosecutor to suspend media outlets; and excessively harsh regime of sanctions for offences that have no defence (Article 19, 2004).

Certain provisions of the current law, especially the ones on government-controlled licensing, the establishment of the Press Council that oversees media activities, and the lack of independent regulatory authorities or intuitions make this law no more useful than being justifications for intensifying the already banned Oromo press freedom and media ownership rights.

Thus, the current Ethiopian press law does unequivocally fail to meet international press freedom and freedom of expression standards. The law defies and shuns Article 19 of the Universal Declaration of Human Rights (UDHR), which is binding on all States in the world. The article states:

> Everyone has the right to freedom of opinion and expression; this right includes the right to hold opinions without interference and to seek, receive and impart information and ideas through any media regardless of frontiers (UN General Assembly, 1948).

Furthermore, the law disregards provisions of press freedom given in the International Covenant on Civil and Political Rights, the African Charter on Human and Peoples' Rights, which Ethiopia ratified in 1993, and 1998 respectively (Article 19, 2004).

The denials of these fundamental rights is disproportionately so for the Oromo people and for all the repressed peoples in Ethiopia, compared to some rights granted to ethnic Tigre and Amhara media and journalists. This is not just a contention as there is staggering amount evidence from various international reports to corroborate it. For instance, regarding widespread discrimination of the Oromo under the EPRDF government, Freedom House (2008: 4) reports this:

> The government has tended to favor the Tigrayan ethnic interest in economic and political matters. Politics within the EPRDF have been dominated by the Tigrayan People Democratic (*sic*) Front. Discrimination against and repression of other groups, especially the Oromo, have been widespread.

Linking Press Freedom to Governance Indicators

From 1973 to 2008 Ethiopia has maintained its 'Not Free' and 'Partly Free' Statuses' in overall freedom, including economic freedom, political rights and civil liberties (Freedom House, 2008). This extended lack of freedom indicates the EPRDF government's un-commitment and its substantial similarities with preceding: the imperial and socialist regimes. While the facts indicate that this government has shown little betterment in leadership, the EPRDF still purports to have demonstrated good and democratic leadership in the country.

In 2007, in a survey rating world countries on a scale of 0-7 in the variables of accountability/public voice, civil liberties, rule of law, anti-corruption/ transparency, the Freedom House finds Ethiopia to be amongst the set of thirty countries that are at a critical crossroads to determine their political future. Ethiopia is at the bottom on all the variables, making it a country that is known for bad governance for too long. In turn, this makes it a necessity for the international community to be seriously concerned in seeking an all-inclusive solution.

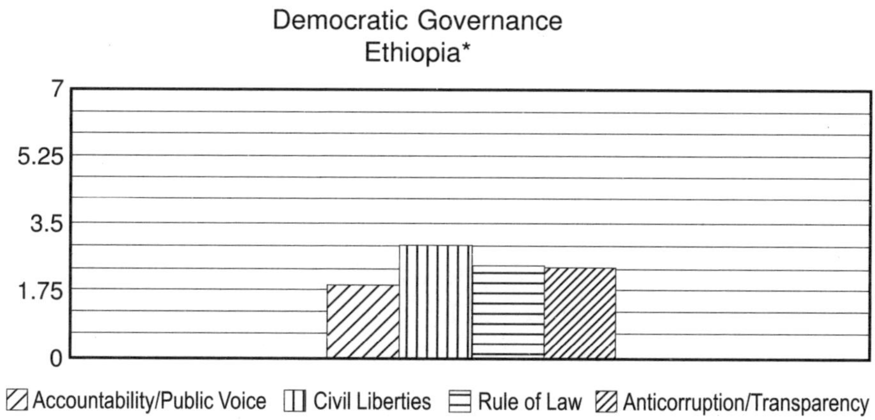

Graphic:* © *Freedom House, Inc 2007.

If there are no political rights and civil liberties, then it is not hard to imagine the ensuing lack of press freedom in Ethiopia particularly for the segregated majority like the Oromos in the country.

Indicators of Physical Threats against Media and Journalists

The Freedom House (2006) report clearly indicates Ethiopia has no press freedom. The criteria Freedom House employed to determine absence of press freedom in Ethiopia include: the legal environment in which the media operate; the degree of independence of the news media from governmental ownership and influence; economic pressures on news content; and diverse violations of press freedom from the murder of journalists to extra-legal abuse and harassment.

This government like its successive governments has systematically denied the existence of Oromo press. In Oromia, the largest and the most populous state in Ethiopia, the EPRDF government has totally shattered the existence of independent Oromo media.

There is not an agreed upon criteria to measure press freedom violations around the world for various media watchdogs to follow. It is often idiosyncratic to each organization. However, there are some similarities of approach. The purpose of press freedom indicators/index is to measure the state of press freedom in the world. The measurement is assumed to reflect the degree of freedom journalists and news organizations enjoy in 169 countries and the efforts made by authorities to ensure the respect for this freedom (Reporters Without Borders, 2005, 2006 & 2007).

The Reporters Without Borders (RWB) compiles its annual press freedom index, using 50 criteria that are distributed in the form of questionnaires. The criteria include violations directly affecting journalists (for instance, murder, imprisonment and physical threats) and the news media in areas of censorship, confiscation of newspaper issues, searches and harassments. At times, the criteria include legislative issues affecting the news media such as whether there is an independent media and communications regulatory body, and types of charges pressed against journalists (2007).

Discussing these criteria is crucial as it explicates what we mean when we say there is or there is no press freedom in one country. I observed documents, reports, and broadcasts often overlook defining the criteria of evaluating press freedom and go into recounting cases. This is tantamount to making a misleading assumption that the populace knows. Without considering the existing criteria and many more emerging variables, the term 'press freedom' will simply be an empty word that it is not concretized for an ordinary person to understand.

So, based on the 50 criteria, RWB (2007) ranks Ethiopia 150th with scores of 63 on all counts of violations of out of 167 countries included in the study. The higher the score the worse the countries are. Ethiopia is amongst the 20 countries of the world that are at the bottom of the index. It in the pack of five Sub-Saharan African countries (Equatorial Guinea, Libya, Somalia and Eriteria) notorious for their press freedom records over a long period of time.

The position of Ethiopia on press freedom indices has a dangerous implication for recreating the non-existing Oromo press. Because the historical circumstances of the Oromos as targets of oppression by the successive Ethiopian regimes, the current state of the country even makes it harder for the Oromo press to emerge from its cemetery. It also means a few Oromo journalists who manage to be employed by the state broadcaster and the non-Oromo independent press in the country will continue to be targeted as evidences show.

We know that independent Oromo media do not exist in Ethiopia. For instance, Freedom House (2006:2) shows Amharic independent newspaper account for 80 % of the newspaper circulation. All newspapers and the state-owned broadcast media are concentrated in few urban areas, particularly Finfinnee (also Addis Ababa). In the context section of this article I indicated about 90% the Oromos live in rural areas and speak only Afan Oromo. They are the ones who have been cut off vital information. State Radios and television have assigned disproportionately few hours (<15 hrs combined) Afan Oromo government propaganda broadcast a week. Whenever there is a general election, student demonstrations, political contestation between Oromo oppositions and the government, and external conflicts with Eritrea and Somalia, the state clamps down even on journalists who work in government media. These journalists are often attacked under the pretext of belonging to or passing over information to the Oromo Liberation Front (CPJ, 2004, 2005; RWB 2007:1)

After 2006, going beyond traditional media, the government propelled itself into censoring and blocking opposition websites from the Diaspora as well as home (ONI, 2008). OpenNet Initiative (ONI) explains this is because opponents of the current government have increasingly used online media to criticize the current government. The state retains all the power to do this because it monopolizes the telecommunications sector and Internet Service Providers (ISPS). Ethiopia performs very low on the test results of Internet freedom as well. Especially, it substantially filters political content. The following graph indicates the current result:

Results at a Glance

	No evidence of filtering	Suspected filtering	Selective filtering	Substantial filtering	Pervasive filtering
Filtering					
Political				•	
Social			•		
Conflict/security			•		
Internet tools			•		
Other factors	**Low**	**Medium**	**High**	**Not applicable**	
Transparency	•				
Consistency			•		

Source: © *ONI 2008.*

A further Internet indicator for Ethiopia shows that currently only 0.2 % of the country's population has access to the Internet, which is far behind the rest of Africa. This percentage is found in a few urban centres. The degree of Oromo exclusion at online new media level clearly exceeds that of radio and television.

The table (on next page) corroborates on the country's low level performance on major indicators according to World Bank et al. (quoted in ONI 2008:2).

The Current State of Oromo Diaspora and New Media

In the above sections, I have indicated how in their own homeland, the Oromo have been deprived of the freedom of expression and the right to own media by the Ethiopian government. The issues of banning freedom of expression and press freedom in Oromia are directly linked to the Abysinian history of conquest and domination of the Oromo and Oromoland. This history is an impetus for the opening up of new frontier of Diaspora communications, via news websites and general-public-rated discussion forums. This section and its subsections will focus on analysing this phenomenon of resort to the new media out of the lack of other options by giving examples from Oromo websites that have been well maintained for at least a decade. These websites are www.oromoliberationfront.org and www.gadaa.com I will look at both one after the other.

The new copyright information of www.oromoliberationfront.org reads 2005. I remember accessing this website for the very first time back in 2001 out of curiosity of what it is doing although this act was violently punishable if detected in Ethiopia. The content and the format has not changed much ever since. This website is a website of Oromo Liberation Front (OLF), a veteran political organization founded in 1973 with the mission of leading the Oromo national struggle from a century-old Abysinian colonial rule (OLF, 2005). The significance of this mission is that it shapes the content produced and distributed on the website and stretches to inform the underpinning goals of several other Oromo websites and blogs. The website specialises in political news and information in its bi-lingual sections-English and Afaan Oromoo. Readers of this website contribute postings to the website that focus on the current political situation at home and in Diaspora. The cons are that all postings are centrally moderated and the website does not allow for comments/feedbacks on postings from readers as many other websites run by Ethiopian political organizations.

The English section of the news caters for the international community and Oromos who understand English, while the Afan Oromo section is meant for Oromos at home and in diaspora.

The recent posting on its both English and Afaan Oromoo sections focuses on the historical event of how university students at home commemorate July13 as a national mourning day for Oromos because of forced expulsion from the city by the EPDF regime. The news section of the OLF website discusses a wide range of political, economic, cultural developments issues in the home country, which are important in the Oromo national struggle for freedom and democracy.

The website also reports on gross human rights abuses. For instance, it covered the March 2007 Gaara Suufii massacre in Eastern Oromia, where 17 people including a 14 year old girl were abducted from home, taken out of prison in to the mountainous area of Gaara Suufii at night and found killed and their bodies fed to beasts. In the same vein, the website reported the May 2008 ethnic cleansing against the Oromo in the Western Oromia, which lead to deaths of

Key Indicators	worst … best
GDP per capita, PPP (constant 2000 international $)	896
Life expectancy at birth (years)	42
Literacy rate (% of people age 15+)	42
Human development index (out of 177)	170
Rule of law (out of 208)	150
Voice and accountability (out of 208)	168
Digital opportunity index (out of 180)	173
Internet users (% of population	0.2

Source: (by indicator): World Bank 2005, 2006a, 2006b; UNDP 2006; World Bank 2006c; ITU 2006, 2006. © *ONI.*

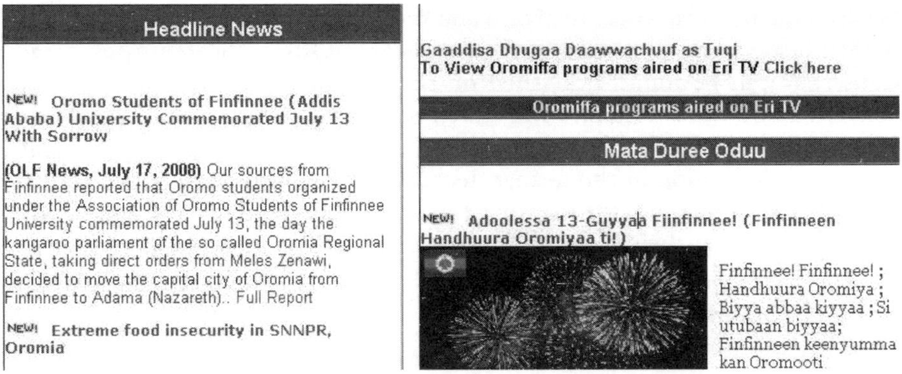

several hundred people. Generally, it reports on human rights abuses and harms that are perpetrated against Oromos.

The oromoliberationfront.org is one the earliest Oromo websites, trying to provide alternative political information for the Oromo people. Trends of new media use like this are common to another nations' experience of new media usage as an alternative media in the Horn of Africa. In a study that focused on Eritrean diaspora's usage of online media, Bernal (2006:161) found that Eritreans abroad use the Internet as a transnational public sphere, where narratives of history, culture, democracy and identity are discussed. The starting of Oromo new media as an alternative public sphere themselves relates to the formation of globally-spread refugees and immigrants because of politically motivated violence and instability at home (Bernal, 2006:163).

The further characteristic of the www.oromoliberationfront.org is its convergence with the SBO/Voice of Oromo Liberation (VOL) radio[3]. VOL broadcasts for one hour a day for seven days from Berlin, Germany in Afaan Oromoo and Amharic. The two languages have been assigned half an hour everyday except for an exclusively Afaan Oromoo service on Saturdays and Sudays. The equal sharing of programme time between the two languages shows how open and democratic the Oromo world view is to ensure diversity and pluralism as opposed to other Ethiopian mono-linguistic fanatic media.

The SBO is at least a decade older than the website as it had celebrated its 20th anniversary this year. The target audience of the SBO is 40 million Oromos in Ethiopia and a few other millions in countries in North East Africa. The objectives of the SBO are: (a) to popularize principles of democracy and human rights; (b) promote public awareness about the importance of environment and ways to safeguard it; (c) promotion of Afaan Oromoo, culture and history; (d) provide basic education on Women in Oromo society and their health (SBO, 2005).

The various aspects of SBO deserve a separate media research in their own rights. It is not the purpose of this paper to do so. The reason of mentioning SBO radio broadcasts here is simply to indicate the existence of a content- sharing between the two platforms: the radio and the Oromo section of the website. This is technically termed as content convergence. Often, the repurposed radio transcripts can be found published on the Internet. Radio programs are also converted into real media files and stored on the website for global access on the Internet. The impact of this is tremendous in terms of giving people opportunities to access information in the format, technology and time most suited to them. Nevertheless, sometimes the streaming audio embedding is delayed and deprived of the freshness of their content.

The following screenshot shows the convergence of between SBO and oromoliberationfront.org:

SBO/VOL RADIO

Afaan Oromoo	*Amharic Program*
07/18/2008	07/18/2008
07/16/2008	07/16/2008
07/15/2008	07/15/2008
07/13/2008	
07/11/2008	07/11/2008
07/09/2008	07/09/2008
07/08/2008	07/08/2008

© 2005. oromoliberationfront.org

Assessed altogether, the oromoliberationfront.org offers diverse political information and news on the Horn of Africa region, shaped by the organization's vision. The Internet aspect of it is only accessed by a population of < 0.02 % in urban areas and who have the money to buy technology, connectivity and skills. The large majority of the Oromo people are clearly technologically unfortunate to access information on the Internet. In a case study focusing an Ertrean dispora website Dehai, Bernal (2005: 665) discusses that interesting ideas and controversies that surface in cyberspace are spread by telephone, word of mouth, and are discussed in face to face meetings off-line. These methods make it possible for the ordinary people at home to get second-hand information. This is very much true for the Oromo people who inhabit the same region as Eritreans.

Gadaa.Com came into the scene of Oromo cyberspace much later in 2004. Gadaa.com is English-language Oromo web portal, encompassing Oromo news, sports, music, politics, human rights, culture and business. It does a good job with regard to automatic newsfeeds from other news sources world-wide. It usually produces its own content. At least in diaspora, Gadaa.com's significance is to provide an alternative voice to Oromo people in the continuous search for freedom and democracy in Ethiopia. Gadaa's exclusive use of the English language might be intimidating and inaccessible to the non-English speaking populace at home.

Oromo Hall of Struggle for Freedom: PaltalkScene

Oromo diaspora's use of the basic service of Paltalk known as 'Black Nick'[4] may represent one of the most vibrant, transnational public sphere in which discussions and heated debates, and advocacy for human rights, freedom and democracy are carried out daily.

Paltalk is an Internet-based instant messaging service with text, voice and video for subscribers all over the world. The basic software is freely downloadable. In this program, the subscribers responsible for starting the chatroom have administrative status, which means they can allow users in, suspend user for period of time, and ban users permanently, and control the microphone. The owner of the room can delegate or grant administrative power to other users to ease the workload (Paltalk, 1999-2007).

That was a brief description of how the program works. I will now analyse a very fascinating topic of ways in which the Oromo diaspora has been using this technology effectively to advocate for political change in its distant home. I will focus one of a few Oromo chat rooms, named 'Galma Qabsoo Bilisummmaa Oromoo", translated literally as "Oromo Hall of Struggle for Freedom". This room is always full of activities and with the highest number of users compared to other Oromo rooms. The room disclaims that it is a G-rated public room intended for a general audience including minors. Galma Qabsoo Bilisummaa Oromoo does not allow for offensive languages. It also disclaims the room is pro OLF, ULFO, and AFD, the three biggest opposition groups in the Ethiopia. It welcomes discussions pertinent to the struggle of these political organizations and rejects hatred amongst any Ethnic group, nationalities and nations.

Topics of politics, human rights, Oromo struggle etc. are discussed in details everyday by people, but Saturday afternoons are characterized by very informed discussions, where experts, politicians or other able guests are invited to educate or brief the users worldwide on the current sate of Oromo struggle.

Political education by invited speakers in the 'Oromo Hall of Freedom' a common practice every Saturday afternoon. The time zone is carefully chosen by administrators for maximum user participation from different world time zones. Experts in sociology, political and international studies, and history volunteer on the paltalk show to educate participants. Experts passionately lecture on topics such as Oromo unity, regional political developments in the Horn of Africa and their influences the Oromo struggle, Oromo history etc.. The lectures last for at least two hours at least two hours, after which users raise their digital hands to get mics to ask questions for an extended number of hours. This is a two-way interactive experience. The Q&A sessions are characterized by impassioned questions based on issues for the day. Generally, people ask substantive questions except for some users who sit in and try to polarize and shift the direction the discussions. Sometimes very few of participants' comments unexpectedly target the character of the presenter with the intent of hurting their feelings and to ultimately discourage them from doing the education they are doing. Very often acrimony between participants happens which calmed down by the amini or by cyber-mediator. Presentations and discussions are generally in Afaan Oromoo to meet the language needs of the audience.

To further indicate the immense amount of activism taking place in the Oromo bitsphere, I will analyse how the room handled a crucial topic-ethnic cleansing. This will serve as an outstanding example of political activism for Oromo rights in the cyberspace.

The following topic was posted and nearly discussed for a week in the room:

> **GUBAAY:** *Baha Wallaggaa keessatti lola mootummaan wayyaanee ummata Oromoo fi Gumuz gidduutti qabsiise gaaga'ama guddaa dhaqqabsiisaa jira*
>
> Translation:
>
> GUBAAY: The Woyane- instigated conflict between the Oromo people and Gumuz in East Wallega caused a huge amount of instability and deaths.

This was a voice discussion topic augmented by simultaneous Instant Messaging. It was one of the discussion topics on current events, taking place thousands of miles from where the participants are located globally. In relation of the above topic posted in the room, many ideas were discussed, including and not limited to, sending home money for humanitarian aid for the Internally Displaced Persons (IDPS). There were also suggestions for holding rallies across cities of hosting nations. I did not know about the money but I have later confirmed that demonstrations happened in Brussels, Oslo, London, Sydney, and Washington D.C and so on opposing ethnic cleansing in Oromia. It is certain that the main alternative communication venues available to the Oromo Diaspora are the websites discussed and powerful multimedia tools such as Paltalk. By means of these technologies, the Oromo diaspora has mobilized the mentioned demonstration protesting ethnic-cleansing in Oromia and asking for international interventions. This is similar to how Bernal (2006) finds the Eritrean diaspora uses the cyberspace.

A unique phenomenon that I observed on discussions of such topics is that individual users corroborate whether the incident happened. They update others in the room with current information and news. As the text discussion goes on, users play streaming audio news from major Oromo radio services such as the Voice of America Afaan Oromoo Service and the SBO for all in the room. A user surely gets unimaginable amount of information from the integration of all media resources replayed in PaltalkScene. The rebroadcast is then paused or stopped and further robust discussions rage until a topic is fully analysed from all possible angles.

Except for when users are banned suspended for violating the rules of the room, the paltalk platform is highly interactive and free. The anonymity of users in Oromo discussion forums does not only keep them safe from Ethiopian spies who pause and eavesdrop, but also seem to encourage them to talk freely. Despite the advantages, there are clear individual differences in participants: some are more knowledgeable than others; some are wise and patient; some are angry and emotional; some are abusive. If used wisely these fora will really be real alternative media.

Conclusion

The Oromo Diasporic communities worldwide have been incrementally using the Internet for pulling together ideas, expertise and resources for political activism; for establishing and maintain communications amongst Oromo communities in disapora and with people in Oromia.

It is particularly striking how the Oromo dispora effectively utilizes free online multimedia interactive programs such as PatalkScene Basic for purposes of political debates, education on human rights, history and identity. It is undoubtedly impossible to form this kind of cyber-association to engage in topics of deep political nature that challenges the EPRDF government in the homeland.

The information and communications mediated by this sort of media are rooted in discourses of Oromo nationalism, identity, the history of conquest and colonization of the Oromo by successive Ethiopian regimes. It is not an overstatement to say that what the Oromo dispora is doing in the cyberspace is a fight in the cyberspace in the quest for freedom, democracy and justice. This is a constitutional right conducted commensurate with the Article 39 of the Ethiopian Constitution, which allows for the rights to self determination and secession of peoples/states if they so wish to. The issues and topics are serious political discussions about the fate of Oromos and other repressed nationalities in Ethiopia.

NOTES

1. 'deterritorialized' and 'tranational' refer to people who originated in land other than in which it currently resides and whose social, economic, and political networks beyond the borders of nation-states or spanning the globe.
2. Major restrictive provisions of other articles of the 1992 draft press law include further justifications for capital physical and financial punishments of media/media workers, which include attack against the state and national and other emblems (art 244), insults of foreign states (art 264), insult of official emblems of foreign states (art 265), insults to inter-state institutions (art 266), contempt of court (art 449), and special cases aggravating the crime (art 618).
3. Sagalee Bilisummaa Oromoo (SBO) broadcasts its programs for one hour a day for seven days a week in Afaan Oromoo and Amharic. It transmits on 9,485 KHz SW on the 31 meter band and focuses on Northeast Africa with special focus on the Horn of Africa. However, listeners in other parts of Africa, Middle East and southern Europe also do tune in. It is also listened to by speakers of Afaan Oromo and Amharic through Internet all over the world.
4. Black Nick-It is a free service of paltalk , called PaltalkScene Basic. People with this service use the program for audio chat, publishing videos and transferring files and adding up to 199 pals.

21

New Media and the Redemption of the Other

Ravi K Dhar

Most communication texts begin with an introduction to communication steeped in the spirit and terminology of the **transmission school of communication**. Most academic programmes begin with an introductory lecture on communication couched in the phraseology of the transmission school of communication.[1] All these introductions to communication are prefixed of course with the standard definition of communication as being a two-way exchange of feelings and thoughts and with the etymological beginnings of the term in the Latin term *communis.*

But as the discussion progresses all that gets lost in the vortex of the transmission school and the inference is clear that communication is nothing more than the sending of verbal and non- verbal messages from a source to a recipient across a channel in such a way that there is minimum noise for maximum understanding of the message and a corresponding behavioural change in the recipient of the message. Thus, the neophyte is brought up on an ideology that privileges the transmission school, and in effect, the mass media discourse.[2]

Against this backdrop, this study attempts to analyze how the mass media discourse has subverted the semantic connotation of the word, 'communication' and helped to create a communication inequality that supports and nurtures a **power inequality** and divide between the privileged and the marginalized in various shapes and forms at the national and international levels[3]. It argues that the quintessentially interactive character of the new media has the potential to resurrect the semantic signification of the word, 'communication' and to restore communication equality which is a necessary pre-requisite for the redemption of the 'other' from the hegemony of the mass media owners[4], an important step in the direction of the ideal of human unity.

To this end, the study has been divided into four sections. The **first section** undertakes a survey of the genesis of **divides in human society** from the mystic, not the intellectual, **standpoint** of the ideal of human unity, the **second section** traces the role of mass media in supporting and nurturing such divides to the point of subverting the semantics of the word communication itself, **the third** section maps the ways in which the new media resurrects communication to pave the way for the redemption of the other and the eventual realization of the mystic ideal of human unity, and the **fourth** sums up the findings.

Genesis of Divides in Human Society

Divides are institutionalized forms of inequalities. **Inequalities between man and the rest of the biosphere and between man and man** have existed ever since Nature evolved Life out of matter.[5] While the inequalities between man and the other members of the biosphere were institutionalized to satisfy the avaricious urge of man, these were justified to begin with by a (mis)interpretation of the religious texts[6] that governed human conduct in traditional societies and in later times by Enlightenment historiography that centralized human development at the expense of his environment.[7]

The inequalities between man and man got institutionalized as man turned social/political from being a lone and independent hunter-gatherer.[8] Though the unalterable inequalities between man and man existed even then, yet these did not form the basis of an institutionalized discrimination as man at that time lived a simple life of subsistence.[9] The hunter-gatherer bands and the pastoral tribes had limited needs which formed the central focus of their lives. With the advent of the agricultural stage of economy, human settlements initially in the form of villages, and later in the form of towns came up alongside the flood plains of rivers. Each of the settlements was a closely knit collection of people, still leading a relatively simple social and economic life with subsistence/primitive agriculture as their mainstay.

As the members of a settlement led a more or less closed group life, the form of interaction that emerged between them was interpersonal and face to face. The frequency of interaction and years/decades of living together made the village an extended version of the family. Differences of perception/understanding were, therefore, easily mitigated through constant and equal interaction as in a family. The **interpersonal face to face interaction between members of the settlement helped to evolve common grounds of understanding between them** so that the settlement turned into a community of people communicating between themselves to lead a mutually beneficial life. Thus, the strength of communication lay in its ability to iron out differences between people to weld them into a community.[10]

The alterable inequalities related to the social, economic, cultural and technological 'development' of humankind got institutionalized with the birth of the advanced agricultural and industrial societies.[11] Intensive agriculture created surpluses that could feed the urban population engaged in the newly established factories and the new trading class engaged in the distribution of the mass produced goods. Industrialization and modernization precipitated/facilitated large scale mobility puncturing the closed balloon of the agricultural society and scattering its commune members over a large geographical expanse, thereby giving birth to the modern nation states/societies.

The process continues well into the 21st century, with citizens/members of the nation states/societies dispersing over the entire globe, creating glimmers of a new global society. The large scale displacement of people from their traditional habitats and their consequent convergence in various urban centers speckled across the globe has, as one sociologist prefers to say, given rise to the modern gesselschaft societies.[12]

Gone is the communion of the gemeinschaft commune members and it is replaced with the atomization of the gesselschaft society members. This marked change in the nature of interpersonal relations between the members of the society paved the way for the foregrounding of the alterable inequalities between man and man. As the saga of human development/civilization further unfolded itself, not only did the alterable inequalities freeze into divides, but the unalterable inequalities too got woven into the meta-narrative of divides between people(s). The divides between people(s) engendered **the dialogic discourse of the Self and the Other**. In its mild form, this discourse centralized the concerns of one social sub-group for survival and growth, while marginalizing the concerns of the Others. In its virulent form, it pruned the Others from the very weltanschauung of the dominant social sub-group.[13]

At the national level, while these divides have manifested themselves in the form of caste, class, linguistic and racial hegemony,[14] at the international level, these have manifested in the pejorative discourse of development and modernization/westernization.[15] While the discourse of the Self and the other based on social, economic and technological divides is understandable, what is surprising is the tendency of such discourses to seek their justification in the physical and psychological inequalities between people.[16] Hitler's diabolic attempt to annihilate the Jews and to run over Europe was grounded in his philosophy of the *sonnenkinder*, which sought justification for such a disastrous course of action in the superiority of the Aryan race. The entire colonial discourse[17] was based on the superiority of the Whites over the blacks and the coloured. In recent times, the much publicized concept of the clash of civilizations was also based on this divide between the White and the non-White people(s).

The tendency to found social, economic, cultural and technological divides on unalterable inequalities between man and man goes to show that divides are never circumscribed within one category. Furthermore, it shows that all these divides are only adventitious to something much more germinal and primary. This is the divide of consciousness. The Bible traces this divide back in/out of time to the parable of the Fall that threw Adam and Eve from the exalted state of unitive consciousness to the lowly one of divided consciousness of good and evil. The Vedic tradition traces it back to the manifestation of the Transcendent Truth-Consciousness in the dualistic and divided phenomenological consciousness of all shapes and forms in the sensory world. The Veda celebrates the unity of all forms of animate and inanimate existence in the Vedic hymn of '*Aum prithvi shantih, apah shantih, vanaspatayah shantih, antariksh shantih, visvedevah shantih, Aum Shantih Shantih Shantih*'. Here is the seed mantra of communion between the animate and the inanimate universe, the manifest and the 'unmanifest' universe and (wo)man and (wo)man.[18]

Bereft of such a unitive consciousness, man pits himself against the universe, though to his own peril ultimately, and one (wo)man against another on the bases of the inequalities spoken of so far, alterable or unalterable for each individual sees him(her)self as a different autonomous unit fighting for survival and/or self-aggrandizement. No amount of intellectualization or conceptualization can substitute for the ideal of human unity realized through unitive consciousness. Notwithstanding the plethora of social and economic utopian theories of egalitarianism, inequalities will continue to harden into divides and all systems built on such utopian theories will crumble or collapse like it happened in the wee hours of the French Revolution or in the twilight of the communist regimes in Eastern Europe and the then USSR. Reform, as James Cardinal Gibbons remarks[19], must come from within and not from without.

Mass Media and the Global Divides

The various transitions in the history of humankind reveal a movement away from individualistic independence to greater and more complex communal/social dependence. Underpinning and sustaining these transitions has been the ability of humankind to evolve the means of mutual and harmonious interaction. But, just as the communalizing/socializing impulse of (wo)man has been clogged with inequalities that have often got transmuted into divides, so has this mutual interaction often been far from harmonious due to the distortions introduced by the nature of the process of communication and the public sphere, or communication space.

As long as (wo)man lived the quasi-independent life of a hunter-gatherer, there was scarcely any urgent need for mutual interaction. But, as (s)he graduated from that stage to the others, the need for interaction grew as well. Also, the interaction took on a more complex form. What began with mere signs and whistles soon evolved into human language. With the advent of language, interaction took on a verbal form. As communal/social interaction continued to grow in content and complexity, the human language too grew in the richness of its lexical and syntactic opulence and complexity. Notwithstanding the evolution of human language and its later luxuriance of expression, non-verbal interaction continued to exert a major influence on human relationships. This use of signs, verbal or non-verbal, in human interaction with a view to evolving a common ground of understanding came to be called communication.

The unrestricted interaction between the members of the commune helped communication to play a great harmonizing role not just at the interpersonal level but at the communal level too. The public discourse in such communes—

often associated with the village green, where the village elders would congregate to discuss the common issues of the commune—was characterized by a communication equality that was underpinned by the power equality between the members. Not surprisingly the community, the commune & communication became complementary to each other.

The advent of the industrial society changed all. With the large scale displacement of the people across their native climes, the frontiers of the community burst at its seams, spilling its contents all over a new terrain, giving birth to the nation-state and a host of urban centers. The new matrix of people's congregation took on the form of the modern society, marked by islands of existence. Media stepped in to bridge the gulf created by the social impact of industrialization/modernization/development, creating a new kind of public sphere that was more a mediated one than spatial.[20]

But what a media! Though immensely capable of reaching out to the largest number of people horizontally as well as vertically and thereby connecting a loosely congregated mass of people scattered over the length and breadth of a country that could be as vast as a (sub)continent, it had seeds of distorting the communication equality. By virtue of its capital intensive character, it paved the way for the spawning and consolidation of mammoth media organizations which as the Transmission school of communication rightly pointed out called for pooling and sieving of information by the media house before it could enter the communication/ public space. In other words, the mass media house became the producer and sender of mass media messages to a mass audience passivized to only consume media messages without having any control over the agenda of public discourse[21]. The advent of the mass media, therefore, signaled the death of communication and communication equality. It gave birth to a communication inequality that was very well suited to prop up a power inequality that thrived on divides among people(s).

Though the mass media are effective instruments of dissemination of information on a mass scale, they suffer from a congenital defect. They are not interactive. The absence of interactivity precludes them from facilitating social and political dialogue on a mass scale. Due to the inability of the mass media to enable collaboration in the public sphere, it tends to include some and exclude some from the public/communication space. As a result, it became the mouthpiece of those who own it or have access to it, while excluding the common man's discourse from its space. In other words, the citizens were marginalized to the periphery of the public space and mass media monopolized the communication space. This transformation robbed the process of communication itself of its quintessential character of evolving communion of thoughts and feelings for the community to think & act as a monolith. Mass communication became a one way traffic starting from the media organization and ending at the public /the consumer as the point of reception.

As interpersonal and group communication got back-grounded from the public domain and the mass communication of messages by the mass media got foregrounded, mass communication appropriated to itself the semantic significance of communication. Obviously, the interpersonal discourse of the local communes got discounted as the non-descript mini-narratives of public life, while the mass media discourse, hereafter referred to as mass communication, of the nation states/post-industrial societies got centralized as the meta-narrative of national life. Its implications were momentous. Where earlier communication was a free interaction among citizens/individuals, it now became the handmaid of media organizations. Only those citizens who had the wherewithal to invest in the acquisition and installation of such media could now communicate in the public domain through the mass media. Thus, communication ceased to be a ubiquitous public activity that could shape the destiny of the community; it became a reified/restricted professional activity determined by the editorial, read business, policy of the media house. Mass media house, the Gatekeeper, sieved all those news that ran counter to its interests. In times to come, there emerged a new nexus of power brokers, which included the mass media house.

As the nation-state was defined by the character of the ruling elite, the mass media served to manufacture narratives justifying its (mis)rule, depending on how much the mass media itself was accommodated by the ruling elite. Where the interests coincided, the two worked in unison to create new discourses, privileging the Self over the Others. In the early stages of the post industrial world order, it created the meta-narrative of the White man's supremacy over the Others, leading to two virulent divides that struck at the roots of human unity: one, Hitler's narrative of Aryan supremacy which wrecked inhuman vengeance on the Jews, reducing them, as one writer has fictionalized, to the status of unseemly mice, and two, the (neo)colonial narrative of Westernization, read development, that enslaved the other peoples of the world and unleashed untold misery for the subject races in the name of colonial governance of otherwise ungovernable savages. Mass media helped to deepen this cleavage between (wo)man and (wo)man and to sustain the discourse of hegemony of the ruling nations over the subject races, ignoring and subverting the real life mini-narratives of harmony generated by interpersonal interaction between individuals across these divides.

As man happened to control the strings of power, it also meant the perpetuation of a myth of the superiority of man over woman[22]. Consequently, women had to fight for their rights even in the so-called developed West. The superiority of man over woman was legitimized by tracing it conveniently to the role played by Eve in the 'Fall of Man.' It was maintained both by the clergy and the laity that woman was the architect of man's fall and that God had rightly punished her for this devious work by making her conceive in pain. To this day, the Roman Catholic Church denies women the right to be priests, which has of late come in for resistance from women priests belonging to the RC Church. In the Indian tradition, the downgrading of the position of woman can be traced to Manu, the ancient Hindu law-giver who equated the status of woman with that of the low-born Hindus. This again is a gross distortion of the mystic truth contained in the Veda/Tantra which holds out woman as the manifestation of Shakti, Supraconscious Energy and as such the active principle of Creation[23]. Mass media continued with the popularization and perpetuation of this heresy with a view to subsist and sustain the centrality of the all-powerful man. So, to this day the mass media perpetuates the myth of manliness, manhood and male chauvinism when it spotlights attention on men's sporting events while edging out to inside pages/non-prime time news pertaining to women's sporting events.

The contours of mass media support and popularization of human divides at the global level get replicated at the national and sub-national levels too. Mass media sustains and disseminates the discourse of hegemony of the ruling establishment within each nation in the name of national stability and governance. In countries like India where the society is fragmented in a multiple and complex way along/across the fault-lines of caste, class, colour, gender, religion, language and geographical location, the mass media runs the dominant discourse of the sub-national groups that have had a vice-like grip on political power since independence. It mainstreams the ruling establishment by using a value-loaded terminology defined and created by the dominant sub-groups. In this way it creates a divide between the Self represented by the ruling establishment and the Others represented by the marginalized and deprived sections of the nation. Mass media sustains this divide by ensuring the hegemony of the ruling establishment through the discourse of democracy. This discourse manufactures the consent of the ruled and helps the ruling establishment to cling on to political power.[24]

With globalization hitting the national shores, media too has undergone transformation. In the new attention economy, it has become the vehicle of the advertiser and circulation figures/TRPs have become the bottom lines of editorial policies. The highbrow mass media has come so close to the lowbrow mass media that the lines of distinction between the two have almost evaporated[25]. The 'vulgarisation' of mass media in pursuit of higher circulation figures/TRPs has further had a deleterious effect on the coverage of issues that demand attention from the point of view of addressing the national divides. The marginalization of issues confronting national unity and the mainstreaming of the trivia and sensational divides has further helped the ruling elite to tighten its hold on the reins of power. What is true for India holds more or less true for other emerging economies of South Asia, East Asia, Africa and Latin America where mass media has either stifled dissent or privileged the discourse of the Self over that of the Others.

Thus, in stark contrast with communication which sought to evolve common grounds of understanding among people(s) of different capabilities and cultures and social sub-groups, mass communication has served to exacerbate differences, both alterable and unalterable, into divides that go to sustaining the hegemony of the Self over the Others at the national and international levels, prompting civil society agencies to root for the citizens' right to communicate as opposed to the right of mass media to communicate.[26]

The discourse of mass media and/or mass communication has been so powerful that communication has come to acquire the semantic connotation of mass communication. By defining communication as the transmission of messages from the sender to the receiver with the maximum possible fidelity, the transmission school defined the process in terms that were appropriate to mass communication undertaken by the mass media. Even when the Semiotic school attempted to correct this fallacy, the mass media discourse grudgingly conceded it as one possible alternative way of communication, thereby retaining all the while its claim to being considered as communication and not as a corruption of the original term[27]. This intellectual heresy diverted attention from the death of communication wrought by the factory-model of mass communication and its role in subverting communication equality with a view to perpetuating and widening divides that underpin the power inequality in the industrial and post-industrial society.

Thus, the advent of mass media and its attendant phenomenon of mass communication not only exacerbated the divides in the society but also turned communication upside down. It usurped the right of the citizen to communicate in the public domain and handed over the right, read power, to communicate to either the government or corporate houses that got to control the mass media. The power equality that characterized communication turned into a power inequality in which the mass media owner monopolized the right to communicate as the 'sender' of mass media messages and the citizen was passivised as a mere recipient of those messages; the maximum extent to which (s)he could make his/her presence felt in the process of communication was to give feedback. The content of public discourse got restricted to the agenda that the mass media organization decided, keeping in mind its editorial and business policy. The communication inequality, therefore, supported and perpetuated a power inequality that kept the human society divided.

New Media and the Communication Epiphany

Nature does not like imbalances. As if to correct the communication imbalance between the Self and the Others at the (sub)national and international levels, the mass media scene was visited by a new communication technology that had the potential of subverting the power and communication inequality inbuilt in mass communication and of resurrecting communication. It was the new media. Variously referred to as web media, new information and communication technology and online media, it is a communication technology that can claim to be a total media as it can synthesize all the communication technologies evolved till then. In other words, it can play the radio and web stream/cast the television and display the newspaper. What's more and what has particularly escaped the attention of many has been its ability to break the barrier of mass media technologies by enabling and facilitating interpersonal communication much better than even the telephone as interactive chats on the net can be face to face too through the use of web cams.[28] What's even more mind boggling, it can perform the mass and the interpersonal communication function simultaneously. In other words, it seeks to blow away all the previously held notions and paradigms of mass communication. It is indeed a hurricane that seeks to uproot the entrenched communication and power inequalities of the mass media and to resurrect communication and power equality of the bygone era of agricultural communities, though in a different form.

While communication in the agricultural communities occurred in the geographical space, the communication of the information societies has started taking place in virtual space/cyberspace. The village green of those communities has got supplanted with the global cyber green of the post-modern societies. While the village green could not absorb the destabilizing impact of the industrial society, the cyber green has the ability to overcome the distortions of the mass media space by opening up the possibility of enabling every citizen to interact freely. Communicating on the cyber green does not require much of an investment like it does in the case of mass media. The possibility has become much more potent with the shift of computer-mediated communication to mobile communication, which can incorporate the PDA into it. With more and still more people accessing the Internet through desktop/laptop/palmtop computers, a large number of citizens, irrespective of their social, economic, cultural and national disabilities, are in a position to communicate on the cyber green both through the interpersonal and the mass mode at one and the same time. New media applications like Virtual Reality Worlds. Wiki, blogs, micro blogs, video sharing, data sharing, social networks, tag clouds, content sharing, cloud computing, search tools, conversion tools, podcasts, online marts, peer networks, writing communities, digital scrapbooking, Voice over Internet Protocol, emailing, and chatting are applications that have revolutionized communication.

Obviously, the New Media has removed the communication advantage of the media house and liberated the communication space from the stranglehold of power brokers, who had used it to run their own discourses of power to subjugate the Others. The cyber space is, therefore, at once a democratic space wherein all citizens can express themselves without any communication/power inequality.

There is, however, a caveat here. Though the new communication space of the cyber green is intrinsically poised to correct the communication inequality and to resurrect communication, its surrounding reality is unlike that of the village communes. While the village communities were characterized by the lack of alterable inequalities of social and economic distinction, the modern nation-societies are hotbeds of such inequalities, with unalterable inequalities too at times played up to justify the former. Compounding this state of divides across regions, classes, colours, races and nationalities is the atomization of social life in a modern society that places a premium on individual growth even at the expense of the societal well being. In an environment of entrenched divides, it is not easy for the new media to achieve its inherent potential of leveling the divides and creating a new social order based on human unity and understanding. Not surprisingly, the success of the new media is hinged on the obliteration of the digital divide and the growing attempts of governments and corporate houses to muzzle freedom of expression on the global cyber green.

Furthermore, the new media is only a communication technology. The medium cannot be the message. It can only be a vehicle. The persistence of the social, economic, cultural and racial divides will continue to frustrate the realization of the promise held out by the new media. To enable the new media to fulfill its role as a great leveler and democratizing technology, it is essential that the cyberspace does not become Babel of conflicting self-interests, which an atomized society has foregrounded. If this happens, there is going to be a deepening of divides and emergence of conflicts. In other words, the human society will become a prisoner of its entrenched divides. But to avert this, it is essential that the basic divide be addressed first of all.

As the basic divide is localized in the human psyche, no amount of systemic change can ever undo or iron out the divides that separate one human being from another. For without the transformation of the post-lapsarian divide of consciousness into the palpable and the living ideal of human unity held up by the advaitic truth of Oneness of Creation and the Biblical truth of prelapsarian unity of existence, divides will continue to ebb and rise in one form or another in the human society/environment. So, if the promise held out by the ever-liberating and ever-democratizing new media has to come true, it is essential that human communication be re-anchored in the mystic wisdom of human unity. Therein lies the key to the rooting out of all human divides and the fulfillment of communication in human society.

Conclusion

The preceding discussion maps the subversion of the semantic connotation of communication and the appropriation of its semantic place by mass communication in an industrial society leading to the privileging of the owners of mass media and their cohorts in the league of the power elite at the expense of the others which include marginalized people(s), thereby creating and sustaining global and local divides. The discussion focuses attention on the role played by the new media in resurrecting communication and redeeming the others from the stranglehold of the mass media on public discourse. At the same time, the paper cautions that the promise of the new media can easily be miscarried if it is not accompanied simultaneously with the reorientation of the content of communication in the mystic ideal of human unity

Notes

1. In one text book, the authors say, "The first school of thought, usually known as the process school, characterises communication as the transmission and reception of messages. The second school of thought, usually known as the semiotic school, conceives

of communication as the generation and sharing of meanings." (A. Beck, P. Bennett and P. Wall, (2005, 2nd edition), ***Communication Studies: The Essential Introduction***, Oxford: Routledge)

2. In another text book, the author says, "The word communication is derived from a Latin word *communis*, which means common. In its application, it means a common ground of understanding. It is a process of exchange of facts, ideas, opinions and as a means that individuals or organisations share meaning and understanding with one another. Communication is a process involving the sorting, selecting and sending of symbols in such a way as to help the listener perceive and recreate in his own mind the meaning contained in the mind of the communicator." (C.S. Rayudu, (2005), ***Communication***, Himalaya Publishing House, Mumbai, p. 2.)
3. This runs counter to the belief generally held that power imbalances distort communication. V. Somasundaran writes, "Communication is systematically distorted by power imbalances that affect participation and expression" (V. Somasundaran, (2005), ***Principles of Communication***, New Delhi: Authors Press, p. 12.)
4. According to Somasundaran, "The phenomenological tradition conceptualises communication as the experience of self and other in dialogue. Such twentieth- century theorists of dialogue as Martin Buber, Hans- George Gadamer, Emanuel Levinas and Carl Rogers can be broadly identified with this tradition. The problem of communication for phenomenology, as for semiotics, is that of a gap between subjective viewpoints. One cannot directly experience another consciousness, and the potential for inter-subjective understanding is thereby limited. The two traditions approach this problem in quite different ways, however". (V. Somasundaran, (2005), ***Principles of Communication***, New Delhi: Authors Press, pp. 8-9)
5. According to Sri Aurobindo, "The creation has descended all the degrees of being from the Supermind to Matter and in each degree it has created a world, reign, plane or order proper to that degree. In the creating of the material world there was a plunge of this descending Consciousness into an apparent Inconscience and an emergence of it out of that Inconscience, degree by degree, until it recovers its highest spiritual and supramental summits and manifests their powers here in Matter." (***Sri Aurobindo's Letters: The Supramental Evolution (1)***, Available at the URL: http://www.indiadivine.org/articles/239/1/Sri-Aurobindos-Letters-The-Supramental-Evolution-1/Page1.html)
6. According to Amy Naylor: "The nature of written Hebrew makes it (The Holy Bible) extremely vulnerable to misinterpretation. If we take a look at ancient texts from a feminist point of view as opposed to a patriarchal one we might be surprised at what we find hidden within the text. Through this reinterpretation and reclaiming of the bible as a text for both men and women we can begin to decide if our "traditional gender roles" are actually what God intended." (Amy Naylor, (2004), 'Sexuality, Gender Roles and the Bible: A Feminist Approach', ***Women's Studies***, 399, 2004 Available at the URL: http://www.stolaf.edu/courses/ws399/ws399_04/Projects/Naylor_Research/index.html)
7. According to Sandra Harding, "Recent "gender, environment, and sustainable development" accounts raise pointed questions about the complicity of Enlightenment philosophies of science with failures of Third World development policies and the current environmental crisis. The strengths of these analyses come from distinctive ways they link androcentric, economistic, and nature-blind aspects of development thinking to "the Enlightenment dream." In doing so they share perspectives with and provide resources for other influential schools of science studies." (Sandra Harding, (Summer, 1988), *Gender, Development, and Post-Enlightenment Philosophies of Science*, ***Hypatia***, Vol

13, No. 3, pp. 146-167. Available at the URL: http://www.accessmylibrary.com/article-1G1-191273924/gender-development-and-post.html)

8. According to Rousseau, "I conceive that there are two kinds of inequality among the human species; one, which I call natural or physical, because it is established by nature, and consists in a difference of age, health, bodily strength, and the qualities of the mind or of the soul: and another, which may be called moral or political inequality, because it depends on a kind of convention, and is established, or at least authorised by the consent of men. This latter consists of the different privileges, which some men enjoy to the prejudice of others; such as that of being more rich, more honoured, more powerful or even in a position to exact obedience." (J. J. Rousseau, (1754), ***A Dissertation On the Origin and Foundation of The Inequality of Mankind***, Available at the URL: http//www.palisade.wordpress.com/2007/02/01/the-inequality-of-man/)
9. Ross Vaughn, 2009, *Thoughts on the Evolution of Social Inequality: A Paradigmatic Analysis*, hosted on October 10, 2009 at the URL: http://integralbuddha.net/thoughts-on-the-evolution-of-social-inequality-a-paradigmatic-analysis
10. Gregory J. Shepherd and Eric W. Rothenbuhler (2001) Communication and Community. Chapters address interpersonal conversation and communal relationships
11. Compared to hunting and gathering societies, the surplus available in agricultural societies led to the creation of more inequality in these societies. Woodburn (1982) argued that hunting and gathering societies have "immediate-return systems" and tend to be egalitarian. In contrast, the aborigines of Australia are examples of the "delayed-return system." Here there is a marked degree of inequality because stored food can be turned into durable and exchangeable goods. This allows the accumulation of wealth and power (Yesner, 1982; Testart, 1982), thereby providing the basis for creating more status distinctions among peoples. http://www.vernonjohns.org/vernjohns/rnagric.html
12. According to Tomislav Sunic, "Peaceful modern societies which respect the individual evolved from age-old familistic ties. The transition from band-type societies, through clan and tribal organizations, into nation-states was peaceful only when accomplished without disruption of the basic ties which link the individual to the larger society by a sense of a common history, culture and kinship. The sense of "belonging" to a nation by virtue of such shared ties promotes cooperation, altruism and respect for other members. In modern times, traditional ties have been weakened by the rise of mass societies and rapid global communication, factors which bring with them rapid social change and new philosophies which deny the significance of the sense of nationhood, and emphasize individualism and individualistic goals. The cohesion of societies has consequently been threatened, and replaced by multicultural and multi-ethnic societies and the overwhelming sense of lost identity in the mass global society in which Western man, at least, has come to conceive himself as belonging. Sociologically, the first theorist to identify this change was the Arab scholar, Ibn Khaldun (1332-1406), who emphasized the tendency for mass urban societies to break down when the social solidarity characteristic of tribal and national societies disappeared. Ibn Khaldun saw dramatically the contrast between the morality of the nationalistic and ethnically unified Berbers of North Africa and the motley collation of peoples who called themselves Arabs under Arabic leadership, but did not possess the unity and sense of identity that had made the relatively small population of true Arabs who had built a widespread and Arabic-speaking Empire. Later it was Ferdinand Tonnies (1855-1936) who introduced this thought to modern sociology. He did so in his theory of gemeinschaft and gesellschaft (Gemeinschaft und Gesellschaft, 1887). This theory revealed how early tribal or national (gemeinschaft) societies achieved harmonious collaboration and cooperation more or less automatically

due to the common culture and sense of common genetic and cultural identity in which all members were raised. This avoided major conflicts concerning basic values since all shared a common set of mores and a common sense of destiny. However, as history progressed, larger multi-ethnic and multi-cultural societies began to develop, and these Tonnies described as being united by gesellschaft ties. These were not united by any common set of values or historical identity, and collaboration was only maintained due to the need to exchange goods and services. In short, their existence came to depend on economic relations, and as a result of the diversity of cultural values, the lack of any "family feeling," and the emphasis on economic exchange and economic wealth, conflict over wealth and basic values was likely to disrupt the harmony of such societies at any time. In political terms, liberalism developed to eulogize the freedom of individuals from claims to national loyalty and support for national destiny, while Marxism grew out of the dissatisfaction felt by those who were less successful in achieving wealth and power, which now came to represent the primary goals of the individuals who were left at the mercy of the modern mass gesellschaft society. Nationalism and any sense of loyalty to the nation as a distinct ethnic, kinship unit came to be anathomized by both liberals and Marxists." Vol. 34, Mankind Quarterly, 04-01-1994, pp 263. Available at the URL: (http://home.alphalink.com.au/~radnat/debenoist/alain6.html)

13. The 'other' has been used here in the sense in which Simone de Beauvois uses it to describe women in male dominated cultures and Edward Said does to refer to the colonized people. http://en.wikipedia.org/wiki/The_other
14. According to Purba Das, Raceless, Casteles "Unity in Diversity": India's Ideological Articulation of National Identity, "This unity in diversity project by the government has been discursively constructed bysuturing selected identity markers like language, ethnicity, religion and excluded caste and race in its articulation. Thus the project was constructed strategically to win and sustain consent from the diverse masses. The aim was to cohere a common senseunderstanding that all are equal, around which people's imagined community is constructed. But internal sessesionist, communal and caste movements, counter narrative of the Dalits in the UN racism conference disrupt this political ideology and attempt to fix or close this particular representation of identity permanently." http://www.allacademic. com/meta/p_mla_apa_research_citation/2/5/7/9/5/pages257954/p257954-18.php
15. According to J. L. Sadie, "Economic development of an underdeveloped people by themselves is not compatible with the maintenance of their traditional customs and mores. A break with the latter is a prerequiste to economic progress. What is needed is a revolution in the totality of social, cultural and religious institutions and habits, and thus in their psychological attitude, their philosophy and their way of life. What is, therefore, required amounts in reality to social disorganization. Unhappiness and discontentment in the sense of wanting more than is obtainable at any moment is to be generated. The suffering and dislocation that may be caused in the process may be objectionable , but it appears to be the price that has to be paid for economic development; the condition of economic progress." J.L. Sadie, "The Social Anthroplogy of Economic Underdevelopment", *The Economic Journal*, No. 70, 1960, p.302, quoted in: Gérald Berthoud, "Market" in: The Development Dictionary, ed. by Wolfgang Sachs, London: Zed Books, 1992, pp. 70-87, citation pp. 72-73, Available at the URL: http://en.wikipedia.org/wiki/Modernization_theory
16. In Portraits of White Racism, David Wellman has defined racism as "culturally sanctioned beliefs, which, regardless of intentions involved, defend the advantages whites have because of the subordinated position of racial minorities". Wellman, David T. (1993).

Portraits of White Racism. New York, NY: Cambridge University Press. Available at the URL: http://en.wikipedia.org/wiki/Racism

17. According to Onyemaechi Udumukwu, "The thrust of colonialist's ideology was white supremacy. Its ultimate goal was to subjugate the black native in order to control the resources of his land." "The Antinomy of Anti-Colonial Discourse: A Revisionist Marxist study of Achebe's Things Fall Apart," Neohelicon, Vol. 18, No. 2 (September 1991), pp. 317-336. Available at the URL: http://www.springerlink.com/content/k54280p77687473k/
18. In the words of Stephen Knapp, "As everything is created from the Supreme Creator, then we should certainly have a high regard for everything as the expansion of God's energies. This not only includes all of our fellow men, but all creatures, as well as all aspects of the planet. Violence toward the planet in the form of not caring for the environment, misusing and polluting our natural resources, not managing the land and forests properly, are all forms of disrespect toward God and the blessings that have been given us." (Stephen Knapp, Environmentalism according to the Vedic View, Available at the URL: http://www.stephen-knapp.com/environmentalism_according_to_the_vedic_view.htm)
19. http://www.worldofquotes.com/author/James-Cardinal-Gibbons/1/index.html
20. According to Thomas Tufte, Analysing global divides in relation to media in everyday life becomes an analysis of experienced mediatized divides related to processes of social inclusion, identity formation and citizenship. It may concern experienced divides in relation to people and nations elsewhere on the globe, but just as likely experienced divides in one's own country or community. In this context, the media are the mediators of lived experience, access-givers to symbolic worlds of entertainment and global news reporting. They also become facilitators of and providers of spaces for public debate and for participation in society. By analysing media and global divides from an everyday perspective, the object of study does not become the technologies per se, but how they facilitate social networking, enhance processes of identity formation, enable access to and participation in public debates and ultimately enhance possibilities for citizens to express themselves and engage in society. Thomas Tufte, Media and the Global Divide: A Bottom-up and Citizen Perspective. Available at the URL: http://www.nordicom.gu.se/common/publ_pdf/283_tufte
21. Agenda-setting theory was introduced in 1972 by Maxwell McCombs and Donald Shaw in their ground breaking study of the role of the media in 1968 presidential campaign in Chapel Hill, North Carolina.[3] The theory explains the correlation between the rate at which media cover a story and the extent that people think that this story is important. This correlation has been shown to occur repeatedly. http://en.wikipedia.org/wiki/Agenda-setting_theory. The Gate keeping Theory, first instituted by Kurt Lewin in 1947 and expanded and applied to media by David Manning White, one of his assistants, complements the Agenda setting Theory as it opines that gatekeeping occurs at all levels in the media, right from source selection by the reporter to the story selection by the editor. http://en.wikipedia.org/wiki/Gatekeeping_%28communication%29
22. Despite the tremendous changes of the twentieth century, discrimination and violence against women and girls remain firmly rooted in cultures around the world, according to a new report, "Lives Together, Worlds Apart—State of World Population 2000", released on 20 September by the United Nations Population Fund (UNFPA). The report demonstrates that while many countries have started taking steps to protect women's rights and promote equality, actual progress has been slow. Inequality between men and women persists-Brief Article, UN Chronicle, Fall, 2000. Available at http://

findarticles.com/p/articles/mi_m1309/is_3_37/ai_70654237/?tag=content;col1

23. The Maha Nirvana Tantra, a sacred book of Tantra reads thus about the significance of Parvati, the Holy Consort of Lord Shiva:
    Sri Sadashiva said,
    Listen, O Thou of high fortune and destiny, to the reasons why Thou shouldst be worshipped, and how thereby the individual becomes united with the Brahman. Thou art the only Para Prakriti of the Supreme Soul Brahman, and from Thee has sprung the whole Universe—O Shiva—its Mother. O gracious One! whatever there is in this world, of things which have and are without motion, from Mahat to an atom, owes its origin to and is dependent on Thee. Thou art the Original of all the manifestations; Thou art the birthplace of even Us; Thou knowest the whole world, yet none know Thee.
    Such is the high place accorded to woman in the Tantric tradition.
    http://www.sacred-texts.com/tantra/maha/index.htm
24. Chomsky argues that the media, especially the large multimedia companies, have one supervening motive apart from profit and that is what he calls the "manufacturing of consent" Essentially, Chomsky argues that the media today are involved in a two pronged process. The first process is to ensure that the top 20 % of the population are satisfied and this is achieved by maintaining their position as policy makers, in control of some rudiments of power. Most of the media are therefore inevitably interested in maintaining the status quo, as is, frequently, the power elite; often the power elite and the media elite are the same group of people. He argues that part of the hegemonic function of media is to keep the remaining 80% of the population happy- a concept called "bread and circuses"- with a diet of celebrity gossip, sport, soap operas and light entertainment. It can therefore be seen that media have vested interests: to maintain the ideological status quo, to cooperate with the govt and to make money. Chomsky argues that this process is a form of control in a democratic society. [Manufacturing Consent: Noam Chomsky as mentioned in the book—Media Studies as the Essential Introduction for AQA 2008 specifications by Philip Rayner and Peter Wall (third edition) Routledge London and New York] pp. 168-69.
25. Pooja Rana (2009) Doctoral Dissertation on Newspaper Supplements—Content Analysis and Readers' Feedback, Accepted by Guru Jambheshwar University of Science & Technology, Hissar, India.
26. The demand for citizens' right to communicate was first voiced by Jean D'Arcy, later by the Non Aligned Movement countries, leading to the call for the New World Information and Communication Order by the UNESCO, which however got aborted. In recent times, the Right to Communicate Group based in Honolulu has been trying to resurrect this issue and its relevance for citizens.
27. In his Introduction to Communication, John Fiske writes, "Shannon and Weaver's Mathematical Theory of Communication (1949; Weaver, 1949b) is widely accepted as one of the main seeds out of which Communication Studies has grown. It is a clear example of the process school, seeing communication as the transmission of messages.' (p.6). He goes on to present in the same book the Semiotic School, as an alternative approach to communication. (John Fiske. 1990. Introduction to Communication, London: Routledge)
28. While discussing the different types of online journalism, Mark Deuze falls into the trap of privileging mass communication at the expense of communication when he embeds online communication within online journalism. Mark Deuze, Online Journalism: Modelling the First Generation of News Media on the World Wide Web, Available at the URL: http://outreach.lib.uic.edu/www/issues/issue6_10/deuze/index.html

Section E

MEDIA AND THE QUEST FOR TRUTH

22

Labourers of the Real "Authenticity Work" in Reality Television

Minna Aslama and Mervi Pantti

The fundamental scholarly claim about television is that as a medium it is, and thrives to be, closest to the "real", and that consequently, it offers mediated experiences of "livens", a sense of shared "witnessing", and the like (e.g., Bourdon, 2000; Ellis, 2000). It could be argued that "manufacturing the real" has been paramount to the allure and success of the medium. It indeed seems that in these times of increased competition for audiences—both in terms of expansion of television output and content in other media, particularly the Internet—the emphasis in "the real" has become one of the key strategies with which television tries to maintain its allure with viewers (Couldry, 2003, p. 104; 2008, p. 23). At the same time, as this chapter argues, it is often forgotten in academic and public debates that the notion and experiences of "the real" in the context of television are not only a product of television as such, or a mere calculated strategy of programme-makers. They are co-created, and equally contested, by several "labourers of the real", including audiences and other media. It is argued here that reality television, with its "unscripted' events, "ordinary people" as participants (e.g. Couldry, 2008, p. 23). and multimedia platforms for this authenticity labour, is a case par excellence for examining this "authenticity work".

The shared labour of the "real" is nothing new. Values such as the real and the authentic have been ascribed to the television medium from its beginning. The essentially evaluative and legitimating notion of authenticity has been used to define what is genuine, sincere, trustworthy and, ultimately, "good", since the notion of authenticity also implies the possibility of inauthenticity, of being fake or false (see Van Leeuwen, 2001). The specificity of television, especially in comparison to cinema, was related to three characteristics: screen size, domestic reception and live broadcasting, which has had a strong emphasis on truth and authenticity (Bourdon, 2000, p. 533). Thus, certain genres have been privileged as more authentic than others. Factual television traditionally drew its trustworthiness from authentic actions, locations and characters (Thornborrow & Leeuwen, 2001).

But reality television has intensified the work for televised "authenticity". First, capturing the "real" is the crucial aim for the program makers, since it is what differentiates reality programming from fictional entertainment (e.g. Fetveit, 1999). Reality TV promises to offer us real thoughts and action and, most importantly, true emotions of people like ourselves (Andrejevic & Colby, 2006; Aslama & Pantti, 2006). Audiences of reality TV are similarly focused on authenticity; negotiating the paradox between authentic and inauthentic elements are among the key attractions of reality programming (Mikos et al., 2000; Hill, 2002; 2005; Jones, 2003; Rose & Wood, 2005). Moreover, much of the public criticism of reality TV has focused on issues around authenticity. The format is frequently claimed to force authenticity by seducing participants into disclosing themselves and to manipulate the audiences to seek truth inside manifest fabrication (e.g. Biltereyst, 2004; Meers & van Bauwel, 2004).

The dilemma of the staged and scripted character of the "reality" is a recurring topic in the research literature (e.g. Andrejevic, 2004; Corner, 2002; Escoffery, 2006; Friedman, 2002; Kilborn, 2003; Holmes & Jermyn, 2004; Jerslev, 2004; Ouellette & Murray, 2004; van Zoonen & Aslama, 2006). At the same time, most analyses of reality TV, all address in some manner, even when only implicitly in their discussions of authenticity, the complex processes that produce a reality TV product. In this light, it is curious that although the claim of authenticity is central for reality TV, discussions of it have often remained at the level of merely re-stating the role of production in the construction of these fabricated realities. More sophisticated analyses of authenticity have not extended beyond particular aspects (mainly consumption) of reality programming.

So while "manufacturing the real" is a crucial function of television but surprisingly little is known how different stakeholders engage in the process. This chapter uses the concept of "authenticity work" to refer to collective or individual efforts to claim authenticity or to reject claims of authenticity made by others. The notion of "work", then, is used to stress that authenticity is socially and culturally constructed; that it is not a given quality, but a "a claim that is made by or for someone, thing, or performance and either accepted or rejected by relevant others" (Peterson, 2005, p. 1086). Accordingly, this notion of authenticity work implies that the experience and judgment of authenticity is pluralistic, in the sense that different groups and individuals might base their assessment of authenticity on different criteria (Van Leeuwen, 2001; Moore, 2002, p. 210; Peterson, 2005). Thus, the question here is not whether reality programs per se provide some kind of authenticity. Rather, the issue is how various classes of actors discursively construct different "authenticities" and how they negotiate the paradox of explicit creation of mediated authenticity (and its fundamental aim to allure audiences).

The aim of this chapter is, through empirical examples, to discuss how authenticity is claimed, questioned and/or rejected in different interrelated spheres and by different "labourers of the real": (1) in the production process, (2) by audiences, (3) by cast members, and (4) in media publicity. To illustrate the complexity of the concept of authenticity, this article also draws upon analysis of interviews with Finnish reality program makers and of interviews with the production team, audiences and cast members of the first *Big Brother Finland* (2005).[1] The goal is the address the importance of addressing authenticity work as a part of a complex process that is simultaneously calculated and manufactured as well as spontaneous, and "real".

Producers: One cannot Script Reality

The production team, which uses authenticity as a differentiation and selling tool, obviously has a central role in authenticity work. There is yet very little empirical work-based, for example, on observation or interviews—that is concerned with the motives, strategies and experiences of program makers (see Roscoe, 2001; Andrejevic, 2002). In the few studies that include evidence from producers of reality programming, the focus is usually on the construction, boundaries and ethics of "reality".

In program makers' attempt to create a sense of authenticity, all evidence points to the importance of ordinary people. The striving for authenticity through the cast members is apparent, to start with, in the adverts for subjects to take part in reality programs; for example, the slogan of the Finnish *Big Brother* gives a promise that "the most authentic person wins"; the British *Experiment* asked "do you really know yourself?" (Biressi and Nunn, 2005, p. 27). Likewise, the participants are selected by the producers with an eye to authenticity. This is for instance illustrated in the following statement from Finnish reality TV producer: "You have to find different people with different backgrounds, different values and who look different. Screen charisma is important. Being authentic is most important; the character must endure through the whole series" (Producer of Finnish dating game show *Escort*). At the same time, however, the "casting" in the reality show is seen as one of the few justifiable means of creating drama and conflict in reality television, but these two interests are not seen as conflicting (Andrejevic, 2004, p. 104).

Ultimately, it is the idea of documentary truth upon which the program makers' claim to authenticity is primarily based. The guarantor of authenticity is the documentary format in the case of *Big Brother*, the objectivity of omnipresent cameras, which reveal authenticity and truth. This emphasis on "technological authenticity", that the truth will be revealed through the eye of the camera lens, seems to be an universal discourse among producers: the co-producer of *The Real World* (Andrejevic 2002, p. 261; 2004, p. 104; see also Holmes 2004, p. 128; Holmes, 2008; Biressi & Nunn 2005, p. 20) as well as the Finnish producer of *Big Brother* argue that perpetual observation makes it impossible to act in ways which are not true to oneself:

> Some *Big Brothers* have tried to put in actors to fool people in the house for a couple of days or for a week, and actually a professional actor cannot keep a mask longer than two days. Because you cannot, you are disclosed really

> fast as an actor. And it is really hard because it is 24 hours and you can't perform for 100 or 96 days. [...] Some people are performing more in normal life and, well, then they perform here too, they try to be a little bit not themselves. In normal life they can get away with it, here they are revealed because we see them all the time, so it is impossible to keep up a role. (Member of the production team of *Big Brother Finland*)

Another common justification for authenticity concerns producers' limited power over what happens in reality TV—their "loss of control" (Andrejevic, 2004, p. 104). Producers claim that the "script" is ultimately written by the participants, rather than by them, even in international formats such as *Big Brother* that come with a "Bible", a detailed production plan (Roscoe, 2001, pp. 481-482). For example, the producer of the Finnish *Big Brother* describes the script as a "natural phenomenon" whose random moves can be controlled by the production crew only to a certain extent: the outcome is always unpredictable, and therefore authentic. Also typically, producers refer to uncontrollable moments of heightened authenticity, such as unexpected outbursts of emotion (cf. Grindstaff, 2002; Gamson, 1998, p. 91; Andrejevic, 2002, p. 262).

It is clear that program makers are also aware that authenticity provides a dilemma for reality TV. Finnish producers confessed that they constantly negotiate the contradictory views about influencing and "just observing" the interaction between participants. On the one hand, they see that the key for capturing authentic moments is that the production team is just observing the action; but, on the other hand, they also see that "pulling strings" or "throwing carrots" is a necessary part of making reality TV. Yet, paradoxically, the manipulation of action also forms a part of the producers' authenticity work. While the manipulation is ultimately explained by making reality programs that appeal to the audiences, the producers also believe that "real selves" are likely to emerge under pressure and that they can push the contestants to become more "authentic", understood in terms of conflict and uninhibited expression of emotion:

> At one point last year we noticed that the atmosphere in the program was flattening and so we decided that the contestants had to go on a 30 km march. Hard physical exercises and the tiredness caused by them create conflicts. Also the change in eating habits, or the lack of food, potentially generates drama. We do not want participants to get depressed, but we want them to be a bit… anxious (The producer of Finnish gamedoc *Extreme Escapades* [Suuri seikkailu])

The relationship between factual entertainment and its participants is often seen in terms of exploitation (Gamson, 1994, p. 89; cf. Teurlings, 2001), of which the above quote undoubtedly also provides an example. In her study on Finnish *Big Brother*, Minna Aslama (2009) however reveals that the ways in which the production team members relate to the participants is more complex and resembles Grindstaff's (2002, p. 141) findings about U.S. talk-show producers. On the one hand, members of the production team view participants as "the cast" or as "performers" who are evaluated, analyzed and controlled from a distance. This includes program makers also putting cast members' authenticity in question. For instance, the Finnish producers complained that participants are increasingly eager to perform in the ways they think the format requires, and that they sometimes also tried to direct producers in making appealing television (see also Syvertsen, 2001). On the other hand, program makers confessed that they are attached to the participants "as real people", and this evokes contradictory feelings in some situations such as evictions.

Participants: Importance of being True

Most literature on reality TV shares the idea that the authenticity of reality TV is first and foremost based in real thoughts, emotions and behaviour of people allegedly like ourselves; that is, it is based in the participants' "ordinariness" (as opposed to professional actors) and willingness to be true to one's self (Andrejevic, 2002, p. 261; Aslama & Pantti, 2006). While the popular fascination with film stars or pop stars derives from revealing their authentic and ordinary self behind the public persona (Dyer, 1987), in reality TV the presence of "ordinary people", at the outset, lays audiences' expectations on the expression of the real self. As Anita Biressi and Heather Nunn (2005) argue, "The contestant, as he or she appears before the media audience, can be courageous, bold, greedy, bitchy or ruthless but they cannot appear pretentious" (pp. 151-152). The importance of the "techniques of the self" are heightened in the reality shows that explicitly deal with self-expression, definition and development, namely therapeutic and "self help" programmes. Those subgenres, from *Dr. Phil* to Extreme Makeover, intend to assist the participants (and viewers) to be even more authentic or true to their "true selves" (e.g. Ouellette & Hay, 2008, pp. 63-98).

While there is a rich body of research on talk shows that discuss the presence of ordinary people on TV, there are only few studies that look at what kind of discourses the cast members of reality TV produce, for instance, what their motivations to participate in reality programs are and what kind of authenticity work they are involved in (see Syvertsen, 2001; Teurlings, 2001; Andrejevic, 2004; Aslama, 2009). Empirical studies on participants reveal that not only audiences but also participants could appropriate mass media for their own goals, rather than participants producing identities in line with "the logic and rules sanctioned by the show's producers and director" (Andrejevic & Colby, 2006, pp. 197-198). The interviews with the cast members of *Big Brother Finland* participants provide rich material on participants' understanding of authenticity in reality TV. They focus on their own quest for authenticity but also discuss the quest of producers, audiences and the media for constructing, interpreting or distorting their identities and behaviour. Most importantly, while the cast members recognize the power of producers, as well as audiences and the media, to create meanings, they still see themselves as sources of the most relevant meanings and authenticity (Aslama, 2009). Regarding casting, for instance, some participants explained that different "types" were selected for the house in order to create tension and drama, while others felt that they were depicted according to certain pre-determined roles that did not correspond to their "real" selves. But, at the same time, they did not doubt their own power to resist the representational strategies "from above" by committing to be real:

> If I am there and I am who I really am they cannot distort that very much, can they? [—] But then I have discussed with them, I think it was with the scriptwriter... And he said that towards the end he wanted to make me a kind of dictator. And at that point I thought how could you possibly do that? But I suppose it did not work out because I did not do enough such things. [—] They think about everything and try but they did not succeed with me. (Participant (f) March 2006)

Above all, the cast members discussed the impact of an extraordinary setting, acknowledging that it blurs the borders between performing and acting in ways that are true to one's inner self. Regarding the quest and ideal of being oneself, there is an interesting difference between producers' and participants' understanding; whereas the producers claim that the participants simply cannot mask their real selves because of being under constant surveillance, the participants argue that they managed to be true to themselves despite the artificial setting. Thus, participants' claim of authenticity derives its guarantee from a "real self" beyond the processes of mediation. The result of participants' authenticity work is that they act "authentically", yet a bit differently, than in real life:

> I don't think that anybody was like really on purpose acting. I mean that everyone was surely just being themselves; so much as it is possible in that situation. But now when I know the people outside the house I see that they are all somehow different. I didn't understand it there then, but it is those circumstances that make you somehow different. (Participant (f) March 2006)

Indeed, the core of participants' authentication work seemed to be in negotiating how being oneself in *Big Brother* house is different from being oneself in real life. Common ideas were that in *Big Brother* house one needs to be a bit more careful with his words and reactions than in real life and also a bit more pleasant or flamboyant. However, these minor adjustments in one's character and behaviour were not understood as a risk for being authentic. In contrast, acting understood as "role-playing" or being "two-faced" was not accepted (see also Andrejevic, 2004, p. 104; Holmes, 2005). For instance, participants who were revealed to be deceitful (pretending to be friends, faking emotions and talking differently behind others' backs or in the diary room) created the most negative reactions among the other cast members. This "being oneself" versus "role-playing" is discussed as a moral issue, but also as an issue which has direct consequences within the show. Some participants pointed out that one of them was (rightly) voted out early because his behaviour changed radically after one week. It is commonly believed that authenticity, remaining consistent, is the most important criteria for winning: "You win, absolutely, by being honest and being completely just yourself." (Participant (f), June 2006) (See also Andrejevic, 2004, p. 125; Holmes, 2005, p. 17)

The same special circumstances that were perceived to set some limits to their authenticity-as-in-normal life were, however, also commonly valued for providing an extraordinary opportunity for learning about one's true self, gaining insights about how one relates to others and reacts under special circumstances. The participants tend to highlight the "therapeutic" value of participating in reality program or their experience as means of self-discovery and personal development (cf. Andrejevic 2002, p. 265; Hill, 2002, p. 336; Couldry 2003, p. 124). The role of media in modern life as a place where the authentic self can be found and refined is clear in one participant's account of her two-step learning process; first, participating in *Big Brother*, and second, watching herself in the show afterwards: "I expect to learn from there [video recordings] too, but it [*Big Brother*] has taught me a lot and is teaching more all the time. Like, how I behave when I'm anxious or how I want to deny something even if I know how things really are." (Participant (f) April 2006)

What emerges from the interviews is that even if cast members occasionally complain about producers' decisions and their power to influence their representations, they felt that they are "in a same boat" with them. Interestingly, comments on the possible power of audiences entail an understanding of different truths about *Big Brother*. The participants stated that audiences could easily misinterpret the characters and events in the house: because audiences did not know what was "really" going on and what kind of people participants "really" were, they made wrong choices in voting. Not even the tabloid press received as much criticism for misunderstanding or misinterpreting the truth as did the fans discussing in the chatrooms. This may indicate that reality TV contestants understand the extensive media coverage around the programs as another part of the entertainment business, while the fans are seen more as "peers"; their assessments of reality thus are more easily targets of contempt. Whatever the case, the participants blamed audiences not understanding the truth and even feeding distorted news to the press, as exemplified by a participant who talks about the chat room:

> When one reads the stories one really has to laugh about how they could possibly interpret something in that way? And then you see that someone had written something and then someone [else] reads it and has not even seen [the situation], for example, because it has been on 24/7. And then those stories escalate, like the snowball effect, and become totally ridiculous. [—] the press did not really bully us at all. And when the press wrote something negative it was basically based on the chatroom [discussions]. (Participant (f) March 2006)

Audiences: Looking for Authenticity

An area that has received most empirical attention is the "epistemology of reception": viewing experience and pleasure, fan culture and participation, and multimedia use (Andrejevic, 2002; 2003; Hill 2002; 2005; Holmes, 2004b; Jones, 2004; Mikos et al., 2000; Roscoe, 2005, in Finland, Hautakangas, 2006;

Rasimus, 2006). The attention to audiences makes sense because of the immense popularity of reality TV, and also because the claim to authenticity is ultimately directed at them. Two important points emerge from the existing literature regarding audiences and authenticity. First, audiences are highly "tele-literate" and critical regarding reality TV's authenticity claims (Andrejevic, 2002, p. 261). As Annette Hill (2005, p. 173) has noted, audiences judge the degree of authenticity in each reality format based on their experience of other types of factual programming and actively negotiate the tensions between the performance and authenticity, between the real and the unreal. However, the fact that the audiences question the authenticity of reality programming does not mean that they reject the idea of authenticity. On the contrary, this critical stance involves an essentialist idea of authenticity, that is, that each individual has a "true" self, and that feelings and actions are authentic when they are true to this inner self."

This is evident in the second key finding of the audience research. The findings of Mikos et al. (2000), replicated in Hill's (2002, 2004, 2005) multi-method research on audiences of popular factual television, is that the principal source of audience fascination with reality programs is that of assessing what is authentic in an artificial environment; of looking for moments when participants are being themselves and not playing up to the camera (cf. Andrejevic, 2002, p. 261; Hill, 2002, p. 327; Jones, 2003; Scannel, 2002, p. 278; Andacht, 2004). Of course, assessing what is not authentic in reality TV participants' interactions and emotions is part of the self-reflexive viewing strategy. An example from *Big Brother Finland* illustrates both points; audiences questioned not only the authenticity of the cast members but also the trustworthiness of the production, suspecting producers of manipulating the representations and of forging and concealing audience votes:

> And then there was the case when Mika votes Tiina, Kate and Perttu to be evicted, those were the moments when I thought: WHAT? We're shown these people who seem so close, Mika and Perttu always smoking together and everything. I thought they had a real friendship going. So THAT's the point where you can sort of see that what we are shown about the BB house. Things are not quite that way and then viewers are surprised like this. But that's again an issue of editing and manipulation. (Fan interview, m, January 2006)

What are then the moments or reasons audiences might have for finding, or failing to find, a particular performance authentic? Here the authenticity of emotional expression is crucial (cf. Johnston, 2006). As Annette Hill (2002, p. 336) argues, the question in audiences' search for authenticity is not about whether a program depicts contestants in a faithful manner, but rather, whether the contestants' behaviour and emotions correspond to their true selves, eventually disclosed at some point. She suggests that the contestants reveal their "true" nature when they are facing emotionally difficult situations. Here the production tools of authenticity facilitate audiences' work as arbiters of authenticity. As we have stated, reality TV programs employ a variety of revelatory narrative strategies through which the impression of the "authenticity of expression" is conveyed.

For instance, different variations of the monologue such as confession, often combined with the use of close-ups, are employed to display those moments when emotions appear uncontrolled and unpremeditated and to judge the authenticity of other contestants (Aslama & Pantti, 2006; Dubrofsky & Hardy, 2007, p. 379; Holmes, 2004a, p. 124). However, as we have pointed out, assessing whether a performance or an individual is valued as authentic relates to the socially and culturally specific norms and expectations of how one should act, and appearing "authentic" might be easier for some contestants than others; as several studies have shown gender and ethnicity seem to be crucial sites or markers of the authenticity production for the participants (e.g. Bell-Jones, 2008; Dubrofsky & Hardy, 2008).

Importantly, this "authenticity spotting", looking for the moments of authentic expression, is connected to audiences' own authentication project. Hill (2002) suggests that assessing whether the participants are presenting an authentic self is connected to viewers' reflection on the performance of self and of authenticity in their everyday lives: "Viewers judge the moment of authenticity in a gamedoc such as BB by referring to their knowledge of the contestants coupled with knowledge of themselves, and how they would act in a similar situation." (p. 335) Correspondingly, Janet Jones (2003, pp. 407-408) argues that the fans use reality programs, the observation of the emotions and behaviour of others, as a "compass" that helps them make sense of their own lives. Thus, what emerges is a complex relationship between "real people" in the audience and "real people" on the television; scrutinizing the disclosed selves in reality TV presents an opportunity to reflect upon moral and social questions related to the self and acceptable behaviour and emotional expression.

In reality programming there has been a shift towards an interactive multi-platform world where audiences can choose to experience more "unmediated" access to "the real" through 24/7 live feeds, or to monitor and comment on the events as well as the publicity around the shows through new interactive features such as chat rooms, message boards and weekly polls (Tincknell & Raghuram, 2002; Jones, 2003; Roscoe, 2004; Holmes, 2004b; Hautakangas, 2006; Rasimus, 2006). These complex intermedial and intertextual relations in reality TV work to facilitate active viewing strategies that focus on negotiating the real and the authentic (Holmes, 2004b). As a result of her longitudinal web based survey, Jones (2003) concludes that the variety of ways in which *Big Brother* fans can access "the house" is seen as increasing the "perception of witnessing reality" (p. 229). In sum, the core authenticity work by audiences in the context of reality programs is all about the power of assessment: whether about a genre, a situation, a person, or an emotion. This is enhanced by opportunities offered in multiple media for investigating and discussing what is real and authentic. At the same time, it is about the proximity and distance needed for making the assessments. It is about identification with emotional or other aspects of content, and about recognition of generic conventions and production choices, but also about the power to step aside and judge.

Media Publicity: What Really Happened?

A point seldom addressed is that the active participation by audiences is also supported by the extensive media coverage surrounding many reality programs. Biltereyst (2004), for instance, argues regarding *Big Brother* publicity that the whipping up of moral panics in the media is an extension of the marketing of reality programs. Public debate was characterized by controversial arguments about, for instance, exploitation and voluntary participation, which certainly contributed to the popularity of the program. In broader terms, inter-media coverage and promotional materials work to enhance the commercial viability and life-span of the program. The many-sided publicity, from chat rooms and sponsors' advertising to gossip and participants' revelations in the tabloid press and critical columns in quality news papers, is a central part of the programs—and also central to authenticating reality TV programs. Yet media publicity has received little sustained analysis in general, let alone in terms of what kind of authenticity work media coverage of reality programs engages in, or in terms of what kind of role it plays for other parties involved in reality TV's quest for authenticity.

What should be considered is how media coverage shapes the audience-text relations, namely, audiences' understanding of what is authentic. As Su Holmes (2004a) suggests, "most sustained and self-conscious attempts to articulate 'the real' around Reality TV take place at the level of its intertextual circulation—in the popular press and magazine" (p. 122). An analysis of the media coverage of the first Finnish *Big Brother* (Herkman et al., 2005) reveals that the media publicity extended from political cartoons to interior design magazines. However, the main divide was straight-forward: the "serious" media engaged in critical readings and even moral panic, while the popular press capitalized on the "untold" and "true" stories from the lives of the new BB celebrities. The intensity of the quest for authenticity is perhaps the most curious phenomenon about the media publicity surrounding reality TV. One reason may be, simply, that the marketing machinery of most large-scale reality programs builds up the momentum and few media outlets can refrain from commenting and capitalizing on the hype.

From the point of view of authenticity discourses, most important studies about the relationship between reality TV and media publicity concern the "ordinary" participants' celebrity status. Due to the intertextual circulation of reality TV programs, appearing on television exposes "ordinary people" to a scrutiny that exceeds the original act of disclosure. As Nick Couldry (2003, p. 127) argues, the press "tend to monitor quite close 'ordinary people' as they pass backwards and forwards across the media/ordinary boundary; not surprisingly, because it is the boundary on which the media's own authority, in part, depends". Couldry's insight on the question of authority is significant here. However, what is also at stake in the popular media's coverage of reality programs are the boundaries between different media (television/press) and the seeking of cultural legitimacy and therefore capital value. In her study about ordinary/extraordinary paradox in *Big Brother*, Su Holmes (2004a) analyses the intertextual relations of the program, namely, the commentary on *Big Brother* that is produced from a range of different media sources (e.g. Internet, the popular press, celebrity magazines). She argues that "In a bid to differentiate itself from the televisual text, running throughout the press and magazine coverage is the claim to offer a higher form of 'truth' on the program, the 'reality', as it were, 'behind' the reality" (p. 122). Thus, the popular press seeks to challenge reality TV's claim to authenticity by using different strategies to reveal the "true story" behind the events in the show; for instance, by interviewing the evictees or by disclosing the authentic selves behind the screen persona by putting emphasis on the participants' past prior to their entrance into the *Big Brother* house, and, thus, prior to their mediated and manipulated identity (Holmes, 2004a, p. 125)

The popular press thus challenges the surveillance system of *Big Brother* as a guarantee of authenticity. By shifting the focus away from the screen events and characters, for instance, through the use of autobiographical rhetoric or by seeking gossip from the fan chat rooms, the popular press claims for the ultimate truths. At the same time, the critical analyses of the "serious" media often concentrate on revealing the manufactured authenticity and manipulative power of commercial reality TV productions, or the causes and curses of the celebrity-obsessed contemporary culture. The arguments or "tools" may be different, but their role as cultural gatekeepers who declare what is authentic, and what is not, seems to be very similar for both the popular and quality media. In other words, the media needs to engage in authenticity work to validate their own authority and to secure audiences. What this also clearly demonstrates is that claims about authenticity are deeply implicated in attempts to create differentiation and legitimacy in media production at large.

Discussion: Labouring for Authenticity—but to what Extent?

Understanding authenticity work of reality TV matters for and as cultural criticism at large. Reality TV epitomizes not only the rise of mediated authenticity but also the paradox of authenticity in contemporary culture. As more or less explicitly noted in most studies on reality television, while "real" and authentic traditionally refer to the opposition between the commercial and the authentic, authenticity is increasingly constructed within commercial processes—the idea of authenticity being increasingly important to the production of cultural objects and consumer choices (e.g. Brown et al., 2003; Grayson & Martinec, 2002). As Richard Peterson (2005) has argued, claiming, defining and manufacturing authenticity through different strategies is the central work of all cultural production today. In addition, while the very idea of authenticity has been claimed to stand in opposition to mass-mediated, highly individualistic (post)modern life (Baudrillard, 1988; Berger, 1973; Boorstin, 1964), at the same time the interest in authenticity has increased (e.g. Boyle, 2004; Erickson, 1995; Taylor, 1991). For instance, studies on tourism have emphasized the searching for authenticity as a modern embodiment of the religious pilgrim and illustrated a new type of tourist who seeks real locales and people behind the artifices of mass tourism

(Cohen, 1988; MacCannell, 1989; Urry, 1990). As Espen Ytreberg (2007) has stated, "the concept of authenticity seems to describe a communicational climate, a certain current mentality".

A part of that mentality is undoubtedly the question of defining and re-defining the individual "self". Authenticity as understood in terms of being true to one's self is both an ideal and a quest: a true self is something to be constructed or to be discovered (Giddens, 1991; Nicholson, 1999). Increasingly, spontaneity and exposures of emotions are seen to play a central role in discovering the authentic self (Lupton, 1998). New monitoring practises and professions have developed to support the authenticity work of the self; in addition, we have witnessed the creation of new forms of public spaces that are explicitly devoted to the analysis of emotion (Nicholson, 1999, p. 152). Certainly, reality TV has contributed to the increased cultural and social value of authenticity by offering individuals' unscripted talk and their emotional self-disclosures as "real" (Aslama & Pantti, 2006).

Indeed, as the examples in this chapter show, the individuality and emotionality seem to be tools for all authenticity labourers. As noted in his analysis of "first person" media, John Dovey (2000) offers the conclusion that the proliferation of publicly mediated, individual experiences and emotions operates as a new regime of truth and guarantor of authenticity (pp. 23, 25; see also Montgomery, 2001, p. 404). The guarantee of the authenticity of reality programs is primarily anchored in the idea of "being true to oneself", which is weighed up by the nature and manner of the expression of individuals and their interaction with other participants. The judgements of contestants' "subjective authenticity" are evidently connected to wider social norms and stereotypes regarding behaviour and expression; as Catherine Squires (2007) states, issues of authenticity "have real world antecedents and consequences" (p. 438), meaning that judgments of authenticity are constructed through such elements as race, class and gender (Bell-Jordan, 2008; Dubrofsky & Hardy, 2008). The issue of "social authenticity" emerges also from studies about indigenized reality television formats in which the construction of authenticity is anchored in national stereotypes and national identity (Dhoest, 2005; Aslama & Pantti, 2007).

Given the importance of authenticity work in contemporary societies, it is crucial to map and understand the processes of discursively "manufacturing the real" in the media. Interestingly, in the case of reality television, the above discussion of the different dimensions of authenticity work illustrates how authenticity is not constructed as a unified concept around reality TV. The analysis of existing research, complemented with the illustrative material of this chapter, clearly indicates that rather than looking at truth or falseness of the "authentic", one needs to approach authenticity critically as a cultural work that is established through discourse and remains in process. While the question regarding how audiences use authenticity as an important framework for interpreting reality television has been addressed by research, other spheres beyond audiences remain unstudied and need further empirical research.

In the context of reality TV, and particularly in *Big Brother*, authenticity work is focused on the idea of being true to one's "core" self. Accordingly, the tension between the "authentic" and the performed self is crucial for all different classes of actors involved in the authenticity work. Their labour might not be constant or straight-forward, but there are still discourses and strategies typical to each group. A couple of specific observations can be made. First, interestingly, reality TV seems to enhance or underline "conventional" positions in authenticity construction. The *production team* discusses the authenticity in terms of technology-based claims (surveillance technology; other conditions that make "performing" impossible) and generic conventions ("documentary"; unscripted production). The *participants*, then, unsurprisingly concentrate in their efforts to remain true to their authentic selves in the artificial reality TV setting and claim authenticity both within and outside the program. *Audiences* gain pleasure by analyzing and judging the authenticity of the disclosed selves. The surrounding *media coverage*, whether critical commentaries or tabloid stories, justifies its claim to authenticity by the critical "watchdog" discourse, that is, by revealing the truth behind the scenes. It is curious, yet perhaps symptomatic for a popular cultural product that these positions are not anything new if we consider any work of the culture industries such as movies or pop music. These positions, however, are intensified especially in the case of *Big Brother* and other reality programming that is distributed intensely during a period of time.

At the same time, these conventional positions are also leaky. They are self-contested within the different spheres and they fluidly shift from one sphere to another. A typical case-in-point is a *Big Brother* fan who suspects that voting results are manipulated by the production team but is still voting frantically for his favourite participant (and puzzled why he is acting that way). Yet another illustration of leakiness is audiences producing content and acting as "watchdogs"; for instance, giving tips in the chatrooms for the popular press to follow in their stories (Aslama, 2009). Similarly, the media coverage, at least in the case of the Finnish *Big Brother*, included stories on the *Big Brother* production, emphasizing the technological aspects of the 24-hour *Big Brother* production team. The producers, in turn, sometimes admit to their paradoxical position, proximity and distance to the participants, and analyse the participants' psyches as well as speculate about their future actions ("I know how Terhi really is, she's just acting nice now"). Furthermore, the participants both claim to be "true" to themselves, but act "untypically" in untypical circumstances. Some also note that they watch themselves (on taped episodes) afterwards, as audiences, to learn about themselves.

As noted, a "new" aspect of the authenticity work regarding reality TV, in contrast to more conventional television genres, for instance, is the multimedia component. Options to follow and to comment, even to create contents (for instance, by voting) are produced and offered for audiences. Consequently, they affect and intensify the authenticity work by audiences. It could be argued that audiences' search for authenticity is increasingly met by offering more opportunities to enter the Goffmanesque "backstage", a space of intimacy, closeness and (prior) reality. As MacCannell (1976), referring to Goffman (1959) argues, what is at stake in a quest for authenticity is a desire to be part of the backstage rather than observing it as an audience. This is an important aspect exemplifying how the authenticity work in general rests with individuals, rather than being based on predefined notions of the authentic.

At the same time, this can be a larger phenomenon regarding mediated realities. Nick Couldry's (2003, p. 116) idea of the media as the "exemplary centre", representing the essence of today's societies, resonates here. He argues that fame is not what allures people to become contestants of reality TV; rather, it is the idea of being in the inner circle of the most important social centre. To follow this line of reasoning, perhaps the producers' self-conscious and conflicting assessments of their role in manufacturing authenticity, or, for the matter, the frantic media publicity around many reality shows, all signify that everyone wants the access and the right to be at the very core of that mythical centre. Producers need to know the best, even about the inner life of the housemates, and work to entertain the audiences, although they claim they cannot control the reality of their shows. Similarly, the press and other coverage about reality shows seem to entail the argument that the real core of the centre is with them, not within a staged reality show in and for the everyday meanings and practices, for different stakeholders.

Most research on reality TV seems to be the "manufactured" nature of authenticity and most of the discussion ends up addressing the way audiences do authenticity work. This discussion bears resemblance to the notion of "audience work" introduced in critical cultural studies in the 1980s, referring to the idea that audiences "work" for programmers and advertisers by watching (e.g. Jhally & Livant, 1986). The discourses around reality TV and authenticity work tend to indicate the same; that audiences work for commercial media enterprises when they are seduced by the manufactured authenticity of reality programming. Yet, as illustrated here, the empirical analyses of audiences seem to indicate that a part of the authenticity work is a work that deals very much with the self—self-development, discovery, identification, and the like. Moreover, there are several other parties that engage in contradictory authenticity production practices. Authenticity work, embedded in complex intertextual relations in and around reality television programs, takes place in reality TV and involves all different classes of actors, While the notion of "manufactured authenticity" is a valid observation and result in many respects, the leaky, multi-dimensional and self-reflective discourses, emerging from the empirical analyses depicted in this article, might suggest a need to re-think and empirically examine the core notion of authenticity, in reality television and in mediated culture in general.

Note

1 The *Big Brother* interviews are a part of a larger project, engaging several postgraduate and Masters' students in 2005–6 with the first Finnish localization of BB. A major part of the research design was to conduct interviews with the three groups most involved in BB; that is, with members of the production team (including the executive producer, casting director and "script writer", and editors and production assistants), with some 30 fans and with all 12 housemates (see Aslama, 2009). Interviews with other Finnish reality program makers (10 interviews in total) have been conducted in 2005.

23

Super Girl and the Expediency of Hybridity

Robert Moses Peaslee, Shu-Ling Chen Berggreen and Sunyoung Kwak

Super Girl, the Chinese version of *American Idol* or Britain's *Pop Idol*, is the most successful program in Chinese television history. Although modeled after them, *Super Girl* is not, however, an iteration of the FreemantleMedia-owned *Idol* format. In addition, unlike other *Idol* shows around the world, *Super Girl*, as its name implies, allows only female contestants. One of these women, Li Yuchun, the 2005 winner, was voted by *Time Asia* magazine as one of the top-10 most influential people in Asia. Judging from the viewership alone—more than four hundred million viewers and eight million mobile phone voters for Li's final contest—*Time Asia* magazine's vote was warranted (Keane, Fung & Moran, 2007, 123).

However, the show's influence far exceeds television ratings and magazine accolades. *Super Girl* is regarded by many Chinese commentators as a spectacle of media convergence. It mobilizes old and new media, such as television, Internet, newspapers, and mobile phones, to both embody platform amalgamation and create a mass-consuming event that is both commercially and culturally groundbreaking. Flying in the face of traditional Chinese cultural and social practices, the show seems to promote female status in a male-dominated society. Furthermore, any citizen is allowed to vote (with a cost), a form of democracy familiar to *Idol* viewers around the world but not practiced in other aspects of Chinese social life. Finally, the audience's embrace of Li Yuchun, a self-confessed tomboy, signifies a new definition of femininity at work in a conservative, gender-traditional society.

This evolution may indicate an important shift from Chinese television's once authoritarian status to a more truly participatory mass medium in an environment of democratization of taste and of flexibility of gender performance. Are these true indicators of a fundamental social change to come? Or are these reconfigurations rather a mirage, a mere reflection of an expediency of hybridity that obscures the continuation of a top-down, elite-centered social, cultural and media landscape? This paper will situate *Super Girl* within the larger discussion of global participatory television formats (Baltruschat, 2009; Moran & Malbon, 2006) and their relationship to issues of globality and locality (Waisbord, 2004), and it will seek to problematize the sometimes emancipatory conclusions drawn by scholars emphasizing "democratic" consumption and its potential for empowerment.

The Chinese Media Environment

In order to appreciate *Super Girl*'s novelty, one must understand the regulatory media context from which it has emerged. From 1948 to 1953, the time of the Chinese Communist Party (CCP)'s consolidation of power post-Civil War, the number of Chinese language newspapers shrank from over 1300 to just 265. By the end of the Cultural Revolution in 1976, there were only 180. Circulation, meanwhile, increased during this time from 4.5 to 177 million (White, 2005, 135). This obviously represents a narrowing of control coupled with an amplification of audience. A similar process unfolded as television was introduced under the auspices of Beijing Television (renamed China Central Television [CCTV] in 1978) in 1958. CCTV began satellite transmission in 1972 and operated a national network by the 1980s. Prior to the beginning of the Reform period in 1979, broadcasters proceeded with aims of publicizing and explaining CCP policies, offering Maoist/Leninist socio-moral standards, helping the Party to maintain order, and preventing anti-Party, anti-government coverage. With the ascension of Deng Xiaoping in 1978, however, the CCP began a slow process of reform, ceasing the jamming of foreign signals in 1980, establishing an English-language channel for foreigners in 1986, and, by 1987, making contact with 120 television companies in 84 foreign countries (Hong, 1998). Importation proceeded quickly; by 1988, China's total volume of imported shows had reached 1,800, more than twice the 1986 level (ibid., 66). This influx of content precipitated an attendant increase in both television stations (from two in 1958 to 837 in 1996) and nationwide broadcast hours (from 2,018 in 1980 to 22,298 in 1990) (ibid., 72, 79).

Alongside the boom in Chinese broadcasting rose, predictably, a similarly expansive advertising industry. Reinstated in 1979, advertising grew from an annual business volume of zero prior to reinstatement to 2 million yuan (Renminbi) in ten years (ibid., p. 83). Shanghai Television's increase in advertising revenue was exponential, skyrocketing from .49 million yuan in 1979 to 170 million yuan in 1992 (ibid., p. 85). Such impressive gains were made possible largely by the penetration of television hardware into the vast Chinese population. Television set ownership increased from just over 12,000 in 1960 to 300 million in 1996, a year in which CCTV broadcasted to an estimated 940 million viewers (ibid., pp. 87-9). Government investment in television followed this pattern as well: from 20 million yuan in 1967 to 6 billion yuan in 1996 (ibid., p. 92).

As White (2005) reports, however, terrestrial broadcasting soon faced competition from satellite transmissions. AsiaSat-1 launched in 1990 with a footprint stretching from Japan to Egypt, Russia to New Zealand. One year later, all of Asia had access to signals from the BBC, CNN, and several other international networks. Satellite dishes were consequently outlawed in China in 1993 under State Council Decree No. 129. By this time, however, an estimated 11 million dishes were already extant in China. By the end of 2001, an estimated 45 million Chinese had gained access to satellite signals. Concurrently, cable television also has exploded as a technology that appears to offer greater consumer choice while remaining controllable at its terrestrial core. Chinese cable subscribers, according to various estimates, numbered roughly 150 million in 2007.[1]

The complications faced by the CCP with the establishment of the Internet, meanwhile, have been the subject of much speculation. Between 2001-2002, China experienced a 72.8% growth in Internet usage (White, 2005, 172). As of 2005, China was the second largest national block of Internet users at 111 million, and in 2006 it was reported that, when factoring in Internet activity made possible via mobile telephony, China had likely surpassed the US in Internet users (Pace, 2006). In this environment, according to one commentator, the vast regulatory edifice built to protect China from Internet influence is akin to the pop-up gopher game at the arcade (White, 2005). Internet activity, alongside China's pollination by special economic zones like Macau and Hong Kong, are therefore said to create consumer broadcasting demands which outpace CCTV's ability to program, resulting in the decision to release some of this responsibility into the market sphere. It is within this political and economic open-door policy that *Super Girl*, the market leader of *Idol* shows in China, burst into the nation's media and cultural scenes.

Super Girl

By the early 2000s, the *Idol* format already had numerous franchised copies and spin-offs in many countries around the world. While it incessantly proclaimed its novelty, this type of talent search show was very popular during television's formative years in East Asia. For example, for three decades or so, watching *Five Star Prize (wu den jiang)* was very much a part of Friday afternoon routine for many people in Taiwan. The show ran from 1965 to 1998.

Just like any other TV station in China, Hunan Satellite Television (HSTV) was in search of a formula to bring in high ratings and increased advertising revenue. The new global *Idol* fever and the old familiar talent search format gave rise to its first *Idol*–esque show, *Super Male Voice (chaoji nansheng)*, a Chinese version of *American Idol*, but with male contestants only. The show failed to generate a desirable market share and was short-lived. However, the local enthusiasm (3000 people applied to be on the show within two weeks of its debut) indicated a profit potential. Thus, repackaging the show, HSTV launched *Super Girl* nationwide in May 2004. It was an instant success. HSTV soon collaborated with other regional TV stations and a Shanghai production company to create a more national edition (Keane, et al., 2007). The show ran from 2004 to 2006, at which point it disappeared from the Chinese television spectrum until being resurrected in 2009 under the slightly modified moniker of *Happy Girls*.

Subsequently, *Super Girl* was a ratings miracle. For example, during the 2005 summer season more than 10 percent of China's television viewers (20 million people) watched the program every Friday. On August 26, more than 400 million viewers – nearly one third of China's population – watched the 2005 season finale. This marked the largest television audience in the country's history ("*Super Girl* in," March 2, 2006). With an astounding 3.53 million votes through mobile phone text messages, Li Yuchun was crowned *Super Girl* 2005. Paralleling this unprecedented viewership, conversations among viewers and fans filled many of China's major Internet portals and blogs. While the show was produced mainly in Changsha, the capital of Hunan Province, China's new media environment allowed fans nationwide to connect with every single development of the show, no matter how far they were from the production center (Madden, 2006). The 2009 iteration of the show has seen similar, if slightly decreased, levels of popularity.

Reasons for this cultural fervor are manifold. First, *Super Girl* is supported by the wave of the global *Idol* popularity. Keane, et al. (2007) advance three success factors in support of the *Idol* format: "the ordinary nature of the entertainers, simple sets and interactivity" (132). China's media environment was ripe for those factors. As Keane, et al. indicate, "interactivity adds value through internet sites and is accounted for by SMS voting. Cross-platform collaboration with internet service providers helped *Super Girl* to maintain consistently high ratings" (133). However, in the Chinese cultural and political contexts, it is perhaps the unique rules of the game that propel *Super Girl*'s extreme national popularity.

The Rules of the Game

While *Super Girl* attracts audiences from all ages, the show's primary fans are those in their 20s, a generation raised in the post-Mao era. This is a cohort with a haunting desire for democracy, some for its ideological import and some for the attendant discourses of consumerism. *Super Girl* epitomizes imagined youth communities interacting within the entertainment marketplace (Wu & Wang, 2008). Within this context, the show's "equal opportunity" and "people's choice" selection and elimination processes became a most significant element of *Super Girl's* gravitational power.

The show went through a pre-selection process called *haixuan* (village election) to choose top contenders, and then text messaging and "player killing" (PK) were used to select winners to advance to each level until the final competition. In the political sphere, *haixuan* refers to "voting by direct ballot at the village level, which is the only democratic poll in the Chinese country side" (Wu & Wang, 2008, 421); many Chinese, however, rarely (such as 3 times in 50 years) participate in their villages' *haixuan* process, seeing such votes as useless with the outcome already predetermined. Factory owners, for example, are said to tell workers whom they should vote for, leaving them with a felt obligation to cast their votes accordingly. Therefore, to some this direct voting has no relation to democracy. However, *haixuan* in *Super Girl* took on a different meaning.

Super Girl used the *haixuan* method to select participants for the show. Five cities (Guangzhou, Zhengzhou, Changsha, Hangzhou and Chengdou) representing five representative geographic areas composed the pre-selection sites. More than 150,000 Chinese women, between the ages four to eighty-nine, entered as contestants in the 2005 preliminary *haixuan*. Fifty from each geographical area advanced to the next stage. In the end, only three from each area were chosen for the final competition. The probability was one out of 10,000 for a contestant to make it from a preliminary *haixuan* to the final competition. This process also resonates with what the phrase *haixuan* implies: "*hai* means sea in Chinese with implications of vastness and mass participation" (Wu & Wang, 2008, 411), and *xuan* means "selection" or "election" in Chinese. Even with an chance of one in 10,000, then, for the first time, every female (or every family with a female member) in the country had, in theory, an equal opportunity to fame, fortune and power – a chance normally available only to the elite and the wealthy. *Haixuan* in *Super Girl*, therefore, symbolized hope to many people in China in a time of uncertainty.

Super Girl then offered another mass participation process: direct voting for one's favorite candidate (contestant) every Friday through text messaging. This "people's will" mentality sharply differs from the "conventional CCTV style of authoritative experts deciding on the contest outcome" (Xiao, 2006, 60). This brought about "a nationwide movement of fantasizing about democracy and modern political enlightenment" (ibid). Even academia engaged in heated debate on the political impacts of *Super Girl*. No matter how one regarded the show, all academia seemed to take the show "seriously as a realistic performance of democracy" (ibid.). Xiao (2006) notes that this phenomenon vividly illustrates ideoscapes as advanced by Appadurai (1990), in that Chinese viewers are subject "the global flows of the Enlightenment worldviews in which democracy is a central term" (Xiao, 60). Keane, et al. (2007) further states that this quasi-democracy through *Super Girl* "reflects a trend by which popular culture destabilized the hegemony of elite cultural forms, echoing global critiques of subsidized state culture" (132).

While democracy no doubt was a central term in discourses about *Super Girl*, the degree to which this participatory consumption ritual truly destabilizes the elite hegemony and de-centers state power remains, in our opinion, an open question. While the 2005 season finale gathered the highest voting record of more than eight million votes (Zhang, 2006), that was eight million out of possible one billion-plus votes. To participate in this voting process, moreover, one had to pay one yuan, about US$0.13, per vote (Madden & Wentz, 2005). This is more like a privilege than a right, considering the average annual earnings for most people in China. For example, Chinese farmers' average annual earnings for 2006 were 1,797 yuan (US$225)(Li, 2006). Therefore, an average farmer would have spent roughly one-seventh of his/her annual income to engaging in the voting process for one season of *Super Girl* (about 6 months), not counting purchasing and subscribing to a mobile phone service. In the end, only those with the communication tools and disposable income could possibly afford a taste of democracy through *Super Girl*.

In addition to this mobile but direct voting, another type of votes was cast through the "player killing" (PK) process. PK is a macho phrase from online computer games, popular with many Chinese male cyber-gamers. *Super Girl* borrowed the phrase and used it to set a rule, which stipulated that one of the two players (contestants) must be killed (eliminated) in every competitive play-off (Wu & Wang, 2008; Xiao, 2006). We return to gender below, but for now it is important to note the irony that a male-oriented phrase should be used to eliminate players in an all-female contest. While there were substantial similarities with other global *Idol* shows, such as judges with strong personalities and audiences' direct voting, *Super Girl* was distinctive with the PK sudden-death process and its integration into the show's presentation.

Each show began with all contestants singing and dancing together as a group in uniforms, smiling and holding hands. It was a highly rehearsed and choreographed performance in a friendly and harmonious environment. The live audience sang along. It was a display of a happy Chinese family with no sign of the competition to come. Then, there was contestants' performance in small groups with the same uplifting, cheery atmosphere among contestants and between the contestants and the live audiences. For example, in the Top-Nine-to-Eight elimination show, the contestants were divided into three groups. The two-hour show included the all-contestant performance, small group performance, and clips of contestants and their life stories. Then after the individual signing contest, judges picked the best performer from each group. After the text messaging votes, one more member from each group was saved. Then the last three went through the PK process. The thirty live audience members walked up to the stage where the three PK players stood nervously next to a see-through ballet box. The audience members, often in T-shirt uniforms, filed past the stage and dropped their vote without much emotion. Cameras often zoomed in to show the teary, nervous, or crying faces of the PK players. This segment contrasted sharply to the earlier harmonious, happy family scenes. The show ended with the "killed" player giving her final performance.

Even though this was the general routine of the show, the rules were not absolute and the process lacked transparency. Judges seemed to have the supreme power to overturn votes from audiences. Sometimes the judges saved certain contestants from each group even before the text voting. Therefore, the contestants who received the least votes from the nationwide audience could still be saved by the judge and advanced to the next level. Conversely, sometimes judges sent contestants with the highest national votes to PK. For example, in the Top Seven-to-Six elimination of the Chengdu regional show, contestant No. 7 received the most votes from the national audience while Li Yuchun came in second. But the judges decided to send No. 7 to PK. She was eliminated while Li advanced to the next level and eventually became the 2005 *Super Girl.*

In a way, this non-transparent decision-making process mirrors somewhat the useless vote sentiment uttered by some villagers about *haixuan*. *Super Girl* judges and the audiences, whose certain privileged and resourceful statuses allow them to attend the competition live, were positioned as the authority and were allowed to dramatically alter what the "people's will" intended. Therefore, *even if* anyone who wished to vote were equipped equally with tools and disposable income, their voices could be arbitrarily silenced.

Gender Politics

One reason HSTV's *Super Male Voice* was short-lived was that the profit-driven strategies employed in *Super Girl* couldn't work well with male contestants in a culture with a long tradition of patriarchic value system. For example, in *Super Girl*, producers employed a melodramatic strategy that evoked much emotion, intensifying the contest and generating historically high ratings. As we mentioned above, through group performances, contestants were first arranged together as a happy family and later paired up as loving sisters. In the end, however, they must turn against each other to survive the PK process. This ambiguous sisterhood love produced endless tears among contestants and among audiences, live or remote. Further, during the PK process, both killed and advanced contestants embraced and shed tears together. The killed cried for her own death and the advanced mourned for the loss of a family member and expressed their guilt for "survival". This particular crying ritual was reminiscent of *kusang*, a ritualistic act of crying in traditional Chinese funerals.

Historically, the Chinese female has occupied a central role in ritualistic crying (which was outlawed during Mao-era), such as *kujia* (wedding lamentation songs) and *kusang* (Wu & Wang, 2008). This type of ritualistic crying is important as it unifies and integrates the event by guiding and leading the rhythm of the ceremony. While the society remains patriarchal, Chinese females symbolize in these roles the faces of unity not only in ritualistic events but also in day-to-day family harmony. *Super Girl's* enactment and showcase of happy Chinese unity and the crying ritual in every competition is achievable only with female contestants. Therefore, while many saw the show as an elevation of female status in the society, opening up possibilities for upward mobility, it could also be seen as a relentless exploitation and commodification of the female's traditional role in a competitive globalizing Chinese economy.

Another national discussion about *Super Girl* centered on the redefinition of Chinese feminine beauty. Deviating from Chinese norms, the 2005 *Super Girl* champion Li Yuchun proudly paraded her androgynous image throughout the season. She was often described as a tomboy with a rather masculine manner and style (Liu, 2006). Xiao's (2006) description best summed up her appearance: "a lanky figure always in pants rather than skirts; orange-tinged spiky hair cut short; deep voice; manly look in the sense of resembling Yao Ming, the macho basketball player and also the embodiment of globalizing sports market of China" (62). While many saw this represent a change of feminine beauty, Xiao also observantly points out that this "can be read as a Chinese translation of new masculinity configurations under the impact of imported male star images in the Pan-Asian media coverage and popular culture" (ibid).

Whether it was a fundamental reexamination of femininity or masculinity, the public endorsement of Li's style may also be in part a result of profit-driven strategies. Li's mannish style may not be free of commercial contamination after all. As soon as public acceptance of Li's "self" was obvious, the show did everything to reinforce that image to the degree of typecasting her. When contestants were grouped, Li and other short-haired females were often assigned together and with pants, shirts, and a loose tie as their group uniform, while contestants with traditionally feminine appearances were put in groups with dresses or skirts as uniforms. Songs chosen for group performance further indicated this intentional distinction. For example, in the Top Five-to-Three elimination show, Li and He Jie (from the skirt group) performed a duet, "Fairy Couple," with Li signing the male part and He the female part. Therefore, this all-female contest also pit two types of femininities (or traditional femininity and new masculinity) against each other to further fuel the already heated competition among fans, a situation guaranteed to garner enormous commercial profit. Nevertheless, it should be said that Li's stage representation, whether commercially contrived or not, did provide a platform for safe multiculturalism where gender perception and identity could be explored. Crucially, however, this exploration was effectively contained.

Idol-izing an Imagined Past

While *Super Girl* was part of the contemporary worldwide *Idol* phenomenon, it also was a show about the past. Nostalgia filled the air through the selection of songs. These songs evoked public emotion about the purity and innocence of the bygone era, something that seems no longer available in China's speedy modernization process. Further, these songs also painted an image of a happy yesterday, which does not reflect the hardship the society experienced in its recent past. Therefore, through *Super Girl*, a new version of the old past was freshly injected into the public's collective memory.

For example, songs from the musical genre *Huangmeìdiao*, made famous by Hong Kong film industry throughout East Asia in the 1960s, were popular numbers in *Super Girl*. However, during the Cultural Revolution of 1960s only revolutionary songs were allowed for public consumption and performance. Live audiences cheered non-stop whenever a *Super Girl* sang "Small Town Stories," an extremely popular song in Taiwan (and in East Asia) in the 1970s. The 1970s witnessed tension between Taiwan and China; it was a time when communication of any kind was outlawed between people divided by the Taiwan Strait and when materials of any kind from the other side, including media products, were absolutely banned. Such songs, then, along with Western songs of the 1980s like

"We Are the World," celebrate what has been termed a "trans-Chinese imagination" (Berggreen & Peaslee, 2007) alongside China's emergent openness and hybridity. The 2005 season finale, however, provided a different celebration of the past. While there were only three competitors, the show lasted four hours. In addition to showing many heart-warming clips of *Super Girls* visiting hospitals and orphanages (Wang, 2008), it also featured songs from the revolutionary era. Performing the role of modest learners, the three *Super Girls* sang along with long-retired singers who were famous for singing traditional folksongs and Mao-era revolutionary numbers. Whether this was an arrangement to glorify the revolutionary past is up to interpretation.

As Hall (1996) observes, people's lived experience, their pleasures, their memories, and their traditions are the basis for popular culture. Popular culture has connections with local hopes and local aspirations. These songs reflected the public craving for regional and global popular culture not available to them in the 1960s, 1970s and 1980s. Through *Super Girl*, the public celebrated and relived an alternative past. Such remembering of an imagined past may serve as a form of confidence building through which people could feel updated and finally in step with the rest of the world and therefore ready to take the new turn in which China is engaging. The question remains, however, whether *Super Girl* is expressive of an actually existing hybridity, where discourses of democracy and meritocracy are truly taking hold and destabilizing traditional power structures, or if, on the other hand, the show provides an opportunity for the display of consumerist hybridity for the purposes of obscuring (and thereby retaining) these same structures of influence.

Super Girl and the Privatization of Propaganda

Chang (2007) has outlined the changes that have taken place in China with regard to political control over media content in the context of increasing marketization. According to Chang, the *Super Girl* phenomenon (as well as the growing popularity of China's YouTube clone, Toodou) emerges in response to a steady movement on the part of the Chinese Communist Party (CCP) toward the commercialization of broadcasting alongside a nevertheless conservative stance toward content. Beginning in 2000, the CCP adopted a posture of adaptation to the waning of its manufacturing economy in favor of one built around knowledge and information. Chang relates that this process evolved quickly; by 2004, the development of the "cultural industry" was officially included as a platform plank in the 10th Five Year Plan (2001-2005). The following year saw the legalized privatization of some cultural industries, a concession that precipitated a perhaps unsurprising tension between commercial broadcasters—struggling for survival in a suddenly highly competitive business environment powered by consumer demand—and government officials unwilling to cede control of content.

In this context, Chang describes *Super Girl* as a manifestation of consumer erosion of the CCP's centralized dominion over culture. The show, Chang suggests, is essentially opposed to both official Chinese policy and traditional Chinese culture, especially, in the latter case, in terms of Li Yuchun's presentation of gender ambiguity. Since *Super Girl* celebrates the larger Western ideals of individuality, meritorious personal achievement, and celebrity, that is, and since its monumental popularity made it difficult for the CCP to compel HSTV to cease broadcasting it, Chang would like to describe *Super Girl* (as well as Toodou's increasingly decentered and user-generated content cluster) in terms of progress toward a more open Chinese society. This assumes, we would suggest, rather too much about the unidirectional nature of historical development toward democratization.[2] We would suggest instead the greater applicability of a recent study by Luo & Hao (2007), who have made a more nuanced argument concerning the presentation of Chinese womanhood on prominent magazine covers, suggesting that "rather than a literal portrayal of the 'reality,' it is a symbolic representation of Chinese women created through the interaction of party ideology, editorial policy, and readers' taste as well as the changing reality of Chinese women's life and work" (281). In this case (and, we would argue, in the case of *Super Girl*'s crying rituals), a modern form of "female" is displayed while leaving aside the strong cultural conservatism faced by most Chinese women. While party control may be disrupted by consumer culture, that is, the reconfiguration that results in Party-approved content (which includes a new presentation of modern Chinese-ness) may in fact be a reinforced bulwark against those who would agitate for tangible political change.

Global Participatory Television Formats and Power Relations

In theorizing the practices of the viewer-participant of the "enhanced" television format on a worldwide scale, commentators have tended to revisit familiar arguments concerning structure and agency. On the one hand, investigators have found reason to be optimistic about the democratic potential of fan activity surrounding shows like *American Idol*, *Big Brother*, and their respective format clones in national television environments around the world. Coleman (2003) and van Zoonen (2004) are emblematic in this regard, making observations concerning the equivalency of political participation and participatory consumption of television product. Van Zoonen, specifically, suggests that, since political constituencies and fan communities share a structural equivalence, exhibit similarities in terms of practice, and each blur the traditional separation between affect and cognition in political activity, the traditional characterization of entertainment as detrimental to political participation (she references Postman [1985] as particularly representative here) should be problematized.

Coutas (2006) is more cautious. Analyzing the cultural work performed by *Indonesian Idol*, Coutas suggests that, since the finalists of the program (referred to locally as the "*Idola*") are the result of the importation of a Western television format, the show might be considered an example of cultural imperialism. By encouraging a commodification and celebritization of the Indonesian cultural context, that is, *Indonesian Idol* exhibits ideological properties. In the end, however, Coutas invokes the cultural imperialism thesis largely as a straw man. Relying upon Appadurai's (1990) description of hybridized, fluid, and co-constitutive "scapes" of cultural production in the age of transnational flows, Coutas suggests that *Indonesian Idol*, as a program which allows (in a way, requires) viewer participation and supports the uploading of a kind of Indonesian locality into the global popular, is a rather more diverse arena of cultural contestation. Coutas closes with—but unfortunately leaves aside—the more crucial question: to what extent does the participatory *Idol* format represent a "*fantasi* of agency that is constructed 'from above'"? (388).

Other commentators, however, have found cause for a more nuanced (Holmes, 2004) or even pessimistic (Kjus, 2009) vision of the "enhanced" television format. Nightingale and Dwyer (2006), for example, position the format as exportable precisely because it conveniently obscures, in its cloying appeal to discourses of democratic empowerment, community building, and patriotism, the relations of production and consumption which ensure that each "vote" is in fact a unit of financial exchange. This "neoliberal rhetoric" of the participation model requires the cultural work of hosts as "salespeople" to promote fan involvement, the end result of which is a cost, in the form of telephony and data fees, to the participant. Critiquing analyses such as Coleman's and van Zoonen's, which "focus on the similarities" between fan involvement in enhanced formats and political participation "at the expense of" recognizing their important differences, Nightingale and Dwyer suggest that, rather than offering true empowerment through interactivity, such programs offer only access, and for a price at that: "...access is renamed 'interactivity' and represented back to the public as a sign of the 'democratic nature' of television voting" (30). In following the "money trail" of fan voting in reference to televised competitions, whereby mobile service providers, 1-900 purveyors, ISPs, external producers, and television networks all benefit financially from such activity, Nightingale and Dwyer are representative of a school of thought which sees enhanced "reality" programming as, essentially, ideological and exploitative. In the case of *Super Girl*, according to Luo Yuanjuan (2005) some of the real "winners" might be HSTV, Short Message Services (SMS), the Mengniu group who sponsored the show, and Tianyu Meida, who own the *Super Girls* brand. Similar advantageous structures exist for any *Idol* program (see Jenkins, 2006 for an account of *American Idol* in these terms). A compelling example from the case of *Super Girl* helps illustrate this argument. According to Chang (2007), "a contestant who was voted out complained that competing on *Super Girl* was a financial disaster for her family. Zhang Meina, 21, from China's Northwest Xinjiang Uyghur Autonomous Region, said her family owed a debt of 90,000 yuan (US$11,250) after friends and family members sent out 45,000 phone text messages to support her during the competition" (9).

The Expediency of Hybridity and the Consolidation of Cultural Authority

James White, writing in 2005, points out that the emerging multi-channel televisual environment necessarily erodes the nation-building ability of a public broadcaster, especially an authoritarian one. Writing in part about CCTV in the late 20th and early 21st centuries, White points out that "the very notion of globalization fundamentally upset the whole idea of community, which suddenly could be as big as the audience for World Cup soccer or Princess Diana's funeral, or as specific as viewers of a channel devoted to golf or subscribers to an online discussion group, situated everywhere and nowhere" (xviii). Such a point of view informs Jaiyan Mi's (2005) investigation of a new "visually imagined community" in China which is effected through television programming displaying "a problematic televisual collage of both Chinese and Western images for national consumption in post-Mao Era" (327).

Here we might again consider Arjun Appadurai's (1990) thesis—certainly still a cogent and crucial one—regarding the hybridization of social and psychological spaces in our time. Appadurai's intent, in part, is to complicate discourses of globalization that amount to facile expositions on cultural imperialism, on the one hand, and celebrations of the "global village" on the other. This spectrum of analyses, with homogenization at one extreme and heterogeneity at the other, is in Appadurai's estimation something to be transcended with an analysis that sees both of these processes occurring simultaneously. To this end, and in an effort to posit the abstract concept of "hybridity" in relatively concrete terms, he proposes the spatial concept of the "scape" in opposition to traditional core/periphery models of globalization analysis. In ethnoscapes, technoscapes, finanscapes, mediascapes and ideoscapes, Appadurai suggests, we can see "imagined worlds" in which people, technology and technological knowledge, capital, cultural products and discourses, respectively, transcend national and ethnic boundaries on a rapid scale. Moreover, such scapes are, rather than strictly bounded categories of culture and practice, prone to cross-pollination, such that diasporic communities should be understood as manifestations of conflict and contestation between the imperatives of the enthno-, finan-, and technoscapes (at least). Therefore, Appadurai suggests that global flows occur through and in "disjunctures" between the "scapes" (11).

Appadurai is very helpful in considering the case of China. He makes a particularly apt observation in pointing out that the (cultivation of) fear of homogenization from some outside force (usually the United States) can effect a more pervasive homogenization from within. At the same time, the scholarship on Chinese media culture outlined above certainly suggest that China represents fertile ground for investigation of Appadurai's "disjunctures" between the scapes. In addition, however, we might consider the degree to which such analyses on the part of cultural commentators morph over time into a mediated strategy on the part of cultural producers; that is, to what degree does performance of "hybridity," "disruption," or "disjuncture" obscure conservative power relationships which aim at the maintenance of cultural and political status quos? In much the same way that George Yúdice (2003) has alerted us to an "expediency of culture" in discourses and actions related to globalization, we would suggest that the discourse of hybridity—imagined as a more nuanced understanding of the relationship between a creeping homogenization and the maintenance of heterogeneity in the global sphere—may also be expedient. We would suggest that *Super Girl* offers an opportunity to analyze the mobilization of the concept of hybridity for the very purposes of maintaining its opposite. In other words, we would propose as an emerging discourse, especially in the Chinese context, an *expediency of hybridity*.

Such a proposal requires further study, and we would suggest that a particularly fecund area of analysis in this regard would be the 2008 Beijing Olympic Games, most notably the mind-boggling opening and closing ceremonies. What messages were being communicated during those spectacular moments, and to whom were they being communicated? Was the net effect greater or lesser control over cultural hegemony on the part of the CCP? We would also suggest that textual research of the kind in which we've engaged here ought to be supplemented with detailed fieldwork investigating the meaning making strategies employed by Chinese (or other) audiences. It is perhaps in this area of activity where the collision of practices of consumption and production may provide novel evidence of cultural contestation beyond the arguments presented here.

Notes

1. See http://www.screendigest.com/reports/08chinacabletv/08chinacable-pdf/view.html and http://www.cmmintelligence.com/ as examples.
2. Chang also underestimates the degree to which media have been participatory for some time (see Griffen-Foley, 2004) without necessarily empowering its participants in meaningful ways.

24

Anime in Asia: Why Not Japanese? Rethinking the Local-Global Cultural Nexus

Umi Khattab and Gin Chee Tong

Japan's mass culture has long had a dominant presence in South and Southeast Asia, and anime is no exception. According to *Asia Week*, 'Japan is Top of the Pops' in Asia, in view of the cultural affinity between Asian consumers and Japanese products (Tesoro, 1996). As Shiraishi (1997) argues, despite the undisputable importance of Hollywood in the production of image-based culture products, contemporary Asian popular culture is not solely Western because Japanese values resonate well within many Asian societies. In illustrating her point, Shiraishi (1997: 264-8) presents several case studies of anime's popularity in various parts of Asia, including a thorough discussion of *Doraemon*'s popularity in Indonesia and Taiwan, as well as citing *Astro Boy* as the first foreign animated television series to run in China. Anime networks and channels are 'mushrooming' all over the Asian region, further signifying the rising popularity of this cultural product. Animax, the world's first-ever 24-hour channel dedicated to Japanese animation, now broadcasts into many parts of Asia, including Taiwan, Hong Kong, South Asia and Southeast Asia (Animax, 2005).

While anime's popularity among Asian consumers is not recent, anime is also slowly finding an appreciative audience in the West. Beginning with the release of Ootomo Katsushiro's hugely popular animation film *Akira* (1988), the quality and attraction of "Japanimation" is gradually being acknowledged by the American market (Iwabuchi, 2002: 30). In November 1995, the animated film *The Ghost in the Shell* was shown simultaneously in Japan, America and Great Britain, while its video sales reached number one on the American *Billboard* video charts (Reesman, 2002). More recently, the *Pokémon* phenomenon has taken America and the rest of the world by storm. Though it came to life as a piece of software to be played on Nintendo's Game Boy, *Pokémon* quickly diversified into a comic book, television show, movie, trading cards, stickers, small toys and other ancillary products such as backpacks and T-shirts (Tobin, 2004: 1). Like the situation in Asia, there is a linear growth of American networks and cable channels dedicated to Japanese animation. As Dong (2005) observes, when the Cartoon Network first started showing anime many years ago, variety was scant and few, but flash forward to now and the differences are phenomenal.

This paper aims to fill in the vacuum by contributing a semiotic reading of anime programmes available in Asia. It situates the study in the context of theoretical debates on cultural imperialism and globalisation, to lend support to the paper's hypothesis that Asia's preference for anime is based on the theory of 'cultural proximity'.

(Re)visiting Cultural Imperialism

Is 'global culture' yet another name for 'American culture'? The media and cultural imperialism thesis argues that the one-way flow of media products and services from the advanced industrial countries to the less advanced nations undermine their existing cultures, morals and values, and its central argument points to the dominant dissemination of Western culture via the mass media. Herbert Schiller (1970, 1976) presses the case that transnational media corporations provide the ideological support for a capitalist world system. He argues that "[transnational media corporations] provide in their imaginary and messagery, the beliefs and perspective that create and reinforce their audiences' attachments to the way things are in the system overall" (in Tomlinson, 1991: 38). Schiller (1970: 79-93) elides capitalist culture with American culture, following America's principal role as a major exporter (and small importer) of movies, popular music, television programmes, news, books, magazines, advertisements, and associated lifestyles and values.

This political-economy approach to cultural hegemony in favour of 'Americanism' remains deeply entrenched in much of the analytical literature on international media systems. As Croteau and Haynes (2000: 346) observe, a supposed conflict of traditional values and the erosion of local culture follows the close ties between ownership and media content, with much of the latter embedded with the values and images of Western society. Herman and McChesney (1997: 35) argue that ownership and control of global media systems in the hands of a few main transnational corporate players has resulted in a dominant and accelerating influence that extends not only within the economic and political spheres, but also basic assumptions and modes of thought. The cultural imperialism thesis therefore claims that the economic and cultural power of the media, and the cultural artefacts of America and other dominant western powers, have allowed them to dominate or unduly influence and put into a dependency relationship the media and cultures of less economically advanced countries (Herman and McChesney, 1997: 152).

Since Herman and McChesney's book, greater and more powerful mergers between media transnationals have emerged, most notably the merger between Time Warner and America Online on January 10, 2000, which has been cited as "the most expensive marriage ceremony in history" (Bagdikian, 2004: 30). Tomlinson (1999) concedes that the claim for a single hegemonic 'homogenised' global culture continues to constitute an important and widely-used critical perspective even to the present day, based on several irrefutable empirical observations and arguments. He maintains that there is a wealth of evidence that Western cultural practises and tastes are becoming global ones, such as clothing, food, music, film and television (Tomlinson, 1999: 83). As the cultural imperialism thesis draws attention to the locus of control of lived experience and underscores distanced influences on our everyday lives, the convergence and the standardisation of cultural goods around the world serve as a pointed reminder on the possible negative effects that our interaction with these goods may bring.

Giddens (2002:15) argues that American names like McDonald's, Coca-cola and CNN are among the world's most visible cultural expressions of globalisation. By declaring that "the media are American", Tunstall (1997) concurs that a non-American way out of the media box is difficult, given that the only way out of experiencing an American dominant hegemony is to construct a new box. Holton (1998: 166) points out that the Americanisation thesis is being further strengthened by the visible capitalist control of various forms of mass media, such as the manufacture and transmission of culture, including satellite systems, information technology manufacture, news agencies, the advertising industry, television programme production and export, and the film industry. With much of the so-termed 'global' mass culture being largely American, the West (or more specifically North America) is often recognised as taking a leading role in many recent phases of globalisation. As Storey (2003: 153) cynically notes, the world is supposedly being slowly reduced to an American 'global village'.

As the debates sketched in favour of the cultural imperialism thesis show, the evolving consensus amongst observers is that globalisation evokes an unrelenting and all-absorbing, linear process of cultural homogenisation. While we do not deny the pervasive influx of global images into our everyday worlds, as media researchers it is also necessary to take into account the complicated relationship between global media and local meanings. Cvetkovich and Kellner (1997: 1) contend that it would be a mistake to focus on one side in favour of exclusive concern with the other, that is, to either reject the local in favour of exclusive concern with the global, or to reject the global for exclusive concern with the local. Instead, they suggest that it is necessary to think through the relationship between the global and the local, by observing how global forces influence and structure local situations, as well as how local forces and situations mediate the global (Cvetkovich and Kellner, 1997: 1-2). Rather than simplifying the concept of globalisation into a one-way flow of Western cultural commodities into non-Western nations, Featherstone (1995: 6) suggests that globalisation needs to be thought of as a "form, a space or field made possible through improved means of communication in which different cultures meet and clash", or simply put, as a "stage for global differences".

Storey (2003:159) expands on Featherstone's point, cautioning against thinking of America as the only global power, in view that this perspective ignores the global economic status of Hong Kong, South Korea, Singapore, and especially Japan. By downplaying the role of nation-states from within the Asian sphere, the cultural imperialism thesis leaves little room for understanding the impact non-Western cultures have been making on the West. Pieterse (1995: 53) disagrees that cultural experiences are moving in the direction of cultural uniformity and standardisation, while Giddens (2002: 16) attest to globalisation as being only partly Westernisation, in view that much of the non-Western countries are increasingly influencing development in the West.

Morley (1998:349) suggests that "modernity (or postmodernity) may perhaps in the future, be located more in the Pacific than in the Atlantic". Sony's purchase of Columbia in 1989 and Matsushita's purchase of MCA-Universal in 1990, have not only dramatised the ascent of Japanese global media conglomerates through the merger of hardware and software, but the acquisitions have also exposed the anxiety that Japanese investors are "buying into America's soul" (Morley and Robins, 1995: 149-50). As Japan continues to outperform the economics of the West, Morley and Robins (1995:160) further claim that the possibility that the West may have to learn from the most (post)modern societies has accordingly "called into question the supposed centrality of the West as a cultural and geographical locus for the project of modernity". With signs of 'reverse colonisation' occurring on a more widespread basis, this phenomenon signifies that the relationships between cultures are becoming increasingly diverse and multilateral. Consequently, not only do the debates surrounding globalisation need to shift away from a homogenisation perspective, we need to seriously consider the power of the local in resisting, negotiating, and appropriating global influences on a daily basis.

Debunking Imperialism, Engaging Audiences

Despite a preponderance of literature citing globalisation as equating Westernisation, or more specifically Americanisation, the media imperialism position has been berated for its reliance on the so-called hypodermic model of media effects. Audience reception theorists question the type of widespread cultural domination portrayed by media imperialism and argue that audiences actively interpret, negotiate and even resist media content (Ang, 1996; Morley, 1992). By refuting the cultural imperialism thesis which claims audiences to be passive and unresponsive recipients of tangible and intangible cultural products, audience reception theorists argue that local and regional ways of thinking and living do not disappear in the face of imported cultural influences, as audiences are shown to be active interpreters of media content, who mediate, negotiate and invent cultural meanings based on existing values and beliefs (see also Liebes and Katz, 1993). As Ang (1996: 153) argues, local responses and negotiations that are both culturally diverse and geographically dispersed need to be taken into account to better understand the complex and contradictory dynamics of today's 'global culture', in view that mass-mediated cultures are actively and differentially responded to and negotiated with in concrete local contexts and conditions.

Likewise, Tomlinson (1999: 84) contends, the receiving culture often brings its own cultural resources to bear, in dialectical fashion, upon 'cultural imports', and as a result, the movement between cultural and geographical areas always involves interpretation, translation, mutation, adaptation and the process of 'indigenisation'. Local discourses and practices are increasingly defining the contemporary scene, and it would be a mistake to focus on one side in favour of exclusive concern with the other. Ang (1996: 152) points out that the cultural imperialism thesis offers a flawed account of 'global culture', conceding to an unambiguous domination of subordinated peoples and cultures by a clearly demarcated powerful culture, usually designated as American or European, or more generally, as 'Western' culture.

Besides debunking the myth of cultural imperialism, audience reception studies support the on-going process of 'glocalisation', a phenomenon Robertson (1995: 28) maintains is formed through "telescoping global and local to make a blend". Following the ongoing influx of global cultures, glocalisation is offered as an alternate viewpoint to cultural homogeneity, as the process of localising the global signifies greater freedom for different people in different places to use external cultural products in different ways, and adapt them for their own uses and to create their own meanings. Lull (2000: 244) argues that through the negotiation of external influences, imported cultural elements are hybridised to take on local features, for the purpose of 'domesticating' the exotic, unfamiliar and foreign. He uses rap music as a case study to illustrate how the unfamiliar, imported cadence and attitude of rap is appropriated by local musicians, resulting in a musical hybrid that adopts local aspects involving lyrics that refer to local personalities, conditions and situations (Lull, 2000:244).

As Lull's example illustrates, cultures simply do not transfer in a unilinear way, but often involves the reworking and reproduction of 'global culture' to suit local flavour. Appadurai (1990:295) concedes that "as rapidly as forces from various metropolises are brought into new societies, they tend to become indigenised in one or other way". This is true of music, housing styles, science and terrorism. Hence, unlike the cultural homogenisation thesis, audience reception studies have shown that increasing global integration does not result in the elimination of cultural diversity, but instead, globalisation provides the context for the production of new cultural forms which are marked by local specificity (Ang, 1996:155). Furthermore, local and regional ways of thinking and living do not disappear in the face of imported cultural influences, as the active audience negotiate the influx of 'global cultures' through incorporating particular elements into their everyday lives.

Studies in Asia and outside of North America by Sinclair (2000) and Straubhaar (2000) suggest that audiences prefer television programming from their own country, and in their own vernacular, so long as national programming can be supported by the local economy. These cross-cultural studies also indicate that viewers tend to actively privilege national or regional programming over its imported counterpart and in fact rarely turn to imported programmes when local alternatives are available (Moragas Spa and Lopez, 2000). Sinclair's (2000) work on the consumption of television programmes in Latin America demonstrates that the most popular imports are those that share the same language and cultural ambit of the local region.

Several scholars argue that in the current global media environment characterised by a plurality of actors and media flows, it is no longer possible to sustain the notion of Western media domination (cf. Banerjee, 2002, 2003; Chang, 2001; Chadha and Kavoori, 2000). Instead, they emphasise the emergence of many developing nations as major producers, gate-keepers and global exporters of audiovisual material which has not only altered the one-way flow of Western media content, but also, their growing importance effectively undermine the 'hegemonic' model represented by media imperialism.

Fears of 'cultural invasion' and 'cultural homogenisation' are frequently voiced by 'Third World' nations who claim that 'cultural disassociation' is the only way of protecting vulnerable indigenous cultures that would otherwise be almost certainly effaced (Sreberny-Mohammadi, 1990). Generally, people tend to lead local lives, and even if certain cultural products have a global spread, meanings offered to them may not be the same everywhere (Sreberny-Mohammadi, 1996: 18). Thussu (1998:69) cites Rupert Murdoch for admitting that "everywhere I go it is local programming which is proving to be the most popular. The majority of our staff everywhere are local. Local producers and editors provide the concepts and ensure the cultural priorities". Consequently, in line with this 'domestication' strategy, STAR has developed Phoenix, a Mandarin-language service just for China, and STAR Plus, the mainly Hindi-language-based channel for India, both of which draw on indigenously made programmes (Thussu, 1998: 69).

MTV, or Music Television, the global music television station of Western origins, is another early adopter of glocalisation, which begun differentiating its content around the world through incorporating local music with local programming and languages, after its initial campaign to establish a pan-Asian television service faltered due to the lack of cultural specificity (Herman and McChesney, 1997: 42; Sturmer in Holton, 1998: 169). Chang (2001) contends that viewers' preference for local programming in their native languages has led to a two-way 'push' and 'pull' process within the global broadcasting networks, following which, local imperatives are taken into consideration. Chang (2001: 9-13) cites CNBC Asia, CNNI and BBC World as leading news channels that have moved towards programme regionalisation and localisation, through the global newscasters' partnerships with the local broadcasting stations.

Despite the deep presence of many Western transnational media organisations within the Asian region, their domination is restricted by the dynamics of audience preference, a factor which significantly forces such global companies to either localise or regionalise their products for financial benefits. As the case studies here demonstrate, in a world characterised by flows of people, goods and images, far from thinking about globalisation in terms of 'fixed' or stagnant points, Meyer and Ceschiere (1999: 4-5) suggest that we should consider the making and unmaking of boundaries, localities and 'cultures' in various forms of power constellations, given that there are no absolute boundaries unaffected by global flows. Thus, rather than thinking of globalisation as a process that uniformly subverts local imperatives, the future of globalisation for the world's leading television news broadcasters, and other types of mass media producers, appears to depend a lot on programme localisation, whereby the local is seen as exercising influences in constituting the global.

Kimonos, Meat-buns and all things Asian

In his study on the cultural products of Japan, Iwabuchi (2002) critically appraised Japanese animation and computer games for their 'non-Japaneseness', or *mukokuseki*, which literally means "something or someone lacking any nationality". He argues that because for the most part the characters of Japanese animation and computer games do not look 'Japanese', such culturally 'odourless' products allow for the erasure of racial or ethnic characteristics or a context, and therefore negates the imprint of a particular culture or country with these features (Iwabuchi, 2002: 28). In this respect, through ridding anime of some of its 'cultural odour' as part of the glocalisation process for non-Japanese markets, it leaves space for anime to blend in easily with the cultural, societal and political values of its consuming audiences. As Sreberny-Mohammadi (1996) asserts, to be successful in Asian markets, the domestication of, or adding of indigenous ingredients to, programming is especially inevitable for many transnational cable channel operators. The business of selling anime outside Japanese borders is no exception, and as the following semiology exercise demonstrates, many of Japan's cultural exports do embody distinct Asian characters and symbols to transform that which is 'exotic' and 'strange', into something that is 'familiar' and 'approachable'.

For textual analysis purpose, the study drew a sample of anime products from Animax, Asia's first and only channel dedicated to broadcasting Japanese animation 24-hours, seven days a week. They are: *Saiyuki Reload Gunlock* (2004), which draws on Chinese mythology, *Otogizoushi* (2004), a story about a female Japanese samurai, and *Gankutsuou* (2004), an anime loosely based on *The Count of Monte Cristo* by French novelist Alexandre Dumas.

Created by Kazuya Minekura and produced by Studio Pierrot, *Saiyuki Reload Gunlock* has 26 episodes and is the third instalment of the *Saiyuki* series. Like its two predecessors, *Gensoumaden Saiyuki* and *Saiyuki Reload*, *Gunlock* continues with the adventures of the four main characters (see figure 1) – the half-demon Sha Gojyo, the demon Cho Hakkai, the monk Genjyo Sanzo and the monkey deity Son Goku—as they journey to India to investigate the reasons behind the recent insanity among the *youkais* ('demons'). The *youkais*, who have formerly coexisted peacefully with humans in Shangri-La, have gone berserk and are turning against the humans.

Asian Chinese viewers face little problems approaching this text, as *Gunlock* draws inspiration from Chengen Wu's must-read Chinese classic *Journey to the West*. In addition to retaining the classic's original 'heroes and villains', character names are also presented in their original Chinese format. As Taylor and Willis (1999: 20) explain, central to the semiotic approach is the idea that language, signs and their meanings are historically, culturally and socially produced. On the other hand, different clothing can send out different social messages involving status, occupation, ethnic and religious affiliation, while accessories can situate the cultural resonance of a particular character. Figure 2 illustrates the traditional Chinese cheongsam commonly worn by women, while the men are clad in conventional peasant-like clothing. The scriptures that hang on either side of Sanzo's shoulders by contrast (see figure 1), are Buddhist sutras that record the oral teachings of Gautama Buddha. In keeping with the Oriental look, the setting and props are also easily distinguishable as being part of Asia, as illustrated by the presence of Buddhist temples, monks and Chinese delicacies (see figure 3). Through using elements which are culturally proximate to most Chinese Asian consumers, such as the aforementioned Chinese scripts and traditional imagery, they anchor the 'Asian-ness' of the otherwise *mukokuseki*-looking characters.

The second sample, *Otogizoushi*, is an original anime created by Production I.G. This anime follows the adventures of the young Japanese protagonist Hikaru, who attempts to save ancient Kyoto through collecting the *Magatama*, legendary gems said to hold mysterious power. Failing the task, Hikaru and her trusted allies are given a second chance when they are reincarnated in modern-day Tokyo to right the wrongs of history made 1000 years ago. Unlike *Gunlock*, *Otogizoushi* draws heavily from Japanese culture and practices, particularly its character designs, costumes and setting. For instance, Hikaru is depicted in traditional samurai costume when masquerading as her brother, but wears the Japanese kimono at home (see figure 4). In modern-day Tokyo, although the cast has traded in their traditional costumes for casual tees and jeans, the 'Japanese-ness' of the anime is retained through the visual presence of typical Japanese 'sailor moon-style' school uniform. Character names also situate the anime in a conventional Japanese setting, as they are distinguishably Japanese in essence, both orally and scripturally.

To further sharpen the 'Japanese-ness', *Abe no Seimei*, an eleventh-century specialist on *onmyodo* ('feng-shui') is featured among the regular cast (see figure 5). Through his inclusion, this gives the anime a sense of what Danesi (1999:19) has described as 'tribal roots', an important factor in establishing the cultural resonance visible within the animated feature. Additionally, there is an abundance of iconic Japanese objects and places, among them *Mizuko Jizou*, bib-and-hood-wearing stone 'protectors' of prematurely dead children, *shinkansen* ('trains'), as well as various shrines and temples dedicated to Japanese deities.

Despite *Otogizoushi*'s outward Japanese appearance, a closer analysis reveals some resemblance to Chinese culture. The practice of *onmyoudou* ('traditional Japanese cosmology') for instance, is based on two Chinese theories, the Five Elements (Water, Wood, Fire, Earth and Metal) and Yin-Yang. By contrast, Hikaru's impersonation of a male samurai in place of her ailing brother parallels Chinese heroine Mulan's substitution as her father in the Chinese army. As Sinclair (2000) argues, the most popular imports are those that share the same language and cultural ambit of the local region, and by adopting distinct Chinese ingredients, it allows anime easier access to those living in the Asian region.

The third anime examined is a Gonzo Digimation production entitled *Gankutsuou*. Loosely based on Alexandre Dumas's *The Count of Monte Cristo*, *Gankutsuou* has been reinterpreted as a sci-fi revenge story and set in a fantasy-like Paris of the future. The anime opens with the chance meeting of 15-year-old Albert de Morcerf with the Count of Monte Cristo, then moves quickly into the main theme, that of the Count's revenge against the three men who framed him for treason more than a decade ago.

Although *Gankutsuou* is inspired by a European (or 'Western') text, a semiotic reading uncovers many examples of the reworking and reproduction of its visual imagery and thematic plots to suit the local 'Asian flavour'. Character designs in particular, are devoid of any significant racial or cultural characteristics (see figure 6), which fall in line with Iwabuchi's (2002) concept of *mukokuseki*-ness. And bearing in mind Lull's (2000: 244) argument that external influences are negotiated at every (local) level, while imported cultural elements are hybridised to take on local features, Haydee's wardrobe of Japanese kimonos (see figure 7) demonstrates the ways in which *Gankutsuou* has been 'domesticated' during the production process to allow for a more 'Asianised' viewing experience.

To further domesticise a text considered 'exotic' by many Asians, *Gankutsuou* focuses on filial piety and arranged marriages, two issues familiar to an Asian audience. Another example of glocalisation to suit a more conservative Asian consumer is the marked absence of homosexuality. Rather than retain Dumas' underlying tone of lesbianism (that of Eugénie eloping with her female piano teacher), *Gankutsuou*'s Eugénie is instead, to marry the fake Italian nobleman, Marquis Cavalcanti.

Conclusion

Globalisation has undoubtedly changed the way we look at the world. Whereas in the past we could only imagine what the other cultures were like, new media technologies have accelerated the speed in which cultures are translated, adapted and experienced. Although proponents of the cultural imperialism thesis like Herman and McChesney (1997) suggest that 'local' cultures are slowly but surely, becoming one homogeneous body that looks suspiciously like American culture, audience reception scholars such as Ang (1996) and Morley (1992) argue that local and regional audiences are 'fighting back' through active interpretation of imported cultural influences. Furthermore, cross-cultural studies almost uniformly indicate that given the option, viewers tend to actively privilege national or regional programming over its imported counterpart (Sinclair, 2000; Straubhaar, 2000). This suggests that globalisation has prompted a return to the 'traditional', whereby media consumers are looking for products that resonate with their own values and beliefs. Suggestively, despite the ubiquity of Western transnational media organisations within the Asian region, their domination is restricted by the dynamics of audience preference, a factor which significantly forces such global companies to either localise or regionalise their products for financial benefits.

To illustrate the effectiveness of glocalisation, this paper has looked at Japanese animation as an example of a cultural export that has successfully found its way into the hearts and minds of many Asian consumers. As the semiotic reading illustrates, anime has adopted a variety of Asian symbols and values, while simultaneously glocalising 'exotic' elements to appeal to the different Chinese cultures located around different parts of Asia. By removing Japanese-ness when necessary, and incorporating cross-cultural history and tradition to depict a hybrid of Asian cultural values, anime has made itself accessible to a local, plural Asian audience.

APPENDIX I: IMAGES

Figures 1-3: Still Not There Yet (2004) 'A Saiyuki Reload Gunlock Screencap Gallery', consulted 15 September 2005: http://www.yareyare.net/Saiyuki/Gunlock/gallery/SaiyukiRELOADGUNLOCKEpisode01Screencaps

Figure 1

Figure 2

Figure 3

Figures 4-5: Yummy Sushi Pajamas (2004) 'Otogizoushi', consulted 15 September, 2005: http://yummysushipajamas.com/ipw-web/gallery/otogizoushi_nohotlinking_02

Figure 4

Figure 5

Figures 6-7: Gankutsuou Official Website (2004) 'Character', consulted 22 September 2005: http://www.gankutsuou.com/world/character.html

Figure 6

Figure 7

Index

Abalo, Ernesto, 114
Access and Bias
  Problems of, 194
Active User, 190
Ad-Edit Space Distribution, 81
Akhter, Jostana, 205, 207
Almiron, Nuria, 46
American culture, 325
American Life Project, 34
Analysis of Information Society Strategy, 148
Anand, Navneet, 186
Anime in Asia: Why Not Japanese?
  Rethinking the Local-Global Cultural Nexus, 322
Annamalai University, 189
Arab Human Development Report, 105
Arab Science and Technology Foundation, 106
Arab Thought Forum, 106
Arab World
  Knowledge Realities in, 105
Araujo, Denize Correa, 126
Aslama, Minna, 295
Attitudes to www.ams.se, 122
Audiences
  Looking for Authenticity, 301
Ayish, Muhammad, 102

Bannerman, Sara, 95
BBC's Video Nation, 164
Begum, Majeda, 204
Begum, Rubia, 203, 205
Begum, Safali, 206
Being Cultural Citizen: Role of Media, 227-37
Bell, Daniel, 104
Bhartiya Janata Party (BJP), 192-93
Brazilian Society: Digital Divide in Contemporary, 126-34
Bush, George W., 36
Business Standard, 190
Business Week, 54

Carpentier, Nico, 155
Chinese Communist Party (CCP), 317
Chinese Media Environment, 310
Coalition for Unity and Democracy (CUD), 266
Collaborative Virtual Environments (CVE), 65
  Democratic Public Discussion on, 69
Collaborative Virtual Environments, 68
Computer Mediated Communications (CMC), 68
Conceptualising Diaspora, 240
Convergence Culture, 161
Cordoba Mosque, 109
Critical Discourse Analysis (CDA), 137-39
Cross-media Production
  Broadcast Culture Meets Role-Playing Culture Consequences for Audience Participation, 17-33
Current Internet Use, 118
cyber journalism, 2

Dahlgren, Peter, 22
Danielsson, Martin, 114
Das, Taposhi Rani, 205
Dasgupta, Satarupa, 174
Data Collection
  Methods of, 80

Debunking Imperialism, Engaging Audiences, 325
Denward, Marie, 17
Development Agenda: Optimists and Pessimists, 97
Dhar, Ravi K., 278
Digital Age
 Democracy in, 124
digital excluded, 126
digital hipertropolis, 130
digital included, 130
digital literacy, 129
Dinur, Amit Lavie, 65
direct financing, 49
Dome of the Rock in Jerusalem, 109
Dugo, Habtamu, 261
Durbar Mohila Samnwaya Committee (DMSC), 183

easy to use, 120
Edit Space
 Distribution of, 83
e-governance, 116
e-government, 116
Emerging Patterns in the Era of E-governance, 114-25
enabling technology, 188
Encapsulating a Freirean Logic of Empowerment, 174-85
Enlightenment and Critique, 99
Ethiopian Peoples Revolutionary Front (EPRDF), 264
Existential-Transcendental Knowledge, 111

Feature Space Accorded to Relationship Features, 86
Feature Space Distribution, 84
financial disintermediation, 49
Flickr, 26
Focus Group Critiques
 on 16plus, 164
 on Barometer, 168
Focus Group Discourses that Legitimise Barometer, 170
Foreign Direct Investment (FDI), 146
form of social practice, 137
Fourth Dimension of the Fourth Estate, 79
Freedom and Democracy
 Quest for, 264
Friedman, Doron, 65
fun, 120
Functional-Ritual Knowledge Processes, 111

Gender Politics, 315
Gender-Based Visual Categorisation, 88
General Electric (GE), 52
 Financial Debt, 59
global culture, 325
Global Information Infrastructure (GII), 136
Global Participatory Television Formats and Power, 318
Global Warming on Second Life, 65-77
global warming, 71
good television, 27
Google, 161
GoogleMaps, 26

HaJoon Chang, 98
Hay bin Yaqthan, 109
history of human civilization, 1
HIV/AIDS, 177, 185
 infection, 181, 182
Holy Book, 108
Hultberg, Linda, 199
Human Society
 Genesis of Divides in, 279
Human Visual Categorisation on the Basis of Gender, 88
Human Visual Presentation
 Manner of, 89
Human Visual Presentation, 89
Hybridity
 Expediency of, 320

IBGE (Brazilian Institute of Geography and Statistics), 130
Identification of Variables for Data Collection, 80

Identities and Media of Brazilian Diaspora, 251-60
image barrier, 36
Indebtedness and Financial Innovation, 58
Indian Youth Congress (IYC), 193
Individual-Community Knowledge, 111
Information and Communication Technologies (ICTs), 105, 141, 143, 144, 145, 147, 149
Information Society Strategy, 152
information society, 104
Innovation Resistance, 37
Institute for Broadband Technology (IBBT), 163
instructive, 120
Intellectual Property (IP), 95
Intellectual Property Rights (IPRs), 148
Interdisciplinary Center in Herzliya, 71
Internally Displaced Persons (IDPS), 276
Internet and Mobile Association of India (IAMAI), 190
Internet and Political Communication Dynamics in India, 186-98
Internet Service Providers (ISPS), 271
Internet today, 187
Internet use, 119
Internet, 2
    Attitudes to the, 119
    experiences of, 117
    The Great Enabler, 188
Islamic Knowledge Model, 110
IT-BPO industry, 188
Ivanova, Elitsa, 238

Jane McGonigal, 19
Jawaharlal Nehru University (JNU), 189, 194
Johansson, Håkan, 114

Karniel, Yuval, 65
Kerry, John, 36
Kimonos, Meat-buns and all things Asian, 328
Knowledge as Empirical/Revealed, 112
Knowledge Project
    Lighthouses of, 128, 133
Knowledge Society as Pathway to Sustainable Development in the Arab World, 102-13
    Dominant Paradigm, 103
Kuhn, Fernando, 251
Kwak, Sunyoung, 309

Labourers of the Real "Authenticity Work" in Reality Television, 295-308
Lane, Robert, 103
Layout of Visuals, 90
Lee, Hyunwoo, 212
Linking Press Freedom to Governance Indicators, 270
Live Action Role-Playing (LARP), 18

Machlup, Fritz, 103
magical consciousness, 178
Mahajan, Deepti, 88
manufacturing the real, 295
Mapping Brazilian Diasporic Media, 257
Mass Media and the Global Divides, 281
massification, 6
Material/Social-Moral Knowledge Drive, 111
Measure Financialization
    Tools to, 47
Media
    in Transition, 8
    Production, 24
Media and Journalists
    Physical Threats against, 271
Media Publicity
    What Really Happened?, 304
Media Research Users Council (MRUC), 88
media technology, 1
Media Usage Patterns, 230
Media, Traditional
    Predominance of, 195
Mediation of Community and Identity, 244
Mission Mode Projects (MMPs), 191

Mohammed bin Rashid Foundation, 106

Natarajan, Jayanthi, 192
Nation's Mobile Phone Service
Characteristics of, 213
National Students Union of India (NSUI), 194
Nationalist Congress Party (NCP), 193
Negotiation of Identities, 254
New Media and Oromo Diaspora, 261-77
New Media and the Communication Epiphany, 285
New Media and the Redemption of other, 278-94
New Media
Emergence of, 7
New World Information and Communication Order (NWICO), 155, 158
News Corp (NWS), 53
News Corp Operating Segments, 57
NGO (non-governmental organization), 126
Normative Islamic Conceptions of Knowledge, 107
Normative Islamic Knowledge Values, 107
Norris, Pippa, 261
Notions of Critical Pedagogy, 178

Olsson, Tobias, 114
online communication, 2
Opening up the Black Box of Participation, 155-73
OpenNet Initiative (ONI), 271
Oromo Diasporic Formations, 262
Oromo Hall of Struggle for Freedom, 275
Oromo Liberation Front (OLF), 266, 272
Oromo People
General Context of, 262
Overview of New Media Theories, 265

Pantti, Mervi, 295
Participants: Importance of being True, 299
Participation
Key Concept of, 156
participation drama, 18
participatory democracy, 36
Peaslee, Robert Moses, 309
Perceived Ease of Use (PEOU), 38-39
Perceived Usefulness (PU), 38
Pew Internet, 34
Political Economy Research Institute (PERI), 46
Possibility of Applying Universal Service Policy Principle on Mobile Phone Service, 212-26
post-Cold War era, 102
Producers
one cannot Script Reality, 297
professional journalists, 167
Prophet Muhammad (PBUH), 103, 107-08
pseudo-participation, 157
Public Sphere Online, 67

Qatar Foundation, 106
Question of 'home', 242

Rana, Pooja, 78
Rashtriya Ekta Yatra, 192
Reception of Participatory Media Products, 162
reciprocal action or influence, 3
Registrar of Newspapers in India (RNI), 80
Reject Now, Accept in the Future?, 34-45
Relationship Feature Space Distribution, 86
Reporters without Borders (RWB), 270
Restricting Press Freedom by Law, 266
Revisiting Cultural Imperialism, 323
RFID (Radio Frequency Identification) technology, 215
Right to Information (RTI) activists, 197
risk barrier, 36
Robock, Karen, 88
Roger's Diffusion of Innovation (DOI) theory, 35
Role-playing nerds strike back, 17
Roy, Dipti, 206
Rules of the Game, 312

Searching for Empowerment, 204
Second Life (SL), 68
Second World War, 99
Securities Exchange Commission (SEC), 52
7th Flemish Science Week, 163
sexually transmitted diseases (STDs), 174
Shan-Shan Li, 227
Shu-Ling Chen Berggreen, 309
Small, Medium and Micro Enterprises (SMMEs), 146
social dialogues, 247
Social Shaping of Technologies (SST), 116
Societal Role-Based Human Visual Categorisation, 87
Sonagachi Project, 175-84
stage for global differences, 324
State Wide Areas Networks (SWANs), 190
Street of Citizenship, 133-34
Structure of the Mobile Phone Service Market, 220
subject-subject dialogue, 176
subliminal messages, 21
Suggested Knowledge Model, 110
Super Girl and Expediency of Hybridity, 309-21
    and Privatization of Propaganda, 317
Supplement Journalism in India, Emergence, 78-94
Swedish Public Employment Service (SPES), 115, 117, 120, 122, 123
    Digital Information, Unemployed, 120
Swedish Television (SVT), 17

Taiwan
    Cyber-campaigning in, 37
Taj Mahal, 109
Technology Acceptance Model (TAM), 8
Text-Visual Space Distribution, 82
The Battle Already Won, 96
The Holy Quran, 9
The Walt Disney Company (DIS), 52
Theorisation
    Need for, 239
Tigrian Peoples Liberation Front (TPLF), 266
Tim Berger Lee's Mosaic browser, 7
Time Warner (TW), 52, 56, 59
Time Warner Operating Segments, 56
Top Six US Media Conglomerates, 50-51
Transmission School of Communication, 6
Turkey's Information Society Strategy, 148
24:7 governmental agencies, 125

Umi Khattab and Gin Chee Tong, 322
Unemployed and the Digitalization of the Contacts, 123
United Nations (UN), 96
    Development Program, 105
Universal Declaration of Human Rights (UDHR), 268
US Media System, Financialization, 46-64
usage barrier, 36

value barrier, 36
Viacom (VIA), 53
Viacom Operating Segments, 57
Videsh Sanchar Nigam Limited (VSNL), 190
Village Pay Phones (VPP), 199-201
    Use, 203
Virtual Diasporas
    Notion of 'Home' and Identity Formation in Cyberspace, 238-50
Virtual Diasporas, 245

Walt Disney Operating Segments, 56
web journalism, 2
web media, 2
West
    Cyber-campaigning in the, 36
Western Knowledge Model, 110
What about the 21st Century (Mass) Media?, 159
What Problems will the Information Society Resolve, 145
What Problems will the Information Society Solve?, 150

Why do People need the Information Society?, 143, 149
Women Empowerment and Poverty Reduction in Bangladesh, 199-211
World Bank, 106
World Health Organization, 174
World Intellectual Property Organization (WIPO), 95
    Development Agenda Forum, 95-101
World Press Freedom Committee (WPFC), 266
World Summit on the Information Society (WSIS), 139-43, 145-49, 151
    Documents, Analysis of, 139
    Turkey and Information Society, 135-54
World Trade Organization (WTO), 95
World Wide Web, 2, 189, 192, 261
www.ams.se
    General Patterns of Use of, 121
    Use of Various Parts of, 122

Yah-Huei Hong, 34
YouTube, 20, 26, 161